Utah County

Community Assessment

2011

Volume 2: Appendix

CIVICUS

ISBN: 978-0-9828092-3-5

Library of Congress Control Number:

Published by Civicus
17612 Highway E
Richmond, MO 64085

www.CivicusConsulting.com

10 9 8 7 6 5 4 3 2 1

–

Utah County

Community Assessment

2011

Volume 2: Appendix

CIVICUS

Acknowledgments

We express gratitude to those agencies that assisted with funding of this project. Without their willingness to help with financial resources, we would not have been able to complete this assessment. Special thanks go to

Center for Women and Children in Crisis

Community Action Services and Food Bank

Kids on the Move

Provo City Housing Authority

Utah County Department of Health

Utah County Housing Authority

Wasatch Mental Health

United Way of Utah County

Contents

15

Foreword

This is Volume 2 of the two-volume Utah County Community Assessment 2011. It contains data only, and is organized and categorized in the same manner as Volume 1: Education, Income, Health, and Looking Forward. Source agencies or organizations are listed for each set of data. When not noted otherwise, the data is for Utah County only.

It is our desire to share this data with other nonprofit organizations, government entities, community leaders, policy makers, grant writers, grant makers, and others.

5 Appendix

5.1 Overview Data

5.1.1 Population

5.1.1.1 Total Population, 2000-2009, Comparison Counties and State

	Utah County	Davis County	Salt Lake County	State
2000	243,049	155,031	624,804	1,514,471
2001	256,845	159,967	638,564	1,562,047
2002	263,139	164,631	648,880	1,598,964
2003	271,005	169,610	659,791	1,635,911
2004	286,323	174,679	669,810	1,679,395
2005	299,425	179,366	679,770	1,723,644
2006	316,724	185,447	698,337	1,781,221
2007	335,630	191,146	710,377	1,834,181
2008	346,214	195,729	721,551	1,876,661
2009	355,853	199,352	733,842	1,915,748

Source: U.S. Census Bureau

5.1.2 Banking

5.1.2.1 Commercial Banks, Comparison Counties and State, 1985-2009

	Utah County	Davis County	Salt Lake County	State
1985	44	33	179	418
1986	51	34	190	445
1987	51	34	192	440
1988	50	35	196	438
1989	49	35	197	440
1990	51	35	195	441
1991	52	36	198	441
1992	51	36	195	435
1993	51	36	195	430
1994	52	36	199	437
1995	53	39	202	453
1996	60	40	204	471
1997	67	44	223	521
1998	72	50	230	547
1999	74	51	237	561
2000	74	54	245	576
2001	78	53	237	574
2002	78	53	235	577
2003	80	50	237	574
2004	81	50	248	583
2005	81	53	252	594
2006	83	52	255	604
2007	87	52	261	615
2008	91	52	260	621
2009	93	54	259	625

Source: U.S. Census Bureau

5.1.2.2 Total Deposits, Comparison Counties and State, 1985-2009, in Thousands

	Utah County	Davis County	Salt Lake County	State
1985	709,896	393,201	4,276,550	7,665,218
1986	764,172	402,244	4,694,085	8,228,189
1987	801,009	426,857	4,868,409	8,520,122
1988	834,060	443,521	4,643,128	8,370,000
1989	894,019	496,972	4,759,016	8,791,260
1990	1,001,862	539,767	5,431,433	9,778,768
1991	1,050,529	603,770	5,709,690	10,250,071
1992	1,088,227	636,359	5,698,407	10,372,356
1993	1,179,245	682,673	5,825,410	10,760,011
1994	1,270,441	732,587	6,313,466	11,563,020
1995	1,401,140	778,139	6,931,737	12,572,048
1996	1,488,275	833,656	7,689,359	13,799,329
1997	1,598,080	917,611	9,861,202	16,398,617
1998	1,789,672	1,045,916	9,962,757	17,129,079
1999	1,876,027	1,076,780	11,768,833	19,248,766
2000	1,966,822	1,155,102	30,245,877	38,208,471
2001	2,066,558	1,333,464	72,695,228	81,362,340
2002	2,234,000	1,418,000	75,013,000	84,226,000
2003	2,373,000	1,473,000	75,341,000	84,962,000
2004	2,440,000	1,584,000	91,777,000	102,048,000
2005	2,676,000	1,759,000	100,828,000	118,114,000
2006	3,059,000	2,209,000	120,603,000	143,266,000
2007	3,312,000	2,397,000	156,251,000	181,652,000
2008	3,362,000	2,551,000	200,839,000	229,330,000
2009	3,377,000	2,462,000	245,964,000	275,292,000

Source: U.S. Census Bureau

24

5.1.3 Business and Industry

5.1.3.1 Total Earnings, By Industry

	Earnings in Thousands $
Earnings in all industries (NAICS, no code) 2001	45,570,562
Earnings in all industries (NAICS, no code) 2002	47,534,147
Earnings in all industries (NAICS, no code) 2003	48,676,208
Earnings in all industries (NAICS, no code) 2004	52,434,746
Earnings in all industries (NAICS, no code) 2005	56,648,640
Earnings in all industries (NAICS, no code) 2006	61,824,993
Earnings in all industries (NAICS, no code) 2007	66,372,417
Earnings in all industries (NAICS, no code), average earnings per job 2004	35,991
Earnings in all industries (NAICS, no code), average earnings per job 2005	37,180
Earnings in all industries (NAICS, no code), average earnings per job 2006	38,579
Earnings in all industries (NAICS, no code), average earnings per job 2007	39,651
Farm earnings (NAICS, no code) 2001	297,529
Farm earnings (NAICS, no code) 2002	180,687
Farm earnings (NAICS, no code) 2003	208,888
Farm earnings (NAICS, no code) 2004	278,957
Farm earnings (NAICS, no code) 2005	246,234
Farm earnings (NAICS, no code) 2006	110,011
Farm earnings (NAICS, no code) 2007	186,047
Earnings in agriculture, forestry, fishing, and hunting (NAICS 11) 2001	55,118
Earnings in agriculture, forestry, fishing, and hunting (NAICS 11) 2002	46,069
Earnings in agriculture, forestry, fishing, and hunting (NAICS 11) 2003	50,461
Earnings in agriculture, forestry, fishing, and hunting (NAICS 11) 2004	50,788
Earnings in agriculture, forestry, fishing, and hunting (NAICS 11) 2005	54,446
Earnings in agriculture, forestry, fishing, and hunting (NAICS 11) 2006	61,100
Earnings in agriculture, forestry, fishing, and hunting (NAICS 11) 2007	70,750
Earnings in mining (NAICS 21) 2001	509,577
Earnings in mining (NAICS 21) 2002	532,637
Earnings in mining (NAICS 21) 2003	540,759
Earnings in mining (NAICS 21) 2004	656,558
Earnings in mining (NAICS 21) 2005	782,327
Earnings in mining (NAICS 21) 2006	1,020,766
Earnings in mining (NAICS 21) 2007	1,168,058
Earnings in utilities (NAICS 22) 2001	395,309

	Earnings in Thousands $
Earnings in utilities (NAICS 22) 2002	459,954
Earnings in utilities (NAICS 22) 2003	366,172
Earnings in utilities (NAICS 22) 2004	407,838
Earnings in utilities (NAICS 22) 2005	419,901
Earnings in utilities (NAICS 22) 2006	473,612
Earnings in utilities (NAICS 22) 2007	481,972
Earnings in construction (NAICS 23) 2001	3,447,200
Earnings in construction (NAICS 23) 2002	3,580,465
Earnings in construction (NAICS 23) 2003	3,510,360
Earnings in construction (NAICS 23) 2004	3,843,588
Earnings in construction (NAICS 23) 2005	4,452,093
Earnings in construction (NAICS 23) 2006	5,334,442
Earnings in construction (NAICS 23) 2007	5,724,470
Earnings in manufacturing (NAICS 31-33) 2001	5,724,441
Earnings in manufacturing (NAICS 31-33) 2002	5,718,329
Earnings in manufacturing (NAICS 31-33) 2003	6,017,090
Earnings in manufacturing (NAICS 31-33) 2004	6,484,455
Earnings in manufacturing (NAICS 31-33) 2005	6,744,183
Earnings in manufacturing (NAICS 31-33) 2006	7,433,295
Earnings in manufacturing (NAICS 31-33) 2007	7,979,603
Earnings in computer and electronic product manufacturing (NAICS 334) 2005	749,335
Earnings in computer and electronic product manufacturing (NAICS 334) 2006	834,913
Earnings in computer and electronic product manufacturing (NAICS 334) 2007	1,005,250
Earnings in motor vehicles, bodies and trailers, and parts manufacturing (NAICS 336) 2005	NA
Earnings in motor vehicles, bodies and trailers, and parts manufacturing (NAICS 336) 2006	NA
Earnings in motor vehicles, bodies and trailers, and parts manufacturing (NAICS 336) 2007	NA
Earnings in chemical manufacturing (NAICS 325) 2005	630,173
Earnings in chemical manufacturing (NAICS 325) 2006	726,865
Earnings in chemical manufacturing (NAICS 325) 2007	728,726

	Earnings in Thousands $
Earnings in wholesale trade (NAICS 42) 2001	2,128,164
Earnings in wholesale trade (NAICS 42) 2002	2,120,316
Earnings in wholesale trade (NAICS 42) 2003	2,164,106
Earnings in wholesale trade (NAICS 42) 2004	2,336,127
Earnings in wholesale trade (NAICS 42) 2005	2,592,648
Earnings in wholesale trade (NAICS 42) 2006	2,854,575
Earnings in wholesale trade (NAICS 42) 2007	3,143,922
Earnings in retail trade (NAICS 44-45) 2001	3,548,428
Earnings in retail trade (NAICS 44-45) 2002	3,639,657
Earnings in retail trade (NAICS 44-45) 2003	3,745,249
Earnings in retail trade (NAICS 44-45) 2004	4,000,677
Earnings in retail trade (NAICS 44-45) 2005	4,256,761
Earnings in retail trade (NAICS 44-45) 2006	4,678,838
Earnings in retail trade (NAICS 44-45) 2007	5,138,055
Earnings in transportation and warehousing (NAICS 48-49) 2001	2,013,069
Earnings in transportation and warehousing (NAICS 48-49) 2002	2,099,374
Earnings in transportation and warehousing (NAICS 48-49) 2003	2,100,420
Earnings in transportation and warehousing (NAICS 48-49) 2004	2,339,759
Earnings in transportation and warehousing (NAICS 48-49) 2005	2,491,349
Earnings in transportation and warehousing (NAICS 48-49) 2006	2,569,311
Earnings in transportation and warehousing (NAICS 48-49) 2007	2,896,873
Earnings in information (NAICS 51) 2001	1,610,334
Earnings in information (NAICS 51) 2002	1,547,549
Earnings in information (NAICS 51) 2003	1,545,802
Earnings in information (NAICS 51) 2004	1,603,195
Earnings in information (NAICS 51) 2005	1,827,679
Earnings in information (NAICS 51) 2006	1,806,953
Earnings in information (NAICS 51) 2007	1,782,130
Earnings in finance and insurance (NAICS 52) 2001	2,603,154
Earnings in finance and insurance (NAICS 52) 2002	2,754,483
Earnings in finance and insurance (NAICS 52) 2003	2,897,209
Earnings in finance and insurance (NAICS 52) 2004	3,089,127
Earnings in finance and insurance (NAICS 52) 2005	3,272,186
Earnings in finance and insurance (NAICS 52) 2006	3,583,994
Earnings in finance and insurance (NAICS 52) 2007	3,850,810

	Earnings in Thousands $
Earnings in real estate and rental and leasing (NAICS 53) 2001	912,975
Earnings in real estate and rental and leasing (NAICS 53) 2002	1,019,539
Earnings in real estate and rental and leasing (NAICS 53) 2003	1,031,170
Earnings in real estate and rental and leasing (NAICS 53) 2004	1,109,328
Earnings in real estate and rental and leasing (NAICS 53) 2005	1,306,144
Earnings in real estate and rental and leasing (NAICS 53) 2006	1,393,782
Earnings in real estate and rental and leasing (NAICS 53) 2007	1,375,197
Earnings in professional and technical services (NAICS 54) 2001	3,759,207
Earnings in professional and technical services (NAICS 54) 2002	4,006,970
Earnings in professional and technical services (NAICS 54) 2003	3,982,146
Earnings in professional and technical services (NAICS 54) 2004	4,464,592
Earnings in professional and technical services (NAICS 54) 2005	4,999,036
Earnings in professional and technical services (NAICS 54) 2006	5,554,775
Earnings in professional and technical services (NAICS 54) 2007	6,032,773
Earnings in management of companies and enterprises (NAICS 55) 2001	1,190,454
Earnings in management of companies and enterprises (NAICS 55) 2002	1,112,339
Earnings in management of companies and enterprises (NAICS 55) 2003	1,038,662
Earnings in management of companies and enterprises (NAICS 55) 2004	1,074,277
Earnings in management of companies and enterprises (NAICS 55) 2005	1,174,582
Earnings in management of companies and enterprises (NAICS 55) 2006	1,300,458
Earnings in management of companies and enterprises (NAICS 55) 2007	1,412,109
Earnings in administrative and support and waste management and remediation services (NAICS 56) 2001	1,585,245
Earnings in administrative and support and waste management and remediation services (NAICS 56) 2002	1,588,025
Earnings in administrative and support and waste management and remediation services (NAICS 56) 2004	1,808,122
Earnings in administrative and support and waste management and remediation services (NAICS 56) 2005	1,975,150
Earnings in administrative and support and waste management and remediation services (NAICS 56) 2006	2,246,054
Earnings in administrative and support and waste management and remediation services (NAICS 56) 2007	2,464,719
Earnings in educational services (NAICS 61) 2001	650,090
Earnings in educational services (NAICS 61) 2002	704,954

	Earnings in Thousands $
Earnings in educational services (NAICS 61) 2003	722,492
Earnings in educational services (NAICS 61) 2004	786,293
Earnings in educational services (NAICS 61) 2005	870,955
Earnings in educational services (NAICS 61) 2006	947,380
Earnings in educational services (NAICS 61) 2007	999,493
Earnings in health care and social assistance (NAICS 62) 2001	3,233,768
Earnings in health care and social assistance (NAICS 62) 2002	3,519,006
Earnings in health care and social assistance (NAICS 62) 2003	3,697,697
Earnings in health care and social assistance (NAICS 62) 2004	3,965,168
Earnings in health care and social assistance (NAICS 62) 2005	4,294,769
Earnings in health care and social assistance (NAICS 62) 2006	4,691,127
Earnings in health care and social assistance (NAICS 62) 2007	4,967,035
Earnings in arts, entertainment, and recreation (NAICS 71) 2001	455,429
Earnings in arts, entertainment, and recreation (NAICS 71) 2002	557,897
Earnings in arts, entertainment, and recreation (NAICS 71) 2003	448,921
Earnings in arts, entertainment, and recreation (NAICS 71) 2004	461,678
Earnings in arts, entertainment, and recreation (NAICS 71) 2005	488,989
Earnings in arts, entertainment, and recreation (NAICS 71) 2006	548,186
Earnings in arts, entertainment, and recreation (NAICS 71) 2007	590,250
Earnings in accommodation and food services (NAICS 72) 2001	1,184,475
Earnings in accommodation and food services (NAICS 72) 2002	1,260,058
Earnings in accommodation and food services (NAICS 72) 2003	1,291,170
Earnings in accommodation and food services (NAICS 72) 2004	1,365,940
Earnings in accommodation and food services (NAICS 72) 2005	1,465,313
Earnings in accommodation and food services (NAICS 72) 2006	1,631,378
Earnings in accommodation and food services (NAICS 72) 2007	1,763,495
Earnings in accommodation (NAICS 721) 2001	341,212
Earnings in accommodation (NAICS 721) 2002	368,126
Earnings in accommodation (NAICS 721) 2003	367,824
Earnings in accommodation (NAICS 721) 2004	382,364
Earnings in accommodation (NAICS 721) 2005	412,879
Earnings in accommodation (NAICS 721) 2006	459,287
Earnings in accommodation (NAICS 721) 2007	493,983
Earnings in food services and drinking places (NAICS 722) 2001	843,263
Earnings in food services and drinking places (NAICS 722) 2002	891,932

	Earnings in Thousands $
Earnings in food services and drinking places (NAICS 722) 2003	923,346
Earnings in food services and drinking places (NAICS 722) 2004	983,576
Earnings in food services and drinking places (NAICS 722) 2005	1,052,434
Earnings in food services and drinking places (NAICS 722) 2006	1,172,091
Earnings in food services and drinking places (NAICS 722) 2007	1,269,512
Earnings in other services, except public administration (NAICS 81) 2001	1,882,784
Earnings in other services, except public administration (NAICS 81) 2002	2,057,669
Earnings in other services, except public administration (NAICS 81) 2003	2,156,493
Earnings in other services, except public administration (NAICS 81) 2004	2,239,753
Earnings in other services, except public administration (NAICS 81) 2005	2,237,620
Earnings in other services, except public administration (NAICS 81) 2006	2,363,826
Earnings in other services, except public administration (NAICS 81) 2007	2,497,959

Source: U.S. Census Bureau

5.2 Education Data

5.2.1   Dropout Rates

	05-06	06-07	07-08
ACADEMY FOR MATH ENGINEERING & SCIENCE (AMES)			2
ALPINE DISTRICT	0.7	5.6	3.2
AMERICAN LEADERSHIP ACADEMY	2.9	1.3	1.9
BEAVER DISTRICT	2.7		0.8
BOX ELDER DISTRICT	3.4	2.2	2.9
CACHE DISTRICT	1.2	1.5	1.5
CARBON DISTRICT	1	1	1.6
CBA CENTER	71	32.1	83.3
CITY ACADEMY		5.8	9.7
DAGGETT DISTRICT	0	0	0
DAVINCI ACADEMY		2.1	20
DAVIS DISTRICT	2.1	4.5	2.8
DUCHESNE DISTRICT	7.1	7.2	5.5
EAST HOLLYWOOD HIGH		2.8	10.7
EMERY DISTRICT	1.7	3.5	2.9
FAST FORWARD HIGH	12.1	28.4	29.8
GARFIELD DISTRICT	2.2		3.9
GRAND DISTRICT		3.4	2.4
GRANITE DISTRICT	2.4	3.2	5.8
IRON DISTRICT	4.8	3.7	3.2
JORDAN DISTRICT	5.7	2.9	3
JUAB DISTRICT		0.9	0.8
KANE DISTRICT		1.4	2.9
LOGAN DISTRICT	1	3.2	2.2
MILLARD DISTRICT	2.8	2.5	2.6
MORGAN DISTRICT	1.5	1.2	1.4

	05-06	06-07	07-08
MURRAY DISTRICT	0.7	1.8	5
NEBO DISTRICT	0.8	2.6	2.3
NO UT ACAD FOR MATH ENGINEERING & SCIENCE (NUAMES)		3.3	6.5
NORTH SANPETE DISTRICT	5.9	7.9	7.6
NORTH SUMMIT DISTRICT		1.7	1.9
OGDEN DISTRICT	17.9	14.7	15.2
PARADIGM HIGH SCHOOL			12.1
PARK CITY DISTRICT	2.6	3.2	2.2
PROVO DISTRICT	1.7	6.1	3.9
SALT LAKE DISTRICT	7	4.9	9.4
SAN JUAN DISTRICT	2.5	2.6	2.8
SEVIER DISTRICT	6.1	5.7	5.2
SOUTH SANPETE DISTRICT	1.8	2.7	2.4
SOUTH SUMMIT DISTRICT	3	3.5	2.9
TINTIC DISTRICT	0		
TOOELE DISTRICT	3.1	7.3	5.8
UINTAH DISTRICT	8.1	6.2	6.8
UINTAH RIVER HIGH	21	25.5	23.5
WASATCH DISTRICT	1.9	5.1	6.2
WASHINGTON DISTRICT	3.1	6.2	3.3
WAYNE DISTRICT		3.9	5
WEBER DISTRICT	2.3	2.5	3.2

Source: National Center for Education Statistics

5.2.2   Total Dropouts, by County, 2006-2008

County	2005-2006	2006-2007	2007-2008
Utah County	242	1,000	933
Davis County	384	633	579
Salt Lake County	2,317	1,287	2,922

Source: National Center for Education Statistics

5.2.3   Averaged Freshman Graduation Rate

	06-07	07-08
ALPINE DISTRICT	78.6	74.6
BEAVER DISTRICT	83.2	77.7
BOX ELDER DISTRICT	74.7	71.1
CACHE DISTRICT	88.5	89.3
CARBON DISTRICT	84.5	79.7
CITY ACADEMY	11.4	9.1
DAGGETT DISTRICT	100	100
DAVIS DISTRICT	80	83.1
DUCHESNE DISTRICT	71.3	73.8
EAST HOLLYWOOD HIGH		38.7
EMERY DISTRICT	81.3	77.1
GARFIELD DISTRICT	70.9	62.2
GRAND DISTRICT	82.5	77
GRANITE DISTRICT	63.3	61.6
IRON DISTRICT	80.6	83.5
JORDAN DISTRICT	80.8	78.4
JUAB DISTRICT	85.2	80
KANE DISTRICT	69.5	67.6
LOGAN DISTRICT	88.5	86.3
MILLARD DISTRICT	86.6	90.4
MORGAN DISTRICT	98.1	91.6
MURRAY DISTRICT	83.7	79.6
NEBO DISTRICT	81.3	74.9
NORTH SANPETE DISTRICT	68	61.6
NORTH SUMMIT DISTRICT	100	100
OGDEN DISTRICT	53.9	51.3
PARK CITY DISTRICT	83.2	82.2
PIUTE DISTRICT	75	75

	06-07	07-08
PROVO DISTRICT	71.4	73
RICH DISTRICT	87	100
SALT LAKE DISTRICT	63.1	62
SAN JUAN DISTRICT	77.5	84.6
SEVIER DISTRICT	77.9	81
SOUTH SANPETE DISTRICT	90.1	85.3
SOUTH SUMMIT DISTRICT	87.3	87
TINTIC DISTRICT		85.7
TOOELE DISTRICT	69.3	67.9
UINTAH DISTRICT	61.6	60.1
WASATCH DISTRICT	83.3	81.3
WASHINGTON DISTRICT	80.5	74.6
WAYNE DISTRICT	81	94.4
WEBER DISTRICT	77.1	76.1
Source: National Center for Education Statistics		

5.2.4   Averaged Freshman Graduation Rate, By State

State	05-06	06-07	07-08
AK	66.5	69.1	69.1
AL	66.2	67.1	69
AR	80.4	74.4	76.4
AZ	70.5	69.6	70.7
CA	69.2	70.7	71.2
CO	75.5	76.6	75.4
CT	80.9	81.8	82.2
DC		54.9	56
DE	76.3	71.9	72.1
FL	63.6	65	66.9
GA	62.4	64.1	65.4
HI	75.5	75.4	76
IA	86.9	86.5	86.4
ID	80.5	80.4	80.1
IL	79.7	79.5	80.4
IN	73.3	73.9	74.1
KS	77.6	78.9	79.1
KY	77.2	76.4	74.4
LA	59.5	61.3	63.5
MA	79.5	80.8	81.5
MD	79.9	80	80.4
ME	76.3	78.5	79.1
MI	72.2	77	76.3
MN	86.2	86.5	86.4

State	05-06	06-07	07-08
MS	63.5	63.6	63.9
MT	81.9	81.5	82
NC	71.8	68.6	72.8
ND	82.1	83.1	83.8
NE	87	86.3	83.8
NH	81.1	81.7	83.4
NJ	84.8	84.4	84.6
NM	67.3	59.1	66.8
NV	55.8	52	51.3
NY	67.4	68.8	70.8
OH	79.2	78.7	79
OK	77.8	77.8	78
OR	73	73.8	76.7
PA		83	82.7
RI	77.8	78.4	76.4
SC		58.9	
SD	84.5	82.5	84.4
TN	70.6	72.6	74.9
TX	72.5	71.9	73.1
UT	78.6	76.6	74.3
VA	74.5	75.5	77
VT	82.3	88.6	89.3
WA	72.9	74.8	71.9
WI	87.5	88.5	89.6
WV	76.9	78.2	77.3
WY	76.1	75.8	76
		USA	75.966
Source: National Center for Education Statistics			

5.2.5   Diploma Recipients, 2004-2008

	Diplomas 04-05	Diplomas 05-06	Diplomas 06-07	Diplomas 07-08	Other Complete 04-05	Other Complete 05-06	Other Complete 06-07	Other Completers 07-08
ACADEMY FOR MATH ENGINEERING & SCIENCE (AMES)	0		83	83	0			
ALPINE DISTRICT	3,295		2,952	2,936	43		109	
AMERICAN LEADERSHIP ACADEMY			50	50			3	
AMERICAN PREPARATORY ACADEMY								
BEAVER DISTRICT	88		94	94	1		3	
BEEHIVE SCIENCE & TECHNOLOGY ACADEMY (BSTA)								
BOX ELDER DISTRICT	762		616	615	0		41	
CACHE DISTRICT	909		914	911	43		54	
CANYON RIM ACADEMY								
CANYONS DISTRICT								
CARBON DISTRICT	276		240	240	0		12	
CBA CENTER	8		6	6	0			
CENTRAL UTAH ED SERVICES								
CHANNING HALL								
CITY ACADEMY	2		4	4	1		2	
CS LEWIS ACADEMY								
DAGGETT DISTRICT	21		13	13	0		1	
DAVINCI ACADEMY	0		47	47	0			
DAVIS DISTRICT	3,690		3,706	3,695	0		426	
DREAM CHARTER SCHOOL	4				0			
DUAL IMMERSION ACADEMY								
DUCHESNE DISTRICT	269		234	234	0		13	

	Diplomas 04-05	Diplomas 05-06	Diplomas 06-07	Diplomas 07-08	Other Complete 04-05	Other Complete 05-06	Other Complete 06-07	Other Completers 07-08
EARLY LIGHT ACADEMY AT DAYBREAK								
EAST HOLLYWOOD HIGH			29	29			5	
EDITH BOWEN LABORATORY SCHOOL								
EMERSON ALCOTT ACADEMY								
EMERY DISTRICT	185		165	165	0		1	
ENTHEOS ACADEMY								
EXCELSIOR ACADEMY								
FAST FORWARD HIGH	10		41	41	0		1	
FREEDOM ACADEMY								
GARFIELD DISTRICT	79		56	56	1		3	
GATEWAY PREPARATORY ACADEMY								
GEORGE WASHINGTON ACADEMY								
GRAND DISTRICT	119		94	94	2		2	
GRANITE DISTRICT	3,916		3,284	3,244	0			
GUADALUPE SCHOOL								
HAWTHORN ACADEMY								
INTECH COLLEGIATE HIGH SCHOOL								
IRON DISTRICT	439		479	477	0		22	
ITINERIS EARLY COLLEGE HIGH	0		41	41	0			
JEAN MASSIEU SCHOOL								
JOHN HANCOCK CHARTER SCHOOL								
JORDAN DISTRICT	4,922		4,632	4,626	0		779	

	Diplomas 04-05	Diplomas 05-06	Diplomas 06-07	Diplomas 07-08	Other Complete 04-05	Other Complete 05-06	Other Complete 06-07	Other Completers 07-08
JUAB DISTRICT	114		121	120	1		3	
KANE DISTRICT	96		73	73	0		3	
KARL G MAESER PREPARATORY ACADEMY								
LAKEVIEW ACADEMY								
LEGACY PREPARATORY ACADEMY								
LIBERTY ACADEMY								
LINCOLN ACADEMY								
LOGAN DISTRICT	415		385	373	0		16	
MERIT COLLEGE PREPARATORY ACADEMY								
MILLARD DISTRICT	252		227	226	0		4	
MOAB COMMUNITY SCHOOL								
MONTICELLO ACADEMY								
MORGAN DISTRICT	159		152	152	0		4	
MOUNTAINVILLE ACADEMY								
MURRAY DISTRICT	460		438	434	4		16	
NAVIGATOR POINTE ACADEMY								
NEBO DISTRICT	1,364		1,346	1,345	0		97	
NO UT ACAD FOR MATH ENGINEERING & SCIENCE (NUAMES)	1		62	62	0		3	
NOAH WEBSTER ACADEMY								
NORTH DAVIS PREPARATORY ACADEMY								
NORTH SANPETE DISTRICT	175		123	122	0			

	Diplomas 04-05	Diplomas 05-06	Diplomas 06-07	Diplomas 07-08	Other Complete 04-05	Other Complete 05-06	Other Complete 06-07	Other Completers 07-08
NORTH STAR ACADEMY								
NORTH SUMMIT DISTRICT	74		80	80	0		2	
NORTHEASTERN UTAH ED SERV								
ODYSSEY CHARTER SCHOOL								
OGDEN DISTRICT	595		466	461	10		85	
OGDEN PREPARATORY ACADEMY								
OPEN CLASSROOM								
OPEN HIGH SCHOOL OF UTAH								
OQUIRRH MOUNTAIN CHARTER SCHOOL								
PARADIGM HIGH SCHOOL			5				3	
PARK CITY DISTRICT	284		287	287	1		6	
PINNACLE CANYON ACADEMY								
PIUTE DISTRICT	23		21	21	0		1	
PROVIDENCE HALL								
PROVO DISTRICT	798		706	707	6		50	
QUEST ACADEMY								
RANCHES ACADEMY								
REAGAN ACADEMY								
RENAISSANCE ACADEMY								
RICH DISTRICT	37		40	40	0		1	
ROCKWELL CHARTER HIGH SCHOOL								
SALT LAKE ARTS ACADEMY								
SALT LAKE CNTR SCIENCE EDUCATN								

	Diplomas 04-05	Diplomas 05-06	Diplomas 06-07	Diplomas 07-08	Other Complete 04-05	Other Complete 05-06	Other Complete 06-07	Other Completers 07-08
SALT LAKE DISTRICT	1,178		1,032	1,036	17		10	
SALT LAKE SCHOOL FOR THE PERFORMING ARTS			8	8				
SAN JUAN DISTRICT	184		207	204	3		20	
SEVIER DISTRICT	298		282	282	0		5	
SOLDIER HOLLOW CHARTER SCHOOL								
SOUTH SANPETE DISTRICT	212		183	180	0		7	
SOUTH SUMMIT DISTRICT	89		96	94	0		1	
SOUTHEAST ED SERVICE CENTER								
SOUTHWEST ED. DEV. CENTER								
SPECTRUM ACADEMY								
SUCCESS ACADEMY								
SUCCESS SCHOOL				2				
SUMMIT ACADEMY								
SYRACUSE ARTS ACADEMY								
THOMAS EDISON - NORTH								
THOMAS EDISON - SOUTH								
TIMPANOGOS ACADEMY								
TINTIC DISTRICT	21			18	0			
TOOELE DISTRICT	504		518	518	1		24	
TUACAHN HIGH SCHOOL FOR THE PERFORMING ARTS	36		46		1		1	
UINTAH DISTRICT	370		253	252	5		34	
UINTAH RIVER HIGH	10		4	4	0		1	
USOE								

	Diplomas 04-05	Diplomas 05-06	Diplomas 06-07	Diplomas 07-08	Other Complete 04-05	Other Complete 05-06	Other Complete 06-07	Other Completers 07-08
UTAH COUNTY ACADEMY OF SCIENCE (UCAS)			42	42			3	
UTAH SCHOOLS FOR DEAF & BLIND	0			5	0		23	
UTAH STATE UNIVERSITY								
UTAH VIRTUAL ACADEMY								
VENTURE ACADEMY								
VISTA AT ENTRADA								
WALDEN SCHOOL OF LIBERAL ARTS								
WASATCH DISTRICT	270		260	260	0		10	
WASATCH PEAK ACADEMY								
WASHINGTON DISTRICT	1,357		1,258	1,254	6		102	
WAYNE DISTRICT	41		34	34	0		2	
WEBER DISTRICT	1,842		1,716	1,719	0		135	

Source: National Center for
Education Statistics

5.2.6 Migrant Students/Free and Reduced-Price Lunch Students

	Migrant Students 04-05	Migrant Students 05-06	Migrant Students 06-07	Free/Reduced Lunch 04-05	Free/Reduced Lunch 05-06	Free/Reduced Lunch 06-07	Free/Reduced Lunch 07-08	Free/Reduced Lunch 08-09
ACADEMY FOR MATH ENGINEERING & SCIENCE (AMES)	0			0	0	0		216
ALPINE DISTRICT	64			12,947	13,561	8,673	10,428	13,273
AMERICAN LEADERSHIP ACADEMY					0	420	396	410
AMERICAN PREPARATORY ACADEMY	0			0	0	11		86
BEAVER DISTRICT	60		78	718	740	747	566	750
BEEHIVE SCIENCE & TECHNOLOGY ACADEMY (BSTA)					0	2		48
BOX ELDER DISTRICT	174		195	3,672	3,606	3,726	3,466	3,889
CACHE DISTRICT	50		42	3,931	4,306	4,193	3,348	4,198
CANYON RIM ACADEMY							81	76
CANYONS DISTRICT								
CARBON DISTRICT	0			1,577	1,520	1,730	1,502	1,825
CBA CENTER	0			0	18	27	21	23
CENTRAL UTAH ED SERVICES								
CHANNING HALL						93	57	60
CITY ACADEMY	0			87	72	84	57	69
CS LEWIS ACADEMY								77
DAGGETT DISTRICT	0			40	53	33	140	27
DAVINCI ACADEMY	0			0	117	147	144	140
DAVIS DISTRICT	69		82	14,373	14,583	16,748	18,019	19,351
DREAM CHARTER SCHOOL				0				
DUAL IMMERSION ACADEMY							200	249
DUCHESNE DISTRICT	0			1,705	1,592	1,507	1,399	1,540
EARLY LIGHT ACADEMY AT DAYBREAK								
EAST HOLLYWOOD HIGH	0			0	0	7		81

	Migrant Students 04-05	Migrant Students 05-06	Migrant Students 06-07	Free/Reduced Lunch 04-05	Free/Reduced Lunch 05-06	Free/Reduced Lunch 06-07	Free/Reduced Lunch 07-08	Free/Reduced Lunch 08-09
EDITH BOWEN LABORATORY SCHOOL							57	80
EMERSON ALCOTT ACADEMY								
EMERY DISTRICT	0			1,138	1,070	1,075	1,033	1,060
ENTHEOS ACADEMY						223	143	178
EXCELSIOR ACADEMY								
FAST FORWARD HIGH	0			0	0	0		9
FREEDOM ACADEMY	0			67	137	237	295	332
GARFIELD DISTRICT	0			424	418	444	568	402
GATEWAY PREPARATORY ACADEMY								
GEORGE WASHINGTON ACADEMY						59		109
GRAND DISTRICT	0			651	687	686	608	696
GRANITE DISTRICT	0			28,403	28,009	20,129	33,130	15,670
GUADALUPE SCHOOL								94
HAWTHORN ACADEMY								
INTECH COLLEGIATE HIGH SCHOOL						30	89	51
IRON DISTRICT	6		8	2,987	2,764	3,678	3,764	2,806
ITINERIS EARLY COLLEGE HIGH	0			0	0	23	20	
JEAN MASSIEU SCHOOL				23				
JOHN HANCOCK CHARTER SCHOOL	0			0	0	3		39
JORDAN DISTRICT	0		81	16,033	16,269	16,414	17,534	17,435
JUAB DISTRICT	0			739	716	833	767	717
KANE DISTRICT	0			359	438	442	481	544
KARL G MAESER PREPARATORY ACADEMY								31
LAKEVIEW ACADEMY						107	79	93

	Migrant Students 04-05	Migrant Students 05-06	Migrant Students 06-07	Free/Reduced Lunch 04-05	Free/Reduced Lunch 05-06	Free/Reduced Lunch 06-07	Free/Reduced Lunch 07-08	Free/Reduced Lunch 08-09
LEGACY PREPARATORY ACADEMY						62	1	93
LIBERTY ACADEMY						46		
LINCOLN ACADEMY					0	21		11
LOGAN DISTRICT	0			1,971	2,475	2,687	3,175	3,092
MERIT COLLEGE PREPARATORY ACADEMY								60
MILLARD DISTRICT	182		99	1,423	1,404	1,340	1,270	1,421
MOAB COMMUNITY SCHOOL	0			68	24	18	28	31
MONTICELLO ACADEMY						139	189	222
MORGAN DISTRICT	0			374	330	329	330	319
MOUNTAINVILLE ACADEMY						29		42
MURRAY DISTRICT	0			1,673	1,676	1,818	2,021	1,961
NAVIGATOR POINTE ACADEMY					0	15		74
NEBO DISTRICT	641		498	7,252	7,005	7,301		8,918
NO UT ACAD FOR MATH ENGINEERING & SCIENCE (NUAMES)	0			0	112	104	87	61
NOAH WEBSTER ACADEMY						35		86
NORTH DAVIS PREPARATORY ACADEMY	0			0	97	206	129	278
NORTH SANPETE DISTRICT	221		105	842	1,170	1,180	1,239	1,204
NORTH STAR ACADEMY					0	84	61	37
NORTH SUMMIT DISTRICT	0			249	224	192	223	215
NORTHEASTERN UTAH ED SERV								
ODYSSEY CHARTER SCHOOL					34	9		93
OGDEN DISTRICT	1,489		632	8,480	8,444	6,865	9,764	10,076
OGDEN PREPARATORY ACADEMY	0			152	235	386	254	305
OPEN CLASSROOM							17	38
OPEN HIGH SCHOOL OF UTAH								

	Migrant Students 04-05	Migrant Students 05-06	Migrant Students 06-07	Free/Reduced Lunch 04-05	Free/Reduced Lunch 05-06	Free/Reduced Lunch 06-07	Free/Reduced Lunch 07-08	Free/Reduced Lunch 08-09
OQUIRRH MOUNTAIN CHARTER SCHOOL								
PARADIGM HIGH SCHOOL						0		110
PARK CITY DISTRICT	0			351	538	582	706	823
PINNACLE CANYON ACADEMY	0			89	148	254	245	271
PIUTE DISTRICT	0		22	227	216	160	208	210
PROVIDENCE HALL								41
PROVO DISTRICT	21		93	5,849	5,959	6,418	6,612	6,980
QUEST ACADEMY								117
RANCHES ACADEMY	0			0	0	16		78
REAGAN ACADEMY					151	304	208	238
RENAISSANCE ACADEMY						32		84
RICH DISTRICT	0			215	197	210	223	226
ROCKWELL CHARTER HIGH SCHOOL								
SALT LAKE ARTS ACADEMY	0			0	0	20		29
SALT LAKE CENTER FOR SCIENCE EDUCATION								78
SALT LAKE DISTRICT	0			12,802	14,334	14,939	16,024	15,967
SALT LAKE SCHOOL FOR THE PERFORMING ARTS						23	16	16
SAN JUAN DISTRICT	0			2,173	2,150	2,148	1,076	2,010
SEVIER DISTRICT	0			1,933	1,936	2,069	2,077	2,165
SOLDIER HOLLOW CHARTER SCHOOL	0			0	0	29		65
SOUTH SANPETE DISTRICT	103			1,393	1,367	1,392	1,468	1,418
SOUTH SUMMIT DISTRICT	0			266	233	254	237	278
SOUTHEAST ED SERVICE CENTER								
SOUTHWEST ED. DEV. CENTER								
SPECTRUM ACADEMY						38		70

	Migrant Students 04-05	Migrant Students 05-06	Migrant Students 06-07	Free/Reduced Lunch 04-05	Free/Reduced Lunch 05-06	Free/Reduced Lunch 06-07	Free/Reduced Lunch 07-08	Free/Reduced Lunch 08-09
SUCCESS ACADEMY					0	43	38	50
SUCCESS SCHOOL	0			0	0	18	9	4
SUMMIT ACADEMY	0			0	0	43		59
SYRACUSE ARTS ACADEMY						146	63	123
THOMAS EDISON - NORTH	0			0	0	51		
THOMAS EDISON - SOUTH					0	63		
TIMPANOGOS ACADEMY	0			0	0	6		
TINTIC DISTRICT	0			160	166	8	130	132
TOOELE DISTRICT	0			4,021	4,289	4,545	4,633	4,777
TUACAHN HIGH SCHOOL FOR THE PERFORMING ARTS	0			0	0	0		
UINTAH DISTRICT	0			2,318	2,112	2,316	2,158	2,067
UINTAH RIVER HIGH	0			0	34	37	35	31
USOE								
UTAH COUNTY ACADEMY OF SCIENCE (UCAS)					26	51	48	54
UTAH SCHOOLS FOR DEAF & BLIND	0					67		
UTAH STATE UNIVERSITY	0			70	72			
UTAH VIRTUAL ACADEMY								
VENTURE ACADEMY								
VISTA AT ENTRADA								
WALDEN SCHOOL OF LIBERAL ARTS	0			0	0	0	63	149
WASATCH DISTRICT	0			1,154	1,174	1,239	1,376	1,511
WASATCH PEAK ACADEMY					56	105	97	68
WASHINGTON DISTRICT	0			7,066	7,268	8,034	8,481	9,492
WAYNE DISTRICT	0			264	248	246	277	290
WEBER DISTRICT	0			7,342	7,675	9,256	8,888	9,277

Source: National Center for Education Statistics

5.2.7 LEP/ELL and IEP Students

	LEP/ELL 04-05	LEP/ELL 05-06	LEP/ELL 06-07	LEP/ELL 07-08	LEP/ELL 08-09	IEP 04-05	IEP -05-06	IEP 06-07	IEP 07-08	IEP 08-09
ACADEMY FOR MATH ENGINEERING & SCIENCE (AMES)	0	0	34	10	26	16	20	19	19	22
ALPINE DISTRICT	2,535	2,581	2,943	2,675	2,747	5,672	6,313	5,639	7,154	6,582
AMERICAN LEADERSHIP ACADEMY		0	0	0	0		138	185	201	225
AMERICAN PREPARATORY ACADEMY	0	0	0	0	0	41	47	39	39	42
BEAVER DISTRICT	61	82	66	61	66	242	240	186	209	213
BEEHIVE SCIENCE & TECHNOLOGY ACADEMY (BSTA)		2	3	9	16		4	16	16	37
BOX ELDER DISTRICT	419	485	503	401	416	1,322	1,447	1,180	1,603	1,325
CACHE DISTRICT	674	724	821	838	726	1,580	1,931	1,607	2,245	1,731
CANYON RIM ACADEMY				2	4					41
CANYONS DISTRICT										
CARBON DISTRICT	7	9	15	31	48	721	699	594	743	610
CBA CENTER	0	1	3	4	4	10	7	8	12	9
CENTRAL UTAH ED SERVICES										
CHANNING HALL				0	0			26	29	84
CITY ACADEMY	1	0	11	7	6	33	34	28	32	23
CS LEWIS ACADEMY				16	29					63
DAGGETT DISTRICT	2	2	2	1	0	22	26	15	18	17
DAVINCI ACADEMY	0	0	1	0	0	8	22	44	45	43
DAVIS DISTRICT	2,576	2,752	3,037	1,982	2,764	6,643	7,463	6,708	8,127	6,754
DREAM CHARTER SCHOOL	0					0				
DUAL IMMERSION ACADEMY				139	165					30
DUCHESNE DISTRICT	74	88	90	70	68	631	731	618	811	717

	LEP/ELL 04-05	LEP/ELL 05-06	LEP/ELL 06-07	LEP/ELL 07-08	LEP/ELL 08-09	IEP 04-05	IEP -05-06	IEP 06-07	IEP 07-08	IEP 08-09
EARLY LIGHT ACADEMY AT DAYBREAK										
EAST HOLLYWOOD HIGH	0	0	0	0	0	8	31	44	51	41
EDITH BOWEN LABORATORY SCHOOL				3	0					30
EMERSON ALCOTT ACADEMY										
EMERY DISTRICT	79	80	80	45	55	353	409	314	413	389
ENTHEOS ACADEMY				0	0			47	50	75
EXCELSIOR ACADEMY										
FAST FORWARD HIGH	0	0	0	0	0	43	62	50	58	31
FREEDOM ACADEMY	0	0	31	42	117	31	38	37	41	80
GARFIELD DISTRICT	33	56	52	31	29	164	176	158	200	125
GATEWAY PREPARATORY ACADEMY					0					45
GEORGE WASHINGTON ACADEMY				0	0			15	21	41
GRAND DISTRICT	45	75	65	96	94	201	259	210	267	200
GRANITE DISTRICT	12,848	16,187	15,130	13,049	13,314	8,890	8,295	7,825	9,145	7,603
GUADALUPE SCHOOL				60	64					8
HAWTHORN ACADEMY										
INTECH COLLEGIATE HIGH SCHOOL				5	4			4	5	9
IRON DISTRICT	460	343	400	280	282	1,093	1,280	1,145	1,453	1,113
ITINERIS EARLY COLLEGE HIGH	5	7	3	0	0	0	0			
JEAN MASSIEU SCHOOL	0					39				
JOHN HANCOCK CHARTER SCHOOL	0	0	4	0	0	21	25	29	30	25
JORDAN DISTRICT	3,981	4,008	4,437	3,854	3,907	9,307	9,993	9,170	11,402	9,185
JUAB DISTRICT	0	0	0	0	0	240	294	252	310	259

	LEP/ELL 04-05	LEP/ELL 05-06	LEP/ELL 06-07	LEP/ELL 07-08	LEP/ELL 08-09	IEP 04-05	IEP -05-06	IEP 06-07	IEP 07-08	IEP 08-09
KANE DISTRICT	14	19	18	14	12	209	246	195	242	195
KARL G MAESER PREPARATORY ACADEMY				0	2					16
LAKEVIEW ACADEMY				0	1			47	58	57
LEGACY PREPARATORY ACADEMY				0	0			35	38	39
LIBERTY ACADEMY				0	0			30	38	40
LINCOLN ACADEMY		0	0	0	0		45	58	58	72
LOGAN DISTRICT	689	816	654	545	684	668	766	671	910	747
MERIT COLLEGE PREPARATORY ACADEMY					0					27
MILLARD DISTRICT	273	288	305	235	235	429	520	479	577	435
MOAB COMMUNITY SCHOOL	0	0	0	3	0	9	11	15	17	13
MONTICELLO ACADEMY				0	0			33	36	62
MORGAN DISTRICT	6	8	11	12	13	136	157	153	181	174
MOUNTAINVILLE ACADEMY				1	1			58	64	84
MURRAY DISTRICT	409	438	421	468	367	623	678	569	722	654
NAVIGATOR POINTE ACADEMY		0	0	0	0		47	60	67	46
NEBO DISTRICT	984	1,041	1,222	1,149	1,138	3,413	3,703	3,279	4,375	3,993
NO UT ACAD FOR MATH ENGINEERING & SCIENCE (NUAMES)	7	5	10	0	7	12	9	13	13	4
NOAH WEBSTER ACADEMY				0	11			34	42	45
NORTH DAVIS PREPARATORY ACADEMY	0	0	0	0	0	23	43	47	53	74
NORTH SANPETE DISTRICT	194	182	202	169	142	330	311	291	321	326

	LEP/ELL 04-05	LEP/ELL 05-06	LEP/ELL 06-07	LEP/ELL 07-08	LEP/ELL 08-09	IEP 04-05	IEP -05-06	IEP 06-07	IEP 07-08	IEP 08-09
NORTH STAR ACADEMY		0	0	2	0		29	39	40	41
NORTH SUMMIT DISTRICT	59	68	71	51	48	115	145	118	152	127
NORTHEASTERN UTAH ED SERV										
ODYSSEY CHARTER SCHOOL		0	0	0	0		14	26	26	31
OGDEN DISTRICT	2,760	2,872	2,101	2,385	2,527	1,665	1,718	1,551	1,720	1,622
OGDEN PREPARATORY ACADEMY	6	4	15	22	20	40	67	79	81	67
OPEN CLASSROOM				8	9					30
OPEN HIGH SCHOOL OF UTAH										
OQUIRRH MOUNTAIN CHARTER SCHOOL										
PARADIGM HIGH SCHOOL				0	0			7	7	28
PARK CITY DISTRICT	421	439	450	496	399	479	485	461	525	378
PINNACLE CANYON ACADEMY	0	0	0	0	0	63	103	84	95	137
PIUTE DISTRICT	10	9	9	14	18	31	54	38	46	52
PROVIDENCE HALL					0					59
PROVO DISTRICT	2,520	2,597	2,751	2,841	2,090	1,723	1,796	1,780	2,171	1,824
QUEST ACADEMY					0					58
RANCHES ACADEMY	0	0	0	0	0	26	40	43	54	32
REAGAN ACADEMY		0	0	0	0		58	68	73	108
RENAISSANCE ACADEMY				0	0			44	47	35
RICH DISTRICT	10	7	6	3	8	47	51	35	45	46
ROCKWELL CHARTER HIGH SCHOOL					0					60
SALT LAKE ARTS ACADEMY	0	0	0	0	0	15	22	22	24	19
SALT LAKE CENTER FOR SCIENCE EDUCATION					13					16

	LEP/ELL 04-05	LEP/ELL 05-06	LEP/ELL 06-07	LEP/ELL 07-08	LEP/ELL 08-09	IEP 04-05	IEP -05-06	IEP 06-07	IEP 07-08	IEP 08-09
SALT LAKE DISTRICT	7,560	8,836	7,377	8,797	6,466	3,315	3,456	3,178	3,994	2,847
SALT LAKE SCHOOL FOR THE PERFORMING ARTS				0	5			7	8	4
SAN JUAN DISTRICT	1,222	573	248	662	624	333	361	322	416	344
SEVIER DISTRICT	127	146	152	101	111	593	636	539	701	645
SOLDIER HOLLOW CHARTER SCHOOL	0	0	0	0	0	5	5	19	23	33
SOUTH SANPETE DISTRICT	194	211	231	226	229	409	421	362	459	513
SOUTH SUMMIT DISTRICT	53	63	65	85	79	153	145	133	167	152
SOUTHEAST ED SERVICE CENTER										
SOUTHWEST ED. DEV. CENTER										
SPECTRUM ACADEMY				0	0			121	141	140
SUCCESS ACADEMY		4	6	2	0		0			1
SUCCESS SCHOOL	25	28	17	7	8	29	9	15	32	9
SUMMIT ACADEMY	0	0	0	0	0	26	47	39	46	67
SYRACUSE ARTS ACADEMY				0	0			31	34	33
THOMAS EDISON - NORTH	0	0	0	0	0	27	36	36	43	91
THOMAS EDISON - SOUTH		0	0	4			27	63	71	
TIMPANOGOS ACADEMY	0	0	0	0	0	18	32	27	28	30
TINTIC DISTRICT	0	0	0	0	0	41	50	35	44	21
TOOELE DISTRICT	491	636	731	650	699	1,505	1,755	1,567	2,064	1,675
TUACAHN HIGH SCHOOL FOR THE PERFORMING ARTS	0	0	0	0	0	0	0	17	17	21
UINTAH DISTRICT	577	41	38	55	79	831	812	754	848	848
UINTAH RIVER HIGH	0	0	0	0	0	0	7	7	7	7
UTAH COUNTY ACADEMY OF SCIENCE		0	0	0	0		0	1	1	1

	LEP/ELL 04-05	LEP/ELL 05-06	LEP/ELL 06-07	LEP/ELL 07-08	LEP/ELL 08-09	IEP 04-05	IEP -05-06	IEP 06-07	IEP 07-08	IEP 08-09
UTAH SCHOOLS FOR DEAF & BLIND	0	0	0	0	0	0	0		425	225
UTAH STATE UNIVERSITY	2	4				38	40	33		
UTAH VIRTUAL ACADEMY					0					43
VENTURE ACADEMY					0					35
VISTA AT ENTRADA										
WALDEN SCHOOL OF LIBERAL ARTS	0	3		26	1	9	17	10	10	21
WASATCH DISTRICT	374	467	518	567	542	572	667	578	746	654
WASATCH PEAK ACADEMY		0	0	0	0		24	22	27	35
WASHINGTON DISTRICT	1,647	2,007	2,222	2,636	2,103	2,494	2,866	2,711	3,299	2,838
WAYNE DISTRICT	0	0	1	2	5	63	60	58	72	59
WEBER DISTRICT	593	679	816	821	823	4,312	4,447	4,062	4,883	3,747

Source: National Center for Education Statistics

5.2.8 Dropout Rates, 2008-2009, by Race and Ethnicity: Comparison Counties

	All Students	Asian	Black	American Indian	White	Hispanic/Latino	Pacific Islander	Economically Disadvantaged	Limited English Proficiency	Studentw with Disabilities
ALPINE DISTRICT	2%	2%	2%	0%	2%	4%	1%	3%	6%	6%
AMERICAN FORK HIGH	1%	0%	0%		1%	2%	0%	2%	0%	1%
EAST SHORE HIGH	31%				33%	29%	18%	29%	36%	56%
LEHI HIGH	2%	0%		0%	2%	0%	0%	3%		5%
LONE PEAK HIGH	1%	0%			1%	0%	0%	2%		1%
MOUNTAIN VIEW HIGH	2%	0%	6%	0%	2%	4%	0%	3%	4%	2%
OREM HIGH	1%	0%			1%	1%	0%	1%	3%	0%
PLEASANT GROVE HIGH	1%	8%	0%		1%	3%	0%	3%	8%	2%
TIMPANOGOS HIGH	2%	3%	8%		2%	6%	0%	3%	5%	6%
WESTLAKE HIGH	2%	0%	0%	0%	2%	2%	2%	2%	11%	4%
DAVIS DISTRICT	2%	2%	3%	8%	2%	5%	3%	5%	4%	3%
BOUNTIFUL HIGH	1%	0%	0%		1%	4%	4%	3%	4%	3%
CANYON HEIGHTS	34%				32%	38%		36%	31%	17%
CLEARFIELD HIGH	3%	3%	0%	20%	3%	5%		5%	3%	6%
DAVIS HIGH	1%	0%	6%		1%	2%		4%	0%	2%
LAYTON HIGH	2%	0%	3%	0%	2%	4%	7%	4%	3%	4%
MOUNTAIN HIGH	26%				28%	27%		28%	20%	15%
NORTHRIDGE HIGH	3%	4%	8%	18%	2%	6%	0%	5%	8%	5%
SYRACUSE HIGH	4%	2%	0%	0%	4%	9%	0%	6%	13%	4%
VIEWMONT HIGH	2%	0%	6%		2%	4%	0%	5%	0%	4%
WOODS CROSS HIGH	3%	0%	0%		2%	5%	4%	5%	5%	6%

	All Students	Asian	Black	American Indian	White	Hispanic/Latino	Pacific Islander	Economically Disadvantaged	Limited English Proficiency	Studentw with Disabilities
GRANITE DISTRICT	5%	3%	3%	7%	4%	7%	4%	6%	8%	5%
COTTONWOOD HIGH	3%	2%	2%	0%	3%	5%	4%	4%	5%	4%
CYPRUS HIGH	7%	5%	11%	14%	6%	10%	4%	8%	15%	5%
GRANGER HIGH	11%	7%	7%	10%	10%	14%	8%	12%	15%	8%
GRANITE PEAKS HIGH	63%		30%	82%	61%	69%	40%	62%	68%	50%
HUNTER HIGH	4%	3%	0%	0%	4%	5%	2%	4%	6%	3%
KEARNS HIGH	4%	8%	2%	5%	3%	6%	5%	4%	8%	3%
OLYMPUS HIGH	2%	0%	4%	6%	2%	3%	0%	4%	2%	6%
SKYLINE HIGH	0%	0%	0%		0%	0%	0%	0%	0%	0%
TAYLORSVILLE HIGH	3%	0%	4%	3%	3%	4%	6%	4%	4%	9%
JORDAN DISTRICT	2%	2%	3%	4%	2%	3%	2%	2%	4%	3%
BINGHAM HIGH	0%	0%	5%		0%	1%	0%	1%	0%	1%
COPPER HILLS HIGH	2%	1%	3%	0%	2%	3%	4%	2%	4%	5%
RIVERTON HIGH	2%	0%	0%	0%	1%	4%	0%	3%	0%	3%
VALLEY HIGH	15%			8%	16%	12%		13%	17%	14%
WEST JORDAN HIGH	3%	2%	4%		2%	5%	10%	4%	7%	2%
MURRAY DISTRICT	2%	3%	0%	0%	2%	5%	4%	3%	4%	5%
MURRAY HIGH	3%	4%	0%	0%	2%	7%	6%	4%	5%	5%

	All Students	Asian	Black	American Indian	White	Hispanic/Latino	Pacific Islander	Economically Disadvantaged	Limited English Proficiency	Studentw with Disabilities
NEBO DISTRICT	2%	2%	6%	3%	1%	3%	2%	3%	4%	3%
LANDMARK HIGH	15%			20%	15%	12%		14%	7%	7%
MAPLE MOUNTAIN HIGH	1%				1%	3%		2%	6%	1%
PAYSON HIGH	2%			0%	1%	5%		2%	9%	5%
SALEM HILLS HIGH	1%			0%	1%	0%		1%	0%	2%
SPANISH FORK HIGH	1%				0%	1%	0%	0%	5%	1%
SPRINGVILLE HIGH	1%	8%	n<10	1%	1%	361	48	122		
PROVO DISTRICT										
ESCHOOL@PSD										
INDEPENDENCE HIGH	6%			0%	6%	7%		6%	10%	10%
PROVO HIGH	0%	0%	0%	0%	0%	1%	0%	0%	0%	1%
TIMPVIEW HIGH	0%	0%	0%	0%	0%	0%	0%	0%	0%	1%
SALT LAKE DISTRICT	7%	6%	6%	17%	4%	10%	5%	9%	8%	10%
EAST HIGH	4%	11%	3%	6%	2%	6%	3%	5%	6%	6%
HIGHLAND HIGH	3%	6%	1%	7%	3%	5%	0%	5%	6%	6%
HORIZONTE INSTR & TRN	39%		53%	59%	32%	40%	37%	38%	41%	32%
CTR										
WEST HIGH	2%	1%	4%	7%	2%	3%	1%	3%	2%	3%

Source: National Center for Education Statistics

5.2.9 Averaged Freshman Graduation Rates, By State, 2005-2008

State	05-06	06-07	07-08
AK	66.5	69.1	69.1
AL	66.2	67.1	69
AR	80.4	74.4	76.4
AZ	70.5	69.6	70.7
CA	69.2	70.7	71.2
CO	75.5	76.6	75.4
CT	80.9	81.8	82.2
DC		54.9	56
DE	76.3	71.9	72.1
FL	63.6	65	66.9
GA	62.4	64.1	65.4
HI	75.5	75.4	76
IA	86.9	86.5	86.4
ID	80.5	80.4	80.1
IL	79.7	79.5	80.4
IN	73.3	73.9	74.1
KS	77.6	78.9	79.1
KY	77.2	76.4	74.4
LA	59.5	61.3	63.5
MA	79.5	80.8	81.5
MD	79.9	80	80.4
ME	76.3	78.5	79.1
MI	72.2	77	76.3
MN	86.2	86.5	86.4
MO	81	81.9	82.4
MS	63.5	63.6	63.9
MT	81.9	81.5	82
NC	71.8	68.6	72.8
ND	82.1	83.1	83.8
NE	87	86.3	83.8
NH	81.1	81.7	83.4
NJ	84.8	84.4	84.6
NM	67.3	59.1	66.8
NV	55.8	52	51.3
NY	67.4	68.8	70.8
OH	79.2	78.7	79
OK	77.8	77.8	78
OR	73	73.8	76.7
PA		83	82.7
RI	77.8	78.4	76.4

State	05-06	06-07	07-08
SC		58.9	
SD	84.5	82.5	84.4
TN	70.6	72.6	74.9
TX	72.5	71.9	73.1
UT	78.6	76.6	74.3
VA	74.5	75.5	77
VT	82.3	88.6	89.3
WA	72.9	74.8	71.9
WI	87.5	88.5	89.6
WV	76.9	78.2	77.3
WY	76.1	75.8	76
		USA	75.966

Source: National Center for Education Statistics

5.2.10 Total Graduation Rates, Utah County School Districts, 2007-2009

	2007	2008	2009
Alpine	93%	92%	89%
Nebo	94%	91%	95%
Provo	83%	89%	87%
Alternative High Schools	40%	48%	46%
Utah County	90%	91%	90%

Source: Utah State Office of Education

5.2.11 Key Education Data, Comparison Counties, and State of Utah

Description	Utah County	Davis County	SL County	State
Public school enrollment Fall 1986-1987	63339	49559	165056	417002
Public school enrollment Fall 1987-1988	63937	50706	164744	419814
Public school enrollment Fall 1988-1989	66787	56217	171357	450536
Public school enrollment Fall 1989-1990	67835	59131	172031	456835
Public school enrollment Fall 1990-1991	68872	60662	174786	467502
Public school enrollment Fall 1991-1992	70001	56002	179926	456545
Public school enrollment Fall 1992-1993	71118	57116	181718	462323
Public school enrollment Fall 1993-1994	73246	57933	182900	470415
Public school enrollment Fall 1994-1995	74023	58122	182006	473308
Public school enrollment Fall 1995-1996	75051	58782	181361	475626
Public school enrollment Fall 1996-1997	76616	59220	181966	480531
Public school enrollment Fall 1997-1998	77999	59220	181130	481740
Public school enrollment Fall 1998-1999	78754	59285	179069	479854
Public school enrollment Fall 1999-2000	79918	59486	177222	478910
Public school enrollment Fall 2000-2001	81513	59578	176334	477914
Public school enrollment Fall 2001-2002	83799	59366	177101	480915
Public school enrollment Fall 2003-2004	89404	60749	177592	491206
Public school enrollment Fall 2004-2005	93165	59429	176216	494574
Public school enrollment Fall 2005-2006	97424	62538	178332	508248
Public school enrollment Fall 2006-2007	102688	64224	182067	523586
Public school enrollment Fall 2007-2008	114564	72378	198932	576244
School enrollment - persons 3 years and over enrolled in school 1980	84597	48839	187076	467638
School enrollment - persons 3 years and over enrolled in college 1980	33846	6599	36750	104176
School enrollment - persons 3 years and over enrolled in school 1990	114352	67833	239033	610696
School enrollment - persons 3 years and over enrolled in preprimary school, kindergarten: 1990	6360	5213	18212	43626
School enrollment - persons 3 years and over enrolled in preprimary school, kindergarten: public 1990	4278	3449	11296	29239
School enrollment - persons 3 years and over enrolled in preprimary school, kindergarten: private 1990	2082	1764	6916	14387
School enrollment - persons 3 years and over enrolled in elementary or high school: 1990	65181	50774	168237	419975

Description	Utah County	Davis County	SL County	State
School enrollment - persons 3 years and over enrolled in elementary or high school: public 1990	63767	49701	161890	409260
School enrollment - persons 3 years and over enrolled in elementary or high school: private 1990	1414	1073	6347	10715
School enrollment - persons 3 years and over enrolled in college: 1990	42811	11846	52584	147095
School enrollment - persons 3 years and over enrolled in college: public 1990	11478	10569	45140	104695
School enrollment - persons 3 years and over enrolled in college: private 1990	31333	1277	7444	42400
School enrollment - persons 3 years and over not enrolled in school: 1990	131486	108213	445229	1010547
School enrollment - persons 3 years and over enrolled in school: 2000	148809	80293	275773	741524
School enrollment - persons 3 years and over enrolled in pre-kindergarten: 2000	8044	5347	18408	46057
School enrollment - persons 3 years and over enrolled in pre-kindergarten: public 2000	3444	2851	8923	24013
School enrollment - persons 3 years and over enrolled in pre-kindergarten: private 2000	4600	2496	9485	22044
School enrollment - persons 3 years and over enrolled in kindergarten: 2000	6568	4461	14561	38261
School enrollment - persons 3 years and over enrolled in kindergarten: public 2000	6320	4217	12826	35481
School enrollment - persons 3 years and over enrolled in kindergarten: private 2000	248	244	1735	2780
School enrollment - persons 3 years and over enrolled in elementary school grades 1 to 8: 2000	51609	36421	116078	305486
School enrollment - persons 3 years and over enrolled in elementary school grades 1 to 8: public 2000	50071	35194	109345	292727
School enrollment - persons 3 years and over enrolled in elementary school grades 1 to 8: private 2000	1538	1227	6733	12759
School enrollment - persons 3 years and over enrolled in elementary and high school: 2000	77195	56218	179290	470463
School enrollment - persons 3 years and over enrolled in elementary and high school: public 2000	74681	54403	169265	451250
School enrollment - persons 3 years and over enrolled in elementary and high school: private 2000	2514	1815	10025	19213
School enrollment - persons 3 years and over enrolled in high school grades 9 to 12: 2000	25586	19797	63212	164977
School enrollment - persons 3 years and over enrolled in high school grades 9 to 12: public 2000	24610	19209	59920	158523

Description	Utah County	Davis County	SL County	State
School enrollment - persons 3 years and over enrolled in high school grades 9 to 12: private 2000	976	588	3292	6454
School enrollment - persons 3 years and over enrolled in college: 2000	57002	14267	63514	186743
School enrollment - persons 3 years and over enrolled in college: public 2000	20294	12569	53479	134939
School enrollment - persons 3 years and over enrolled in college: private 2000	36708	1698	10035	51804
School enrollment - persons 3 years and over enrolled in college, undergraduate years: 2000	52299	12558	53404	165035
School enrollment - persons 3 years and over enrolled in college, undergraduate years: public 2000	19198	11250	45266	119878
School enrollment - persons 3 years and over enrolled in college, undergraduate years: private 2000	33101	1308	8138	45157
School enrollment - persons 3 years and over enrolled in graduate or professional school: 2000	4703	1709	10110	21708
School enrollment - persons 3 years and over enrolled in graduate or professional school: public 2000	1096	1319	8213	15061
School enrollment - persons 3 years and over enrolled in graduate or professional school: private 2000	3607	390	1897	6647
School enrollment - persons 3 years and over not enrolled in school 2000	193665	144368	573098	1361513
Persons 25 years and over 1980 (population used to calculate educational attainment rates)	88199	66838	314739	704790
Persons 25 years and over 1990 (population used to calculate educational attainment rates)	114438	93502	398673	897321
Persons 25 years and over 2000 (population used to calculate educational attainment rates)	166240	125532	509453	1197892
Years of school completed - persons 25 years and over completing 0 to 8 years of school 1980	4961	3014	21571	49582
Educational attainment - persons 25 years and over completing less than 9th grade 1990	3150	1825	12137	30379
Educational attainment - persons 25 years and over completing less than 9th grade 2000	4234	1967	18214	38426
Years of school completed - persons 25 years and over completing 1 to 3 years of high school 1980	10265	6466	40288	91236
Educational attainment - persons 25 years and over completing 9th to 12th grade, no diploma 1990	10689	7662	46409	102936
Educational attainment - persons 25 years and over completing 9th to 12th grade, no diploma 2000	10943	7768	48871	108585
Years of school completed - persons 25 years and over completing 12 years or more of school 1980	72973	57358	252880	563972
Educational attainment - persons 25 years and over completing 12 years or more of school 1990	100599	84015	340127	764006

Description	Utah County	Davis County	SL County	State
Educational attainment - persons 25 years and over completing 12 years or more of school 2000	151063	115797	442368	1050881
Educational attainment - persons 25 years and over - percent high school graduate or higher 1980	82.7	85.8	80.3	80
Educational attainment - persons 25 years and over - percent high school graduate or higher 1990	87.9	89.9	85.3	85.1
Educational attainment - persons 25 years and over - percent high school graduate or higher 2000	90.9	92.2	86.8	87.7
Years of school completed - persons 25 years and over completing high school only 1980	27417	26014	111210	253495
Educational attainment - persons 25 years and over - high school graduate (includes equivalency) 1990	25013	24646	105528	244132
Educational attainment - persons 25 years and over - high school graduate (includes equivalency) 2000	31855	29278	122409	294426
Years of school completed - persons 25 years and over completing 1 to 3 years of college 1980	24942	17689	73479	170375
Educational attainment - persons 25 years and over - some college or associate degree 1990	45583	37380	139572	320121
Educational attainment - persons 25 years and over - some college or associate degree 2000	66915	50387	180328	443492
Educational attainment - persons 25 years and over - some college, no degree 2000	50827	39276	142287	348680
Educational attainment - persons 25 years and over - associate degree 2000	16088	11111	38041	94812
Years of school completed - persons 25 years and over completing 4 years or more of college 1980	20614	13655	68191	140102
Educational attainment - persons 25 years and over - bachelor's, graduate, or professional degree 1990	30003	21989	95027	199753
Educational attainment - persons 25 years and over - bachelor's, graduate, or professional degree 2000	52293	36132	139631	312963
Educational attainment - persons 25 years and over - percent bachelor's degree or higher 1980	23.4	20.4	21.7	19.9
Educational attainment - persons 25 years and over - percent bachelor's degree or higher 1990	26.2	23.5	23.8	22.3
Educational attainment - persons 25 years and over - percent bachelor's degree or higher 2000	31.5	28.8	27.4	26.1
Educational attainment - persons 25 years and over - bachelor's degree 2000	35908	25935	93213	213959
Educational attainment - persons 25 years and over - graduate or professional degree 2000	16385	10197	46418	99004
Persons 16 to 19 years 1990 (population used to calculate high school dropout rates)	24571	13262	44398	120248
Persons 16 to 19 years 2000 (population used to calculate high school dropout rates)	34454	18896	62241	173747

Description	Utah County	Davis County	SL County	State
Persons 16 to 19 years not enrolled in school and not a high school graduate 1990	1412	1118	5008	10481
Persons 16 to 19 years not enrolled in school and not a high school graduate 2000	2154	1293	6861	15185

Source: U.S. Census Bureau

5.2.12 Educational Attainment, Comparison Counties

	Utah County	Davis County	Salt Lake County
Universe: POPULATION 25 YEARS AND OVER: No schooling completed	593	1060	5040
None	0.2%	0.6%	0.8%
Universe: POPULATION 25 YEARS AND OVER: Nursery to 4th grade	578	114	4549
< 5th Grade	0.2%	0.1%	0.7%
Universe: POPULATION 25 YEARS AND OVER: 5th and 6th grade (Estimate)	1209	476	9542
5th or 6th	0.5%	0.3%	1.5%
Universe: POPULATION 25 YEARS AND OVER: 7th and 8th grade (Estimate)	1710	412	7121
7th or 8th	0.7%	0.2%	1.1%
Universe: POPULATION 25 YEARS AND OVER: 9th grade (Estimate)	1875	1661	9670
9th	0.8%	1.0%	1.5%
Universe: POPULATION 25 YEARS AND OVER: 10th grade (Estimate)	3312	1319	10767
10th	1.3%	0.8%	1.7%
Universe: POPULATION 25 YEARS AND OVER: 11th grade (Estimate)	3621	1722	14301
11th	1.5%	1.0%	2.2%
Universe: POPULATION 25 YEARS AND OVER: 12th grade, no diploma	3849	1248	11862
12th, no diploma	1.6%	0.7%	1.9%
Universe: POPULATION 25 YEARS AND OVER: Regular high school diploma	38306	34868	139340
HS Diploma	15.5%	20.4%	21.9%
Universe: POPULATION 25 YEARS AND OVER: GED or alternative credential (Estimate)	5007	3655	16212
GED	2.0%	2.1%	2.5%
Universe: POPULATION 25 YEARS AND OVER: Some college, less than 1 year (Estimate)	18742	14369	49557
Less than 1 yr college	7.6%	8.4%	7.8%

	Utah County	Davis County	Salt Lake County
Universe: POPULATION 25 YEARS AND OVER: Some college, 1 or more years, no degree (Estimate)	58323	34608	114206
1 or more yrs college, no degree	23.6%	20.3%	18.0%
Universe: POPULATION 25 YEARS AND OVER: Associate's degree	26768	17209	54848
Associate's	10.8%	10.1%	8.6%
Universe: POPULATION 25 YEARS AND OVER: Bachelor's degree	55412	39465	126453
Bachelor's	22.4%	23.1%	19.9%
Universe: POPULATION 25 YEARS AND OVER: Master's degree (Estimate)	19059	13549	43592
Master's	7.7%	7.9%	6.9%
Universe: POPULATION 25 YEARS AND OVER: Professional school degree (Estimate)	4365	2949	11329
Professional degree	1.8%	1.7%	1.8%
Universe: POPULATION 25 YEARS AND OVER: Doctorate degree	4439	2177	7523
Doctorate	1.8%	1.3%	1.2%

Source: American Community Survey, U.S. Census Bureau

5.2.13 Student-Teacher and Student-Adult Ratios, All Utah Districts, 2009-2010

District	Median Student-Teacher Ratio	Median Student-Adult Ratio
Alpine	22.50	21.23
Beaver	19.74	15.32
Box Elder	22.82	21.21
Cache	22.42	18.78
Carbon	19.67	13.32
Daggett	13.00	13.00
Davis	22.40	21.45
Duchesne	17.33	14.67
Emery	17.44	15.09
Garfield	12.52	9.55
Grand	17.35	13.75
Granite	22.70	21.59
Iron	21.29	17.95
Jordan	23.51	21.79
Juab	22.12	19.33
Kane	16.41	10.12
Logan	19.21	16.20
Millard	17.68	11.73
Morgan	21.19	20.41
Murray	20.73	18.32

District	Median Student-Teacher Ratio	Median Student-Adult Ratio
Nebo	21.41	18.64
North Sanpete	18.74	11.09
North Summit	16.39	15.12
Ogden	22.38	15.35
Park City	16.56	14.91
Piute	13.52	9.63
Provo	20.69	19.53
Rich	13.66	11.59
Salt Lake	19.80	13.51
San Juan	15.24	10.37
Sevier	20.10	19.12
South Sanpete	19.19	10.01
South Summit	17.55	16.28
Tintic	11.21	8.96
Tooele	21.40	18.99
Uintah	22.28	15.45
Wasatch	18.46	17.23
Washington	20.51	19.61
Wayne	13.35	12.87
Weber	22.57	20.94
DISTRICT MEDIAN	21.42	19.22
CHARTER MEDIAN	19.62	17.32
STATE MEDIAN	21.33	19.11

Source: Utah State Office of Education

5.2.14 Expenditures per Pupil based on Fall Enrollment, 2005-2009, All Utah Districts

District	Current Expenditures Per Pupil SOURCE: USOE					FY 2008-2009
	2005	2006	2007	2008	2009	CHNGE
Alpine	$4,687	$4,972	5,085	5,777	5,938	2.79%
Beaver	6,806	6,825	6,251	7,185	7,049	-1.89%
Box Elder	5,314	5,410	5,593	6,371	6,450	1.24%
Cache	5,193	5,297	5,556	6,379	6,807	6.71%
Carbon	7,450	7,692	7,395	8,271	8,626	4.29%
Daggett	14,219	13,819	16,750	20,956	19,978	-4.67%
Davis	5,075	5,166	5,499	6,244	6,400	2.50%
Duchesne	6,462	6,552	6,783	7,251	7,444	2.66%
Emery	6,976	7,145	7,755	8,715	9,154	5.04%
Garfield	8,867	9,470	9,767	11,398	12,774	12.07%
Grand	7,068	7,205	6,829	7,300	8,453	15.79%
Granite	5,027	5,074	5,408	6,213	6,427	3.44%
Iron	5,077	5,140	5,463	6,293	6,571	4.42%
Jordan	4,734	4,940	5,083	5,761	6,128	6.37%
Juab	5,029	5,346	5,496	6,191	6,350	2.57%
Kane	7,801	8,672	9,200	10,135	10,339	2.01%
Millard	7,452	7,713	7,963	8,986	9,326	3.78%
Morgan	5,218	5,317	5,534	5,730	6,418	12.01%
Nebo	4,721	4,959	5,284	5,909	6,081	2.91%
No. Sanpete	6,419	6,616	7,002	7,819	7,872	0.68%
No. Summit	6,735	7,194	7,464	8,302	9,157	10.30%
Park City	7,113	7,743	8,009	8,964	9,991	11.46%
Piute	9,950	11,127	12,010	13,263	12,857	-3.06%
Rich	10,458	10,910	10,945	12,711	12,198	-4.04%
San Juan	10,295	10,319	10,757	12,675	12,682	0.06%
Sevier	5,564	5,796	6,515	7,135	6,812	-4.53%
So. Sanpete	6,439	6,435	6,568	7,735	8,046	4.02%
So. Summit	6,742	7,052	7,033	7,941	7,929	-0.15%
Tintic	12,346	-	13,456	15,285	16,981	11.10%
Tooele	4,790	4,902	5,195	5,903	6,122	3.71%
Uintah	6,324	6,650	6,326	6,933	6,606	-4.72%
Wasatch	5,323	5,509	6,058	6,857	7,225	5.37%
Washington	4,826	5,038	5,338	6,195	6,570	6.05%
Wayne	8,595	8,759	10,255	9,235	10,004	8.33%
Weber	5,015	5,222	5,507	5,963	6,253	4.86%
Salt Lake	6,408	6,530	6,878	7,694	7,904	2.73%

District	Current Expenditures Per Pupil SOURCE: USOE					FY 2008-2009
	2005	2006	2007	2008	2009	CHNGE
Provo	5,683	5,737	6,206	7,040	6,906	-1.90%
Logan	5,473	5,654	6,085	7,125	7,239	1.60%
Murray	5,584	5,740	5,885	6,441	6,664	3.46%
Charters	4,919	5,051	5,055	5,572	5,620	0.86%
STATE:	$5,250	5,397	5,645	6,353	6,564	3.32%

Source: Utah State Office of Education

5.2.15 Licensed and Classified Personnel, Instruction, FY 2009, All Utah Districts

	INSTRUCTION							
	CLASSROOM TEACHERS						Instructional Aides	Instructional Coordinators and Supervisors
	Pre-Kindergarten		Kindergarten	Elementary	Secondary	Special Education		
	Regular	Special						
	CACTUS Database	CACTUS Database	CACTUS Database	CACTUS Database	CACTUS Database	CACTUS Database	Classified Personnel Report	CACTUS Database
Alpine	8.000	16.530	105.120	1,203.710	966.720	222.860	599.190	108.340
Beaver	0.500	0.000	3.000	37.450	30.280	7.350	36.020	1.600
Box Elder	1.000	8.000	24.030	168.390	220.330	44.820	213.000	9.060
Cache	0.000	5.000	26.500	235.680	271.310	56.850	301.560	33.690
Carbon	0.000	2.000	11.000	67.010	65.130	20.740	80.860	16.030
Daggett	0.000	0.000	1.000	4.900	6.290	0.580	5.130	2.960
Davis	2.670	15.830	129.090	1,204.140	1,143.090	286.500	1,131.550	158.860
Duchesne	0.000	1.000	11.500	94.640	85.740	24.860	88.760	2.980
Emery	0.000	1.000	6.510	49.000	50.550	12.020	35.510	2.670
Garfield	0.500	0.000	3.660	23.840	31.180	5.930	24.710	4.820
Grand	0.000	1.000	5.000	30.540	39.470	8.500	45.500	2.830
Granite	11.000	26.250	142.920	1,221.270	1,142.420	310.200	616.930	278.220
Iron	2.000	6.500	22.000	163.610	160.590	46.570	234.100	8.900
Jordan	7.900	34.180	131.270	1,494.600	1,231.960	321.250	917.920	243.410
Juab	0.000	1.000	5.000	44.040	35.700	11.800	42.830	2.080
Kane	1.500	0.000	3.590	25.570	35.700	5.900	33.240	0.340
Logan	0.570	3.000	15.290	100.330	119.910	27.120	151.750	26.990
Millard	0.000	3.500	6.330	51.730	70.530	9.780	60.880	6.380
Morgan	0.000	1.000	5.000	46.330	46.250	8.800	30.460	1.670
Murray	0.000	1.500	12.330	116.930	126.680	26.100	103.680	9.610
Nebo	4.000	14.000	60.000	510.220	408.810	115.920	399.880	93.380
North Sanpete	0.000	1.000	5.000	53.000	51.330	9.830	58.410	2.170

	INSTRUCTION							
	CLASSROOM TEACHERS						Instructional Aides	Instructional Coordinators and Supervisors
	Pre-Kindergarten		Kindergarten	Elementary	Secondary	Special Education		
	Regular	Special						
	CACTUS Database	CACTUS Database	CACTUS Database	CACTUS Database	CACTUS Database	CACTUS Database	Classified Personnel Report	CACTUS Database
North Summit	0.500	0.000	2.060	18.840	22.840	6.340	19.250	3.510
Ogden	0.000	4.500	37.600	225.070	177.650	58.990	200.350	64.000
Park City	0.000	0.000	9.000	78.310	122.950	21.740	74.480	21.410
Piute	0.000	0.750	1.340	8.820	13.900	1.920	10.700	0.200
Sevier	0.000	3.500	11.000	74.800	99.560	31.840	69.810	4.680
South Sanpete	0.000	1.710	7.500	63.190	75.420	13.930	110.000	4.250
South Summit	0.000	0.130	2.000	33.840	31.410	5.870	25.250	4.310
Tintic	0.000	0.250	0.750	8.400	10.410	1.670	7.250	0.700
Tooele	1.500	7.110	27.750	256.200	242.150	70.060	178.970	32.270
Uintah	0.000	3.000	16.540	111.850	96.860	27.410	94.250	12.400
Wasatch	0.000	3.000	8.500	85.000	87.470	26.000	88.920	23.820
Washington	0.000	8.700	61.910	452.690	504.440	105.380	250.390	84.450
Wayne	0.000	0.500	1.630	13.280	18.060	2.850	9.170	1.420
Weber	0.000	9.000	58.500	545.180	502.180	154.020	332.980	44.070
DISTRICT TOTAL	43.640	196.250	1,094.010	9,680.440	9,055.620	2,350.640	7,471.230	1,486.340
CHARTER TOTAL	3.500	0.000	54.300	583.690	506.810	85.240	461.210	39.470
GRAND TOTAL	47.140	196.250	1,148.310	10,264.130	9,562.430	2,435.880	7,932.440	1,525.810

Source: Utah State Office of Education

5.2.16 Licensed and Classified Personnel, Support, FY 2009, All Utah Districts

District	SUPPORT			
	Elementary Guidance Counselors	Secondary Guidance Counselors	Librarians and Media Specialists	Library and Media Support Staff
	CACTUS Database	CACTUS Database	CACTUS Database	Classified Personnel Report
Alpine	0.000	66.880	18.500	57.160
Beaver	0.000	2.010	0.000	2.860
Box Elder	0.500	15.000	5.000	12.000
Cache	0.000	18.880	20.000	0.000
Carbon	1.000	6.240	0.830	3.430
Daggett	0.000	0.000	0.250	0.000
Davis	37.650	87.300	17.500	60.270
Duchesne	0.000	3.850	6.000	4.930
Emery	0.000	0.500	1.100	8.520
Garfield	0.800	1.700	0.000	4.490
Grand	0.000	2.000	2.000	0.000
Granite	1.000	83.180	20.580	32.970
Iron	4.000	11.500	3.000	10.100
Jordan	1.710	76.060	29.720	77.830
Juab	1.000	2.000	0.000	3.650
Kane	0.000	1.200	0.360	3.250
Logan	1.000	6.410	2.000	7.500
Millard	0.550	1.960	1.000	4.500
Morgan	0.000	3.000	1.200	4.000
Murray	1.000	8.330	2.000	6.750
Nebo	10.900	28.990	8.080	17.880
North Sanpete	0.000	0.000	1.000	3.500
North Summit	0.250	1.750	0.830	1.670
Ogden	11.130	14.320	17.330	3.500
Park City	4.550	6.830	6.840	1.990
Piute	0.500	0.500	0.000	0.800
Provo	0.000	13.000	4.330	11.420
Rich	0.500	0.450	0.000	1.500
Salt Lake	14.000	21.500	38.000	6.060
San Juan	3.000	4.160	2.500	7.820
Sevier	0.000	5.460	0.000	8.610

District	SUPPORT			
	Elementary Guidance Counselors	Secondary Guidance Counselors	Librarians and Media Specialists	Library and Media Support Staff
	CACTUS Database	CACTUS Database	CACTUS Database	Classified Personnel Report
South Sanpete	0.000	6.450	0.000	8.000
South Summit	1.000	1.000	1.500	1.500
Tintic	0.170	0.410	0.500	1.260
Wasatch	3.250	6.350	6.830	1.500
Washington	12.300	32.750	15.010	36.540
Wayne	0.000	0.860	0.000	1.860
Weber	16.150	38.150	12.830	27.200
DISTRICT TOTAL	133.180	603.570	249.680	477.360
CHARTER TOTAL	4.580	22.000	11.970	24.500
GRAND TOTAL	137.760	625.570	261.650	501.860

Source: Utah State Office of Education

5.2.17 Fall Enrollment, Alpine School District, 2009, by Grade, Gender, Race and Ethnicity

SCHOOL NAME	TOTAL	K-2	3-5	6-8	9-12	MALE	FEMALE	ETHNIC MINORITY	ASIAN	BLACK	HISPANIC	AMERICAN INDIAN	PACIFIC ISLANDER	WHITE	UNKNOWN
Alpine School	652	223	306	123	0	315	337	24	0	14	4	1	5	628	0
Aspen School	511	225	211	75	0	275	236	71	6	1	52	6	6	438	2
Barratt School	641	241	287	113	0	330	311	36	11	3	10	5	7	604	1
Bonneville School	779	345	322	112	0	378	401	179	3	14	147	1	14	567	33
Cascade School	505	217	211	77	0	244	261	44	6	1	28	0	9	460	1
Cedar Ridge School	1049	468	435	146	0	535	514	59	9	12	28	2	8	990	0
Cedar Valley School	151	54	70	27	0	86	65	10	2	0	7	1	0	141	0
Central School	540	242	235	63	0	265	275	88	10	1	69	2	6	446	6
Cherry Hill School	727	289	335	103	0	357	370	236	8	16	169	9	34	491	0
Deerfield School	972	396	446	130	0	498	474	50	17	7	11	5	10	917	5
Eaglecrest School	954	432	406	116	0	496	458	57	4	9	35	3	6	896	1
Eagle Valley School	1226	644	457	125	0	628	598	120	6	9	78	6	21	1102	4
Foothill School	624	235	289	100	0	331	293	61	5	6	35	5	10	558	5
Forbes School	610	274	264	72	0	310	300	56	2	5	43	0	6	554	0
Freedom School	1155	501	493	161	0	597	558	26	3	13	5	1	4	1129	0
Fox Hollow Elementary	918	473	344	101	0	442	476	82	8	7	50	4	13	836	0
Geneva School	476	231	198	47	0	246	230	262	6	3	230	10	13	213	1
Greenwood School	612	277	264	71	0	314	298	142	7	4	122	5	4	467	3
Grovecrest School	733	313	320	100	0	388	345	69	4	13	33	1	18	664	0
Harvest Elementary	1049	542	412	95	0	531	518	66	4	10	37	1	14	983	0
Hidden Hollow Elementary	1048	512	410	126	0	569	479	115	7	13	86	4	5	933	0

SCHOOL NAME	TOTAL	K-2	3-5	6-8	9-12	MALE	FEMALE	ETHNIC MINORITY	ASIAN	BLACK	HISPANIC	AMERICAN INDIAN	PACIFIC ISLANDER	WHITE	UNKNOWN
Highland School	887	317	425	145	0	458	429	31	11	3	5	0	12	856	0
Hillcrest School	400	201	144	55	0	209	191	94	9	2	70	6	7	305	1
Legacy School	945	381	438	126	0	481	464	35	7	3	13	2	10	908	2
Lehi School	641	306	263	72	0	326	315	61	2	6	39	8	6	580	0
North Point Elementary	856	441	329	86	0	443	413	56	7	1	37	1	10	799	1
Orchard School	699	286	306	107	0	343	356	118	5	9	84	4	16	581	0
Pony Express School	1120	569	447	104	0	558	562	120	10	11	78	4	17	1000	0
Meadow School	964	482	375	107	0	519	445	103	10	11	55	2	25	860	1
Northridge School	737	320	310	107	0	383	354	92	19	4	54	3	12	645	0
Lindon School	604	263	242	99	0	311	293	84	13	4	55	3	9	517	3
Orem School	639	270	287	82	0	334	305	98	10	12	56	2	18	541	0
Scera Park School	425	189	198	38	0	222	203	86	6	8	61	2	9	339	0
Manila School	815	340	361	114	0	419	396	44	6	4	27	3	4	771	0
Mount Mahogany School	983	502	380	101	0	515	468	135	8	4	114	1	8	848	0
Rocky Mountain School	573	222	268	83	0	297	276	37	2	4	27	2	2	536	0
Saratoga Shores School	1092	490	488	114	0	561	531	77	9	8	45	1	14	1013	2
Sego Lily School	995	427	440	128	0	500	495	89	12	10	47	8	12	904	2
Ridgeline Elementary	1203	592	461	150	0	602	601	106	27	5	50	7	17	1096	1
Sage Hills Elementary	750	379	291	80	0	401	349	73	7	6	45	0	15	677	0
Sharon School	449	222	160	67	0	240	209	227	3	1	217	4	2	222	0
Shelley School	1082	463	494	125	0	583	499	54	14	6	24	2	8	1028	0
Snow Springs School	959	478	390	91	0	470	489	103	9	5	74	4	11	856	0
Suncrest School	448	213	178	57	0	227	221	199	0	1	191	4	3	247	2

SCHOOL NAME	TOTAL	K-2	3-5	6-8	9-12	MALE	FEMALE	ETHNIC MINORITY	ASIAN	BLACK	HISPANIC	AMERICAN INDIAN	PACIFIC ISLANDER	WHITE	UNKNOWN
Valley View School	522	226	215	81	0	268	254	44	4	8	24	2	6	475	3
Vineyard School	677	324	256	97	0	352	325	193	14	4	159	2	14	481	3
Westmore School	436	210	165	61	0	214	222	156	8	8	130	8	2	278	2
Westfield School	864	326	396	142	0	460	404	44	10	6	10	0	18	820	0
Windsor School	585	251	252	82	0	285	300	216	11	2	180	15	8	343	26
Alpine Online School	382	132	141	109	0	205	177	14	0	1	13	0	0	361	7
American Fork Jr High	1699	0	0	1136	563	889	810	132	24	12	77	2	17	1566	1
Canyon View Jr High	1142	0	0	780	362	596	546	248	21	12	186	5	24	892	2
Lakeridge Jr High	1196	0	0	791	405	611	585	323	19	15	248	15	26	871	2
Lehi Jr High	1311	0	0	886	425	688	623	110	26	8	53	8	15	1201	0
Mountain Ridge Jr High	1318	0	0	848	470	668	650	42	4	3	22	0	13	1274	2
Oak Canyon Jr High	1180	0	0	734	446	590	590	136	23	10	84	10	9	1044	0
Orem Jr High	858	0	0	548	310	415	443	259	11	10	211	9	18	596	3
Pleasant Grove Jr High	1386	0	0	912	474	735	651	148	10	14	100	6	18	1237	1
Timberline Middle	1364	0	0	907	457	687	677	73	19	7	26	4	17	1287	4
Willowcreek Middle	1692	0	0	1506	186	890	802	192	17	18	129	7	21	1500	0
Alpine Transition & Employment Center	112	0	0	0	112	70	42	10	0	1	6	1	2	102	0
American Fork High	1892	0	0	0	1892	966	926	134	9	15	85	7	18	1758	0
Lehi High	1603	0	0	0	1603	838	765	133	19	9	78	13	14	1469	1
Lone Peak High School	2058	0	0	0	2058	1033	1025	89	21	6	37	7	18	1968	1
Mountain View High	1351	0	0	0	1351	677	674	353	27	17	264	12	33	995	3

SCHOOL NAME	TOTAL	K-2	3-5	6-8	9-12	MALE	FEMALE	ETHNIC MINORITY	ASIAN	BLACK	HISPANIC	AMERICAN INDIAN	PACIFIC ISLANDER	WHITE	UNKNOWN
Orem High	1098	0	0	0	1098	580	518	186	16	5	148	4	13	909	3
Pleasant Grove High	1819	0	0	0	1819	930	889	157	12	16	107	8	14	1662	0
Timpanogos High	1412	0	0	0	1412	737	675	266	29	12	207	7	11	1146	0
East Shore High	347	0	0	0	347	176	171	83	2	4	69	1	7	264	0
Summit High School (YIC)	0	0	0	0	0	0	0	0	0	0	0	0	0	0	0
At Risk-Summit Jr High	11	0	0	0	11	4	7	2	0	0	2	0	0	9	0
Westlake High	1712	0	0	0	1712	877	835	246	27	17	149	11	42	1466	0
Dan W. Peterson	109	19	12	19	59	68	41	23	3	0	17	3	0	86	0
Serv By Appt	17	5	3	2	7	10	7	1	0	0	0	1	0	16	0

Source: Utah State Office of Education

5.2.18 Fall Enrollment, Nebo School District, 2009, by Grade, Gender, Race and Ethnicity

SCHOOL NAME	TOTAL	K-2	3-5	6-8	9-12	MALE	FEMALE	ETHNIC MINORITY	ASIAN	BLACK	HISPANIC	AMERICAN INDIAN	PACIFIC ISLANDER	WHITE	UNKNOWN
Art City School	689	291	291	107	0	369	320	57	3	1	40	3	10	632	0
Barnett School	743	332	307	104	0	386	357	100	1	4	79	8	8	643	0
Brockbank School	559	280	221	58	0	283	276	60	3	3	44	2	8	499	0
Brookside School	694	325	275	94	0	363	331	98	5	3	77	6	7	595	1
Canyon School	720	287	322	111	0	358	362	57	8	6	30	0	13	662	1
Cherry Creek Elementary	594	282	236	76	0	308	286	146	2	12	120	3	9	448	0
East Meadows Elementary	764	375	306	83	0	395	369	86	13	5	65	2	1	678	0
Foothills Elementary	608	266	258	84	0	310	298	18	2	4	8	3	1	590	0
Goshen School	406	177	180	49	0	215	191	57	6	3	39	6	3	349	0
Hobble Creek School	715	280	320	115	0	359	356	26	5	6	8	1	6	689	0
Larsen School	543	212	239	92	0	249	294	64	1	2	41	5	15	479	0
Mapleton School	810	334	371	105	0	457	353	62	6	11	28	5	12	748	0
Mt Loafer School	466	200	200	66	0	240	226	15	2	0	9	4	0	451	0
Orchard Hills Elementary	712	313	307	92	0	375	337	69	2	8	55	4	0	643	0
Park School	522	239	207	76	0	267	255	65	2	2	47	5	9	456	1
Park View School	560	254	237	69	0	289	271	64	3	3	48	4	6	496	0
Rees School	699	343	280	76	0	362	337	115	1	7	83	7	17	584	0

SCHOOL NAME	TOTAL	K-2	3-5	6-8	9-12	MALE	FEMALE	ETHNIC MINORITY	ASIAN	BLACK	HISPANIC	AMERICAN INDIAN	PACIFIC ISLANDER	WHITE	UNKNOWN
Riverview School	759	387	280	92	0	381	378	93	1	10	73	3	6	666	0
Sage Creek School	745	315	327	103	0	403	342	107	3	21	74	3	6	638	0
Salem School	463	203	189	71	0	224	239	30	0	8	16	4	2	432	1
Santaquin School	577	261	251	65	0	298	279	96	0	5	72	19	0	481	0
Spanish Oaks School	845	366	359	120	0	439	406	76	2	9	53	5	7	768	1
Spring Lake School	730	345	292	93	0	383	347	93	5	5	79	0	4	637	0
Taylor School	353	143	173	37	0	173	180	84	4	6	65	6	3	269	0
Westside School	707	321	296	90	0	359	348	189	9	8	151	10	11	518	0
Wilson School	539	236	222	81	0	277	262	118	2	3	108	4	1	421	0
Diamond Fork Junior High	1211	0	0	843	368	639	572	156	8	3	115	11	19	1052	3
Mapleton Junior High	1086	0	0	743	343	545	541	88	16	7	58	3	4	998	0
Mt. Nebo Junior High	848	0	0	594	254	448	400	129	5	8	91	17	8	719	0
Payson Jr High	990	0	0	705	285	510	480	131	4	3	111	9	4	859	0
Spanish Fork Jr High	1179	0	0	777	402	618	561	101	2	8	78	5	8	1077	1
Springville Jr High	857	0	0	585	272	438	419	132	5	4	108	6	9	725	0
Springville Observation And Assessment (YIC)	0	0	0	0	0	0	0	0	0	0	0	0	0	0	0
Oakridge School	29	3	6	4	16	13	16	2	0	1	0	1	0	27	0
Maple Mountain High	1038	0	0	0	1038	524	514	95	6	4	71	8	6	943	0

SCHOOL NAME	TOTAL	K-2	3-5	6-8	9-12	MALE	FEMALE	ETHNIC MINORITY	ASIAN	BLACK	HISPANIC	AMERICAN INDIAN	PACIFIC ISLANDER	WHITE	UNKNOWN
Payson High	1032	0	0	0	1032	548	484	166	4	5	144	13	0	866	0
Salem Hills High	1085	0	0	0	1085	561	524	75	2	8	46	10	9	1009	1
Spanish Fork High	923	0	0	0	923	475	448	126	3	3	97	6	17	797	0
Springville High	1167	0	0	0	1167	601	566	146	11	8	111	7	9	1021	0
Landmark High	285	0	0	0	285	167	118	78	2	3	58	10	5	207	0
Ascent, Inc., Mona Country Residential (YIC)	0	0	0	0	0	0	0	0	0	0	0	0	0	0	0
The Journey: Blazing New Trails LLC, Impact Ranch	0	0	0	0	0	0	0	0	0	0	0	0	0	0	0
Legacy High School	30	0	0	0	30	0	30	10	0	0	9	0	1	20	0

Source: Utah State Office of Education

5.2.19 Fall Enrollment, Provo School District, 2009 by Grade, Gender, Race and Ethnicity

SCHOOL NAME	TOTAL	K-2	3-5	6-8	9-12	MALE	FEMALE	ETHNIC MINORITY	ASIAN	BLACK	HISPANIC	AMERICAN INDIAN	PACIFIC ISLANDER	WHITE	UNKNOWN
Amelia Earhart School	569	247	245	77	0	282	287	193	2	6	165	4	16	376	0
Canyon Crest School	469	171	221	77	0	239	230	36	6	4	14	2	10	433	0
Edgemont School	505	231	209	65	0	244	261	79	9	9	48	3	10	424	2
Farrer School	412	211	156	45	0	226	186	286	4	2	266	4	10	126	0
Franklin School	544	235	224	85	0	253	291	311	3	7	282	6	13	232	1
Lakeview Elementary	693	315	277	101	0	356	337	195	7	15	146	3	24	496	2
Provost School	434	197	190	47	0	219	215	158	5	2	136	7	8	273	3
Rock Canyon School	580	247	255	78	0	284	296	104	39	0	48	6	11	442	34
Spring Creek School	567	267	230	70	0	295	272	324	7	6	271	15	25	242	1
Sunset View School	568	252	239	77	0	302	266	233	12	2	201	10	8	330	5
Timpanogos School	621	294	251	76	0	313	308	348	4	6	304	22	12	273	0
Wasatch School	704	351	264	89	0	353	351	129	49	11	54	0	15	565	10
Westridge School	862	357	372	133	0	410	452	181	19	11	116	7	28	677	4
Centennial Middle	1030	0	0	1030	0	510	520	323	52	9	229	12	21	701	6
Dixon Middle	854	0	0	854	0	467	387	331	7	12	281	13	18	519	4
Eschool@psd	19	9	3	2	5	11	8	4	0	1	3	0	0	15	0
Central Utah Enterprises	24	0	0	0	24	15	9	3	0	1	1	0	1	21	0
Early Intervention	0	0	0	0	0	0	0	0	0	0	0	0	0	0	0

SCHOOL NAME	TOTAL	K-2	3-5	6-8	9-12	MALE	FEMALE	ETHNIC MINORITY	ASIAN	BLACK	HISPANIC	AMERICAN INDIAN	PACIFIC ISLANDER	WHITE	UNKNOWN
Provo High	1696	0	0	0	1696	879	817	588	20	26	485	13	44	1104	4
Timpview High School	1822	0	0	0	1822	916	906	467	83	16	313	17	38	1346	9
Independence High	265	0	0	0	265	148	117	142	0	4	115	14	9	123	0
Center For High School Studies	3	0	0	0	3	0	3	1	0	0	1	0	0	2	0

Source: Utah State Office of Education

5.2.20 Educator Salary and Benefits, All Utah School Districts, FY 2009

DISTRICT	School Administrators' Median Salary	Classroom Teachers											
		Median Beginning Salary	Median Salary	Soc. Sec.	Retirement	Health Insurance	Dental Insurance	Life Insurance	Industrial Insurance	Unemployment Insurance	Long-Term Disability	Total Benefits	Total Compensation
Alpine	$83,961	$32,023	$42,266	$3,233	$6,644	$12,228	$0	$43	$148	$13	$128	$22,437	$64,703
Beaver	75,488	32,858	47,007	3,596	7,390	10,772	798	60	306	0	128	23,048	70,055
Box Elder	75,087	30,624	45,978	3,517	7,228	7,931	0	98	145	46	0	18,965	64,943
Cache	84,825	31,255	48,551	3,714	7,632	10,145	0	26	127	49	121	21,813	70,364
Carbon	67,908	32,913	47,269	3,616	7,431	14,065	0	63	360	47	72	25,654	72,923
Daggett	45,487		47,446	3,630	7,459	15,013	0	60	393	0	155	26,709	74,155
Davis	85,526	33,368	48,721	3,727	7,659	11,554	909	57	69	49	88	24,112	72,833
Duchesne	71,404	32,120	44,751	3,423	7,035	9,200	0	69	154	13	134	20,030	64,781
Emery	79,625	33,810	52,890	4,046	8,314	12,648	655	56	340	0	69	26,129	79,019
Garfield	64,056	32,876	49,001	3,749	7,703	11,838	1,138	119	158	49	174	24,928	73,929
Grand	69,064	31,121	43,639	3,338	6,860	8,179	0	63	355	44	182	19,022	62,661
Granite	80,257	33,870	47,274	3,616	7,431	7,593	0	63	331	16	0	19,051	66,325
Iron	72,330	29,127	39,984	3,059	6,285	11,546	731	71	156	0	147	21,995	61,979
Jordan	86,331	32,407	44,921	3,436	7,062	10,614	0	61	338	45	157	21,713	66,634
Juab	75,929	33,290	47,379	3,624	7,448	7,646	0	93	184	47	220	19,263	66,642
Kane	60,088	37,456	46,057	3,523	7,240	15,660	1,128	56	145	46	232	28,031	74,088
Logan	71,008	33,012	47,772	3,655	7,510	12,192	0	0	243	18	102	23,720	71,492
Millard	72,659	33,296	52,610	4,025	8,270	12,192	1,174	49	391	0	146	26,247	78,857
Morgan	71,453	33,430	41,529	3,177	6,528	13,544	0	99	209	42	84	23,683	65,212
Murray	87,482	35,756	49,739	3,805	8,316	10,479	0	104	254	50	144	23,152	72,891
Nebo	81,968	32,605	44,663	3,417	7,021	10,268	0	62	148	45	77	21,037	65,700
North Sanpete	64,847	32,098	42,885	3,281	6,742	17,124	0	58	284	38	98	27,624	70,509

	School Administrators' Median Salary	Classroom Teachers											
		Median Beginning Salary	Median Salary	Soc. Sec.	Retirement	Health Insurance	Dental Insurance	Life Insurance	Industrial Insurance	Unemployment Insurance	Long-Term Disability	Total Benefits	Total Compensation
North Summit	68,763		46,738	3,575	7,347	12,866	876	42	266	47	174	25,194	71,932
Ogden	80,837	34,565	50,033	3,828	7,865	11,428	804	28	125	125	300	24,504	74,537
Park City	98,668	41,270	54,422	4,163	8,555	7,960	722	79	653	34	120	22,287	76,709
Piute	48,617		46,014	3,520	7,233	13,380	0	61	190	46	39	24,469	70,483
Provo	82,549	34,999	50,785	3,885	7,983	9,156	0	38	508	51	193	21,814	72,599
Rich	69,023	32,060	50,901	3,894	8,002	14,832	923	53	413	51	350	28,518	79,419
Salt Lake	70,518	37,280	49,896	3,817	8,093	7,860	585	96	175	50	245	20,921	70,817
San Juan	77,062	37,320	53,409	4,086	8,396	8,808	0	116	427	53	202	22,088	75,497
Sevier	72,720	30,984	43,656	3,340	6,863	7,072	0	50	279	0	171	17,775	61,431
South Sanpete	71,147	32,959	49,910	3,818	7,846	12,211	0	60	360	50	226	24,571	74,481
South Summit	74,910	36,652	47,474	3,632	7,463	12,192	600	109	248	0	117	24,360	71,834
Tintic	76,793	32,101	56,408	4,315	8,867	10,788	1,320	73	3	56	248	25,671	82,078
Tooele	80,421	33,009	41,765	3,195	6,565	9,944	388	41	193	42	64	20,432	62,197
Uintah	73,561	33,091	49,172	3,762	7,730	12,060	0	125	418	49	212	24,356	73,528
Wasatch	83,242	35,033	49,325	3,773	7,754	12,108	1,320	33	148	49	195	25,381	74,706
Washington	80,460	34,696	44,001	3,366	6,917	10,093	737	36	271	44	91	21,555	65,556
Wayne	57,366	30,058	45,469	3,478	7,148	12,555	1,202	89	93	0	226	24,791	70,260
Weber	76,781	29,227	46,331	3,544	7,283	10,749	0	54	158	46	102	21,937	68,268
DISTRICT MEDIAN	$80,492	$33,169	$46,713	$3,620	$7,440	$11,487	$0	$60	$245	$45	$145	$23,044	$69,757
CHARTER MEDIAN	$68,588	$33,000	$35,294	$2,663	$5,140	$6,358	$0	$0	$137	$38	$0	$14,337	$49,631
GRAND TOTAL MEDIAN	$80,257	$33,091	$45,923	$2,998	$5,895	$8,100	$0	$41	$158	$44	$39	$17,275	$63,198

Source: Utah State Office of Education

5.2.21 Educational Attainment by Metropolitan Statistical Areas in Utah

	HS grads	Some College	Associates Degree	Bachelor's degree	Master's degree	Professional Degree	PhD	Any Post-secondary education	College Degree
Logan, UT-ID MSA	92.7%	25.2%	11.7%	20.7%	7.8%	1.0%	3.4%	69.8%	44.6%
Ogden-Clearfield, UT MSA	92.3%	29.5%	10.0%	18.9%	6.4%	1.4%	0.7%	66.9%	37.4%
Provo-Orem, UT MSA	93.5%	30.0%	11.7%	24.2%	6.9%	1.3%	1.5%	75.6%	45.6%
St. George, UT MSA	90.9%	29.5%	7.0%	17.5%	5.5%	2.0%	0.7%	62.2%	32.8%
Salt Lake City, UT MSA	88.9%	25.3%	8.6%	19.7%	7.2%	1.9%	1.2%	63.9%	38.6%

Source: American Community Survey, U.S. Census Bureau

5.2.22 School District Indebtedness, FY 2009, All Utah Districts

Indebtedness at End of FY 2009
Long-Term Debt

District	General Obligation Bonded Indebtedness Year End	Non-Bonded Indebtedness at Year End Contingencies, Comp., etc.	School Building Loan Fund	Capital Leases	TOTAL	TOTAL LONG-TERM DEBT 6/30/2009
Alpine	$ 419,395,000	$2,162,513	$ -	$2,509,000	$ 4,671,513	$ 424,066,513
Beaver	11,410,000	570,221	0	0	570,221	11,980,221
Box Elder	25,000,000	4,795,874		287,429	5,083,303	30,083,303
Cache	88,465,000	728,989	0	0	728,989	89,193,989
Carbon	11,275,000	512,902	0	58,529	571,431	11,846,431
Daggett	170,000	227,377	0	0	227,377	397,377
Davis	315,500,000	13,390,034	0	5,020,299	18,410,333	333,910,333
Duchesne	19,723,781	710,923	2,060,000	0	2,770,923	22,494,704
Emery	279,000	1,378,656	0	0	1,378,656	1,657,656
Garfield	4,905,000	430,781	0	134,683	565,464	5,470,464
Grand	34,130,000	588,022	0	271,450	859,472	34,989,472
Granite	0	26,946,125	0	0	26,946,125	26,946,125
Iron	60,797,000		0	0	-	60,797,000
Jordan	293,015,000	15,431,737	0	0	15,431,737	308,446,737
Juab	23,428,765	2,228,099		361,074	2,589,173	26,017,938
Kane	3,815,000	2,450,632	0	0	2,450,632	6,265,632
Logan	17,575,000	11,977,715	0	0	11,977,715	29,552,715
Millard	0	460,248	0	18,750	478,998	478,998
Morgan	26,160,000	5,921	0	1,872,469	1,878,390	28,038,390
Murray	22,460,000	755,516	0	0	755,516	23,215,516

District	General Obligation Bonded Indebtedness Year End	Non-Bonded Indebtedness at Year End Contingencies, Comp., etc.	School Building Loan Fund	Capital Leases	TOTAL	TOTAL LONG-TERM DEBT 6/30/2009
Nebo	174,315,000	17,323,902	0	0	17,323,902	191,638,902
No. Sanpete	2,360,000	299,781	0	0	299,781	2,659,781
No. Summit	9,263,618	0	0	3,262,498	3,262,498	12,526,116
Ogden	89,000,329	7,361,205	0	0	7,361,205	96,361,534
Park City	25,890,000	1,295,591	0	0	1,295,591	27,185,591
Piute	0	165,322	0	120,781	286,103	286,103
Provo	56,384,000	904,990	0	285,128	1,190,118	57,574,118
Rich	3,960,000	328,929	0	0	328,929	4,288,929
Salt Lake	132,538,722	8,797,025	0	0	8,797,025	141,335,747
San Juan	0	1,309,017	0	0	1,309,017	1,309,017
Sevier	12,651,000	868,802	1,160,000	0	2,028,802	14,679,802
So. Sanpete	24,400,000	1,994,744	1,001,031	0	2,995,775	27,395,775
So. Summit	0	4,163,571	0	0	4,163,571	4,163,571
Tintic	330,000	448,987	0	0	448,987	778,987
Tooele	109,191,867	5,642,042	0	25,012,220	30,654,262	139,846,129
Uintah	46,227,000	2,367,227	0	6,181,000	8,548,227	54,775,227
Wasatch	74,170,000	761,154	0	0	761,154	74,931,154
Washington	250,472,498	5,162,479	0	0	5,162,479	255,634,977
Wayne	0	1,526,600	0	182,922	1,709,522	1,709,522
Weber	109,510,519	13,698,982	0	0	13,698,982	123,209,501

Source: Utah State Office of Education

5.2.23 Fee Waivers, All Utah Districts. FY 2009

District	Students Granted Fee Waivers	Students Worked in Lieu of Fee Waiver	Total Fees Waived in Dollars	Total Fees Collected in Dollars
ALPINE DISTRICT	2,976	0	432,319	3,756,715
BEAVER DISTRICT	69	18	5,487	179,604
BOX ELDER DISTRICT	817	0	98,094	589,249
CACHE DISTRICT	584	3	71,060	981,978
CARBON DISTRICT	272	5	12,674	89,402
DAGGETT DISTRICT	0	0	0	0
DAVIS DISTRICT	3,248	10	286,518	11,383,766
DUCHESNE DISTRICT	230	0	13,444	142,728
EMERY DISTRICT	174	0	12,243	129,579
GARFIELD DISTRICT	47	4	2,906	24,979
GRAND DISTRICT	121	0	18,424	74,797
GRANITE DISTRICT	8,096	4	889,736	2,609,905
IRON DISTRICT	942	0	69,747	448,552
JORDAN DISTRICT	4,145	0	302,080	6,795,623
JUAB DISTRICT	159	0	12,001	88,370
KANE DISTRICT	99	0	7,979	44,683
LOGAN DISTRICT	744	0	78,337	235,501
MILLARD DISTRICT	76	27	8,903	194,472
MORGAN DISTRICT	52	0	6,534	6,534
MURRAY DISTRICT	449	0	23,823	217,605
NEBO DISTRICT	1,409	114	87,757	876,444
NORTH SANPETE DISTRICT	222	0	15,039	144,235
NORTH SUMMIT DISTRICT	11	0	430	0
OGDEN DISTRICT	3,161	0	294,273	1,102,593
PARK CITY DISTRICT	291	0	62,480	518,465
PIUTE DISTRICT	53	0	1,762	4,493
PROVO DISTRICT	1,681	7	244,872	3,098,775
RICH DISTRICT	3	0	110	14,930
SALT LAKE DISTRICT	4,903	0	436,568	986,308
SAN JUAN DISTRICT	850	0	50,688	57,666
SEVIER DISTRICT	262	6	27,182	289,690

District	Students Granted Fee Waivers	Students Worked in Lieu of Fee Waiver	Total Fees Waived in Dollars	Total Fees Collected in Dollars
SOUTH SANPETE DISTRICT	147	0	8,237	276,166
SOUTH SUMMIT DISTRICT	8	0	3,010	33,247
TINTIC DISTRICT	0	237	0	0
TOOELE DISTRICT	647	0	121,427	658,238
UINTAH DISTRICT	190	0	27,052	192,169
WASATCH DISTRICT	384	0	16,581	232,300
WASHINGTON DISTRICT	2,002	0	148,145	1,621,435
WAYNE DISTRICT	28	0	2,644	19,676
WEBER DISTRICT	1,737	0	182,647	2,322,272
DISTRICT SUBTOTAL	41,289	435	4,083,213	40,443,144
CHARTER SUBTOTAL	1,651	64	211,938	1,019,721
GRAND TOTAL	42,940	499	4,295,151	41,462,865

Source: Utah State Office of Education

5.2.24   Iowa Test Summary by District, Grade 3 Core, Comparison Counties, 2009

	Grade 3											
	Reading			Language			Math			CORE TOTAL		
	Nsize	NCE	Natl Percentile	Nsize	NCE	Natl Percentile	Nsize	NCE	Natl Percentile	Nsize	NCE	Natl Percentile
ALPINE DISTRICT	4902	57	62	4954	50	51	4882	52	53	4801	53	56
NEBO DISTRICT	2131	54	57	2177	48	47	2138	50	50	2084	51	51
PROVO DISTRICT	1032	54	58	1040	46	43	1025	49	49	1010	50	50
DAVIS DISTRICT	5100	56	62	5119	50	50	5051	51	52	4981	53	55
GRANITE DISTRICT	5275	47	44	5362	44	39	5276	44	38	5143	45	40
JORDAN DISTRICT	6462	54	58	6536	49	48	6456	49	49	6339	51	52
MURRAY DISTRICT	477	51	52	473	46	43	469	47	44	463	48	47
SALT LAKE DISTRICT	1927	49	48	1970	42	36	1929	45	40	1881	45	42

Source: Utah State Office of Education

Key:
n<10 = there are too few tests for reporting criteria
blank = the school did not test students for that grade

Core Total = Reading, Language, and Mathematics
Total Composite = Reading, Language, Mathematics, Social Studies, and Science.

Nsize = Number of Tests
Natl Percentile = National Percentile Rank (NPR), should not be averaged
NCE = Normal Curve Equivalent of Average Scaled Score, can be averaged

For explanations:
http://www.schools.utah.gov/assessment/DOCUMENTS/Iowa_Technical_Questions_ITBS.pdf

Grade 3	Social Science			Science			TOTAL COMPOSITE		
	Nsize	NCE	Natl Percentile	Nsize	NCE	Natl Percentile	Nsize	NCE	Natl Percentile
ALPINE DISTRICT	4949	58	65	4947	60	69	4772	57	62
NEBO DISTRICT	2174	56	61	2166	58	64	2071	54	58
PROVO DISTRICT	1041	54	58	1041	56	62	1007	53	56
DAVIS DISTRICT	5128	57	63	5119	60	68	4958	56	61
GRANITE DISTRICT	5378	50	49	5346	50	49	5104	48	45
JORDAN DISTRICT	6538	56	61	6525	58	64	6307	54	58
MURRAY DISTRICT	476	56	62	473	58	65	459	53	55
SALT LAKE DISTRICT	1970	52	55	1956	53	56	1862	49	49

Source: Utah State Office of Education

Key:
n<10 = there are too few tests for reporting criteria
blank = the school did not test students for that grade

Core Total = Reading, Language, and Mathematics
Total Composite = Reading, Language, Mathematics, Social Studies, and Science.

Nsize = Number of Tests
Natl Percentile = National Percentile Rank (NPR), should not be averaged
NCE = Normal Curve Equivalent of Average Scaled Score, can be averaged

For explanations:
http://www.schools.utah.gov/assessment/DOCUMENTS/Iowa_Technical_Questions_ITBS.pdf

5.2.26 Iowa Test Summary by District, Grade 5 Core, Comparison Counties, 2009

Grade 5	Reading			Language			Math			CORE TOTAL		
	Nsize	NCE	Natl Percentile	Nsize	NCE	Natl Percentile	Nsize	NCE	Natl Percentile	Nsize	NCE	Natl Percentile
ALPINE DISTRICT	4609	56	62	4617	54	58	4600	54	58	4581	54	58
NEBO DISTRICT	2164	54	58	2162	51	52	2157	52	54	2152	52	54
PROVO DISTRICT	1031	53	56	1031	51	53	1021	55	60	1018	53	55
DAVIS DISTRICT	4875	56	62	4875	52	54	4847	53	56	4833	53	56
GRANITE DISTRICT	5138	46	43	5144	46	43	5110	46	43	5087	46	42
JORDAN DISTRICT	6187	53	56	6192	51	53	6167	50	51	6153	52	53
MURRAY DISTRICT	474	54	57	474	51	51	473	50	50	473	51	52
SALT LAKE DISTRICT	1749	47	44	1760	47	44	1746	45	41	1730	46	42

Source: Utah State Office of Education

Key:
n<10 = there are too few tests for reporting criteria
blank = the school did not test students for that grade

Core Total = Reading, Language, and Mathematics
Total Composite = Reading, Language, Mathematics, Social Studies, and Science.

Nsize = Number of Tests
Natl Percentile = National Percentile Rank (NPR), should not be averaged
NCE = Normal Curve Equivalent of Average Scaled Score, can be averaged

For explanations:
http://www.schools.utah.gov/assessment/DOCUMENTS/Iowa_Technical_Questions_ITBS.pdf

5.2.27 Iowa Test Summary by District, Grade 5 Expanded, Comparison Counties, 2009

Grade 5	Social Science			Science			TOTAL COMPOSITE		
	Nsize	NCE	Natl Percentile	Nsize	NCE	Natl Percentile	Nsize	NCE	Natl Percentile
ALPINE DISTRICT	4616	55	60	4605	61	70	4564	57	63
NEBO DISTRICT	2159	54	57	2155	58	66	2141	55	59
PROVO DISTRICT	1026	52	54	1025	59	66	1012	55	59
DAVIS DISTRICT	4864	54	58	4863	60	68	4823	56	61
GRANITE DISTRICT	5137	46	42	5131	51	52	5067	47	45
JORDAN DISTRICT	6174	53	56	6165	58	65	6120	54	58
MURRAY DISTRICT	474	55	60	474	58	65	473	54	58
SALT LAKE DISTRICT	1754	49	47	1753	53	56	1719	49	48

Source: Utah State Office of Education

Key:
n<10 = there are too few tests for reporting criteria
blank = the school did not test students for that grade

Core Total = Reading, Language, and Mathematics
Total Composite = Reading, Language, Mathematics, Social Studies, and Science.

Nsize = Number of Tests
Natl Percentile = National Percentile Rank (NPR), should not be averaged
NCE = Normal Curve Equivalent of Average Scaled Score, can be averaged

For explanations:
http://www.schools.utah.gov/assessment/DOCUMENTS/Iowa_Technical_Questions_ITBS.pdf

5.2.28 Iowa Test Summary by District, Grade 5 Core, Comparison Counties, 2009

Grade 8	Reading			Language			Math			CORE TOTAL		
	Nsize	NCE	Natl Percentile	Nsize	NCE	Natl Percentile	Nsize	NCE	Natl Percentile	Nsize	NCE	Natl Percentile
ALPINE DISTRICT	4363	59	66	4364	54	58	4348	54	58	4331	55	60
NEBO DISTRICT	1786	57	62	1806	51	53	1775	52	55	1738	53	56
PROVO DISTRICT	921	55	60	922	52	53	921	51	52	918	52	55
DAVIS DISTRICT	4773	58	65	4773	54	58	4764	54	58	4755	55	60
GRANITE DISTRICT	4625	50	49	4631	47	45	4614	46	43	4543	48	45
JORDAN DISTRICT	5906	56	62	5919	54	57	5850	53	55	5820	54	58
MURRAY DISTRICT	479	54	57	479	51	53	476	50	51	475	52	53
SALT LAKE DISTRICT	1567	48	46	1581	46	42	1514	46	42	1489	47	44

Source: Utah State Office of Education

Key:
n<10 = there are too few tests for reporting criteria
blank = the school did not test students for that grade

Core Total = Reading, Language, and Mathematics
Total Composite = Reading, Language, Mathematics, Social Studies, and Science.

Nsize = Number of Tests
Natl Percentile = National Percentile Rank (NPR), should not be averaged
NCE = Normal Curve Equivalent of Average Scaled Score, can be averaged

For explanations:
http://www.schools.utah.gov/assessment/DOCUMENTS/Iowa_Technical_Questions_ITBS.pdf

5.2.29 Iowa Test Summary by District, Grade 5 Expanded, Comparison Counties, 2009

Grade 8	Social Science			Science			TOTAL COMPOSITE		
	Nsize	NCE	Natl Percentile	Nsize	NCE	Natl Percentile	Nsize	NCE	Natl Percentile
ALPINE DISTRICT	4359	53	56	4349	62	71	4304	56	62
NEBO DISTRICT	1784	51	52	1776	59	66	1704	54	58
PROVO DISTRICT	921	50	50	919	57	64	915	53	56
DAVIS DISTRICT	4767	52	54	4763	61	69	4742	56	61
GRANITE DISTRICT	4630	46	43	4632	53	55	4497	49	47
JORDAN DISTRICT	5900	52	54	5875	59	67	5777	55	59
MURRAY DISTRICT	478	49	48	479	59	67	473	53	55
SALT LAKE DISTRICT	1567	45	41	1565	53	55	1460	48	47

Source: Utah State Office of Education

Key:
n<10 = there are too few tests for reporting criteria
blank = the school did not test students for that grade

Core Total = Reading, Language, and Mathematics
Total Composite = Reading, Language, Mathematics, Social Studies, and Science.

Nsize = Number of Tests
Natl Percentile = National Percentile Rank (NPR), should not be averaged
NCE = Normal Curve Equivalent of Average Scaled Score, can be averaged

For explanations:
http://www.schools.utah.gov/assessment/DOCUMENTS/Iowa_Technical_Questions_ITBS.pdf

5.2.30   Iowa Test Detail, Alpine School District, Grade 3 Core, 2009

	Grade 3											
	Reading			Language			Math			CORE TOTAL		
	Nsize	NCE	Natl Percentile	Nsize	NCE	Natl Percentile	Nsize	NCE	Natl Percentile	Nsize	NCE	Natl Percentile
ALPINE DISTRICT	4902	57	62	4954	50	51	4882	52	53	4801	53	56
ALPINE ONLINE SCHOOL	42	59	67	44	46	43	43	49	48	41	52	53
ALPINE SCHOOL	104	65	76	104	57	63	103	63	73	103	62	72
AMERICAN FORK JR HIGH												
ASPEN SCHOOL	66	51	53	68	45	41	67	48	45	65	48	47
BARRATT SCHOOL	70	63	73	70	62	71	66	54	58	66	60	69
BONNEVILLE SCHOOL	86	52	54	90	41	34	84	46	42	82	46	43
CANYON VIEW JR HIGH												
CASCADE SCHOOL	63	61	70	64	56	61	64	54	57	63	57	63
CEDAR RIDGE SCHOOL	151	59	66	151	54	57	146	56	62	145	56	62
CEDAR VALLEY SCHOOL	21	44	39	23	42	35	23	45	41	21	44	38
CENTRAL SCHOOL	64	51	51	67	44	39	66	49	48	63	49	47
CHERRY HILL SCHOOL	91	50	50	91	45	41	89	47	45	89	47	45
DEERFIELD SCHOOL	148	63	73	151	53	55	148	55	60	145	57	64
EAGLE VALLEY SCHOOL	145	53	56	148	44	39	149	47	44	142	48	47
EAGLECREST SCHOOL	127	56	62	127	52	53	125	54	58	125	54	57

	Reading			Language			Math			CORE TOTAL		
	Nsize	NCE	Natl Percentile	Nsize	NCE	Natl Percentile	Nsize	NCE	Natl Percentile	Nsize	NCE	Natl Percentile
FOOTHILL SCHOOL	84	65	77	89	58	65	91	62	72	82	63	73
FORBES SCHOOL	82	54	57	82	50	49	81	51	53	80	52	53
FOX HOLLOW ELEMENTARY	137	57	64	140	58	65	137	50	51	134	56	61
FREEDOM SCHOOL	155	58	65	155	57	63	154	54	57	152	56	62
GENEVA SCHOOL	65	42	35	65	42	35	65	41	33	64	41	34
GREENWOOD SCHOOL	85	52	54	87	49	48	85	50	50	83	50	51
GROVECREST SCHOOL	103	59	66	103	54	57	103	58	65	103	56	62
HARVEST ELEMENTARY	177	59	67	176	51	52	173	55	60	173	55	60
HIDDEN HOLLOW ELEMENTARY	117	54	57	122	47	44	122	48	47	115	50	49
HIGHLAND SCHOOL	133	66	78	133	60	68	133	64	75	133	64	74
HILLCREST SCHOOL	55	57	64	55	49	48	54	50	50	53	52	54
LAKERIDGE JR HIGH												
LEGACY SCHOOL	156	61	70	157	52	54	153	51	53	152	55	60
LEHI JR HIGH												
LEHI SCHOOL	90	52	55	94	47	44	93	46	43	87	49	49
LINDON SCHOOL	57	55	60	59	48	46	57	52	55	56	52	54
MANILA SCHOOL	123	57	63	123	48	46	120	53	55	120	53	55
MEADOW SCHOOL	133	52	54	134	47	44	131	46	43	130	48	47

	Reading			Language			Math			CORE TOTAL		
	Nsize	NCE	Natl Percentile	Nsize	NCE	Natl Percentile	Nsize	NCE	Natl Percentile	Nsize	NCE	Natl Percentile
MOUNT MAHOGANY SCHOOL	117	52	54	116	48	46	116	50	50	115	50	49
MOUNTAIN RIDGE JR HIGH												
NORTHRIDGE SCHOOL	113	62	72	113	55	60	113	59	66	113	59	66
OAK CANYON JR HIGH												
ORCHARD SCHOOL	90	55	59	90	51	52	89	49	48	87	51	53
OREM JR HIGH												
OREM SCHOOL	77	61	69	78	48	47	76	49	49	76	53	55
PLEASANT GROVE JR HIGH												
PONY EXPRESS SCHOOL	137	54	58	135	44	39	131	50	51	127	49	49
RIDGELINE ELEMENTARY	134	61	69	135	58	65	133	58	65	132	59	67
ROCKY MOUNTAIN SCHOOL	90	58	64	90	49	49	89	54	58	89	53	56
SARATOGA SHORES SCHOOL	174	53	56	173	43	38	167	46	43	167	47	45
SCERA PARK SCHOOL	58	55	60	58	52	53	58	50	50	58	52	54
SEGO LILY SCHOOL	136	59	66	137	58	64	136	52	54	135	56	62

	Reading			Language			Math			CORE TOTAL		
	Nsize	NCE	Natl Percentile	Nsize	NCE	Natl Percentile	Nsize	NCE	Natl Percentile	Nsize	NCE	Natl Percentile
SHARON SCHOOL	53	47	45	53	41	34	53	41	33	53	43	36
SHELLEY SCHOOL	161	59	66	160	50	49	159	53	56	159	54	57
SNOW SPRINGS SCHOOL	193	55	59	195	50	50	191	50	50	189	51	53
SUNCREST SCHOOL	60	49	47	60	46	43	60	42	35	60	45	41
TIMBERLINE MIDDLE												
VALLEY VIEW SCHOOL	66	54	57	66	46	43	66	47	44	66	49	47
VINEYARD SCHOOL	72	56	62	73	52	53	72	54	58	71	54	58
WESTFIELD SCHOOL	106	59	67	107	56	61	107	56	62	106	57	63
WESTMORE SCHOOL	55	46	42	59	38	28	58	42	35	53	42	35
WILLOWCREEK MIDDLE												
WINDSOR SCHOOL	80	49	49	84	42	35	83	47	44	78	46	43

Source: Utah State Office of Education

Key:
n<10 = there are too few tests for reporting criteria
blank = the school did not test students for that grade

Core Total = Reading, Language, and Mathematics
Total Composite = Reading, Language, Mathematics, Social Studies, and Science.

Nsize = Number of Tests
Natl Percentile = National Percentile Rank (NPR), should not be averaged
NCE = Normal Curve Equivalent of Average Scaled Score, can be averaged

For explanations:
http://www.schools.utah.gov/assessment/DOCUMENTS/Iowa_Technical_Questions_ITBS.pdf

5.2.31 Iowa Test Detail, Alpine School District, Grade 3 Expanded, 2009

	Grade 3								
	Social Science			Science			TOTAL COMPOSITE		
	Nsize	NCE	Natl Percentile	Nsize	NCE	Natl Percentile	Nsize	NCE	Natl Percentile
ALPINE DISTRICT	4949	58	65	4947	60	69	4772	57	62
ALPINE ONLINE SCHOOL	44	57	63	44	57	63	41	55	59
ALPINE SCHOOL	104	66	77	104	66	77	103	65	77
AMERICAN FORK JR HIGH									
ASPEN SCHOOL	68	56	61	68	57	64	65	53	55
BARRATT SCHOOL	70	63	73	70	67	79	66	64	75
BONNEVILLE SCHOOL	90	53	56	91	52	55	82	49	49
CANYON VIEW JR HIGH									
CASCADE SCHOOL	64	61	70	64	62	72	63	60	69
CEDAR RIDGE SCHOOL	152	61	71	151	62	71	144	60	69
CEDAR VALLEY SCHOOL	23	53	56	23	55	59	21	49	48
CENTRAL SCHOOL	65	55	60	67	53	56	62	52	54
CHERRY HILL SCHOOL	91	55	59	91	55	59	89	51	52
DEERFIELD SCHOOL	149	61	69	149	63	73	143	61	69
EAGLE VALLEY SCHOOL	148	55	59	150	57	63	141	52	54
EAGLECREST SCHOOL	126	58	65	125	61	71	123	58	65

	Social Science			Science			TOTAL COMPOSITE		
	Nsize	NCE	Natl Percentile	Nsize	NCE	Natl Percentile	Nsize	NCE	Natl Percentile
FOOTHILL SCHOOL	92	66	77	92	70	82	82	67	80
FORBES SCHOOL	83	56	61	82	57	62	80	54	58
FOX HOLLOW ELEMENTARY	140	59	67	139	61	70	133	59	67
FREEDOM SCHOOL	154	60	68	154	62	71	151	59	67
GENEVA SCHOOL	66	49	48	66	50	50	64	45	41
GREENWOOD SCHOOL	87	55	60	87	57	63	83	54	57
GROVECREST SCHOOL	103	61	70	103	64	75	103	61	69
HARVEST ELEMENTARY	176	62	71	176	64	75	172	60	69
HIDDEN HOLLOW ELEMENTARY	123	56	61	123	57	63	115	53	56
HIGHLAND SCHOOL	133	68	81	132	70	83	132	69	81
HILLCREST SCHOOL	55	57	63	55	63	74	53	57	63
LAKERIDGE JR HIGH									
LEGACY SCHOOL	157	60	68	157	63	74	152	59	67
LEHI JR HIGH									
LEHI SCHOOL	95	57	63	95	58	65	87	54	58
LINDON SCHOOL	58	58	65	59	60	69	55	56	62
MANILA SCHOOL	124	55	60	122	57	63	119	55	59
MEADOW SCHOOL	134	53	55	132	57	63	128	52	54

	Social Science			Science			TOTAL COMPOSITE		
	Nsize	NCE	Natl Percentile	Nsize	NCE	Natl Percentile	Nsize	NCE	Natl Percentile
MOUNT MAHOGANY SCHOOL	116	55	60	115	57	63	115	53	56
MOUNTAIN RIDGE JR HIGH									
NORTHRIDGE SCHOOL	113	61	70	113	64	74	113	62	71
OAK CANYON JR HIGH									
ORCHARD SCHOOL	90	55	60	91	60	69	86	55	60
OREM JR HIGH									
OREM SCHOOL	78	60	68	76	64	74	75	58	65
PLEASANT GROVE JR HIGH									
PONY EXPRESS SCHOOL	133	54	57	138	56	61	127	53	55
RIDGELINE ELEMENTARY	133	62	71	131	65	76	128	63	73
ROCKY MOUNTAIN SCHOOL	89	61	69	89	63	73	89	58	65
SARATOGA SHORES SCHOOL	168	55	60	170	58	64	162	52	54
SCERA PARK SCHOOL	58	57	64	58	57	63	58	55	59
SEGO LILY SCHOOL	136	58	64	136	62	72	133	59	67

	Social Science			Science			TOTAL COMPOSITE		
	Nsize	NCE	Natl Percentile	Nsize	NCE	Natl Percentile	Nsize	NCE	Natl Percentile
SHARON SCHOOL	54	52	54	53	50	50	53	46	43
SHELLEY SCHOOL	161	58	65	160	63	73	158	58	65
SNOW SPRINGS SCHOOL	195	57	63	195	59	67	189	55	60
SUNCREST SCHOOL	60	52	54	60	49	48	60	48	46
TIMBERLINE MIDDLE									
VALLEY VIEW SCHOOL	66	54	57	66	61	70	66	53	56
VINEYARD SCHOOL	73	60	69	73	63	73	71	59	66
WESTFIELD SCHOOL	107	60	68	107	62	71	106	60	68
WESTMORE SCHOOL	60	50	50	60	53	56	53	46	43
WILLOWCREEK MIDDLE									
WINDSOR SCHOOL	85	56	60	85	53	55	78	51	52

Source: Utah State Office of Education

Key:
n<10 = there are too few tests for reporting criteria
blank = the school did not test students for that grade

Core Total = Reading, Language, and Mathematics
Total Composite = Reading, Language, Mathematics, Social Studies, and Science.

Nsize = Number of Tests
Natl Percentile = National Percentile Rank (NPR), should not be averaged
NCE = Normal Curve Equivalent of Average Scaled Score, can be averaged

For explanations:
http://www.schools.utah.gov/assessment/DOCUMENTS/Iowa_Technical_Questions_ITBS.pdf

5.2.32 Iowa Test Detail, Alpine School District, Grade 5 Core, 2009

| | Grade 5 | | | | | | | | | | | |
| | Reading | | | Language | | | Math | | | CORE TOTAL | | |
	Nsize	NCE	Natl Percentile	Nsize	NCE	Natl Percentile	Nsize	NCE	Natl Percentile	Nsize	NCE	Natl Percentile
ALPINE DISTRICT	4609	56	62	4617	54	58	4600	54	58	4581	54	58
ALPINE ONLINE SCHOOL	42	60	69	42	47	45	42	50	51	42	52	54
ALPINE SCHOOL	118	58	65	118	55	59	118	57	63	118	56	62
AMERICAN FORK JR HIGH												
ASPEN SCHOOL	76	51	53	76	55	59	76	54	57	76	53	55
BARRATT SCHOOL	106	62	72	106	63	73	106	61	69	106	62	72
BONNEVILLE SCHOOL	115	53	55	115	51	53	115	50	50	115	51	52
CANYON VIEW JR HIGH												
CASCADE SCHOOL	77	62	72	77	58	65	74	60	69	74	61	70
CEDAR RIDGE SCHOOL	141	63	74	141	59	67	140	59	67	140	61	69
CEDAR VALLEY SCHOOL	25	52	53	25	54	58	25	49	49	25	52	54
CENTRAL SCHOOL	62	53	56	62	49	47	62	46	42	62	49	48
CHERRY HILL SCHOOL	100	59	67	100	56	62	100	59	66	100	57	64
DEERFIELD SCHOOL	126	56	61	126	57	63	126	59	66	126	57	63
EAGLE VALLEY SCHOOL	125	53	56	125	49	48	125	48	46	125	50	49
EAGLECREST SCHOOL	114	56	62	115	57	63	115	59	67	114	57	63

	Reading			Language			Math			CORE TOTAL		
	Nsize	NCE	Natl Percentile	Nsize	NCE	Natl Percentile	Nsize	NCE	Natl Percentile	Nsize	NCE	Natl Percentile
FOOTHILL SCHOOL	94	66	77	98	62	71	95	63	73	91	64	74
FORBES SCHOOL	72	51	52	72	48	46	72	45	40	72	48	46
FOX HOLLOW ELEMENTARY	113	54	58	114	52	53	114	47	44	113	51	52
FREEDOM SCHOOL	155	62	71	155	60	68	155	58	64	155	60	68
GENEVA SCHOOL	45	45	41	46	38	28	45	43	36	44	41	34
GREENWOOD SCHOOL	58	50	50	58	50	49	57	43	37	55	48	46
GROVECREST SCHOOL	98	58	64	98	55	58	98	54	57	98	55	59
HARVEST ELEMENTARY	108	55	60	108	54	57	108	55	59	108	54	58
HIDDEN HOLLOW ELEMENTARY	109	52	53	111	47	44	110	48	47	108	49	48
HIGHLAND SCHOOL	142	64	74	143	61	70	143	63	73	142	63	72
HILLCREST SCHOOL	44	55	60	44	54	58	44	51	53	44	53	56
LAKERIDGE JR HIGH												
LEGACY SCHOOL	126	62	71	125	58	64	124	60	68	124	60	68
LEHI JR HIGH												
LEHI SCHOOL	72	52	53	72	49	49	71	50	51	71	50	50
LINDON SCHOOL	95	58	64	94	58	65	94	59	66	94	58	65
MANILA SCHOOL	113	53	55	113	54	57	112	55	60	112	53	56
MEADOW SCHOOL	106	52	54	106	50	49	106	49	49	103	50	50

	Reading			Language			Math			CORE TOTAL		
	Nsize	NCE	Natl Percentile	Nsize	NCE	Natl Percentile	Nsize	NCE	Natl Percentile	Nsize	NCE	Natl Percentile
MOUNT MAHOGANY SCHOOL	95	50	50	95	51	52	96	49	48	94	50	50
MOUNTAIN RIDGE JR HIGH												
NORTHRIDGE SCHOOL	108	61	70	108	56	61	106	58	64	106	58	64
OAK CANYON JR HIGH												
ORCHARD SCHOOL	113	52	54	113	53	56	113	54	57	113	53	55
OREM JR HIGH												
OREM SCHOOL	80	56	62	80	55	59	80	55	59	80	55	59
PLEASANT GROVE JR HIGH												
PONY EXPRESS SCHOOL	94	51	52	94	51	51	94	46	43	94	49	48
RIDGELINE ELEMENTARY	127	59	67	127	58	65	126	58	65	126	58	65
ROCKY MOUNTAIN SCHOOL	80	57	64	80	55	59	80	55	60	80	56	60
SARATOGA SHORES SCHOOL	161	58	65	161	54	57	160	53	55	160	54	58
SCERA PARK SCHOOL	45	54	58	45	50	50	45	48	46	45	51	51
SEGO LILY SCHOOL	123	55	59	123	55	59	122	53	55	122	54	58

	Reading			Language			Math			CORE TOTAL		
	Nsize	NCE	Natl Percentile	Nsize	NCE	Natl Percentile	Nsize	NCE	Natl Percentile	Nsize	NCE	Natl Percentile
SHARON SCHOOL	66	46	42	67	47	44	67	48	47	66	46	43
SHELLEY SCHOOL	119	57	62	119	56	62	119	56	61	119	56	61
SNOW SPRINGS SCHOOL	144	54	57	144	50	50	143	48	46	143	50	50
SUNCREST SCHOOL	52	45	40	52	47	44	52	47	44	52	45	41
TIMBERLINE MIDDLE												
VALLEY VIEW SCHOOL	75	63	73	75	58	64	75	57	63	75	59	66
VINEYARD SCHOOL	83	53	56	83	51	53	83	51	53	83	52	53
WESTFIELD SCHOOL	135	56	61	135	54	58	135	54	57	135	54	58
WESTMORE SCHOOL	50	55	59	49	50	50	50	47	45	49	50	51
WILLOWCREEK MIDDLE												
WINDSOR SCHOOL	82	54	57	82	51	51	82	52	55	82	52	54

Source: Utah State Office of Education

Key:
n<10 = there are too few tests for reporting criteria
blank = the school did not test students for that grade

Core Total = Reading, Language, and Mathematics
Total Composite = Reading, Language, Mathematics, Social Studies, and Science.

Nsize = Number of Tests
Natl Percentile = National Percentile Rank (NPR), should not be averaged
NCE = Normal Curve Equivalent of Average Scaled Score, can be averaged

For explanations:
http://www.schools.utah.gov/assessment/DOCUMENTS/Iowa_Technical_Questions_ITBS.pdf

5.2.33 Iowa Test Detail, Alpine School District, Grade 5 Expanded, 2009

	Grade 5								
	Social Science			Science			TOTAL COMPOSITE		
	Nsize	NCE	Natl Percentile	Nsize	NCE	Natl Percentile	Nsize	NCE	Natl Percentile
ALPINE DISTRICT	4616	55	60	4605	61	70	4564	57	63
ALPINE ONLINE SCHOOL	41	57	63	41	56	62	41	55	59
ALPINE SCHOOL	118	57	63	118	60	68	118	58	65
AMERICAN FORK JR HIGH									
ASPEN SCHOOL	76	52	54	76	58	66	76	55	59
BARRATT SCHOOL	106	59	67	106	65	76	106	63	73
BONNEVILLE SCHOOL	114	57	63	115	59	66	114	55	59
CANYON VIEW JR HIGH									
CASCADE SCHOOL	77	61	70	76	64	75	74	63	73
CEDAR RIDGE SCHOOL	141	65	76	140	67	78	139	64	74
CEDAR VALLEY SCHOOL	24	51	53	24	56	61	24	53	56
CENTRAL SCHOOL	62	54	57	62	59	66	62	53	55
CHERRY HILL SCHOOL	100	56	61	100	64	74	100	59	67
DEERFIELD SCHOOL	126	56	61	126	60	69	126	58	65
EAGLE VALLEY SCHOOL	125	50	50	125	57	63	125	52	54
EAGLECREST SCHOOL	115	56	60	115	63	73	114	59	67

	Social Science			Science			TOTAL COMPOSITE		
	Nsize	NCE	Natl Percentile	Nsize	NCE	Natl Percentile	Nsize	NCE	Natl Percentile
FOOTHILL SCHOOL	97	64	75	98	69	82	91	66	78
FORBES SCHOOL	72	50	49	72	55	59	72	50	50
FOX HOLLOW ELEMENTARY	113	55	58	113	58	65	112	54	58
FREEDOM SCHOOL	155	58	66	155	66	77	155	62	71
GENEVA SCHOOL	46	44	39	46	53	56	44	45	41
GREENWOOD SCHOOL	60	53	56	60	54	57	55	51	52
GROVECREST SCHOOL	98	57	63	98	61	70	98	58	64
HARVEST ELEMENTARY	108	55	60	108	60	69	108	56	62
HIDDEN HOLLOW ELEMENTARY	111	50	49	110	60	68	107	52	55
HIGHLAND SCHOOL	143	63	72	143	66	78	142	64	75
HILLCREST SCHOOL	44	54	58	44	59	67	44	56	61
LAKERIDGE JR HIGH									
LEGACY SCHOOL	125	57	64	125	64	75	122	61	70
LEHI JR HIGH									
LEHI SCHOOL	72	54	57	72	58	65	71	53	56
LINDON SCHOOL	94	58	65	95	65	77	94	61	69
MANILA SCHOOL	113	52	54	108	60	68	107	55	60
MEADOW SCHOOL	106	51	51	105	57	64	103	52	55
	Social Science			Science			TOTAL COMPOSITE		

	Nsize	NCE	Natl Percentile	Nsize	NCE	Natl Percentile	Nsize	NCE	Natl Percentile
MOUNT MAHOGANY SCHOOL	96	50	50	95	56	61	93	52	53
MOUNTAIN RIDGE JR HIGH									
NORTHRIDGE SCHOOL	108	57	63	108	64	75	106	60	68
OAK CANYON JR HIGH									
ORCHARD SCHOOL	113	51	52	113	56	61	113	54	57
OREM JR HIGH									
OREM SCHOOL	80	56	62	80	60	68	80	57	63
PLEASANT GROVE JR HIGH									
PONY EXPRESS SCHOOL	94	50	50	94	57	63	94	52	53
RIDGELINE ELEMENTARY	127	58	64	127	65	76	126	60	69
ROCKY MOUNTAIN SCHOOL	80	55	60	80	59	66	80	57	63
SARATOGA SHORES SCHOOL	161	56	61	160	62	72	160	57	63
SCERA PARK SCHOOL	45	53	55	45	59	67	45	54	57
SEGO LILY SCHOOL	123	56	60	123	61	70	122	57	62

	Social Science			Science			TOTAL COMPOSITE		
	Nsize	NCE	Natl Percentile	Nsize	NCE	Natl Percentile	Nsize	NCE	Natl Percentile
SHARON SCHOOL	67	50	50	67	54	57	66	49	48
SHELLEY SCHOOL	119	58	65	119	60	68	119	58	65
SNOW SPRINGS SCHOOL	144	52	54	144	59	67	143	54	57
SUNCREST SCHOOL	52	49	47	51	54	57	51	49	47
TIMBERLINE MIDDLE									
VALLEY VIEW SCHOOL	75	58	64	75	62	71	75	60	68
VINEYARD SCHOOL	83	55	59	83	60	68	83	55	59
WESTFIELD SCHOOL	135	55	59	135	61	71	135	57	62
WESTMORE SCHOOL	50	49	48	49	56	61	48	52	53
WILLOWCREEK MIDDLE									
WINDSOR SCHOOL	82	53	56	81	60	68	81	55	59

Source: Utah State Office of Education

Key:
n<10 = there are too few tests for reporting criteria
blank = the school did not test students for that grade

Core Total = Reading, Language, and Mathematics
Total Composite = Reading, Language, Mathematics, Social Studies, and Science.

Nsize = Number of Tests
Natl Percentile = National Percentile Rank (NPR), should not be averaged
NCE = Normal Curve Equivalent of Average Scaled Score, can be averaged

For explanations:
http://www.schools.utah.gov/assessment/DOCUMENTS/Iowa_Technical_Questions_ITBS.pdf

5.2.34 Iowa Test Detail, Alpine School District, Grade 8 Core, 2009

	Grade 8											
	Reading			Language			Math			CORE TOTAL		
	Nsize	NCE	Natl Percentile	Nsize	NCE	Natl Percentile	Nsize	NCE	Natl Percentile	Nsize	NCE	Natl Percentile
ALPINE DISTRICT	4363	59	66	4364	54	58	4348	54	58	4331	55	60
ALPINE ONLINE SCHOOL	37	62	72	37	53	55	37	46	43	37	53	56
ALPINE SCHOOL												
AMERICAN FORK JR HIGH	524	57	64	526	54	58	523	54	58	521	55	59
ASPEN SCHOOL												
BARRATT SCHOOL												
BONNEVILLE SCHOOL												
CANYON VIEW JR HIGH	371	58	65	371	53	56	366	56	61	364	55	60
CASCADE SCHOOL												
CEDAR RIDGE SCHOOL												
CEDAR VALLEY SCHOOL												
CENTRAL SCHOOL												
CHERRY HILL SCHOOL												
DEERFIELD SCHOOL												
EAGLE VALLEY SCHOOL												

	Reading			Language			Math			CORE TOTAL		
	Nsize	NCE	Natl Percentile	Nsize	NCE	Natl Percentile	Nsize	NCE	Natl Percentile	Nsize	NCE	Natl Percentile
EAGLECREST SCHOOL												
FOOTHILL SCHOOL												
FORBES SCHOOL												
FOX HOLLOW ELEMENTARY												
FREEDOM SCHOOL												
GENEVA SCHOOL												
GREENWOOD SCHOOL												
GROVECREST SCHOOL												
HARVEST ELEMENTARY												
HIDDEN HOLLOW ELEMENTARY												
HIGHLAND SCHOOL												
HILLCREST SCHOOL												
LAKERIDGE JR HIGH	390	57	64	392	52	54	389	52	53	386	54	57
LEGACY SCHOOL												

	Reading			Language			Math			CORE TOTAL		
	Nsize	NCE	Natl Percentile	Nsize	NCE	Natl Percentile	Nsize	NCE	Natl Percentile	Nsize	NCE	Natl Percentile
LEHI JR HIGH	414	58	66	414	54	57	412	53	56	412	55	59
LEHI SCHOOL												
LINDON SCHOOL												
MANILA SCHOOL												
MEADOW SCHOOL												
MOUNT MAHOGANY SCHOOL												
MOUNTAIN RIDGE JR HIGH	447	64	74	446	58	65	445	57	63	443	59	67
NORTHRIDGE SCHOOL												
OAK CANYON JR HIGH	426	62	71	427	58	65	425	59	66	424	59	67
ORCHARD SCHOOL												
OREM JR HIGH	286	51	53	285	47	44	288	47	45	284	48	46
OREM SCHOOL												
PLEASANT GROVE JR HIGH	458	57	63	458	54	57	456	54	57	456	54	58
PONY EXPRESS SCHOOL												
RIDGELINE ELEMENTARY												

	Reading			Language			Math			CORE TOTAL		
	Nsize	NCE	Natl Percentile	Nsize	NCE	Natl Percentile	Nsize	NCE	Natl Percentile	Nsize	NCE	Natl Percentile
ROCKY MOUNTAIN SCHOOL												
SARATOGA SHORES SCHOOL												
SCERA PARK SCHOOL												
SEGO LILY SCHOOL												
SHARON SCHOOL												
SHELLEY SCHOOL												
SNOW SPRINGS SCHOOL												
SUNCREST SCHOOL												
TIMBERLINE MIDDLE	413	64	75	412	59	67	412	59	67	410	61	70
VALLEY VIEW SCHOOL												
VINEYARD SCHOOL												
WESTFIELD SCHOOL												
WESTMORE SCHOOL												
WILLOWCREEK MIDDLE	597	55	60	596	51	52	595	49	49	594	52	53
WINDSOR SCHOOL												

Source: Utah State Office of Education

Key:
n<10 = there are too few tests for reporting criteria
blank = the school did not test students for that grade

Core Total = Reading, Language, and Mathematics
Total Composite = Reading, Language, Mathematics, Social Studies, and Science.

Nsize = Number of Tests
Natl Percentile = National Percentile Rank (NPR), should not be averaged
NCE = Normal Curve Equivalent of Average Scaled Score, can be averaged

For explanations:
http://www.schools.utah.gov/assessment/DOCUMENTS/Iowa_Technical_Questions_ITBS.pdf

5.2.35 Iowa Test Detail, Alpine School District, Grade 8 Expanded, 2009

	Grade 8								
	Social Science			Science			TOTAL COMPOSITE		
	Nsize	NCE	Natl Percentile	Nsize	NCE	Natl Percentile	Nsize	NCE	Natl Percentile
ALPINE DISTRICT	4359	53	56	4349	62	71	4304	56	62
ALPINE ONLINE SCHOOL	37	49	49	37	57	62	37	53	56
ALPINE SCHOOL									
AMERICAN FORK JR HIGH	525	51	53	524	62	72	519	56	61
ASPEN SCHOOL									
BARRATT SCHOOL									
BONNEVILLE SCHOOL									
CANYON VIEW JR HIGH	370	53	56	368	62	71	360	57	62
CASCADE SCHOOL									
CEDAR RIDGE SCHOOL									
CEDAR VALLEY SCHOOL									
CENTRAL SCHOOL									
CHERRY HILL SCHOOL									
DEERFIELD SCHOOL									
EAGLE VALLEY SCHOOL									

	Social Science			Science			TOTAL COMPOSITE		
	Nsize	NCE	Natl Percentile	Nsize	NCE	Natl Percentile	Nsize	NCE	Natl Percentile
EAGLECREST SCHOOL									
FOOTHILL SCHOOL									
FORBES SCHOOL									
FOX HOLLOW ELEMENTARY									
FREEDOM SCHOOL									
GENEVA SCHOOL									
GREENWOOD SCHOOL									
GROVECREST SCHOOL									
HARVEST ELEMENTARY									
HIDDEN HOLLOW ELEMENTARY									
HIGHLAND SCHOOL									
HILLCREST SCHOOL									
LAKERIDGE JR HIGH	392	51	52	391	60	67	385	54	58
LEGACY SCHOOL									

	Social Science			Science			TOTAL COMPOSITE		
	Nsize	NCE	Natl Percentile	Nsize	NCE	Natl Percentile	Nsize	NCE	Natl Percentile
LEHI JR HIGH	409	55	60	412	60	68	408	56	62
LEHI SCHOOL									
LINDON SCHOOL									
MANILA SCHOOL									
MEADOW SCHOOL									
MOUNT MAHOGANY SCHOOL									
MOUNTAIN RIDGE JR HIGH	447	57	63	443	65	77	438	61	70
NORTHRIDGE SCHOOL									
OAK CANYON JR HIGH	427	54	57	427	62	71	424	59	66
ORCHARD SCHOOL									
OREM JR HIGH	285	48	47	281	56	62	278	50	51
OREM SCHOOL									
PLEASANT GROVE JR HIGH	456	52	54	457	61	70	455	55	60
PONY EXPRESS SCHOOL									
RIDGELINE ELEMENTARY									

	Social Science			Science			TOTAL COMPOSITE		
	Nsize	NCE	Natl Percentile	Nsize	NCE	Natl Percentile	Nsize	NCE	Natl Percentile
ROCKY MOUNTAIN SCHOOL									
SARATOGA SHORES SCHOOL									
SCERA PARK SCHOOL									
SEGO LILY SCHOOL									
SHARON SCHOOL									
SHELLEY SCHOOL									
SNOW SPRINGS SCHOOL									
SUNCREST SCHOOL									
TIMBERLINE MIDDLE	415	59	66	413	67	79	407	62	72
VALLEY VIEW SCHOOL									
VINEYARD SCHOOL									
WESTFIELD SCHOOL									
WESTMORE SCHOOL									
WILLOWCREEK MIDDLE	596	49	48	596	60	69	593	53	56
WINDSOR SCHOOL									

Source: Utah State Office of Education

Key:
n<10 = there are too few tests for reporting criteria
blank = the school did not test students for that grade

Core Total = Reading, Language, and Mathematics
Total Composite = Reading, Language, Mathematics, Social Studies, and Science.

Nsize = Number of Tests
Natl Percentile = National Percentile Rank (NPR), should not be averaged
NCE = Normal Curve Equivalent of Average Scaled Score, can be averaged

For explanations:
http://www.schools.utah.gov/assessment/DOCUMENTS/Iowa_Technical_Questions_ITBS.pdf

5.2.36 Iowa Test Detail, Nebo School District, Grade 3 Core, 2009

| | Grade 3 | | | | | | | | | | | |
| | Reading | | | Language | | | Math | | | CORE TOTAL | | |
	Nsize	NCE	Natl Percentile	Nsize	NCE	Natl Percentile	Nsize	NCE	Natl Percentile	Nsize	NCE	Natl Percentile
ART CITY SCHOOL	90	61	70	93	52	54	91	53	56	89	56	61
BARNETT SCHOOL	89	50	50	91	45	41	89	48	46	88	48	46
BROCKBANK SCHOOL	72	58	65	72	55	59	72	56	61	72	56	61
BROOKSIDE SCHOOL	76	53	56	79	49	49	79	49	48	76	50	50
CANYON SCHOOL	92	57	63	93	45	41	91	52	53	90	51	53
CHERRY CREEK ELEMENTARY	71	50	50	73	43	37	70	44	39	68	46	42
DIAMOND FORK JUNIOR HIGH												
EAST MEADOWS ELEMENTARY	101	58	64	101	49	49	101	50	50	101	52	54
FOOTHILLS ELEMENTARY	85	55	60	84	53	55	84	55	59	83	54	58
GOSHEN SCHOOL	51	43	37	52	39	29	49	40	32	48	41	33
HOBBLE CREEK SCHOOL	99	61	69	103	51	52	101	53	55	97	55	60
LARSEN SCHOOL	83	54	57	83	51	52	83	51	51	83	51	53

	Reading			Language			Math			CORE TOTAL		
	Nsize	NCE	Natl Percentile	Nsize	NCE	Natl Percentile	Nsize	NCE	Natl Percentile	Nsize	NCE	Natl Percentile
MAPLETON JUNIOR HIGH												
MAPLETON SCHOOL	96	54	57	101	49	49	99	51	51	93	52	53
MT LOAFER SCHOOL	58	61	70	58	58	64	58	59	67	58	60	68
MT. NEBO JUNIOR HIGH												
NEBO DISTRICT	2131	54	57	2177	48	47	2138	50	50	2084	51	51
ORCHARD HILLS ELEMENTARY	89	49	47	97	46	42	96	48	46	88	48	46
PARK SCHOOL	70	49	48	72	45	41	70	47	45	68	47	45
PARK VIEW SCHOOL	74	58	64	75	48	46	71	51	52	71	52	54
PAYSON JR HIGH												
REES SCHOOL	78	53	57	79	44	38	79	49	48	75	49	48
RIVERVIEW SCHOOL	79	52	53	82	48	46	78	48	46	75	50	50
SAGE CREEK SCHOOL	117	55	59	120	48	46	113	54	57	111	52	55
SALEM SCHOOL	54	54	57	54	50	51	54	46	43	53	50	50
SANTAQUIN SCHOOL	65	53	56	67	42	36	66	49	49	64	49	48

	Reading			Language			Math			CORE TOTAL		
	Nsize	NCE	Natl Percentile	Nsize	NCE	Natl Percentile	Nsize	NCE	Natl Percentile	Nsize	NCE	Natl Percentile
SPANISH FORK JR HIGH												
SPANISH OAKS SCHOOL	130	57	63	130	52	53	130	52	53	129	53	56
SPRING LAKE SCHOOL	102	53	55	102	49	48	102	50	51	102	50	51
SPRINGVILLE JR HIGH												
TAYLOR SCHOOL	59	49	48	60	43	37	58	45	41	55	47	44
WESTSIDE SCHOOL	90	50	50	94	48	47	94	46	43	88	49	47
WILSON SCHOOL	61	44	39	62	39	30	60	44	38	59	42	35

Source: Utah State Office of Education

Key:
n<10 = there are too few tests for reporting criteria
blank = the school did not test students for that grade

Core Total = Reading, Language, and Mathematics
Total Composite = Reading, Language, Mathematics, Social Studies, and Science.

Nsize = Number of Tests
Natl Percentile = National Percentile Rank (NPR), should not be averaged
NCE = Normal Curve Equivalent of Average Scaled Score, can be averaged

For explanations:
http://www.schools.utah.gov/assessment/DOCUMENTS/Iowa_Technical_Questions_ITBS.pdf

5.2.37 Iowa Test Detail, Nebo School District, Grade 3 Expanded, 2009

	Grade 3								
	Social Science			Science			TOTAL COMPOSITE		
	Nsize	NCE	Natl Percentile	Nsize	NCE	Natl Percentile	Nsize	NCE	Natl Percentile
ART CITY SCHOOL	94	61	69	94	62	71	89	60	68
BARNETT SCHOOL	91	54	58	91	54	57	88	51	53
BROCKBANK SCHOOL	72	62	71	72	61	71	72	60	68
BROOKSIDE SCHOOL	79	55	59	79	58	65	76	54	57
CANYON SCHOOL	92	56	62	92	59	66	90	55	59
CHERRY CREEK ELEMENTARY	73	52	54	73	50	50	68	49	48
DIAMOND FORK JUNIOR HIGH									
EAST MEADOWS ELEMENTARY	101	58	65	101	59	67	101	55	60
FOOTHILLS ELEMENTARY	84	55	59	83	58	64	82	56	61
GOSHEN SCHOOL	50	44	39	50	44	38	48	43	36
HOBBLE CREEK SCHOOL	103	59	67	103	62	71	97	59	66
LARSEN SCHOOL	83	57	63	83	59	67	83	55	59

	Social Science			Science			TOTAL COMPOSITE		
	Nsize	NCE	Natl Percentile	Nsize	NCE	Natl Percentile	Nsize	NCE	Natl Percentile
MAPLETON JUNIOR HIGH									
MAPLETON SCHOOL	100	58	65	99	61	70	92	56	62
MT LOAFER SCHOOL	58	62	72	58	66	77	58	63	73
MT. NEBO JUNIOR HIGH									
NEBO DISTRICT	2174	56	61	2166	58	64	2071	54	58
ORCHARD HILLS ELEMENTARY	96	56	61	97	56	61	87	52	55
PARK SCHOOL	72	56	62	72	58	65	68	52	54
PARK VIEW SCHOOL	75	55	59	74	57	63	70	54	58
PAYSON JR HIGH									
REES SCHOOL	81	55	60	80	56	61	74	52	55
RIVERVIEW SCHOOL	81	55	59	81	62	71	74	55	59
SAGE CREEK SCHOOL	118	59	67	119	61	69	111	57	63
SALEM SCHOOL	52	56	61	54	58	64	52	54	57
SANTAQUIN SCHOOL	67	55	59	66	57	64	63	53	56

	Social Science			Science			TOTAL COMPOSITE		
	Nsize	NCE	Natl Percentile	Nsize	NCE	Natl Percentile	Nsize	NCE	Natl Percentile
SPANISH FORK JR HIGH									
SPANISH OAKS SCHOOL	131	57	64	129	60	68	128	56	62
SPRING LAKE SCHOOL	102	55	59	102	55	59	102	53	55
SPRINGVILLE JR HIGH									
TAYLOR SCHOOL	61	47	44	61	52	55	55	49	48
WESTSIDE SCHOOL	95	53	56	92	56	61	86	52	53
WILSON SCHOOL	63	47	45	61	52	54	57	46	42

Source: Utah State Office of Education

Key:
n<10 = there are too few tests for reporting criteria
blank = the school did not test students for that grade

Core Total = Reading, Language, and Mathematics
Total Composite = Reading, Language, Mathematics, Social Studies, and Science.

Nsize = Number of Tests
Natl Percentile = National Percentile Rank (NPR), should not be averaged
NCE = Normal Curve Equivalent of Average Scaled Score, can be averaged

For explanations:
http://www.schools.utah.gov/assessment/DOCUMENTS/Iowa_Technical_Questions_ITBS.pdf

5.2.38 Iowa Test Detail, Nebo School District, Grade 5 Core, 2009

	Grade 5											
	Reading			Language			Math			CORE TOTAL		
	Nsize	NCE	Natl Percentile	Nsize	NCE	Natl Percentile	Nsize	NCE	Natl Percentile	Nsize	NCE	Natl Percentile
ART CITY SCHOOL	107	61	70	107	57	63	106	57	64	106	58	65
BARNETT SCHOOL	100	53	55	99	46	43	99	47	44	98	48	46
BROCKBANK SCHOOL	56	49	49	56	52	53	56	47	45	56	49	48
BROOKSIDE SCHOOL	98	54	58	98	54	57	98	51	51	98	53	55
CANYON SCHOOL	110	54	58	110	51	52	107	54	58	107	53	55
CHERRY CREEK ELEMENTARY	70	49	47	71	41	33	71	44	38	70	44	39
DIAMOND FORK JUNIOR HIGH												
EAST MEADOWS ELEMENTARY	79	59	67	79	55	59	79	57	63	79	56	62
FOOTHILLS ELEMENTARY	82	55	59	82	54	57	82	53	55	82	53	56
GOSHEN SCHOOL	47	47	45	47	43	37	47	49	48	47	46	42
HOBBLE CREEK SCHOOL	109	63	74	109	59	67	109	60	69	109	61	70
LARSEN SCHOOL	92	54	57	92	53	55	92	53	56	92	53	55

	Reading			Language			Math			CORE TOTAL		
	Nsize	NCE	Natl Percentile	Nsize	NCE	Natl Percentile	Nsize	NCE	Natl Percentile	Nsize	NCE	Natl Percentile
MAPLETON JUNIOR HIGH												
MAPLETON SCHOOL	96	64	74	96	59	67	96	58	65	96	60	69
MT LOAFER SCHOOL	65	60	69	65	61	71	65	64	74	65	62	71
MT. NEBO JUNIOR HIGH												
NEBO DISTRICT	2164	54	58	2162	51	52	2157	52	54	2152	52	54
ORCHARD HILLS ELEMENTARY	95	52	54	95	50	50	94	49	48	94	50	51
PARK SCHOOL	73	46	42	71	44	38	71	47	45	71	45	40
PARK VIEW SCHOOL	64	49	47	65	45	41	65	48	46	64	47	44
PAYSON JR HIGH												
REES SCHOOL	78	47	45	78	44	38	78	51	52	78	46	43
RIVERVIEW SCHOOL	93	54	57	93	49	48	93	52	55	93	51	52
SAGE CREEK SCHOOL	101	57	64	101	53	56	100	54	57	100	54	58
SALEM SCHOOL	68	52	54	68	50	51	68	52	55	68	51	53
SANTAQUIN SCHOOL	55	50	50	55	47	44	55	53	56	55	49	48

	Reading			Language			Math			CORE TOTAL		
	Nsize	NCE	Natl Percentile	Nsize	NCE	Natl Percentile	Nsize	NCE	Natl Percentile	Nsize	NCE	Natl Percentile
SPANISH FORK JR HIGH												
SPANISH OAKS SCHOOL	125	57	63	125	54	58	125	53	57	125	54	58
SPRING LAKE SCHOOL	89	56	61	89	55	60	89	51	52	89	54	57
SPRINGVILLE JR HIGH												
TAYLOR SCHOOL	45	48	45	45	46	43	44	50	51	44	48	46
WESTSIDE SCHOOL	86	50	51	85	45	40	87	45	40	85	46	43
WILSON SCHOOL	81	48	45	81	43	37	81	49	47	81	46	42

Source: Utah State Office of Education

Key:
n<10 = there are too few tests for reporting criteria
blank = the school did not test students for that grade

Core Total = Reading, Language, and Mathematics
Total Composite = Reading, Language, Mathematics, Social Studies, and Science.

Nsize = Number of Tests
Natl Percentile = National Percentile Rank (NPR), should not be averaged
NCE = Normal Curve Equivalent of Average Scaled Score, can be averaged

For explanations:
http://www.schools.utah.gov/assessment/DOCUMENTS/Iowa_Technical_Questions_ITBS.pdf

5.2.39 Iowa Test Detail, Nebo School District, Grade 5 Expanded, 2009

	Grade 5								
	Social Science			Science			TOTAL COMPOSITE		
	Nsize	NCE	Natl Percentile	Nsize	NCE	Natl Percentile	Nsize	NCE	Natl Percentile
ART CITY SCHOOL	104	60	69	102	63	74	101	61	70
BARNETT SCHOOL	98	49	47	96	57	63	95	51	52
BROCKBANK SCHOOL	56	52	54	56	57	63	56	52	54
BROOKSIDE SCHOOL	98	54	57	98	58	65	98	55	59
CANYON SCHOOL	110	54	58	110	61	69	107	55	60
CHERRY CREEK ELEMENTARY	71	48	46	71	55	59	70	48	46
DIAMOND FORK JUNIOR HIGH									
EAST MEADOWS ELEMENTARY	79	58	65	79	62	72	79	59	66
FOOTHILLS ELEMENTARY	82	54	57	82	58	65	82	55	60
GOSHEN SCHOOL	47	44	38	47	55	60	47	48	46
HOBBLE CREEK SCHOOL	109	61	70	109	66	78	109	63	73
LARSEN SCHOOL	92	51	52	92	56	61	92	54	57

	Social Science			Science			TOTAL COMPOSITE		
	Nsize	NCE	Natl Percentile	Nsize	NCE	Natl Percentile	Nsize	NCE	Natl Percentile
MAPLETON JUNIOR HIGH									
MAPLETON SCHOOL	96	58	66	96	65	76	96	62	71
MT LOAFER SCHOOL	65	58	65	65	64	75	65	62	72
MT. NEBO JUNIOR HIGH									
NEBO DISTRICT	2159	54	57	2155	58	66	2141	55	59
ORCHARD HILLS ELEMENTARY	95	54	57	95	57	63	94	53	56
PARK SCHOOL	71	47	43	72	50	50	70	47	45
PARK VIEW SCHOOL	65	49	48	65	54	57	64	50	49
PAYSON JR HIGH									
REES SCHOOL	78	51	53	78	54	57	78	50	49
RIVERVIEW SCHOOL	93	52	54	93	58	65	93	54	57
SAGE CREEK SCHOOL	100	54	58	100	61	70	99	57	62
SALEM SCHOOL	68	53	56	68	56	62	68	53	56
SANTAQUIN SCHOOL	55	53	56	55	55	60	55	52	53

	Social Science			Science			TOTAL COMPOSITE		
	Nsize	NCE	Natl Percentile	Nsize	NCE	Natl Percentile	Nsize	NCE	Natl Percentile
SPANISH FORK JR HIGH									
SPANISH OAKS SCHOOL	125	57	63	124	60	68	124	57	62
SPRING LAKE SCHOOL	89	53	55	89	61	71	89	56	61
SPRINGVILLE JR HIGH									
TAYLOR SCHOOL	45	48	47	45	54	58	44	50	50
WESTSIDE SCHOOL	87	49	48	87	52	53	85	49	48
WILSON SCHOOL	81	49	47	81	54	57	81	49	47

Source: Utah State Office of Education

Key:
n<10 = there are too few tests for reporting criteria
blank = the school did not test students for that grade

Core Total = Reading, Language, and Mathematics
Total Composite = Reading, Language, Mathematics, Social Studies, and Science.

Nsize = Number of Tests
Natl Percentile = National Percentile Rank (NPR), should not be averaged
NCE = Normal Curve Equivalent of Average Scaled Score, can be averaged

For explanations:
http://www.schools.utah.gov/assessment/DOCUMENTS/Iowa_Technical_Questions_ITBS.pdf

5.2.40 Iowa Test Detail, Nebo School District, Grade 8 Core, 2009

	Grade 8											
	Reading			Language			Math			CORE TOTAL		
	Nsize	NCE	Natl Percentile	Nsize	NCE	Natl Percentile	Nsize	NCE	Natl Percentile	Nsize	NCE	Natl Percentile
ART CITY SCHOOL												
BARNETT SCHOOL												
BROCKBANK SCHOOL												
BROOKSIDE SCHOOL												
CANYON SCHOOL												
CHERRY CREEK ELEMENTARY												
DIAMOND FORK JUNIOR HIGH	315	56	62	321	51	51	319	52	53	313	53	55
EAST MEADOWS ELEMENTARY												
FOOTHILLS ELEMENTARY												
GOSHEN SCHOOL												
HOBBLE CREEK SCHOOL												
LARSEN SCHOOL												
MAPLETON JUNIOR HIGH	328	62	71	329	56	61	326	57	63	325	58	65
MAPLETON SCHOOL												
MT LOAFER SCHOOL												

	Reading			Language			Math			CORE TOTAL		
	Nsize	NCE	Natl Percentile	Nsize	NCE	Natl Percentile	Nsize	NCE	Natl Percentile	Nsize	NCE	Natl Percentile
MT. NEBO JUNIOR HIGH	242	52	54	238	48	47	233	46	43	230	49	48
NEBO DISTRICT	1786	57	62	1806	51	53	1775	52	55	1738	53	56
ORCHARD HILLS ELEMENTARY												
PARK SCHOOL												
PARK VIEW SCHOOL												
PAYSON JR HIGH	283	57	62	285	50	50	274	52	54	268	53	55
REES SCHOOL												
RIVERVIEW SCHOOL												
SAGE CREEK SCHOOL												
SALEM SCHOOL												
SANTAQUIN SCHOOL												
SPANISH FORK JR HIGH	345	55	59	360	50	50	350	53	56	329	52	54
SPANISH OAKS SCHOOL												
SPRING LAKE SCHOOL												
SPRINGVILLE JR HIGH	273	57	64	273	54	57	273	51	52	273	54	57
TAYLOR SCHOOL												
WESTSIDE SCHOOL												
WILSON SCHOOL												

Source: Utah State Office of Education

Key:
n<10 = there are too few tests for reporting criteria
blank = the school did not test students for that grade

Core Total = Reading, Language, and Mathematics
Total Composite = Reading, Language, Mathematics, Social Studies, and Science.

Nsize = Number of Tests
Natl Percentile = National Percentile Rank (NPR), should not be averaged
NCE = Normal Curve Equivalent of Average Scaled Score, can be averaged

For explanations: 138
http://www.schools.utah.gov/assessment/DOCUMENTS/Iowa_Technical_Questions_ITBS.pdf

5.2.41 Iowa Test Detail, Nebo School District, Grade 8 Expanded, 2009

	Grade 8								
	Social Science			Science			TOTAL COMPOSITE		
	Nsize	NCE	Natl Percentile	Nsize	NCE	Natl Percentile	Nsize	NCE	Natl Percentile
ART CITY SCHOOL									
BARNETT SCHOOL									
BROCKBANK SCHOOL									
BROOKSIDE SCHOOL									
CANYON SCHOOL									
CHERRY CREEK ELEMENTARY									
DIAMOND FORK JUNIOR HIGH	319	51	52	318	59	66	312	54	57
EAST MEADOWS ELEMENTARY									
FOOTHILLS ELEMENTARY									
GOSHEN SCHOOL									
HOBBLE CREEK SCHOOL									
LARSEN SCHOOL									
MAPLETON JUNIOR HIGH	327	54	58	326	63	73	322	59	66
MAPLETON SCHOOL									
MT LOAFER SCHOOL									
MT. NEBO JUNIOR HIGH	232	48	46	232	52	55	228	50	50
NEBO DISTRICT	1784	51	52	1776	59	66	1704	54	58

	Social Science			Science			TOTAL COMPOSITE		
	Nsize	NCE	Natl Percentile	Nsize	NCE	Natl Percentile	Nsize	NCE	Natl Percentile
ORCHARD HILLS ELEMENTARY									
PARK SCHOOL									
PARK VIEW SCHOOL									
PAYSON JR HIGH	281	51	52	272	60	68	252	54	58
REES SCHOOL									
RIVERVIEW SCHOOL									
SAGE CREEK SCHOOL									
SALEM SCHOOL									
SANTAQUIN SCHOOL									
SPANISH FORK JR HIGH	352	51	51	355	59	67	317	53	57
SPANISH OAKS SCHOOL									
SPRING LAKE SCHOOL									
SPRINGVILLE JR HIGH	273	51	52	273	59	66	273	54	58
TAYLOR SCHOOL									
WESTSIDE SCHOOL									
WILSON SCHOOL									

Source: Utah State Office of Education

Key:
n<10 = there are too few tests for reporting criteria
blank = the school did not test students for that grade

Core Total = Reading, Language, and Mathematics
Total Composite = Reading, Language, Mathematics, Social Studies, and Science.

Nsize = Number of Tests
Natl Percentile = National Percentile Rank (NPR), should not be averaged
NCE = Normal Curve Equivalent of Average Scaled Score, can be averaged

For explanations:
http://www.schools.utah.gov/assessment/DOCUMENTS/Iowa_Technical_Questions_ITBS.pdf

5.2.42 Iowa Test Detail, Provo School District, Grade 3 Core, 2009

Grade 3	Reading			Language			Math			CORE TOTAL		
	Nsize	NCE	Natl Percentile	Nsize	NCE	Natl Percentile	Nsize	NCE	Natl Percentile	Nsize	NCE	Natl Percentile
AMELIA EARHART SCHOOL	78	52	54	79	44	39	76	46	42	76	47	45
CANYON CREST SCHOOL	66	60	69	66	52	54	65	61	69	65	58	65
CENTENNIAL MIDDLE												
DIXON MIDDLE												
EDGEMONT SCHOOL	88	61	70	89	54	57	88	54	57	87	56	62
FARRER SCHOOL	53	43	36	55	40	31	54	39	30	53	41	33
FRANKLIN SCHOOL	74	42	35	76	37	27	72	41	34	71	40	31
LAKEVIEW ELEMENTARY	94	51	52	94	40	32	93	48	46	89	47	44
OAK SPRINGS SCHOOL	n<10	n<10	n<10	n<10	n<10	n<10	n<10	n<10	n<10	n<10	n<10	n<10
PROVO DISTRICT	1032	54	58	1040	46	43	1025	49	49	1010	50	50
PROVOST SCHOOL	52	56	61	52	55	59	52	51	51	52	54	57
ROCK CANYON SCHOOL	87	63	73	88	49	47	88	55	59	87	55	60
SPRING CREEK SCHOOL	84	47	45	84	43	36	80	45	40	80	45	41
SUNSET VIEW SCHOOL	81	47	44	81	38	28	82	42	34	77	42	35

	Reading			Language			Math			CORE TOTAL		
	Nsize	NCE	Natl Percentile	Nsize	NCE	Natl Percentile	Nsize	NCE	Natl Percentile	Nsize	NCE	Natl Percentile
TIMPANOGOS SCHOOL	70	42	36	69	39	30	69	40	32	69	40	32
WASATCH SCHOOL	90	69	81	92	56	62	92	60	68	90	63	73
WESTRIDGE SCHOOL	114	59	66	114	49	48	113	56	61	113	54	58

Source: Utah State Office of Education

Key:
n<10 = there are too few tests for reporting criteria
blank = the school did not test students for that grade

Core Total = Reading, Language, and Mathematics
Total Composite = Reading, Language, Mathematics, Social Studies, and Science.

Nsize = Number of Tests
Natl Percentile = National Percentile Rank (NPR), should not be averaged
NCE = Normal Curve Equivalent of Average Scaled Score, can be averaged

For explanations:
http://www.schools.utah.gov/assessment/DOCUMENTS/Iowa_Technical_Questions_ITBS.pdf

5.2.43 Iowa Test Detail, Provo School District, Grade 3 Expanded, 2009

	Grade 3								
	Social Science			Science			TOTAL COMPOSITE		
	Nsize	NCE	Natl Percentile	Nsize	NCE	Natl Percentile	Nsize	NCE	Natl Percentile
AMELIA EARHART SCHOOL	79	50	50	79	53	55	76	50	50
CANYON CREST SCHOOL	66	59	66	66	64	74	65	61	70
CENTENNIAL MIDDLE									
DIXON MIDDLE									
EDGEMONT SCHOOL	89	59	67	89	62	71	87	59	67
FARRER SCHOOL	52	44	39	53	48	46	51	44	39
FRANKLIN SCHOOL	76	44	39	76	44	39	71	42	35
LAKEVIEW ELEMENTARY	94	52	54	94	51	53	88	50	50
OAK SPRINGS SCHOOL	n<10	n<10	n<10	n<10	n<10	n<10	n<10	n<10	n<10
PROVO DISTRICT	1041	54	58	1041	56	62	1007	53	56
PROVOST SCHOOL	52	53	56	52	58	65	52	55	60
ROCK CANYON SCHOOL	88	60	69	88	67	79	87	61	70
SPRING CREEK SCHOOL	84	50	49	84	50	49	80	47	45
SUNSET VIEW SCHOOL	84	49	48	83	47	45	77	45	41
TIMPANOGOS SCHOOL	70	46	42	70	50	51	69	44	38
WASATCH SCHOOL	92	65	76	92	67	80	90	66	78
WESTRIDGE SCHOOL	114	57	62	114	61	71	113	57	63

Source: Utah State Office of Education

Key:
n<10 = there are too few tests for reporting criteria
blank = the school did not test students for that grade

Core Total = Reading, Language, and Mathematics
Total Composite = Reading, Language, Mathematics, Social Studies, and Science.

Nsize = Number of Tests
Natl Percentile = National Percentile Rank (NPR), should not be averaged
NCE = Normal Curve Equivalent of Average Scaled Score, can be averaged

For explanations:
http://www.schools.utah.gov/assessment/DOCUMENTS/Iowa_Technical_Questions_ITBS.pdf

5.2.44 Iowa Test Detail, Provo School District, Grade 5 Core, 2009

| | Grade 5 | | | | | | | | | | | |
| | Reading | | | Language | | | Math | | | CORE TOTAL | | |
	Nsize	NCE	Natl Percentile	Nsize	NCE	Natl Percentile	Nsize	NCE	Natl Percentile	Nsize	NCE	Natl Percentile
AMELIA EARHART SCHOOL	73	52	53	73	48	47	72	57	63	72	52	53
CANYON CREST SCHOOL	63	59	67	63	57	63	63	60	68	63	58	65
CENTENNIAL MIDDLE												
DIXON MIDDLE												
EDGEMONT SCHOOL	66	61	69	65	56	61	65	64	75	65	59	67
FARRER SCHOOL	50	41	33	50	38	29	47	42	35	47	39	30
FRANKLIN SCHOOL	81	43	38	81	44	39	79	47	45	79	44	38
LAKEVIEW ELEMENTARY	103	51	52	103	47	45	101	51	52	101	49	48
OAK SPRINGS SCHOOL	n<10	n<10	n<10	n<10	n<10	n<10	n<10	n<10	n<10	n<10	n<10	n<10
PROVO DISTRICT	1031	53	56	1031	51	53	1021	55	60	1018	53	55
PROVOST SCHOOL	55	57	63	55	54	57	55	55	59	55	55	59
ROCK CANYON SCHOOL	88	56	61	87	55	59	88	57	63	87	56	60
SPRING CREEK SCHOOL	69	51	51	70	50	50	70	49	49	69	50	50
SUNSET VIEW SCHOOL	75	45	40	75	48	45	75	48	46	75	46	43
TIMPANOGOS SCHOOL	70	41	33	70	38	28	69	43	36	69	39	31
WASATCH SCHOOL	90	66	77	90	61	69	90	64	75	90	63	74
WESTRIDGE SCHOOL	143	63	74	143	58	66	143	64	74	143	62	71

Source: Utah State Office of Education

Key:
n<10 = there are too few tests for reporting criteria
blank = the school did not test students for that grade

Core Total = Reading, Language, and Mathematics
Total Composite = Reading, Language, Mathematics, Social Studies, and Science.

Nsize = Number of Tests
Natl Percentile = National Percentile Rank (NPR), should not be averaged
NCE = Normal Curve Equivalent of Average Scaled Score, can be averaged

For explanations:
http://www.schools.utah.gov/assessment/DOCUMENTS/Iowa_Technical_Questions_ITBS.pdf

5.2.45 Iowa Test Detail, Provo School District, Grade 5 Expanded, 2009

	Grade 5								
	Social Science			Science			TOTAL COMPOSITE		
	Nsize	NCE	Natl Percentile	Nsize	NCE	Natl Percentile	Nsize	NCE	Natl Percentile
AMELIA EARHART SCHOOL	73	50	49	73	59	67	72	54	57
CANYON CREST SCHOOL	63	60	69	63	64	75	63	61	70
CENTENNIAL MIDDLE									
DIXON MIDDLE									
EDGEMONT SCHOOL	65	59	66	64	67	78	63	62	72
FARRER SCHOOL	50	42	35	50	48	46	47	41	34
FRANKLIN SCHOOL	78	41	34	78	50	49	77	45	41
LAKEVIEW ELEMENTARY	103	49	48	103	57	62	101	52	53
OAK SPRINGS SCHOOL	n<10	n<10	n<10	n<10	n<10	n<10	n<10	n<10	n<10
PROVO DISTRICT	1026	52	54	1025	59	66	1012	55	59
PROVOST SCHOOL	54	55	60	55	60	69	54	57	63
ROCK CANYON SCHOOL	88	53	55	88	58	64	87	56	62
SPRING CREEK SCHOOL	70	49	49	69	60	68	68	53	56
SUNSET VIEW SCHOOL	75	46	43	75	54	58	75	49	47
TIMPANOGOS SCHOOL	70	39	30	70	45	41	69	41	33
WASATCH SCHOOL	90	64	74	90	66	78	90	65	76
WESTRIDGE SCHOOL	143	58	65	143	65	77	143	62	72

Source: Utah State Office of Education

Key:
n<10 = there are too few tests for reporting criteria
blank = the school did not test students for that grade

Core Total = Reading, Language, and Mathematics
Total Composite = Reading, Language, Mathematics, Social Studies, and Science.

Nsize = Number of Tests
Natl Percentile = National Percentile Rank (NPR), should not be averaged
NCE = Normal Curve Equivalent of Average Scaled Score, can be averaged

For explanations:
http://www.schools.utah.gov/assessment/DOCUMENTS/Iowa_Technical_Questions_ITBS.pdf

5.2.46 Iowa Test Detail, Provo School District, Grade 8 Core, 2009

	Grade 8											
	Reading			Language			Math			CORE TOTAL		
	Nsize	NCE	Natl Percentile	Nsize	NCE	Natl Percentile	Nsize	NCE	Natl Percentile	Nsize	NCE	Natl Percentile
AMELIA EARHART SCHOOL												
CANYON CREST SCHOOL												
CENTENNIAL MIDDLE	497	60	68	497	55	59	497	55	59	496	56	62
DIXON MIDDLE	417	50	51	418	48	46	417	47	45	415	48	47
EDGEMONT SCHOOL												
FARRER SCHOOL												
FRANKLIN SCHOOL												
LAKEVIEW ELEMENTARY												
OAK SPRINGS SCHOOL	n<10	n<10	n<10	n<10	n<10	n<10	n<10	n<10	n<10	n<10	n<10	n<10
PROVO DISTRICT	921	55	60	922	52	53	921	51	52	918	52	55
PROVOST SCHOOL												
ROCK CANYON SCHOOL												
SPRING CREEK SCHOOL												
SUNSET VIEW SCHOOL												
TIMPANOGOS SCHOOL												
WASATCH SCHOOL												
WESTRIDGE SCHOOL												

Source: Utah State Office of Education

Key:
n<10 = there are too few tests for reporting criteria
blank = the school did not test students for that grade

Core Total = Reading, Language, and Mathematics
Total Composite = Reading, Language, Mathematics, Social Studies, and Science.

Nsize = Number of Tests
Natl Percentile = National Percentile Rank (NPR), should not be averaged
NCE = Normal Curve Equivalent of Average Scaled Score, can be averaged

For explanations:
http://www.schools.utah.gov/assessment/DOCUMENTS/Iowa_Technical_Questions_ITBS.pdf

5.2.47   Iowa Test Detail, Provo School District, Grade 8 Expanded, 2009

	Grade 8								
	Social Science			Science			TOTAL COMPOSITE		
	Nsize	NCE	Natl Percentile	Nsize	NCE	Natl Percentile	Nsize	NCE	Natl Percentile
AMELIA EARHART SCHOOL									
CANYON CREST SCHOOL									
CENTENNIAL MIDDLE	498	52	53	497	61	70	495	56	62
DIXON MIDDLE	416	49	47	415	54	57	413	50	49
EDGEMONT SCHOOL									
FARRER SCHOOL									
FRANKLIN SCHOOL									
LAKEVIEW ELEMENTARY									
OAK SPRINGS SCHOOL	n<10	n<10	n<10	n<10	n<10	n<10	n<10	n<10	n<10
PROVO DISTRICT	921	50	50	919	57	64	915	53	56
PROVOST SCHOOL									
ROCK CANYON SCHOOL									
SPRING CREEK SCHOOL									
SUNSET VIEW SCHOOL									
TIMPANOGOS SCHOOL									
WASATCH SCHOOL									
WESTRIDGE SCHOOL									

Source: Utah State Office of Education

Key:
n<10 = there are too few tests for reporting criteria
blank = the school did not test students for that grade

Core Total = Reading, Language, and Mathematics
Total Composite = Reading, Language, Mathematics, Social Studies, and Science.

Nsize = Number of Tests
Natl Percentile = National Percentile Rank (NPR), should not be averaged
NCE = Normal Curve Equivalent of Average Scaled Score, can be averaged

For explanations:
http://www.schools.utah.gov/assessment/DOCUMENTS/Iowa_Technical_Questions_ITBS.pdf

5.2.48 Incidents of Prohibited Behavior, 2008-2009, Elementary Schools, All Utah Districts

Elementary Schools

	Alcohol	Tobacco	Other Drugs	Aggravated Assault	Arson	Weapon: Handgun	Weapon: Rifle	Other Firearm	Other Weapon	Truancy	Total
Alpine	0	1	3	0	1	0	0	0	7	0	12
Beaver	0	0	0	0	0	0	0	0	0	0	0
Box Elder	0	3	0	15	0	0	0	0	3	3	24
Cache	0	0	0	0	0	0	0	0	0	3	3
Carbon	0	0	1	0	0	0	0	0	2	0	3
Daggett	0	0	0	0	0	0	0	0	0	0	0
Davis	2	2	1	0	3	0	0	0	44	2	54
Duchesne	0	0	0	4	0	0	0	0	3	0	7
Emery	0	0	0	0	0	0	0	0	0	0	0
Garfield	0	0	0	0	0	0	0	0	0	0	0
Grand	0	0	0	0	0	0	0	0	4	7	11
Granite	1	11	9	2	4	0	0	0	35	2792	2854
Iron	0	0	0	0	0	0	0	0	4	0	4
Jordan	0	1	1	0	4	0	0	0	15	0	21
Juab	0	0	0	0	0	0	0	0	0	2	2
Kane	0	0	0	0	0	0	0	0	0	0	0
Logan	0	1	1	1	0	0	0	1	5	32	41
Millard	0	0	0	0	0	0	0	0	4	0	4
Morgan	0	0	0	0	0	0	0	0	0	0	0
Murray	0	0	0	0	0	0	0	0	6	613	619
Nebo	0	2	0	0	0	0	0	0	9	1301	1312
North Sanpete	0	0	0	0	0	0	0	0	0	1	1
North Summit	0	0	0	0	0	0	0	0	0	0	0
Ogden	2	2	21	5	6	0	0	1	29	20	86
Park City	0	0	0	0	0	0	0	0	1	0	1
Piute	0	0	0	0	0	0	0	0	0	0	0

	Alcohol	Tobacco	Other Drugs	Aggravated Assault	Arson	Weapon: Handgun	Weapon: Rifle	Other Firearm	Other Weapon	Truancy	Total
Provo	0	1	0	0	0	0	0	0	7	173	181
Rich	0	0	0	0	0	0	0	0	0	0	0
Salt Lake	0	4	5	0	0	0	0	0	13	100	122
San Juan	0	0	0	0	0	0	0	0	3	3	6
Sevier	0	0	0	0	0	0	0	0	0	0	0
South Sanpete	0	0	0	0	0	0	0	0	0	0	0
South Summit	0	0	0	2	0	0	0	0	4	1	7
Tintic	0	0	0	0	0	0	0	0	0	0	0
Tooele	0	0	0	0	0	0	0	0	4	0	4
Uintah	0	1	1	0	0	0	0	0	8	213	223
Wasatch	0	0	0	0	0	0	0	0	1	0	1
Washington	0	0	0	0	0	0	0	0	5	0	5
Wayne	0	0	0	0	0	0	0	0	0	11	11
Weber	0	0	0	0	0	0	0	1	3	0	4
TOTAL	5	29	43	29	18	0	0	3	219	5277	5623

Source: Utah State Office of Education

5.2.49 Incidents of Prohibited Behavior, 2008-2009, Middle Schools, All Utah Districts

Middle Schools

	Alcohol	Tobacco	Other Drugs	Aggravated Assault	Arson	Weapon: Handgun	Weapon: Rifle	Other Firearm	Other Weapon	Truancy	Total
Alpine	3	12	29	2	0	0	0	0	16	32	94
Beaver	0	0	0	0	0	0	0	0	0	0	0
Box Elder	1	8	9	2	0	0	0	0	4	75	99
Cache	5	10	2	0	0	0	0	0	10	120	147
Carbon	2	4	8	0	0	0	0	0	0	13	27
Daggett											0
Davis	10	13	53	1	4	0	0	2	35	6	124
Duchesne	1	2	1	0	0	0	0	0	0	0	4
Emery	0	1	0	0	0	0	0	0	0	0	1
Garfield	0	0	0	0	0	0	0	0	0	1	1
Grand	0	0	5	0	0	0	0	0	2	69	76
Granite	19	37	92	3	6	0	0	1	31	2850	3039
Iron	7	9	0	0	2	0	0	0	1	41	60
Jordan	9	0	107	0	4	1	0	5	22	0	148
Juab	1	0	3	1	1	0	0	0	0	3	9
Kane	0	0	0	0	0	0	0	0	0	0	0
Logan	0	0	0	1	0	0	0	0	0	0	1
Millard	0	2	0	0	0	0	0	0	0	9	11
Morgan	0	0	0	0	0	0	0	0	2	0	2
Murray	1	0	0	0	0	0	0	0	2	88	91
Nebo	0	1	0	0	0	0	0	0	0	0	1
North Sanpete	0	3	0	1	0	0	0	0	0	0	4
North Summit	0	0	0	0	0	0	0	0	0	11	11
Ogden	0	15	23	35	0	0	0	0	19	433	525
Park City	0	0	0	1	0	0	0	0	0	0	1
Piute											0

	Alcohol	Tobacco	Other Drugs	Aggravated Assault	Arson	Weapon: Handgun	Weapon: Rifle	Other Firearm	Other Weapon	Truancy	Total
Provo	0	1	2	0	0	0	0	0	5	241	249
Rich	0	0	0	0	0	0	0	0	0	1	1
Salt Lake	3	3	20	0	0	0	0	0	17	70	113
San Juan	0	1	1	0	0	0	0	0	0	1	3
Sevier	0	1	0	0	0	0	0	0	1	0	2
South Sanpete	0	0	1	0	1	0	0	0	1	0	3
South Summit	0	0	0	0	0	0	0	0	0	0	0
Tintic											0
Tooele	0	0	4	0	0	0	0	0	4	30	38
Uintah	0	17	8	0	0	0	0	0	3	195	223
Wasatch	0	1	5	0	0	0	0	0	0	0	6
Washington	2	6	17	0	0	0	0	0	6	9	40
Wayne	0	1	0	0	0	0	0	0	0	0	1
Weber	9	5	20	3	1	0	0	0	18	23	79
TOTAL	73	153	410	50	19	1	0	8	199	4321	5234

Source: Utah State Office of Education

5.2.50 Incidents of Prohibited Behavior, 2008-2009, High Schools, All Utah Districts

High Schools

	Alcohol	Tobacco	Other Drugs	Aggravated Assault	Arson	Weapon: Handgun	Weapon: Rifle	Other Firearm	Other Weapon	Truancy	Total
Alpine	7	31	42	3	6	0	0	0	14	31	134
Beaver	7	6	1	0	0	0	0	0	0	21	35
Box Elder	5	21	7	0	0	0	0	0	0	281	314
Cache	21	20	8	0	0	0	0	0	0	261	310
Carbon	0	15	5	2	0	1	1	0	3	34	61
Daggett	0	2	0	0	0	0	0	0	0	0	2
Davis	13	33	53	1	4	0	1	0	11	3	119
Duchesne	0	8	2	0	0	0	0	0	0	215	225
Emery	1	8	4	0	0	0	0	0	1	86	100
Garfield	0	0	1	0	0	0	0	0	0	29	30
Grand	4	3	1	1	0	0	0	0	1	18	28
Granite	23	36	125	4	1	1	1	1	18	0	210
Iron	5	33	63	2	0	0	0	0	8	276	387
Jordan	24	0	134	0	3	0	0	0	13	0	174
Juab	1	4	1	0	0	0	0	0	1	0	7
Kane	0	1	0	0	0	0	0	0	0	0	1
Logan	0	4	1	0	0	0	0	0	0	10	15
Millard	3	4	0	0	0	0	0	1	1	876	885
Morgan	1	0	0	0	0	0	0	0	0	39	40
Murray	4	16	13	0	0	0	0	0	2	179	214
Nebo	0	0	0	0	0	0	0	0	1	26	27
North Sanpete	0	0	0	2	0	0	0	0	0	0	2
North Summit	1	4	0	0	0	0	0	0	0	4	9
Ogden	7	5	11	8	0	0	0	0	2	1288	1321
Park City	2	8	9	1	0	0	0	0	1	0	21
Piute	1	4	0	0	0	0	0	0	0	0	5

	Alcohol	Tobacco	Other Drugs	Aggravated Assault	Arson	Weapon: Handgun	Weapon: Rifle	Other Firearm	Other Weapon	Truancy	Total
Provo	1	1	11	0	0	2	0	0	6	637	658
Rich	0	0	0	0	0	0	0	0	0	0	0
Salt Lake	12	13	46	0	0	0	0	0	22	9	102
San Juan	2	8	21	0	0	0	0	0	1	13	45
Sevier	0	0	0	0	0	0	0	0	1	0	1
South Sanpete	1	3	0	0	1	0	0	0	0	8	13
South Summit	0	2	5	0	0	0	0	0	2	9	18
Tintic	0	8	0	0	0	0	0	0	0	0	8
Tooele	3	33	4	0	0	0	0	0	0	12	52
Uintah	3	57	26	2	0	0	0	3	6	954	1051
Wasatch	0	16	16	0	0	0	1	0	0	0	33
Washington	3	25	41	0	0	0	0	0	7	11	87
Wayne	0	2	0	0	0	0	0	0	1	0	3
Weber	13	10	15	0	0	0	0	0	2	86	126
TOTAL	168	444	666	26	15	4	4	5	125	5416	6873

Source: Utah State Office of Education

5.2.51 Incidents of Prohibited Behavior, 2008-2009, All Grade Levels, All Utah Districts

All Grade Levels

	Alcohol	Tobacco	Other Drugs	Aggravated Assault	Arson	Weapon: Handgun	Weapon: Rifle	Other Firearm	Other Weapon	Truancy	Total
Alpine	10	44	74	5	7	0	0	0	37	63	240
Beaver	7	6	1	0	0	0	0	0	0	21	35
Box Elder	6	32	16	17	0	0	0	0	7	359	437
Cache	26	30	10	0	0	0	0	0	10	384	460
Carbon	2	19	14	2	0	1	1	0	5	47	91
Daggett	0	2	0	0	0	0	0	0	0	0	2
Davis	25	48	107	2	11	0	1	2	90	11	297
Duchesne	1	10	3	4	0	0	0	0	3	215	236
Emery	1	9	4	0	0	0	0	0	1	86	101
Garfield	0	0	1	0	0	0	0	0	0	30	31
Grand	4	3	6	1	0	0	0	0	7	94	115
Granite	43	84	226	9	11	1	1	2	84	5642	6103
Iron	12	42	63	2	2	0	0	0	13	317	451
Jordan	33	1	242	0	11	1	0	5	50	0	343
Juab	2	4	4	1	1	0	0	0	1	5	18
Kane	0	1	0	0	0	0	0	0	0	0	1
Logan	0	5	2	2	0	0	0	1	5	42	57
Millard	3	6	0	0	0	0	0	1	5	885	900
Morgan	1	0	0	0	0	0	0	0	2	39	42
Murray	5	16	13	0	0	0	0	0	10	880	924
Nebo	0	3	0	0	0	0	0	0	10	1327	1340
North Sanpete	0	3	0	3	0	0	0	0	0	1	7
North Summit	1	4	0	0	0	0	0	0	0	15	20
Ogden	9	22	55	48	6	0	0	1	50	1741	1932
Park City	2	8	9	2	0	0	0	0	2	0	23
Piute	1	4	0	0	0	0	0	0	0	0	5

	Alcohol	Tobacco	Other Drugs	Aggravated Assault	Arson	Weapon: Handgun	Weapon: Rifle	Other Firearm	Other Weapon	Truancy	Total
Provo	1	3	13	0	0	2	0	0	18	1051	1088
Rich	0	0	0	0	0	0	0	0	0	1	1
Salt Lake	15	20	71	0	0	0	0	0	52	179	337
San Juan	2	9	22	0	0	0	0	0	4	17	54
Sevier	0	1	0	0	0	0	0	0	2	0	3
South Sanpete	1	3	1	0	2	0	0	0	1	8	16
South Summit	0	2	5	2	0	0	0	0	6	10	25
Tintic	0	8	0	0	0	0	0	0	0	0	8
Tooele	3	33	8	0	0	0	0	0	8	42	94
Uintah	3	75	35	2	0	0	0	3	17	1362	1497
Wasatch	0	17	21	0	0	0	1	0	1	0	40
Washington	5	31	58	0	0	0	0	0	18	20	132
Wayne	0	3	0	0	0	0	0	0	1	11	15
Weber	22	15	35	3	1	0	0	1	23	109	209
TOTAL	246	626	1119	105	52	5	4	16	543	15014	17730

Source: Utah State Office of Education

5.2.52 Home School Enrollment by District, 2003, 2004, All Utah Districts

	2003 Home Schooled Count	Share	Fall 2002 Public School Enrollment	Home Schooled per 1,000 Public School Students	2004 Home Schooled Count	Share	Fall 2003 Public School Enrollment	Home Schooled per 1,000 Public School Students
Alpine	1,148	16.3%	49,159	23.4	927	13.3%	51,118	18.1
Beaver	11	0.2%	1,469	7.5	22	0.3%	1,472	14.9
Box Elder	205	2.9%	10,660	19.2	177	2.5%	10,529	16.8
Cache	150	2.1%	13,081	11.5	147	2.1%	13,315	11.0
Carbon	0	0.0%	3,827	0.0	35	0.5%	3,622	9.7
Daggett	2	0.0%	130	15.4	2	0.0%	132	15.2
Davis*	852	12.1%	59,536	14.3	896	12.9%	60,025	14.9
Duchesne	44	0.6%	3,993	11.0	45	0.6%	3,900	11.5
Emery	62	0.9%	2,442	25.4	55	0.8%	2,434	22.6
Garfield	0	0.0%	1,040	0.0	3	0.0%	969	3.1
Grand	33	0.5%	1,455	22.7	34	0.5%	1,474	23.1
Granite	517	7.3%	69,600	7.4	571	8.2%	69,072	8.3
Iron	159	2.3%	7,240	22.0	215	3.1%	7,443	28.9
Jordan	1,030	14.6%	73,808	14.0	1,071	15.4%	74,761	14.3
Juab	72	1.0%	1,872	38.5	77	1.1%	1,939	39.7
Kane	7	0.1%	1,235	5.7	15	0.2%	1,200	12.5
Logan	94	1.3%	5,858	16.0	98	1.4%	5,872	16.7
Millard	44	0.6%	3,142	14.0	54	0.8%	3,083	17.5
Morgan	7	0.1%	1,984	3.5	14	0.2%	1,955	7.2
Murray	49	0.7%	6,336	7.7	44	0.6%	6,482	6.8
Nebo	437	6.2%	23,078	18.9	420	6.0%	23,900	17.6
North Sanpete	64	0.9%	2,443	26.2	78	1.1%	2,370	32.9
North Summit	6	0.1%	968	6.2	4	0.1%	969	4.1

	2003 Home Schooled Count	Share	Fall 2002 Public School Enrollment	Home Schooled per 1,000 Public School Students	2004 Home Schooled Count	Share	Fall 2003 Public School Enrollment	Home Schooled per 1,000 Public School Students
Ogden	198	2.8%	13,141	15.1	169	2.4%	12,963	13.0
Park City	72	1.0%	3,957	18.2	77	1.1%	4,059	19.0
Piute	0	0.0%	312	0.0	4	0.1%	307	13.0
Provo	222	3.2%	13,177	16.8	239	3.4%	13,103	18.2
Rich	4	0.1%	473	8.5	4	0.1%	454	8.8
Salt Lake*	172	2.4%	24,382	7.1	82	1.2%	23,966	3.4
San Juan	35	0.5%	2,978	11.8	26	0.4%	2,979	8.7
Sevier	54	0.8%	4,370	12.4	63	0.9%	4,316	14.6
South Sanpete	0	0.0%	2,792	0.0	0	0.0%	2,772	0.0
South Summit	20	0.3%	1,320	15.2	18	0.3%	1,312	13.7
Tintic	0	0.0%	275	0.0	0	0.0%	250	0.0
Tooele	253	3.6%	10,034	25.2	277	4.0%	10,508	26.4
Uintah	214	3.0%	5,682	37.7	204	2.9%	5,607	36.4
Wasatch	56	0.8%	3,916	14.3	56	0.8%	4,022	13.9
Washington	319	4.5%	19,617	16.3	342	4.9%	20,317	16.8
Wayne	6	0.1%	520	11.5	4	0.1%	518	7.7
Weber	419	6.0%	28,315	14.8	381	5.5%	28,196	13.5
TOTAL	7,037	2.5%	479,617	14.7	6,950	2.5%	483,685	14.4

Source: Utah State Office of Education

5.2.53 Home School Enrollment by District, 2005, 2006, All Utah Districts

	2005 Home Schooled Count	Share	Fall 2004 Public School Enrollment	Home Schooled per 1,000 Public School Students	2006 Home Schooled Count	Share	Fall 2005 Public School Enrollment	Home Schooled per 1,000 Public School Students
Alpine	938	12.4%	52,825	17.8	952	11.1%	54,773	17.4
Beaver	21	0.3%	1,508	13.9	2	0.0%	1,536	1.3
Box Elder	181	2.4%	10,561	17.1	201	2.4%	10,625	18.9
Cache	149	2.0%	13,388	11.1	120	1.4%	13,428	8.9
Carbon	34	0.4%	3,488	9.7	41	0.5%	3,389	12.1
Daggett	2	0.0%	136	14.7	2	0.0%	156	12.8
Davis*	960	12.7%	60,606	15.8	1,690	19.8%	62,456	27.1
Duchesne	49	0.6%	3,894	12.6	86	1.0%	3,993	21.5
Emery	30	0.4%	2,366	12.7	35	0.4%	2,335	15.0
Garfield	6	0.1%	947	6.3	8	0.1%	940	8.5
Grand	45	0.6%	1,418	31.7	40	0.5%	1,470	27.2
Granite	697	9.2%	68,568	10.2	699	8.2%	69,048	10.1
Iron	231	3.1%	7,788	29.7	199	2.3%	8,230	24.2
Jordan	1,248	16.5%	75,716	16.5	1,340	15.7%	77,369	17.3
Juab	70	0.9%	1,963	35.7	69	0.8%	1,992	34.6
Kane	20	0.3%	1,196	16.7	21	0.2%	1,194	17.6
Logan	96	1.3%	5,821	16.5	73	0.9%	5,737	12.7
Millard	50	0.7%	2,957	16.9	70	0.8%	2,952	23.7
Morgan	11	0.1%	1,967	5.6	15	0.2%	2,029	7.4
Murray	43	0.6%	6,492	6.6	36	0.4%	6,469	5.6
Nebo	526	6.9%	24,887	21.1	412	4.8%	24,742	16.7
North Sanpete	72	1.0%	2,313	31.1	75	0.9%	2,321	32.3
North Summit	4	0.1%	986	4.1	12	0.1%	982	12.2

	2005 Home Schooled Count	Share	Fall 2004 Public School Enrollment	Home Schooled per 1,000 Public School Students	2006 Home Schooled Count	Share	Fall 2005 Public School Enrollment	Home Schooled per 1,000 Public School Students
Ogden	181	2.4%	12,684	14.3	161	1.9%	12,542	12.8
Park City	70	0.9%	4,212	16.6	62	0.7%	4,367	14.2
Piute	0	0.0%	345	0.0	5	0.1%	302	16.6
Provo	252	3.3%	13,359	18.9	288	3.4%	13,273	21.7
Rich	0	0.0%	429	0.0	2	0.0%	416	4.8
Salt Lake*	135	1.8%	23,595	5.7	208	2.4%	23,728	8.8
San Juan	27	0.4%	2,957	9.1	28	0.3%	2,908	9.6
Sevier	51	0.7%	4,305	11.8	56	0.7%	4,288	13.1
South Sanpete	0	0.0%	2,739	0.0	27	0.3%	2,764	9.8
South Summit	33	0.4%	1,322	25.0	29	0.3%	1,344	21.6
Tintic	0	0.0%	262	0.0	0	0.0%	274	0.0
Tooele	296	3.9%	11,039	26.8	257	3.0%	11,793	21.8
Uintah	227	3.0%	5,642	40.2	217	2.5%	5,539	39.2
Wasatch	58	0.8%	4,136	14.0	58	0.7%	4,303	13.5
Washington	350	4.6%	21,584	16.2	496	5.8%	23,189	21.4
Wayne	5	0.1%	517	9.7	15	0.2%	514	29.2
Weber	405	5.3%	28,527	14.2	433	5.1%	28,774	15.0
TOTAL	7,573	2.5%	489,445	15.5	8,540	2.5%	498,484	17.1

Source: Utah State Office of Education

5.2.54   Home School Enrollment by District, 2007, 2008, All Utah Districts

	2007 Home Schooled Count	Share	Fall 2006 Public School Enrollment	Home Schooled per 1,000 Public School Students	2008 Home Schooled Count	Share	Fall 2007 Public School Enrollment	Home Schooled per 1,000 Public School Students
Alpine	1,365	15.5%	56,051	24.4	977	11.0%	58,665	16.7
Beaver	5	0.1%	1,564	3.2	4	0.0%	1,562	2.6
Box Elder	134	1.5%	10,641	12.6	183	2.1%	10,931	16.7
Cache	107	1.2%	13,560	7.9	135	1.5%	14,194	9.5
Carbon	42	0.5%	3,475	12.1	48	0.5%	3,562	13.5
Daggett	2	0.0%	150	13.3	5	0.1%	134	37.3
Davis*	1,474	16.7%	62,832	23.5	1,844	20.7%	64,551	28.6
Duchesne	85	1.0%	3,982	21.3	70	0.8%	4,224	16.6
Emery	30	0.3%	2,320	12.9	35	0.4%	2,262	15.5
Garfield	5	0.1%	938	5.3	5	0.1%	933	5.4
Grand	39	0.4%	1,500	26.0	35	0.4%	1,486	23.6
Granite	622	7.1%	68,483	9.1	620	7.0%	67,948	9.1
Iron	266	3.0%	8,486	31.3	326	3.7%	8,643	37.7
Jordan	1,216	13.8%	78,708	15.4	1,314	14.8%	80,187	16.4
Juab	64	0.7%	2,071	30.9	49	0.6%	2,147	22.8
Kane	33	0.4%	1,188	27.8	21	0.2%	1,178	17.8
Logan	89	1.0%	5,641	15.8	105	1.2%	5,755	18.2
Millard	70	0.8%	2,897	24.2	54	0.6%	2,852	18.9
Morgan	23	0.3%	2,083	11.0	28	0.3%	2,183	12.8
Murray	55	0.6%	6,352	8.7	61	0.7%	6,426	9.5
Nebo	465	5.3%	25,615	18.2	478	5.4%	26,588	18.0
North Sanpete	67	0.8%	2,321	20.9	65	0.7%	2,340	27.8
North Summit	10	0.1%	981	10.2	26	0.3%	1,000	26.0

	2007 Home Schooled Count	Share	Fall 2006 Public School Enrollment	Home Schooled per 1,000 Public School Students	2008 Home Schooled Count	Share	Fall 2007 Public School Enrollment	Home Schooled per 1,000 Public School Students
Ogden	158	1.8%	12,358	12.8	191	2.1%	12,603	15.2
Park City	30	0.3%	4,336	6.9	25	0.3%	4,443	5.6
Piute	2	0.0%	298	6.7	5	0.1%	300	16.7
Provo	359	4.1%	13,272	27.0	309	3.5%	13,083	23.6
Rich	2	0.0%	436	4.6	1	0.0%	431	2.3
Salt Lake*	179	2.0%	23,894	7.5	194	2.2%	23,536	8.2
San Juan	48	0.5%	2,871	16.7	45	0.5%	2,844	15.8
Sevier	61	0.7%	4,374	13.9	75	0.8%	4,475	16.8
South Sanpete	44	0.5%	2,855	15.4	44	0.5%	2,911	15.1
South Summit	23	0.3%	1,362	16.9	32	0.4%	1,374	23.3
Tintic	0	0.0%	260	0.0	0	0.0%	238	0.0
Tooele	323	3.7%	12,507	25.8	344	3.9%	12,988	26.5
Uintah	232	2.6%	5,772	40.2	203	2.3%	5,952	34.1
Wasatch	61	0.7%	4,398	13.9	68	0.8%	4,588	14.8
Washington	466	5.3%	24,297	19.2	353	4.0%	25,295	14.0
Wayne	12	0.1%	531	22.6	8	0.1%	548	14.6
Weber	540	6.1%	29,132	18.5	510	5.7%	30,097	16.9
TOTAL	8,808	2.5%	504,792	17.4	8,895	2.5%	515,457	17.3

Source: Utah State Office of Education

5.2.55 Home School Enrollment by District, 2009, All Utah Districts

	2009 Home Schooled Count	Share	Fall 2008 Public School Enrollment	Home Schooled per 1,000 Public School Students
Alpine	1,083	11.8%	61,223	17.7
Beaver	14	0.2%	1,577	8.9
Box Elder	176	1.9%	11,132	15.8
Cache	225	2.5%	14,579	15.4
Carbon	65	0.7%	3,502	18.6
Daggett	1	0.0%	142	7.0
Davis*	1,622	17.7%	65,014	24.9
Duchesne	115	1.3%	4,355	26.4
Emery	49	0.5%	2,256	21.7
Garfield	9	0.1%	911	9.9
Grand	26	0.3%	1,498	17.4
Granite	571	6.2%	68,403	8.3
Iron	266	2.9%	8,344	31.9
Jordan	1,226	13.4%	81,017	15.1
Juab	43	0.5%	2,203	19.5
Kane	20	0.2%	1,202	16.6
Logan	116	1.3%	5,960	19.5
Millard	54	0.6%	2,829	19.1
Morgan	43	0.5%	2,276	18.9
Murray	51	0.6%	6,458	7.9
Nebo	395	4.3%	27,592	14.3
North Sanpete	77	0.8%	2,329	33.1
North Summit	7	0.1%	988	7.1

	2009 Home Schooled Count	Share	Fall 2008 Public School Enrollment	Home Schooled per 1,000 Public School Students
Ogden	180	2.0%	12,884	14.0
Park City	18	0.2%	4,477	4.0
Piute	8	0.1%	319	25.1
Provo	309	3.4%	13,288	23.3
Rich	9	0.1%	450	20.0
Salt Lake*	232	2.5%	23,678	9.8
San Juan	45	0.5%	2,889	15.6
Sevier	73	0.8%	4,511	16.2
South Sanpete	52	0.6%	2,955	17.6
South Summit	19	0.2%	1,427	13.3
Tintic	1	0.0%	232	4.3
Tooele	286	3.1%	13,406	21.3
Uintah	192	2.1%	6,408	30.0
Wasatch	63	0.7%	4,745	13.3
Washington	1,018	11.1%	25,775	39.5
Wayne	7	0.1%	531	13.2
Weber	411	4.5%	29,879	13.8
TOTAL	9,177	2.5%	523,644	17.5

Source: Utah State Office of Education

166

5.2.56 College Enrollment, Males, Age 15 and Older, Comparison Counties

	Utah County	Davis County	Salt Lake County
Total Population 15 Years and Older	381,544	214,002	777,394
Total Male Population 15 Years and Older	186,827	106,668	391,575
Enrolled in public college or graduate school	21,228	10,269	35,719
15- to 17-year-olds enrolled in public college or graduate school	0	0	244
18- to 24-year-olds enrolled in public college or graduate school	13,305	4,623	15,466
25- to 34-year-olds enrolled in public college or graduate school	6,098	4,165	16,016
35 years and older enrolled in public college or graduate school	1,825	1,481	3,993
Enrolled in private college or graduate school	21,399	2,808	7,265
15- to 17-year-olds enrolled in private college or graduate school	42	0	0
18- to 24-year-olds enrolled in private college or graduate school	16,588	1,449	2,634
25- to 34-year-olds enrolled in private college or graduate school	3,399	718	3,366
35 years and older enrolled in private college or graduate school	1,370	641	1,265
15 years and older, not enrolled in college or graduate school	144,200	93,591	348,591
15- to 17-year-olds not enrolled in college or graduate school	13,182	7,308	22,106
18- to 24-year-olds not enrolled in college or graduate school	23,342	9,206	32,636
25- to 34-year-olds not enrolled in college or graduate school	24,849	20,409	80,195
35 years and older not enrolled in college or graduate school	82,827	56,668	213,654

Source: American Community Survey 2009, U.S. Census Bureau

5.2.57 College Enrollment, Females, Age 15 and Older, Comparison Counties

	Utah County	Davis County	Salt Lake County
Total Population 15 Years and Older	381,544	214,002	777,394
Total Female Population 15 Years and Older	194,717	107,334	385,819
Enrolled in public college or graduate school	17,713	8,068	30,215
15- to 17-year-olds enrolled in public college or graduate school	0	0	64
18- to 24-year-olds enrolled in public college or graduate school	12,216	3,367	15,510
25- to 34-year-olds enrolled in public college or graduate school	2,763	2,403	8,214
35 years and older enrolled in public college or graduate school	2,734	2,298	6,427
Enrolled in private college or graduate school	24,585	2,011	8,880
15- to 17-year-olds enrolled in private college or graduate school	184	0	0
18- to 24-year-olds enrolled in private college or graduate school	20,310	1,035	4,526
25- to 34-year-olds enrolled in private college or graduate school	2,459	603	2,387
35 years and older enrolled in private college or graduate school	1,632	373	1,967
15 years and older, not enrolled in college or graduate school	152,419	97,255	346,724
15- to 17-year-olds not enrolled in college or graduate school	12,284	7,362	21,142
18- to 24-year-olds not enrolled in college or graduate school	22,923	8,791	27,154
25- to 34-year-olds not enrolled in college or graduate school	32,010	20,861	83,294
35 years and older not enrolled in college or graduate school	85,202	60,241	215,134

Source: American Community Survey 2009, U.S. Census Bureau

5.2.58 Current College Enrollment as Percent by Age and Gender, Utah County Adults

	Male 18-24	Female 18-24	Male 25-34	Female 25-34	Male 35+	Female 35+
Public College	25.0%	22.0%	17.8%	7.4%	2.1%	3.1%
Private College	31.2%	36.6%	9.9%	6.6%	1.6%	1.8%
Not Enrolled	43.8%	41.3%	72.3%	86.0%	96.3%	95.1%
Total	100.0%	100.0%	100.0%	100.0%	100.0%	100.0%

Source: American Community Survey 2009, U.S. Census Bureau

5.2.59 Educational Attainment, Age 15 and Older, Comparison Counties

	Male						
	< 9th Grade	9th to 12th Grade	HS Grad or GED	Some College	Associate's	Bachelor's	Graduate or Professional
Utah County	1.5%	5.0%	16.2%	28.3%	9.7%	23.3%	16.1%
Davis County	0.9%	3.2%	19.0%	27.9%	9.5%	24.0%	15.6%
Salt Lake County	4.3%	8.3%	24.1%	24.2%	8.3%	19.7%	11.1%

	Female						
	< 9th Grade	9th to 12th Grade	HS Grad or GED	Some College	Associate's	Bachelor's	Graduate or Professional
Utah County	1.8%	5.3%	18.8%	33.9%	11.9%	21.6%	6.7%
Davis County	1.5%	3.7%	26.0%	29.4%	10.7%	22.3%	6.4%
Salt Lake County	3.9%	6.4%	24.9%	27.3%	9.0%	20.0%	8.5%

5.2.60   Public School Students in Poverty, 2009-2010, All Utah Districts

	Total students, ages 5 to 17	Students in Poverty	Percent in Poverty
Alpine School District	73,558	6,718	9.1%
Beaver School District	1,463	189	12.9%
Box Elder School District	11,754	1,340	11.4%
Cache School District	16,349	1,543	9.4%
Canyons School District	46,776	4,189	9.0%
Carbon School District	3,792	649	17.1%
Daggett School District	134	7	5.2%
Davis School District	70,431	5,286	7.5%
Duchesne School District	4,278	515	12.0%
Emery School District	2,389	323	13.5%
Garfield School District	894	148	16.6%
Grand School District	1,590	356	22.4%
Granite School District	80,672	10,739	13.3%
Iron School District	9,032	1,843	20.4%
Jordan School District	40,663	3,158	7.8%
Juab School District	2,342	312	13.3%
Kane School District	1,144	191	16.7%
Logan School District	7,231	1,472	20.4%
Millard School District	2,859	499	17.5%
Morgan School District	2,211	116	5.2%
Murray School District	7,154	605	8.5%
Nebo School District	32,838	2,966	9.0%
North Sanpete School District	2,701	463	17.1%
North Summit School District	1,134	155	13.7%
Ogden School District	15,881	3,740	23.6%
Park City School District	4,653	328	7.0%
Piute School District	297	81	27.3%

	Total students, ages 5 to 17	Students in Poverty	Percent in Poverty
Provo School District	21,818	3,387	15.5%
Rich School District	484	62	12.8%
Salt Lake City School District	30,259	6,254	20.7%
San Juan School District	3,703	1,131	30.5%
Sevier School District	4,729	690	14.6%
South Sanpete School District	2,924	493	16.9%
South Summit School District	1,368	111	8.1%
Tintic School District	326	67	20.6%
Tooele School District	14,538	1,242	8.5%
Uintah School District	7,024	800	11.4%
Wasatch School District	4,957	502	10.1%
Washington School District	27,138	4,809	17.7%
Wayne School District	569	122	21.4%
Weber School District	31,044	2,642	8.5%

Source: Utah State Office of Education

5.3 Income Data

5.3.1 Personal, Family, and Household Income

5.3.1.1 Median Household Income by Age, Comparison Counties

	Utah County	Davis County	Salt Lake County
All Households	$57,732	$66,098	$57,006
25 or Younger	$29,136	$38,796	$32,837
Age 25 to 44	$60,728	$65,069	$57,765
Age 45 to 64	$74,438	$88,455	$71,128
Age 65 or Older	$46,226	$47,216	$39,163

Source: U.S. Census Bureau

5.3.1.2 Household Income by Age of Householder

	Householders Under Age 25	Householders Age 25 to 44	Householders Age 45 to 64	Householders Age 65 and Older
<$10,000	10.8%	4.5%	4.3%	5.0%
$10,000 to $14,999	10.5%	3.4%	2.4%	6.7%
$15,000 to $19,999	11.0%	2.8%	2.2%	8.3%
$20,000 to $24,999	9.8%	2.5%	3.0%	3.8%
$25,000 to $$29,999	10.6%	3.3%	3.1%	7.5%
$30,000 to $34,999	6.0%	5.2%	3.8%	5.6%
$35,000 to $39,999	9.8%	4.9%	3.5%	5.9%
$40,000 to $44,999	8.3%	5.6%	3.4%	5.7%
$45,000 to $49,999	4.2%	5.6%	4.5%	5.9%
$50,000 to $59,999	6.9%	11.4%	7.8%	6.2%
$60,000 to $74,999	5.5%	15.1%	12.7%	12.0%
$75,000 to $99,999	5.2%	16.4%	16.0%	12.2%
$100,000 to $124,999	0.5%	9.5%	11.5%	5.3%
$125,000 to $149,999	0.9%	3.4%	7.9%	2.2%
$150,000 to $199,999	0.0%	3.4%	8.1%	6.1%
$200,000 or more	0.0%	3.0%	5.8%	1.7%

Source: U.S. Census Bureau

173

5.3.1.3 Median Household Income by Race and Ethnicity, Comparison Counties

	Utah County	Davis County	Salt Lake County
Median Household Income	$57,732	$66,098	$57,006
White	$59,161	$67,281	$58,725
White, Not Hispanic	$60,578	$68,208	$60,944
Hispanic or Latino	$38,647	$49,690	$39,916
Black	-	-	$27,412
American Indian or Alaska Native	-	$41,814	$42,459
Asian	$41,875	$64,269	$46,579
Native Hawaiian or Other Pacific Islander	$31,636	-	$43,461
Some other race	$42,866	$53,563	$36,832
Two or more races	$60,486	$49,434	$51,361

Source: U.S. Census Bureau

5.3.1.4 Historical Median Household Income, Comparison Counties and State

	Utah County	Davis County	Salt Lake County	State
Median household income in 1979	$16,197	$20,862	$18,418	$17,671
Median household income in 1989	$27,432	$35,108	$30,149	$29,470
Median household income in 1999	$45,833	$53,726	$48,373	$45,726

Source: U.S. Census Bureau

5.3.1.5 Historical Household Income, Comparison Counties and State

	Utah County	Davis County	Salt Lake County	State
Households with income less than $10,000 in 1979	16,299	6,122	47,604	110,934
Households with income less than $10,000 in 1989	9,253	3,867	28,852	67,805
Households with income less than $10,000 in 1999	5,132	2,441	16,589	41,959
Households with income of $10,000 to $14,999 in 1979	10,568	5,972	31,437	73,483
Households with income of $10,000 to $14,999 in 1989	7,675	3,465	21,184	49,726
Households with income of $10,000 to $14,999 in 1999	4,801	2,119	12,804	33,952
Households with income of $15,000 to $19,999 in 1979	8,954	6,608	31,345	71,475
Households with income of $15,000 to $19,999 in 1989	7,309	4,068	22,599	51,467
Households with income of $15,000 to $19,999 in 1999	5,702	2,836	14,872	39,004
Households with income of $20,000 to $24,999 in 1979	7,590	6,749	29,196	64,369
Households with income of $20,000 to $24,999 in 1989	7,093	4,660	24,114	53,197
Households with income of $20,000 to $24,999 in 1999	6,585	3,401	17,390	44,117
Households with income of $25,000 to $29,999 in 1979	5,435	5,020	20,733	44,723
Households with income of $25,000 to $29,999 in 1989	6,798	5,232	22,700	51,260
Households with income of $25,000 to $29,999 in 1999	6,337	3,646	17,728	44,920
Households with income of $30,000 to $34,999 in 1979	3,603	3,625	14,639	30,792
Households with income of $30,000 to $34,999 in 1989	6,258	5,430	21,562	49,395

Households with income of $30,000 to $34,999 in 1999	6,906	4,486	19,142	48,199
Households with income of $35,000 to $39,999 in 1979	2,147	2,102	8,809	18,537
Households with income of $35,000 to $39,999 in 1989	5,727	4,804	18,401	42,391
Households with income of $35,000 to $39,999 in 1999	6,972	4,607	18,232	46,478
Households with income of $40,000 to $49,999 in 1979	2,105	2,211	9,227	18,860
Households with income of $40,000 to $49,999 in 1989	7,936	7,646	29,557	65,225
Households with income of $40,000 to $49,999 in 1999	12,357	8,615	35,992	86,943
Households with income of $40,000 to $44,999 in 1989	4,391	4,312	16,564	37,145
Households with income of $40,000 to $44,999 in 1999	6,615	4,452	18,868	45,900
Households with income of $45,000 to $49,999 in 1989	3,545	3,334	12,993	28,080
Households with income of $45,000 to $49,999 in 1999	5,742	4,163	17,124	41,043
Households with income of $50,000 to $74,999 in 1979	1,333	1,232	6,482	11,806
Households with income of $50,000 to $74,999 in 1989	8,242	10,540	33,998	74,290
Households with income of $50,000 to $74,999 in 1999	22,899	18,440	67,731	158,405
Households with income of $50,000 to $59,999 in 1989	4,525	5,535	19,056	41,968
Households with income of $50,000 to $59,999 in 1999	11,046	8,278	31,486	73,739
Households with income of $60,000 to $74,999 in 1989	3,717	5,005	14,942	32,322
Households with income of $60,000 to $74,999 in 1999	11,853	10,162	36,245	84,666

Households with income of $75,000 or more in 1979	386	332	2,737	4,545
Households with income of $75,000 or more in 1989	3,720	3,931	17,400	32,440
Households with income of $75,000 or more in 1999	22,473	20,524	74,810	157,956
Households with income of $75,000 to $99,999 in 1989	2,203	2,346	9,689	18,939
Households with income of $75,000 to $99,999 in 1999	11,351	10,489	36,370	79,659
Households with income of $100,000 to $124,999 in 1989	646	807	3,409	6,154
Households with income of $100,000 to $124,999 in 1999	5,420	4,817	17,718	36,557
Households with income of $125,000 to $149,999 in 1989	274	322	1,473	2,571
Households with income of $125,000 to $149,999 in 1999	2,209	2,063	7,982	16,084
Households with income of $150,000 or more in 1989	597	456	2,829	4,776
Households with income of $150,000 or more in 1999	3,493	3,155	12,740	25,656
Households with income of $150,000 to $199,999 in 1999	1,941	1,706	6,233	12,924
Households with income of $200,000 or more in 1999	1,552	1,449	6,507	12,732

Source: U.S. Census Bureau

5.3.1.6 Historical Median Family Income, Comparison Counties and State

	Utah County	Davis County	Salt Lake County	State
Median family income 1969	$8,359	$10,869	$9,770	$9,320
Median family income 1979	$17,768	$21,948	$21,064	$20,024
Median family income 1989	$30,536	$38,050	$34,699	$33,246
Median family income 1999	$50,196	$58,329	$54,470	$51,022

Source: U.S. Census Bureau

5.3.1.7 Historical Family Income, Comparison Counties and State

	Utah County	Davis County	Salt Lake County	State
Families with income of less than $10,000 in 1979	10,748	4,128	23,020	60,783
Families with income of less than $10,000 in 1989	5,327	2,106	11,837	31,218
Families with income of less than $10,000 in 1999	3,024	1,225	6,847	19,106
Families with income of $10,000 to $14,999 in 1979	8,404	4,898	22,007	55,884
Families with income of $10,000 to $14,999 in 1989	5,241	2,042	11,903	30,156
Families with income of $10,000 to $14,999 in 1999	2,807	1,194	5,753	17,333
Families with income of $15,000 to $19,999 in 1979	7,467	5,808	25,255	60,104
Families with income of $15,000 to $19,999 in 1989	5,592	3,054	14,204	35,732
Families with income of $15,000 to $19,999 in 1999	3,988	1,713	7,860	23,646
Families with income of $20,000 to $24,999 in 1979	6,710	6,340	25,383	57,690
Families with income of $20,000 to $24,999 in 1989	5,753	3,812	16,817	40,004
Families with income of $20,000 to $24,999 in 1999	4,637	2,321	10,454	28,717
Families with income of $25,000 to $29,999 in 1979	5,020	4,818	18,767	41,192
Families with income of $25,000 to $29,999 in 1989	5,790	4,343	17,045	41,004
Families with income of $25,000 to $29,999 in 1999	4,711	2,641	11,275	31,324
Families with income of $30,000 to $34,999 in 1979	3,414	3,486	13,182	28,626
Families with income of $30,000 to $34,999 in 1989	5,458	4,917	17,157	41,508

Families with income of $30,000 to $34,999 in 1999	5,550	3,478	12,607	35,457
Families with income of $35,000 to $39,999 in 1979	1,926	2,006	8,048	17,118
Families with income of $35,000 to $39,999 in 1989	5,151	4,287	15,304	36,810
Families with income of $35,000 to $39,999 in 1999	5,587	3,700	13,245	35,798
Families with income of $40,000 to $49,999 in 1979	1,947	2,132	8,477	17,569
Families with income of $40,000 to $49,999 in 1989	7,255	7,157	25,511	58,384
Families with income of $40,000 to $49,999 in 1999	10,281	7,200	27,317	70,438
Families with income of $40,000 to $44,999 in 1989	3,973	4,016	14,123	32,979
Families with income of $40,000 to $44,999 in 1999	5,518	3,693	14,230	36,732
Families with income of $45,000 to $49,999 in 1989	3,282	3,141	11,388	25,405
Families with income of $45,000 to $49,999 in 1999	4,763	3,507	13,087	33,706
Families with income of $50,000 to $74,999 in 1979	1,270	1,196	6,027	10,952
Families with income of $50,000 to $74,999 in 1989	7,739	10,120	30,566	68,634
Families with income of $50,000 to $74,999 in 1999	20,406	16,650	55,860	136,848
Families with income of $50,000 to $59,999 in 1989	4,231	5,300	16,923	38,511
Families with income of $50,000 to $59,999 in 1999	9,690	7,364	25,584	62,986
Families with income of $60,000 to $74,999 in 1989	3,508	4,820	13,643	30,123
Families with income of $60,000 to $74,999 in 1999	10,716	9,286	30,276	73,862

Families with income of $75,000 or more in 1979	362	326	2,536	4,253
Families with income of $75,000 or more in 1989	3,444	3,783	15,750	29,807
Families with income of $75,000 or more in 1999	20,684	19,401	64,646	141,061
Families with income of $75,000 to $99,999 in 1989	2,016	2,276	8,683	17,359
Families with income of $75,000 to $99,999 in 1999	10,520	9,942	31,258	71,213
Families with income of $100,000 to $124,999 in 1989	634	758	3,143	5,718
Families with income of $100,000 to $124,999 in 1999	4,908	4,488	15,223	32,443
Families with income of $125,000 to $149,999 in 1989	240	313	1,342	2,341
Families with income of $125,000 to $149,999 in 1999	2,010	1,962	6,988	14,420
Families with income of $150,000 or more in 1989	554	436	2,582	4,389
Families with income of $150,000 to $199,999 in 1999	1,797	1,610	5,474	11,553
Families with income of $200,000 or more in 1999	1,449	1,399	5,703	11,432

Source: U.S. Census Bureau

5.3.1.8 Historical Per Capita Income, Comparison Counties and State

	Utah County	Davis County	Salt Lake County	State
Per capita income in 1969	$2,218	$2,689	$2,963	$2,697
Per capita income in 1979	$5,199	$6,275	$7,013	$6,305
Per capita income in 1989	$9,051	$11,611	$12,222	$11,029
Per capita income in 1999	$15,557	$19,506	$20,190	$18,185

Source: U.S. Census Bureau

5.3.1.9 Historical Aggregate Income, Comparison Counties and State, in Thousands $

	Utah County	Davis County	Salt Lake County	State
Aggregate income in 1969	$305,587	$266,286	$1,358,853	$2,856,859
Aggregate income in 1979	$1,133,933	$919,539	$4,341,510	$9,211,838
Aggregate income in 1989	$2,385,859	$2,182,175	$8,872,910	$19,000,982
Aggregate income in 1999	$5,733,184	$4,661,757	$18,138,308	$40,610,136

Source: U.S. Census Bureau

5.3.1.10 Median Household Income, Comparison Counties and State, 1995-2008

	Utah County	Davis County	Salt Lake County	State
1995	$39,285	$45,861	$40,420	$35,160
1997	$41,509	$48,690	$44,118	$38,884
1998	$42,419	$50,168	$45,484	$41,380
1999	$44,178	$52,577	$46,183	$43,778
2000	$47,499	$55,115	$48,688	$45,934
2001	$46,198	$54,973	$48,348	$45,914
2002	$45,773	$55,623	$47,892	$46,165
2003	$46,399	$56,760	$49,003	$46,709
2004	$47,544	$58,808	$50,420	$47,224
2005	$47,718	$57,492	$48,398	$48,155
2006	$50,661	$61,323	$52,951	$51,373
2007	$57,133	$65,767	$56,378	$55,220
2008	$59,701	$67,004	$59,168	$56,820

Source: U.S. Census Bureau

5.3.1.11　Personal Income, in Millions $

	Utah County
2001	$55,594
2002	$58,172
2003	$59,412
2004	$63,565
2005	$69,747
2006	$75,598
2007	$79,618

Source: U.S. Census Bureau

5.3.1.12　Per Capita Personal Income, 2001-2007

	Utah County
2001	$24,702
2002	$24,919
2003	$24,958
2004	$26,053
2005	$27,885
2006	$29,243
2007	$29,831

Source: U.S. Census Bureau

5.3.1.13 Aggregate Personal Income, in Thousands $, All Utah Counties, Metropolitan Statistical Areas, and Micropolitan Statistical Areas

Area Name	2004	2005	2006	2007	2008
Utah state total	65,453,353	71,533,174	78,382,304	84,709,328	87,411,357
Utah Metropolitan Portion	59,481,475	65,038,757	71,316,660	76,993,133	79,189,869
Utah Nonmetropolitan Portion	5,971,878	6,494,417	7,065,644	7,716,195	8,221,488
Beaver, UT	161,013	161,349	141,196	148,828	156,916
Box Elder, UT	1,051,292	1,122,031	1,199,880	1,328,891	1,395,675
Cache, UT	2,258,291	2,356,969	2,483,356	2,728,999	2,903,678
Carbon, UT	502,173	551,730	590,923	609,911	655,348
Daggett, UT	17,720	18,919	19,347	20,159	21,728
Davis, UT	7,351,105	8,020,474	8,776,034	9,528,967	9,820,631
Duchesne, UT	362,745	416,904	489,543	560,898	645,834
Emery, UT	224,164	236,619	254,202	255,304	265,360
Garfield, UT	103,909	111,755	113,076	118,985	127,744
Grand, UT	206,854	227,731	245,273	264,784	278,529
Iron, UT	744,630	834,408	913,976	984,017	1,022,972
Juab, UT	183,021	201,770	215,553	232,002	243,780
Kane, UT	158,870	171,967	189,980	204,808	209,977
Millard, UT	276,531	282,231	287,406	323,001	348,288
Morgan, UT	186,030	207,459	227,930	257,179	269,732
Piute, UT	27,262	30,909	29,153	32,550	34,684
Rich, UT	51,172	53,204	56,484	59,474	64,710
Area Name	2004	2005	2006	2007	2008
Salt Lake, UT	29,659,586	32,325,960	35,532,198	37,888,312	38,730,205
San Juan, UT	222,182	236,199	245,172	264,450	278,100
Sanpete, UT	403,342	430,598	453,742	501,924	539,923
Sevier, UT	393,905	420,284	453,565	484,690	508,050
Summit, UT	1,673,558	1,861,469	2,041,323	2,271,016	2,311,245
Tooele, UT	1,042,151	1,159,858	1,271,175	1,391,571	1,463,170
Uintah, UT	581,500	661,761	798,008	898,909	992,648
Utah, UT	8,999,992	10,048,630	11,056,529	12,136,946	12,609,664
Wasatch, UT	428,683	469,274	528,998	591,375	609,570
Washington, UT	2,471,312	2,882,099	3,223,602	3,473,083	3,512,116
Wayne, UT	53,931	56,544	55,720	63,237	65,432

Weber, UT	5,656,429	5,974,069	6,488,960	7,085,058	7,325,648
Logan, UT-ID (MSA)	2,523,908	2,635,410	2,772,433	3,052,177	3,236,307
Ogden-Clearfield, UT (MSA)	13,193,564	14,202,002	15,492,924	16,871,204	17,416,011
Provo-Orem, UT (MSA)	9,183,013	10,250,400	11,272,082	12,368,948	12,853,444
St. George, UT (MSA)	2,471,312	2,882,099	3,223,602	3,473,083	3,512,116
Salt Lake City, UT (MSA)	32,375,295	35,347,287	38,844,696	41,550,899	42,504,620
Brigham City, UT Micropolitan SA	1,051,292	1,122,031	1,199,880	1,328,891	1,395,675
Cedar City, UT Micropolitan SA	744,630	834,408	913,976	984,017	1,022,972
Heber, UT Micropolitan SA	428,683	469,274	528,998	591,375	609,570
Price, UT Micropolitan SA	502,173	551,730	590,923	609,911	655,348
Vernal, UT Micropolitan SA	581,500	661,761	798,008	898,909	992,648
Salt Lake City-Ogden-Clearfield, UT (CSA)	47,048,834	51,140,594	56,066,498	60,342,369	61,925,876
Salt Lake City-Ogden-Clearfield, UT (EA)	62,211,419	67,793,762	74,234,961	80,262,914	82,880,761

Source: U.S. Census Bureau

5.3.1.14   Self-Reported Per Capita Income, Comparison Counties, 2009

	Utah County	Davis County	Salt Lake County
Per Capita Income, 2009	$19,052	$24,763	$24,440

Source: U.S. Census Bureau

185

5.3.1.15   Household Income, All Households, Comparison Counties

	Utah County	Davis County	Salt Lake County
Less than $10,000	5.2%	3.9%	5.2%
$10,000 to $14,999	4.4%	2.6%	4.2%
$15,000 to $24,999	8.1%	5.7%	8.4%
$25,000 to $34,999	9.6%	7.8%	10.6%
$35,000 to $49,999	15.5%	15.1%	14.6%
$50,000 to $74,999	21.7%	23.0%	21.5%
$75,000 to $99,999	14.3%	16.6%	14.3%
$100,000 to $149,999	12.8%	17.0%	13.4%
$150,000 to $200,000	4.9%	5.7%	3.9%
> $200,000	3.4%	2.7%	3.7%

Source: U.S. Census Bureau

5.3.1.16   Household Income, Hispanic Householder, 2009, Comparison Counties

	Utah County	Davis County	Salt Lake County
Less than $10,000	9.1%	5.0%	7.1%
$10,000 to $14,999	11.4%	6.0%	4.5%
$15,000 to $24,999	9.6%	9.9%	14.6%
$25,000 to $34,999	14.8%	4.9%	14.6%
$35,000 to $49,999	20.8%	24.4%	19.0%
$50,000 to $74,999	17.2%	26.0%	21.8%
$75,000 to $99,999	7.2%	11.4%	9.3%
$100,000 to $149,999	7.7%	11.1%	7.8%
$150,000 to $200,000	1.1%	1.3%	1.1%
> $200,000	1.1%	0.0%	0.1%

Source: U.S. Census Bureau

5.3.1.17 Annual Household Income, Hispanic or Latino vs. Not Hispanic or Latino, 2009

	Hispanic or Latino	Not Hispanic or Latino
Less than $10,000	9.1%	4.9%
$10,000 to $14,999	11.4%	3.8%
$15,000 to $24,999	9.6%	8.0%
$25,000 to $34,999	14.8%	9.2%
$35,000 to $49,999	20.8%	15.1%
$50,000 to $74,999	17.2%	22.1%
$75,000 to $99,999	7.2%	14.9%
$100,000 to $149,999	7.7%	13.2%
$150,000 to $200,000	1.1%	5.2%
> $200,000	1.1%	3.5%

Source: U.S. Census Bureau

5.3.1.18 Number and Percent of Households with Self-Employment Income, 2009

	Utah County	Davis County	Salt Lake County
Number of Households	22,321	11,603	42,564
Percent of All Households	16.3%	12.7%	12.7%

Source: U.S. Census Bureau

5.3.1.19   Average Sales and Use Tax Rates, Comparison Counties

Utah County	Davis County	Salt Lake County
6.66%	6.53%	6.95%

Source: Utah Tax Commission

5.3.1.20   Local Sales and Use Tax Rates, Utah County Municipalities

	ST*	LS	MT	MF	HH	MZ	CO	Total Rate
Utah County	4.7%	1%		0.3%	0.25%		0.25%	**6.50%**
Alpine	4.7%	1%	0.25%	0.3%	0.25%		0.25%	**6.75%**
American Fork	4.7%	1%	0.25%	0.3%	0.25%		0.25%	**6.75%**
Cedar Fort	4.7%	1%		0.3%	0.25%		0.25%	**6.50%**
Draper City South	4.7%	1%		0.3%	0.25%		0.25%	**6.50%**
Eagle Mountain	4.7%	1%	0.25%	0.3%	0.25%		0.25%	**6.75%**
Fairfield	4.7%	1%		0.3%	0.25%		0.25%	**6.50%**
Genola	4.7%	1%		0.3%	0.25%		0.25%	**6.50%**
Goshen	4.7%	1%		0.3%	0.25%		0.25%	**6.50%**
Lehi	4.7%	1%	0.25%	0.3%	0.25%		0.25%	**6.75%**
Lindon	4.7%	1%	0.25%	0.3%	0.25%		0.25%	**6.75%**
Mapleton	4.7%	1%	0.25%	0.3%	0.25%		0.25%	**6.75%**
Orem	4.7%	1%	0.25%	0.3%	0.25%	0.1%	0.25%	**6.85%**
Payson	4.7%	1%	0.25%	0.3%	0.25%		0.25%	**6.75%**
Pleasant Grove	4.7%	1%	0.25%	0.3%	0.25%		0.25%	**6.75%**
Provo	4.7%	1%	0.25%	0.3%	0.25%		0.25%	**6.75%**
Provo Canyon	4.7%	1%	0.25%	0.3%	0.25%		0.25%	**6.75%**
Salem	4.7%	1%	0.25%	0.3%	0.25%		0.25%	**6.75%**
Santaquin	4.7%	1%		0.3%	0.25%		0.25%	**6.50%**
Saratoga Springs	4.7%	1%	0.25%	0.3%	0.25%		0.25%	**6.75%**
Highland	4.7%	1%	0.25%	0.3%	0.25%		0.25%	**6.75%**
Spanish Fork	4.7%	1%	0.25%	0.3%	0.25%		0.25%	**6.75%**
Springville	4.7%	1%	0.25%	0.3%	0.25%		0.25%	**6.75%**
Vineyard	4.7%	1%		0.3%	0.25%		0.25%	**6.50%**
Cedar Hills	4.7%	1%	0.25%	0.3%	0.25%	0.1%	0.25%	**6.85%**
Elk Ridge	4.7%	1%		0.3%	0.25%		0.25%	**6.50%**
Woodland Hills	4.7%	1%		0.3%	0.25%		0.25%	**6.50%**

Source: Utah Tax Commission

Key:

ST*	State Sales & Use Tax
LS	Local Sales & Use Tax
MT	Mass Transit Tax
MF	Mass Trans Fixed Guideway
HH	County Airport, Highway, Public Transit
MZ	Botanical, Cultural, Zoo Tax (Municipality)
CO	County Option Sales Tax

Note: The following taxes are not collected by any municipality in Utah County:

TO	Town Option Tax
TN	City or Town Option Tax
RR	Resort Community Tax
RA	Additional Resort Community Tax
MA	Additional Mass Transit Tax
RH	Rural Hospital Tax
CZ	Botanical, Cultural, Zoo Tax (County)
HT	Highways Tax
CT	County Option Transportation
SM	Supplemental State Sales & Use

5.3.1.21 Social Security

5.3.1.21.1 Social Security Benefit Recipients (End of Year), Comparison Counties and State

	Utah County	Davis County	Salt Lake County	State
1970	12,041	4,940	44,816	102,016
1975	16,445	6,849	54,870	128,273
1980	19,816	9,103	62,645	148,873
1985	21,994	10,975	69,403	164,813
1990	25,280	13,870	80,440	191,542
1991	25,645	15,270	82,865	198,453
1992	26,450	15,935	86,055	205,797
1993	27,370	16,845	88,350	212,907
1994	28,225	17,675	89,685	218,862
1995	28,758	18,540	90,266	222,751
1996	29,200	19,181	90,646	226,305
1997	29,749	19,698	90,564	228,411
1998	30,119	20,309	90,524	230,745
1999	30,774	20,855	90,959	234,587
2000	31,655	21,923	92,918	241,086
2001	32,300	22,665	94,025	245,624
2002	33,010	23,400	95,470	250,878
2003	33,780	24,245	97,000	256,551
2004	35,030	24,905	98,775	263,267
2005	36,860	26,035	101,510	273,045
2006	38,505	27,140	104,095	282,158
2007	39,765	28,115	106,440	290,128
2008	41,495	29,205	109,280	299,088
2009	43,700	30,710	113,630	312,029

Source: U.S. Census Bureau

5.3.1.21.2 Social Security Benefit Payments (EOY), Comparison Counties and State (in Thousands $)

	Utah County	Davis County	Salt Lake County	State
1970	$1,242	$481	$4,859	$10,464
1975	$3,038	$1,177	$10,612	$23,400
1980	$6,235	$2,635	$20,352	$45,672
1985	$9,715	$4,477	$32,066	$71,714
1990	$14,001	$7,073	$46,249	$104,320
1991	$14,802	$8,102	$49,642	$112,522
1992	$15,811	$8,777	$53,106	$120,676
1993	$16,829	$9,553	$56,054	$128,501
1994	$17,926	$10,406	$58,863	$136,613
1995	$18,865	$11,322	$61,242	$143,713
1996	$19,924	$12,200	$63,845	$151,601
1997	$20,918	$12,956	$65,858	$157,910
1998	$21,717	$13,630	$67,342	$163,132
1999	$22,906	$14,533	$70,008	$171,612
2000	$24,770	$16,104	$75,163	$185,445
2001	$26,257	$17,318	$78,942	$196,165
2002	$27,495	$18,449	$81,997	$205,398
2003	$29,032	$19,770	$85,850	$216,796
2004	$31,171	$21,111	$90,683	$230,988
2005	$34,364	$23,225	$97,843	$251,829
2006	$37,425	$25,293	$104,370	$271,195
2007	$39,863	$27,077	$110,235	$288,039
2008	$44,287	$30,138	$120,675	$317,103
2009	$46,923	$32,083	$126,721	$334,190

Source: U.S. Census Bureau

5.3.1.21.3 Retired Worker Benefit Recipients (EOY), Comparison Counties

	Utah County	Davis County	Salt Lake County	State
1990	14,770	8,950	50,610	119,955
1991	14,970	9,765	52,050	123,930
1992	15,375	10,120	53,510	127,651
1993	15,850	10,635	54,490	131,283
1994	16,285	11,165	55,060	134,423
1995	16,655	11,795	55,645	137,285
1996	17,025	12,265	56,105	139,982
1997	17,555	12,775	56,955	143,202
1998	17,865	13,195	57,395	145,637
1999	18,300	13,655	58,100	148,879
2000	19,095	14,460	60,045	154,713
2001	19,645	15,040	61,075	158,455
2002	20,185	15,555	62,055	162,256
2003	20,620	16,185	63,095	166,211
2004	21,455	16,650	64,320	171,031
2005	22,515	17,355	66,005	177,447
2006	23,560	17,995	67,450	182,948
2007	24,395	18,530	68,855	187,950
2008	25,330	19,315	70,625	193,781
2009	26,710	20,295	74,005	203,464

Source: U.S. Census Bureau

5.3.1.21.4 Retired Worker Benefit Payments (EOY), Comparison Counties and State (in Thousands $)

	Utah County	Davis County	Salt Lake County	State
1990	$9,445	$5,054	$32,585	$73,116
1991	$9,985	$5,764	$34,938	$78,731
1992	$10,622	$6,185	$37,128	$83,985
1993	$11,279	$6,699	$38,988	$89,075
1994	$11,985	$7,282	$40,759	$94,355
1995	$12,637	$7,963	$42,482	$99,412
1996	$13,367	$8,577	$44,342	$104,878
1997	$14,145	$9,206	$46,201	$110,150
1998	$14,710	$9,699	$47,454	$114,214
1999	$15,551	$10,391	$49,553	$120,588
2000	$17,016	$11,639	$53,715	$131,499
2001	$18,080	$12,559	$56,601	$139,451
2002	$18,979	$13,369	$58,792	$146,183
2003	$19,977	$14,389	$61,485	$154,292
2004	$21,472	$15,362	$64,931	$164,516
2005	$23,618	$16,855	$69,863	$179,136
2006	$25,763	$18,241	$74,270	$192,393
2007	$27,516	$19,450	$78,363	$204,258
2008	$30,505	$21,742	$85,779	$225,088
2009	$32,442	$23,128	$90,815	$238,908

Source: U.S. Census Bureau

5.3.1.21.5 Social Security Widow and Widower Benefit Recipients (EOY), Comparison Counties and State

	Utah County	Davis County	Salt Lake County	State
1990	2,915	1,380	9,015	21,621
1991	2,910	1,520	9,125	22,010
1992	2,985	1,575	9,315	22,442
1993	3,045	1,635	9,370	22,707
1994	3,075	1,700	9,410	23,018
1995	3,075	1,745	9,425	23,207
1996	3,090	1,760	9,350	23,219
1997	3,085	1,730	9,015	22,785
1998	3,115	1,765	8,810	22,703
1999	3,135	1,775	8,755	22,734
2000	3,115	1,815	8,690	22,743
2001	3,160	1,840	8,580	22,660
2002	3,150	1,865	8,540	22,625
2003	3,185	1,875	8,510	22,687
2004	3,185	1,935	8,480	22,754
2005	3,250	1,980	8,440	22,847
2006	3,240	2,020	8,445	22,884
2007	3,240	2,055	8,370	22,835
2008	3,255	2,050	8,350	22,777
2009	3,320	2,095	8,300	22,829

Source: U.S. Census Bureau

5.3.1.21.6 Widow and Widower Benefit Payments Received (EOY), Comparison Counties and State (in Thousands $)

	Utah County	Davis County	Salt Lake County	State
1990	$1,712	$735	$5,380	$12,294
1991	$1,799	$847	$5,705	$13,118
1992	$1,924	$923	$6,057	$13,933
1993	$2,031	$994	$6,320	$14,619
1994	$2,140	$1,072	$6,602	$15,392
1995	$2,221	$1,136	$6,853	$16,094
1996	$2,331	$1,204	$7,122	$16,833
1997	$2,404	$1,233	$7,112	$17,110
1998	$2,488	$1,289	$7,135	$17,469
1999	$2,590	$1,341	$7,341	$18,085
2000	$2,685	$1,420	$7,652	$18,947
2001	$2,841	$1,499	$7,844	$19,614
2002	$3,039	$1,654	$8,197	$20,773
2003	$3,156	$1,778	$8,456	$21,596
2004	$3,392	$1,902	$8,823	$22,768
2005	$3,508	$2,029	$9,191	$23,764
2006	$3,647	$2,120	$9,381	$24,461
2007	$3,910	$2,269	$10,011	$26,085
2008	$4,007	$2,360	$10,038	$26,414

Source: U.S. Census Bureau

5.3.1.21.7 Disabled Worker Benefit Recipients (EOY), Comparison Counties and State

	Utah County	Davis County	Salt Lake County	State
1990	1,555	770	5,940	12,214
1991	1,600	880	6,455	13,303
1992	1,765	1,020	7,255	15,029
1993	1,955	1,160	7,945	16,700
1994	2,120	1,310	8,510	18,197
1995	2,185	1,380	8,740	18,925
1996	2,310	1,455	8,815	19,648
1997	2,415	1,475	8,800	19,902
1998	2,515	1,580	8,945	20,549
1999	2,620	1,635	9,030	21,205
2000	2,745	1,730	9,145	21,848
2001	2,835	1,825	9,465	22,868
2002	2,975	1,975	9,950	24,185
2003	3,210	2,090	10,470	25,579
2004	3,440	2,205	11,080	27,157
2005	3,775	2,480	12,150	29,729
2006	4,080	2,735	13,030	32,274
2007	4,350	3,010	13,950	34,726
2008	4,735	3,225	14,860	37,238
2009	5,095	3,450	15,620	39,318

Source: U.S. Census Bureau

5.3.1.21.8 Disabled Worker Benefit Payments Received (EOY), Comparison Counties and State (in Thousands $)

	Utah County	Davis County	Salt Lake County	State
1990	$924	$444	$3,441	$7,123
1991	$984	$526	$3,859	$8,011
1992	$1,104	$625	$4,433	$9,273
1993	$1,239	$724	$4,974	$10,525
1994	$1,376	$839	$5,475	$11,804
1995	$1,451	$929	$5,799	$12,643
1996	$1,576	$1,014	$6,024	$13,551
1997	$1,682	$1,043	$6,169	$14,065
1998	$1,785	$1,129	$6,384	$14,753
1999	$1,921	$1,212	$6,648	$15,697
2000	$2,088	$1,326	$7,057	$16,896
2001	$2,240	$1,444	$7,562	$18,317
2002	$2,416	$1,602	$8,138	$19,839
2003	$2,688	$1,749	$8,859	$21,703
2004	$3,004	$1,913	$9,715	$23,959
2005	$3,452	$2,257	$11,200	$27,585
2006	$3,906	$2,617	$12,536	$31,295
2007	$4,269	$2,946	$13,834	$34,581
2008	$4,947	$3,344	$15,584	$39,241
2009	$5,283	$3,633	$16,386	$41,410

Source: U.S. Census Bureau

5.3.1.21.9 Supplemental Security Income Benefit Recipients (EOY), Comparison Counties and State

	Utah County	Davis County	Salt Lake County	State
1990	1,936	582	5,676	12,616
1991	2,050	691	6,430	14,024
1992	2,257	760	7,628	16,306
1993	2,479	868	8,537	18,198
1994	2,667	1,005	9,375	19,807
1995	2,778	1,080	9,547	20,462
1996	2,851	1,146	9,525	21,011
1997	2,870	1,119	9,002	20,304
1998	2,858	1,179	8,883	20,242
1999	2,860	1,175	8,713	19,999
2000	2,879	1,206	8,800	20,174
2001	3,055	1,240	8,994	20,566
2002	3,164	1,264	9,174	21,042
2003	3,217	1,221	9,338	21,394
2004	3,185	1,348	9,435	21,686
2005	3,190	1,636	9,733	22,606
2006	3,339	1,758	10,115	23,518
2007	3,420	1,911	10,527	24,486
2008	3,618	1,933	10,891	25,447
2009	3,808	2,008	11,465	26,693

Source: U.S. Census Bureau

5.3.1.21.10 Supplemental Security Income Benefits Received (EOY), Comparison Counties and State (in Thousands $)

	Utah County	Davis County	Salt Lake County	State
1990	$466	$162	$1,710	$3,606
1991	$563	$231	$2,077	$4,329
1992	$649	$241	$2,718	$5,659
1993	$713	$282	$2,805	$5,853
1994	$821	$324	$3,106	$6,471
1995	$879	$365	$3,251	$6,935
1996	$940	$378	$3,270	$7,266
1997	$1,008	$405	$3,210	$7,261
1998	$1,021	$435	$3,293	$7,530
1999	$1,023	$438	$3,245	$7,396
2000	$1,051	$457	$3,557	$7,875
2001	$1,175	$520	$3,739	$8,375
2002	$1,249	$499	$3,722	$8,584
2003	$1,331	$496	$4,024	$9,027
2004	$1,374	$584	$4,145	$9,579
2005	$1,388	$842	$4,721	$10,718
2006	$1,488	$836	$4,851	$11,095
2007	$1,692	$935	$5,355	$12,254
2008	$1,715	$975	$5,440	$12,572
2009	$1,861	$1,025	$6,022	$13,708

Source: U.S. Census Bureau

5.3.1.21.11 Supplemental Security Income Average Monthly Benefit Received (EOY), Comparison Counties and State

	Utah County	Davis County	Salt Lake County	State
1990	$241	$278	$301	$286
1991	$275	$334	$323	$309
1992	$288	$317	$356	$347
1993	$288	$325	$329	$322
1994	$308	$322	$331	$327
1995	$316	$338	$341	$339
1996	$330	$330	$343	$346
1997	$351	$362	$357	$358
1998	$357	$369	$371	$372
1999	$358	$373	$372	$370
2000	$365	$379	$404	$390
2001	$385	$419	$416	$407
2002	$395	$395	$406	$408
2003	$414	$406	$431	$422
2004	$431	$433	$439	$442
2005	$435	$515	$485	$474
2006	$446	$476	$480	$472
2007	$495	$489	$509	$500
2008	$474	$504	$499	$494
2009	$489	$510	$525	$514

Source: U.S. Census Bureau

5.3.2 Employment

5.3.2.1 Current Employment by Occupation and Industry

	Total	Management, professional, and related occupations	Service occupations	Sales and office occupations	Farming, fishing, and forestry occupations	Construction, extraction, maintenance, and repair occupations	Production, transportation, and material moving occupations
Civilian employed population 16 years and over	235,219	36.0%	16.1%	29.9%	0.2%	7.6%	10.2%
Agriculture, forestry, fishing and hunting, and mining	2,422	33.9%	6.9%	12.6%	18.7%	20.7%	7.1%
Construction	16,074	19.9%	0.3%	10.9%	0.0%	64.9%	4.0%
Manufacturing	25,292	29.1%	0.9%	20.1%	0.0%	4.7%	45.1%
Wholesale trade	6,892	23.9%	0.0%	53.0%	0.0%	1.8%	21.2%
Retail trade	33,546	13.9%	2.7%	72.4%	0.0%	2.4%	8.5%
Transportation and warehousing, and utilities	5,695	14.8%	7.8%	37.1%	0.0%	9.2%	31.2%
Information	5,243	46.8%	6.1%	33.2%	0.0%	13.0%	0.9%
Finance and insurance, and real estate and rental and leasing	14,508	37.7%	1.2%	57.4%	0.0%	2.5%	1.2%
Professional, scientific, and management, and administrative and waste management services	27,440	51.6%	11.0%	31.3%	0.0%	1.7%	4.5%
Educational services, and health care and social assistance	58,970	58.4%	20.6%	16.2%	0.0%	1.0%	3.9%

	Total	Management, professional, and related occupations	Service occupations	Sales and office occupations	Farming, fishing, and forestry occupations	Construction, extraction, maintenance, and repair occupations	Production, transportation, and material moving occupations
Arts, entertainment, and recreation, and accommodation and food services	20,789	17.9%	66.1%	11.7%	0.0%	0.7%	3.7%
Other services, except public administration	10,783	25.6%	34.9%	13.0%	0.0%	15.7%	10.9%
Public administration	7,565	41.5%	38.6%	15.0%	0.0%	4.9%	0.0%

Source: U.S. Census Bureau

5.3.2.2 Employment Status Characteristics of Families

	Total	Families with own children under 18 years
Families	**110,465**	**64,671**
EMPLOYMENT STATUS CHARACTERISTICS		
Married-couple families	**94,852**	**56,551**
Both husband and wife in labor force	48.8%	49.0%
Husband in labor force, wife not in labor force	37.3%	47.7%
Wife in labor force, husband not in labor force	4.3%	2.1%
Both husband and wife not in labor force	9.7%	1.1%
Other families	**15,613**	**8,120**
Female householder, no husband present	69.9%	72.0%
In labor force	48.1%	59.0%
Not in labor force	21.8%	13.0%
Male householder, no wife present	30.1%	28.0%
In labor force	24.1%	24.6%
Not in labor force	6.0%	3.4%

Source: U.S. Census Bureau

5.3.2.3 Work Status Characteristics of Families

	Total	Families with own children under 18 years
Families	**110,465**	**64,671**
WORK STATUS CHARACTERISTICS		
Families	**110,465**	**64,671**
No workers in the past 12 months	7.8%	2.3%
1 worker in the past 12 months	30.7%	37.4%
2 or more workers in the past 12 months	61.4%	60.3%
Married-couple families	**94,852**	**56,551**
Householder worked full-time, year-round in the past 12 months	55.6%	64.5%
Spouse worked full-time, year-round in the past 12 months	16.8%	16.2%
Householder worked part-time or part-year in the past 12 months	26.8%	24.0%
Spouse worked part-time or part-year in the past 12 months	10.6%	8.2%
Householder did not work in the past 12 months	17.6%	11.4%
Spouse did not work in the past 12 months	8.5%	0.7%

Source: U.S. Census Bureau

5.3.2.4 Percent Working in County of Residence, Comparison Counties

	Work in County of Residence	Work in County Other than County of Residence
Utah County	83.4%	16.6%
Davis County	54.0%	46.0%
Salt Lake County	92.8%	7.2%

Source: U.S. Census Bureau

5.3.2.5 Working in County of Residence, by Gender, Comparison Counties

	Utah County	Davis County	Salt Lake County
Total Workers 16 and Older	230,754	136,671	499,823
Workers 16 and Older working in county of residence	192,419	73,775	464,023
Workers 16 and older working outside county of residence	38,335	62,896	35,800
Male workers 16 and over	129,221	77,602	275,848
Male workers 16 and over working in county of residence	102,090	38,337	251,090
Male workers 16 and over working outside county of residence	27,131	39,265	24,758
Female workers 16 and over	101,533	59,069	223,975
Female workers 16 and over working in county of residence	90,329	35,438	212,933
Female workers 16 and older working outside county of residence	11,204	23,631	11,042

Source: U.S. Census Bureau

5.3.3 Poverty

5.3.3.1 Persons in Poverty, Comparison Counties and State, 1995-2008

	Utah County	Davis County	Salt Lake County	State
1995	34,240	14,337	73,245	197,121
1997	34,817	15,666	77,360	210,783
1998	35,051	16,017	78,046	213,244
1999	32,412	13,621	69,159	188,053
2000	34,205	14,159	73,343	198,434
2001	38,668	15,273	80,691	214,675
2002	41,589	16,545	86,305	224,715
2003	44,333	19,048	90,075	236,637
2004	46,714	20,025	95,394	251,092
2005	53,187	16,315	92,956	254,761
2006	58,292	15,842	102,636	269,611
2007	53,899	18,090	89,473	254,385
2008	61,648	17,875	89,216	261,556

Source: U.S. Census Bureau

5.3.3.2 Percent Persons in Poverty, Comparison Counties and State, 1995-2008

	Utah County	Davis County	Salt Lake County	State
1995	10.8	6.4	8.8	9.7
1997	10.3	6.6	9.1	10
1998	10.1	6.6	9.1	10
1999	9	5.7	7.8	8.5
2000	9.2	5.8	8.2	8.8
2001	10.1	6.2	8.9	9.4
2002	10.6	6.5	9.4	9.7
2003	11.2	7.4	9.8	10
2004	10.7	7.5	10.2	10.3
2005	12.3	6.2	10	10.5
2006	12.8	5.8	10.6	10.7
2007	11.4	6.3	9	9.8
2008	11.8	6.1	8.8	9.7

Source: U.S. Census Bureau

5.3.3.3 Children in Poverty, Comparison Counties and State, 1995-2008

	Utah County	Davis County	Salt Lake County	State
1995	11,517	5,809	28,051	73,381
1997	13,580	6,918	32,501	89,867
1998	14,263	7,587	34,044	92,016
1999	11,242	5,827	25,627	70,949
2000	12,704	5,886	28,543	78,481
2001	14,244	5,979	31,105	82,494
2002	14,571	6,257	31,592	80,892
2003	16,775	7,821	35,619	92,610
2004	16,418	7,888	35,836	92,251
2005	14,376	5,820	31,673	85,446
2006	17,241	6,532	37,456	95,887
2007	14,936	7,722	33,530	91,064
2008	17,945	7,364	32,267	91,706

Source: U.S. Census Bureau

5.3.3.4 Percent Children in Poverty, Comparison Counties and State, 1995-2008

	Utah County	Davis County	Salt Lake County	State
1995	10	6.9	10.2	10.5
1997	11.3	7.9	11.7	12.5
1998	11.7	408.5	12.2	12.7
1999	9	7	9.5	10
2000	10	7.1	10.6	11.1
2001	10.7	7.1	11.3	11.3
2002	10.6	7.3	11.3	10.9
2003	12.2	9.2	12.9	12.5
2004	11.1	9.3	13.2	12.4
2005	9.9	6.9	11.8	11.7
2006	10.7	7.4	13.1	12.3
2007	9.1	8.3	11.5	11.3
2008	9.8	7.7	10.8	10.9

Source: U.S. Census Bureau

5.3.3.5 Related Children in Families in Poverty, Ages 5-17, 1995-2008

	Utah County	Davis County	Salt Lake County	State
1995	5,694	3,016	14,014	38,046
1997	7,913	4,067	18,142	52,139
1998	8,000	4,180	18,612	54,173
1999	6,517	3,291	14,966	43,158
2000	6,941	3,212	15,286	43,761
2001	8,202	3,443	17,243	47,462
2002	8,791	3,563	18,031	48,236
2003	8,914	4,010	18,369	49,493
2004	9,446	4,335	19,587	52,513
2005	8,018	3,507	19,590	51,517
2006	9,711	3,795	22,442	57,412
2007	9,176	4,590	20,866	55,841
2008	9,932	4,588	20,236	55,278

Source: U.S. Census Bureau

5.3.3.6 Percent Related Children in Families in Poverty, Ages 5-17, 1995-2008

	Utah County	Davis County	Salt Lake County	State
1995	7.1	5	7.3	7.7
1997	9.7	6.6	9.5	10.5
1998	9.6	6.7	9.7	10.7
1999	7.9	5.6	7.9	8.7
2000	8.3	5.4	8.2	8.9
2001	9.4	5.7	9	9.4
2002	10	5.9	9.5	9.6
2003	10.2	6.7	9.8	9.9
2004	10	7.4	10.7	10.5
2005	8.5	6	10.8	10.4
2006	9.2	6.2	11.4	10.7
2007	8.5	7.2	10.4	10.2
2008	8.1	7.1	9.9	9.7

Source: U.S. Census Bureau

5.3.3.7 Families in Poverty, Comparison Counties, by Family Type, 2009

	Utah County		Davis County		Salt Lake County	
	Number	Percent	Number	Percent	Number	Percent
Families in poverty	9863	8.9%	3655	4.9%	16289	6.9%
Married-couple families in poverty	5855	59.4%	2292	62.7%	8804	54.0%
Married-couple families without children in poverty	2205	22.4%	518	14.2%	2823	17.3%
Married-couple families with children in poverty	3650	37.0%	1774	48.5%	5981	36.7%
Other families in poverty	4008	40.6%	1363	37.3%	7485	46.0%
Male householder, no wife present, in poverty	1068	10.8%	160	4.4%	1216	7.5%
Single father with own children in poverty	742	7.5%	160	4.4%	535	3.3%
Female householder, no husband present, in poverty	2940	29.8%	1203	32.9%	6269	38.5%
Single mother with own chldren in poverty	2226	22.6%	956	26.2%	5135	31.5%

Source: U.S. Census Bureau

5.3.3.8 Households in Poverty by Household Type, Comparison Counties

	Utah County	Davis County	Salt Lake County
Percent of Households in Poverty who are Families	57.2%	59.1%	49.7%
Percent of Households in Poverty who are Married Couples	34.0%	37.1%	26.9%
Percent of Households in Poverty who are Married Couples Under Age 25	7.2%	8.6%	1.2%
Percent of Households in Poverty who are Married Couples Age 25 to 44	18.9%	20.6%	16.4%
Percent of Households in Poverty who are Married Couples Age 45 to 64	6.8%	6.3%	6.1%
Percent of Households in Poverty who are Married Couples Age 65 and Over	1.1%	1.5%	3.1%
Percent of Households in Poverty who are Other Family Units	23.2%	22.1%	22.8%
Percent of Households in Poverty who are Male Householder, No Wife	6.2%	2.6%	3.7%
Percent of Households in Poverty who are Male Householder, No Wife, Under 25 Years	2.9%	0.0%	0.1%
Percent of Households in Poverty who are Male Householder, No Wife, 25 to 44 Years	1.8%	2.6%	2.3%
Percent of Households in Poverty who are Male Householder, No Wife, Age 45 to 64	1.4%	0.0%	0.5%
Percent of Households in Poverty who are Male Householder, No Wife, Age 65 and Older	0.0%	0.0%	0.7%

Percent of Households in Poverty who are Female Householder, No Husband	17.1%	19.5%	19.1%
Percent of Households in Poverty who are Female Householder, No Husband, Under 25 Years	2.5%	0.5%	2.9%
Percent of Households in Poverty who are Female Householder, No Husband, Age 25 to 44	10.1%	12.0%	10.7%
Percent of Households in Poverty who are Female Householder, No Husband, Age 45 to 64	3.2%	4.9%	4.9%
Percent of Households in Poverty who are Female Householder, No Husband, Age 65 and Over	1.3%	2.0%	0.6%
Percent of Households in Poverty who are Nonfamily Households	42.8%	40.9%	50.3%
Percent of Households in Poverty who are Nonfamily Households, Male Householder	16.5%	15.7%	24.6%
Percent of Households in Poverty who are Nonfamily Households, Male Householder, Under 25 Years	8.7%	1.1%	4.2%
Percent of Households in Poverty who are Nonfamily Households, Male Householder, Age 25 to 44	2.6%	10.9%	6.5%
Percent of Households in Poverty who are Nonfamily Households, Male Householder, Age 45 to 64	3.0%	2.9%	9.3%
Percent of Households in Poverty who arc Nonfamily Households, Male Householder, Age 65 and Over	2.1%	0.9%	4.7%

Percent of Households in Poverty who are Nonfamily Households, Female Householder	26.3%	25.1%	25.7%
Percent of Households in Poverty who are Nonfamily Households, Female Householder, Under Age 25	15.8%	2.3%	4.6%
Percent of Households in Poverty who are Nonfamily Households, Female Householder, Age 25 to 44	2.7%	5.7%	5.0%
Percent of Households in Poverty who are Nonfamily Households, Female Householder, Age 45 to 64	3.9%	8.6%	7.9%
Percent of Households in Poverty who are Nonfamily Households, Female Householder, Age 65 and Over	3.9%	8.5%	8.3%

Source: U.S. Census Bureau

5.3.3.9 Percent of Persons in Poverty by Race/Ethnicity

	White, Not Hispanic	Native Hawaiian or Other Pacific Islander	Hispanic or Latino
Percent in Poverty	12.9%	14.9%	19.5%

Source: U.S. Census Bureau

5.3.3.10   Persons in Poverty by Race/Ethnicity and Age, Comparison Counties

	Utah County		Davis County		Salt Lake County	
	Number	Percent	Number	Percent	Number	Percent
All races and ethnicities, < 18	12981	22.1%	5617	35.9%	15255	27.7%
All races and ethnicities, 18-64	44319	75.3%	8958	57.3%	34706	62.9%
All races and ethnicities, 65+	1544	2.6%	1062	6.8%	5180	9.4%
White alone, < 18	140853	30.8%	77889	30.2%	182418	23.8%
White alone, 18-64	225272	49.3%	143484	55.7%	455435	59.5%
White alone, 65+	31619	6.9%	20657	8.0%	71899	9.4%
Hispanic or Latino, < 18	18731	39.3%	8773	41.3%	51857	47.7%
Hispanic or Latino, 18 to 64 years	5853	57.0%	2095	58.7%	15937	48.7%
Hispanic or Latino, 65 years and over	383	3.7%	0	0.0%	1149	3.5%

Source: U.S. Census Bureau

5.3.3.11   Persons in Poverty by Educational Attainment, Comparison Counties

	Utah County		Davis County		Salt Lake County	
	Number	Percent	Number	Percent	Number	Percent
Population 25 or older living in poverty	21180	8.6%	9329	5.5%	53180	8.5%
Population 25 or older living in poverty who have less than a high school education	3439	16.2%	1415	15.2%	14555	27.4%
Population 25 or older living in poverty who have attained HS diploma or equivalent	4609	21.8%	3394	36.4%	17520	32.9%
Population 25 or older living in poverty who have attained associate's degree or attended some college	9727	45.9%	3584	38.4%	13878	26.1%
Population 25 or older living in poverty who have attained bachelor's degree or higher	3405	16.1%	936	10.0%	7227	13.6%

Source: U.S. Census Bureau

5.3.3.12 Grandparents with Grandchildren in Poverty, Comparison Counties, 2009

	Utah County		Davis County		Salt Lake County	
	Number	Percent	Number	Percent	Number	Percent
Grandparents living with own grandchildren	9616		-		22793	
Grandparents living with own grandchildren living below poverty level	304	3.2%	-		1739	7.6%
Grandparents living with and responsible for own grandchildren, living below poverty level	304	3.2%	-		811	3.6%
Grandparents age 30 to 59 living with and responsible for own grandchildren, living below poverty level	216	2.2%	-		626	2.7%
Grandparents age 60 or older living with and responsible for own grandchildren, living below poverty level	88	0.9%	-		185	0.8%
Grandparents living with but not responsible for grandchildren, living below poverty level	0	0.0%	-		928	4.1%

Source: U.S. Census Bureau

5.3.3.13 Households Receiving Cash Public Assistance or Food Stamps, Comparison Counties, 2009

	Utah County		Davis County		Salt Lake County	
	Number	Percent	Number	Percent	Number	Percent
Total Households	136,789		91,542		336,350	
Households receiving cash public assistance or food stamps	9,988	7.3%	6,016	6.6%	27,267	8.1%

Source: U.S. Census Bureau

5.3.3.14 Persons in Poverty Age 5 and Older by Language Spoken at Home, Comparison Counties

	Utah County		Davis County		Salt Lake County	
	Number	Percent	Number	Percent	Number	Percent
Population age 5 and older living in poverty	69723	14.7%	17321	6.5%	92968	10.0%
Population age 5 and older living in poverty who speak only English at home	60346	12.7%	14143	5.3%	62412	6.7%
Speak Spanish at home	5596	1.2%	2086	0.8%	20246	2.2%
Speak other Indo-European language at home	2167	0.5%	1004	0.4%	3097	0.3%
Speak Asian and Pacific Island languages at home	1369	0.3%	88	0.0%	6082	0.7%
Speak other languages at home	245	0.1%	0	0.0%	1131	0.1%

Source: U.S. Census Bureau

5.3.4 Housing

5.3.4.1 Number of Housing Units, Comparison Counties and State, 2000-2009

	Utah County	Davis County	Salt Lake County	State
Housing unit estimates as of July 1, 2000	105,243	74,551	312,013	772,756
Housing unit estimates as of July 1, 2001	109,238	76,312	316,243	790,672
Housing unit estimates as of July 1, 2002	113,376	78,613	321,132	809,249
Housing unit estimates as of July 1, 2003	117,390	80,983	326,350	828,036
Housing unit estimates as of July 1, 2004	121,860	83,707	333,257	850,049
Housing unit estimates as of July 1, 2005	126,643	86,591	339,487	874,194
Housing unit estimates as of July 1, 2006	132,068	89,677	346,579	900,904
Housing unit estimates as of July 1, 2007	138,151	92,259	352,146	924,870
Housing unit estimates as of July 1, 2008	142,792	93,976	356,011	943,688
Housing unit estimates as of July 1, 2009	143,960	94,789	359,002	952,999

Source: U.S. Census Bureau

5.3.4.2 Net Cumulative Change in Housing Units, Comparison Counties and State, 2000-2009

	Utah County	Davis County	Salt Lake County	State
Housing unit estimates - net change, April 1, 2000 (base) to July 1, 2000	927	437	1,017	4,153
Housing unit estimates - net change, April 1, 2000 (base) to July 1, 2001	4,922	2,198	5,247	22,069
Housing unit estimates - net change, April 1, 2000 (base) to July 1, 2002	9,060	4,499	10,136	40,646
Housing unit estimates - net change, April 1, 2000 (base) to July 1, 2003	13,074	6,869	15,354	59,433
Housing unit estimates - net change, April 1, 2000 (base) to July 1, 2004	17,544	9,593	22,261	81,446
Housing unit estimates - net change, April 1, 2000 (base) to July 1, 2005	22,327	12,477	28,491	105,591
Housing unit estimates - net change, April 1, 2000 (base) to July 1, 2006	27,752	15,563	35,583	132,301
Housing unit estimates - net change, April 1, 2000 (base) to July 1, 2007	33,835	18,145	41,150	156,267
Housing unit estimates - net change, April 1, 2000 (base) to July 1, 2008	38,476	19,862	45,015	175,085
Housing unit estimates - net change, April 1, 2000 (base) to July 1, 2009	39,644	20,675	48,006	184,396

Source: U.S. Census Bureau

5.3.4.3 Net Cumulative Change in Housing Units as Percent, Comparison Counties and State, 2000-2009

	Utah County	Davis County	Salt Lake County	State
Housing unit estimates - percent change, April 1, 2000 (base) to July 1, 2000	0.9	0.6	0.3	0.5
Housing unit estimates - percent change, April 1, 2000 (base) to July 1, 2001	4.7	3	1.7	2.9
Housing unit estimates - percent change, April 1, 2000 (base) to July 1, 2002	8.7	6.1	3.3	5.3
Housing unit estimates - percent change, April 1, 2000 (base) to July 1, 2003	12.5	9.3	4.9	7.7
Housing unit estimates - percent change, April 1, 2000 (base) to July 1, 2004	16.8	12.9	7.2	10.6
Housing unit estimates - percent change, April 1, 2000 (base) to July 1, 2005	21.4	16.8	9.2	13.7
Housing unit estimates - percent change, April 1, 2000 (base) to July 1, 2006	26.6	21	11.4	17.2
Housing unit estimates - percent change, April 1, 2000 (base) to July 1, 2007	32.4	24.5	13.2	20.3
Housing unit estimates - percent change, April 1, 2000 (base) to July 1, 2008	36.9	26.8	14.5	22.8
Housing unit estimates - percent change, April 1, 2000 (base) to July 1, 2009	38	27.9	15.4	24

Source: U.S. Census Bureau

5.3.4.4 Decennial Count of Housing Units, Comparison Counties and State, 1940-2000

	Utah County	Davis County	Salt Lake County	State
Total housing units 1940 (complete count)	14,324	3,862	59,071	147,291
Total housing units 1950 (complete count)	21,976	8,438	81,490	200,554
Total housing units 1960 (complete count)	28,561	16,426	114,425	262,670
Total housing units 1970 (complete count)	35,963	24,223	139,593	315,765
Total housing units 1980 (complete count)	62,337	41,566	214,572	490,006
Total housing units 1990 (complete count)	72,820	55,777	257,339	598,388
Total housing units 2000 (complete count)	104,315	74,114	310,988	768,594

Source: U.S. Census Bureau

5.3.4.5 Housing Units by Structure, Comparison Counties and State

	Utah County	Davis County	Salt Lake County	State
Housing units by units in structure - one unit, detached 1990 (sample)	46,969	39,774	161,650	392,386
Housing units by units in structure - one unit, detached 2000 (sample)	68,002	54,813	202,040	520,101
Housing units by units in structure - one unit, attached 1990 (sample)	2,135	2,465	11,106	24,354
Housing units by units in structure - one unit, attached 2000 (sample)	6,471	3,507	14,739	37,902
Housing units by units in structure - two units, 1990 (sample)	5,376	1,468	13,511	27,508
Housing units by units in structure - two units, 2000 (sample)	5,879	1,855	13,057	29,243
Housing units by units in structure - three or four units, 1990 (sample)	5,148	3,314	12,553	31,122
Housing units by units in structure - three or four units, 2000 (sample)	6,355	3,599	13,869	36,998
Housing units by units in structure - five to nine units, 1990 (sample)	2,454	1,336	11,186	20,476
Housing units by units in structure - five to nine units, 2000 (sample)	3,947	1,859	14,642	27,677
Housing units by units in structure - 10 to 19 units, 1990 (sample)	3,368	2,343	17,533	29,188
Housing units by units in structure - 10 to 19 units, 2000 (sample)	5,068	2,439	16,613	30,357
Housing units by units in structure - 20 to 49 units 1990 (sample)	2,918	1,528	13,899	22,521
Housing units by units in structure - 20 to 49 units, 2000 (sample)	3,255	1,357	13,226	22,720
Housing units by units in structure - 50 or more units, 1990 (sample)	733	317	7,210	9,701
Housing units by units in structure - 50 or more units, 2000 (sample)	2,388	1,358	14,785	22,128

Source: U.S. Census Bureau

5.3.4.6 Housing Units by Structure, Mobile Homes, Comparison Counties and State

	Utah County	Davis County	Salt Lake County	State
Housing units by units in structure - mobile home or trailer, 1990 (sample)	3,033	2,975	6,568	35,245
Housing units by units in structure - mobile home, 2000 (sample)	2,900	3,297	7,840	39,267

Source: U.S. Census Bureau

5.3.4.7 Housing Units by Year Built, Comparison Counties and State

	Utah County	Davis County	Salt Lake County	State
Housing units by year structure built 1999 to March 2000, 2000 (sample)	6,139	3,625	8,874	32,366
Housing units by year structure built 1995 to 1998, 2000 (sample)	17,415	10,903	32,814	101,022
Housing units by year structure built 1990 to 1994, 2000 (sample)	11,766	7,358	22,279	66,058
Housing units by year structure built 1980 to 1989, 2000 (sample)	13,209	14,446	51,067	124,012
Housing units by year structure built 1989 to March 1990, 1990 (sample)	1,247	1,152	2,554	8,984
Housing units by year structure built 1985 to 1988, 1990 (sample)	5,843	7,196	24,966	56,664
Housing units by year structure built 1980 to 1984, 1990 (sample)	8,235	8,097	33,791	80,250
Housing units by year structure built 1970 to 1979, 1990 (sample)	23,324	17,113	71,156	168,147
Housing units by year structure built 1970 to 1979, 2000 (sample)	23,820	16,256	72,799	169,025
Housing units by year structure built 1960 to 1969, 1990 (sample)	10,102	9,320	38,011	82,603
Housing units by year structure built 1960 to 1969, 2000 (sample)	9,482	8,927	36,399	80,217
Housing units by year structure built 1950 to 1959, 1990 (sample)	8,437	7,591	35,941	74,474
Housing units by year structure built 1950 to 1959, 2000 (sample)	8,735	7,350	35,838	75,348
Housing units by year structure built 1940 to 1949, 1990 (sample)	6,763	2,868	19,255	46,487
Housing units by year structure built 1940 to 1949, 2000 (sample)	5,642	2,709	18,655	43,679
Housing units by year structure built 1939 or earlier, 1990 (sample)	8,869	2,440	31,665	80,779
Housing units by year structure built 1939 or earlier, 2000 (sample)	8,107	2,540	32,263	76,867

Source: U.S. Census Bureau

5.3.4.8 Occupied vs. Vacant Housing Units, Comparison Counties and State

	Utah County	Davis County	Salt Lake County	State
Vacant housing units 1970 (complete count)	1,490	464	4,667	17,831
Vacant housing units 1980 (complete count)	3,822	1,572	12,830	41,403
Vacant housing units 1990 (complete count)	2,652	2,179	16,659	61,115
Vacant housing units 2000 (complete count)	4,378	2,913	15,847	67,313
Occupied housing units 1970 (complete count)	34,473	23,759	134,926	297,934
Occupied housing units 1980 (complete count)	58,515	39,994	201,742	448,603
Occupied housing units 1990 (complete count)	70,168	53,598	240,680	537,273
Occupied housing units 2000 (complete count)	99,937	71,201	295,141	701,281

Source: U.S. Census Bureau

5.3.4.9 Occupied Housing Units by Persons Per Room, Comparison Counties and State

	Utah County	Davis County	Salt Lake County	State
Occupied housing units with 1.00 or less persons per room 1980 (complete count)	53,197	38,116	192,628	422,779
Occupied housing units with 1.00 or less persons per room 1990 (complete count)	64,328	51,185	229,421	507,696
Occupied housing units with 1.00 or less persons per room 2000 (sample)	91,884	68,633	277,384	659,183
Occupied housing units with 1.01 or more persons per room 1980 (complete count)	5,318	1,878	9,114	25,824
Occupied housing units with 1.01 or more persons per room 1990 (complete count)	5,840	2,413	11,259	29,577
Occupied housing units with 1.01 or more persons per room 2000 (sample)	8,053	2,568	17,757	42,098
Occupied housing units with 1.01 to 1.50 persons per room 1990 (complete count)	4,541	1,859	8,193	21,849
Occupied housing units with 1.01 to 1.50 persons per room 2000 (sample)	5,649	1,720	10,023	26,186
Occupied housing units with 1.51 or 2.00 persons per room 1990 (complete count)	1,058	473	2,406	5,956
Occupied housing units with 1.51 or 2.00 persons per room 2000 (sample)	1,814	616	5,442	11,314
Occupied housing units with 2.01 or more persons per room 1990 (complete count)	241	81	660	1,772
Occupied housing units with 2.01 or more persons per room 2000 (sample)	590	232	2,292	4,598

Source: U.S. Census Bureau

5.3.4.10   Occupied Housing Units Lacking Plumbing, Comparison Counties and State

	Utah County	Davis County	Salt Lake County	State
Occupied housing units lacking complete plumbing facilities 1990 (sample)	122	79	612	2,163
Occupied housing units lacking complete plumbing facilities 2000 (sample)	258	88	1,074	2,906
Occupied housing units with 1.01 or more persons per room lacking complete plumbing facilities 1990 (sample)	9	13	46	606
Occupied housing units with 1.01 or more persons per room lacking complete plumbing facilities 2000 (sample)	61	20	218	786

Source: U.S. Census Bureau

5.3.4.11 Occupied Housing Units by Heating Fuel Type, Comparison Counties and State

	Utah County	Davis County	Salt Lake County	State
Occupied housing units by house heating fuel - utility gas 1980 (sample)	51,518	36,841	186,381	362,961
Occupied housing units by house heating fuel - utility gas 1990 (sample)	62,517	49,519	219,538	440,040
Occupied housing units by house heating fuel - utility gas 2000 (sample)	88,243	65,603	266,709	594,702
	Utah County	Davis County	Salt Lake County	State
Occupied housing units by house heating fuel - bottled, tank, or LP gas 1990 (sample)	1,012	288	1,432	12,279
Occupied housing units by house heating fuel - bottled, tank, or LP gas 2000 (sample)	2,094	435	2,241	20,911
Occupied housing units by house heating fuel - electricity 1980 (sample)	4,855	2,590	12,376	45,896
Occupied housing units by house heating fuel - electricity 1990 (sample)	4,509	3,208	16,687	51,047
Occupied housing units by house heating fuel - electricity 2000 (sample)	8,760	4,952	24,284	68,433
Occupied housing units by house heating fuel - fuel oil, kerosene, etc. 1980 (sample)	503	108	611	11,132
Occupied housing units by house heating fuel - fuel oil, kerosene, etc. 1990 (sample)	257	19	391	7,048
Occupied housing units by house heating fuel - fuel oil, kerosene, etc. 2000 (sample)	161	23	159	3,851
Occupied housing units by house heating fuel - coal or coke 1980 (sample)	577	55	621	9,734
Occupied housing units by house heating fuel - coal or coke 1990 (sample)	586	18	285	7,202
Occupied housing units by house heating fuel - coal or coke 2000 (sample)	127	0	81	2,691
Occupied housing units by house heating fuel - wood 1980 (sample)	473	219	539	7,476

	Utah County	Davis County	Salt Lake County	State
Occupied housing units by house heating fuel - wood 1990 (sample)	1,065	449	1,218	17,349
Occupied housing units by house heating fuel - wood 2000 (sample)	289	112	329	7,756
Occupied housing units by house heating fuel - solar energy 1990 (sample)	110	40	119	525
Occupied housing units by house heating fuel - solar energy 2000 (sample)	17	0	85	261
Occupied housing units by house heating fuel - other fuel used 1990 (sample)	66	57	765	1,326
	Utah County	**Davis County**	**Salt Lake County**	**State**
Occupied housing units by house heating fuel - other fuel used 2000 (sample)	189	41	821	1,899
Occupied housing units by house heating fuel - no fuel used 1980 (sample)	18	0	37	131
Occupied housing units by house heating fuel - no fuel used 1990 (sample)	46	0	245	457
Occupied housing units by house heating fuel - no fuel used 2000 (sample)	57	35	432	777

Source: U.S. Census Bureau

5.3.4.12   Occupied Housing Units by Vehicles Available, Comparison Counties and State

	Utah County	Davis County	Salt Lake County	State
Occupied housing units with no vehicles available 1980 (sample)	2,624	943	14,803	26,894
Occupied housing units with no vehicles available 1990 (sample)	2,825	1,454	16,209	29,068
Occupied housing units with no vehicles available 2000 (sample)	3,402	2,245	18,574	35,610
Occupied housing units with one vehicle available 1980 (sample)	17,754	10,221	63,939	131,897
Occupied housing units with one vehicle available 1990 (sample)	18,720	12,477	75,033	152,986
Occupied housing units with one vehicle available 2000 (sample)	23,678	16,028	86,847	188,899
Occupied housing units with 2 or more vehicles available 1980 (sample)	38,137	28,830	123,000	289,812
Occupied housing units with 2 or more vehicles available 1990 (sample)	48,623	39,667	149,438	355,219
Occupied housing units with 2 or more vehicles available 2000 (sample)	72,857	52,928	189,720	476,772
Occupied housing units with 2 vehicles available 1990 (sample)	29,102	25,156	98,999	224,752
Occupied housing units with 2 vehicles available 2000 (sample)	43,338	31,632	121,793	293,769
Occupied housing units with 3 vehicles available 1990 (sample)	12,542	10,164	36,286	91,347
Occupied housing units with 3 vehicles available 2000 (sample)	18,254	14,132	45,431	120,676
Occupied housing units with 4 vehicles available 1990 (sample)	4,926	3,057	10,449	28,211
Occupied housing units with 4 vehicles available 2000 (sample)	7,601	4,721	15,653	42,789
Occupied housing units with 5 or more vehicles available 1990 (sample)	2,053	1,290	3,704	10,909
Occupied housing units with 5 or more vehicles available 2000 (sample)	3,664	2,443	6,843	19,538

Source: U.S. Census Bureau

5.3.4.13 Historical Owner-Occupied Housing Values, Comparison Counties and State

	Utah County	Davis County	Salt Lake County	State
Specified owner-occupied housing units with value less than $20,000 1980 (complete count)	673	255	1,635	7,317
Specified owner-occupied housing units with value less than $20,000 1990 (complete count)	187	48	546	3,598
Specified owner-occupied housing units with value less than $20,000 2000 (sample)	103	8	234	1,477
Specified owner-occupied housing units with value of $20,000 to $29,999 1980 (complete count)	1,044	570	3,842	12,581
Specified owner-occupied housing units with value of $20,000 to $29,999 1990 (complete count)	437	136	1,515	6,449
Specified owner-occupied housing units with value of $20,000 to $29,999 2000 (sample)	5	21	187	1,038
Specified owner-occupied housing units with value of $30,000 to $39,999 1980 (complete count)	2,151	1,543	9,795	24,829

	Utah County	Davis County	Salt Lake County	State
Specified owner-occupied housing units with value of $30,000 to $39,999 1990 (complete count)	1,617	560	6,175	16,522
Specified owner-occupied housing units with value of $30,000 to $39,999 2000 (sample)	34	48	257	1,571
Specified owner-occupied housing units with value of $40,000 to $49,999 1980 (complete count)	4,706	3,668	21,609	46,690
Specified owner-occupied housing units with value of $40,000 to $49,999 1990 (complete count)	4,154	2,149	15,658	34,486
Specified owner-occupied housing units with value of $40,000 to $49,999 2000 (sample)	65	48	253	2,233
Specified owner-occupied housing units with value of $50,000 to $99,999 1980 (complete count)	19,526	17,311	66,652	143,580
Specified owner-occupied housing units with value of $50,000 to $99,999 1990 (complete count)	23,675	23,620	83,883	188,574
Specified owner-occupied housing units with value of $50,000 to $99,999 2000 (sample)	3,760	4,073	13,463	62,324
Specified owner-occupied housing units with value of $100,000 to $149,999 1980 (complete count)	2,668	2,544	9,020	18,275
Specified owner-occupied housing units with value of $100,000 to $149,999 1990 (complete count)	4,376	5,294	16,923	35,185
Specified owner-occupied housing units with value of $100,000 to $149,999 2000 (sample)	22,034	17,786	66,673	158,172
Specified owner-occupied housing units with value of $150,000 to $199,999 1980 (complete count)	644	480	2,540	4,399
Specified owner-occupied housing units with value of $150,000 to $199,999 1990 (complete count)	1,278	1,426	5,715	10,641
Specified owner-occupied housing units with value of $150,000 to $199,999 2000 (sample)	16,118	13,995	48,241	101,538

	Utah County	Davis County	Salt Lake County	State
Specified owner-occupied housing units with value of $200,000 or more 1980 (complete count)	406	217	1,814	2,847
Specified owner-occupied housing units with value of $200,000 or more 1990 (complete count)	1,050	732	4,964	8,269
Specified owner-occupied housing units with value of $200,000 or more 2000 (sample)	14,876	12,405	49,012	98,891
Specified owner-occupied housing units with value of $200,000 to $299,999 1990 (complete count)	726	588	3,366	5,727
Specified owner-occupied housing units with value of $200,000 to $299,999 2000 (sample)	9,978	8,443	31,248	64,318
Specified owner-occupied housing units with value of $300,000 to $399,999 1990 (complete count)	175	87	910	1,439
Specified owner-occupied housing units with value of $300,000 to $399,999 2000 (sample)	2,770	2,417	9,460	18,632
Specified owner-occupied housing units with value of $400,000 to $499,999 1990 (complete count)	56	25	317	489
Specified owner-occupied housing units with value of $400,000 to $499,999 2000 (sample)	937	777	4,045	7,452
Specified owner-occupied housing units with value of $500,000 or more 1990 (complete count)	93	32	371	614
Specified owner-occupied housing units with value of $500,000 or more 2000 (sample)	1,191	768	4,259	8,489
Specified owner-occupied housing units with value of $500,000 to $749,999 2000 (sample)	676	549	2,811	5,333
Specified owner-occupied housing units with value of $750,000 to $999,999 2000 (sample)	260	142	778	1,582
Specified owner-occupied housing units with value of $1,000,000 or more 2000 (sample)	255	77	670	1,574

Source: U.S. Census Bureau

5.3.4.14   Housing Values, Homes with a Mortgage

Owner-occupied housing units with a mortgage	73,274
VALUE	
Less than $50,000	1.10%
$50,000 to $99,999	0.80%
$100,000 to $149,999	8.40%
$150,000 to $199,999	22.00%
$200,000 to $299,999	36.70%
$300,000 to $499,999	24.10%
$500,000 or more	6.80%
Median (dollars)	238,400

Source: U.S. Census Bureau

5.3.4.15   Mortgage Status

With either a second mortgage, or home equity loan, but not both	29.90%
Second mortgage only	11.30%
Home equity loan only	18.60%
Both second mortgage and home equity loan	0.70%
No second mortgage and no home equity loan	69.40%

Source: U.S. Census Bureau

5.3.4.16   Household Income, Households with a Mortgage

Less than $10,000	2.20%
$10,000 to $24,999	3.90%
$25,000 to $34,999	5.50%
$35,000 to $49,999	12.90%
$50,000 to $74,999	27.20%
$75,000 to $99,999	19.40%
$100,000 to $149,999	18.60%
$150,000 or more	10.30%
Median household income (dollars)	73,594

Source: U.S. Census Bureau

5.3.4.17   Ratio of Home Value to Household Income, Homes with a Mortgage

Less than 2.0	16.40%
2.0 to 2.9	27.30%
3.0 to 3.9	22.90%
4.0 or more	32.80%
Not computed	0.70%

Source: U.S. Census Bureau

5.3.4.18   Monthly Housing Costs, Homes with a Mortgage

Less than $200	0.0%
$200 to $299	0.1%
$300 to $399	0.3%
$400 to $499	0.8%
$500 to $599	0.5%
$600 to $699	1.5%
$700 to $799	2.2%
$800 to $899	3.0%
$900 to $999	3.6%
$1,000 to $1,249	15.5%
$1,250 to $1,499	19.2%
$1,500 to $1,999	27.4%
$2,000 or more	25.8%
Median (dollars)	1,550

Source: U.S. Census Bureau

5.3.4.19 Monthly Housing Costs as a Percent of Household Income

Less than $20,000	4.00%
Less than 20 percent	0.00%
20 to 29 percent	0.00%
30 percent or more	4.00%
$20,000 to $34,999	7.00%
Less than 20 percent	0.20%
20 to 29 percent	0.50%
30 percent or more	6.30%
$35,000 to $49,999	12.90%
Less than 20 percent	0.90%
20 to 29 percent	2.00%
30 percent or more	10.00%
$50,000 to $74,999	27.20%
Less than 20 percent	3.60%
20 to 29 percent	12.70%
30 percent or more	10.80%
$75,000 or more	48.20%
Less than 20 percent	25.50%
20 to 29 percent	17.50%
30 percent or more	5.20%
Zero or negative income	0.70%

Source: U.S. Census Bureau

5.3.4.20 Real Estate Taxes Paid

Less than $800	11.20%
$800 to $1,499	51.90%
$1,500 or more	35.70%
No real estate taxes paid	1.20%
Median (dollars)	1,313

Source: U.S. Census Bureau

5.3.4.21 Real Estate Taxes Paid, Owner-Occupied Homes with a Mortgage vs. Owner-Occupied Homes without a Mortgage

	Utah County	Davis County	Salt Lake County
All Owner-Occupied Units	$1,309	$1,405	$1,578
Units with a Mortgage	$1,313	$1,432	$1,587
Units without a Mortgage	$1,296	$1,296	$1,544

Source: U.S. Census Bureau

5.3.4.22 Historical Median Rent, Comparison Counties and State

	Utah County	Davis County	Salt Lake County	State
Median contract rent of specified renter-occupied housing units paying cash rent 1980 (complete count)	$ 174	$ 211	$ 204	$ 190
Median contract rent of specified renter-occupied housing units paying cash rent 1990 (complete count)	$ 288	$ 329	$ 316	$ 300
Median contract rent of specified renter-occupied housing units paying cash rent 2000 (sample)	$ 523	$ 573	$ 578	$ 534

Source: U.S. Census Bureau

5.3.4.23   Historical Contract Rent, Comparison Counties and State

	Utah County	Davis County	Salt Lake County	State
Specified renter-occupied housing units with contract rent of less than $100 1990 (complete count)	415	533	1,875	5,120
Specified renter-occupied housing units with contract rent of $100 to $199 1990 (complete count)	3,071	793	6,179	18,324
Specified renter-occupied housing units with contract rent of $100 to $199 2000 (sample)	731	439	2,249	6,702
Specified renter-occupied housing units with contract rent of $200 to $299 1990 (complete count)	10,547	3,799	27,573	57,142
Specified renter-occupied housing units with contract rent of $200 to $299 2000 (sample)	3,296	381	2,567	11,840
Specified renter-occupied housing units with contract rent of $300 to $399 1990 (complete count)	5,142	4,292	27,911	47,773
Specified renter-occupied housing units with contract rent of $300 to $399 2000 (sample)	2,507	1,273	5,745	19,899
Specified renter-occupied housing units with contract rent of $400 to $499 1990 (complete count)	1,928	2,271	11,273	19,137
Specified renter-occupied housing units with contract rent of $400 to $499 2000 (sample)	7,116	2,149	16,291	38,547
Specified renter-occupied housing units with contract rent of $500 to $599 1990 (complete count)	965	620	3,524	6,579
Specified renter-occupied housing units with contract rent of $500 to $599 2000 (sample)	6,468	3,886	21,326	40,413
Specified renter-occupied housing units with contract rent of $600 to $699 1990 (complete count)	1,141	261	1,432	3,550
Specified renter-occupied housing units with contract rent of $600 to $699 2000 (sample)	4,161	2,899	17,335	29,140

Specified renter-occupied housing units with contract rent of $700 to $999 1990 (complete count)	1,492	146	1,167	3,293
Specified renter-occupied housing units with contract rent of $700 to $999 2000 (sample)	4,411	2,584	16,829	28,510
Specified renter-occupied housing units with contract rent of $700 to $799 2000 (sample)	2,191	1,256	8,327	14,099
Specified renter-occupied housing units with contract rent of $800 to $899 2000 (sample)	1,225	967	5,253	8,955
Specified renter-occupied housing units with contract rent of $900 to $999 2000 (sample)	995	361	3,249	5,456
Specified renter-occupied housing units with contract rent of $1,000 or more 1990 (complete count)	131	33	379	690
Specified renter-occupied housing units with contract rent of $1,000 or more 2000 (sample)	2,434	646	5,335	10,466
Specified renter-occupied housing units with contract rent of $1,000 to $1,499 2000 (sample)	2,139	576	4,135	8,402
Specified renter-occupied housing units with contract rent of $1,500 to $1,999 2000 (sample)	265	70	853	1,552
Specified renter-occupied housing units with contract rent of $2,000 or more 2000 (sample)	30	0	347	512

Source: U.S. Census Bureau

5.3.4.24   Owner- vs. Renter-Occupied Rates, Utah MSAs, 2009

	Owner Occupied	Renter Occupied
Logan, UT-ID Metro Area	66.3%	33.7%
Ogden-Clearfield, UT Metro Area	76.8%	23.2%
Provo-Orem, UT Metro Area	71.9%	28.1%
St. George, UT Metro Area	69.6%	30.4%
Salt Lake City, UT Metro Area	69.5%	30.5%

Source: U.S. Census Bureau

5.3.4.25   Owner-Occupied Units, by Year Built, Utah MSAs

	Logan, UT-ID Metro Area	Ogden-Clearfield, UT Metro Area	Provo-Orem, UT Metro Area	St. George, UT Metro Area	Salt Lake City, UT Metro Area
Total owner occupied units	25,035	129,945	98,925	32,141	253,160
Built 2005 or later	9.6%	7.6%	11.0%	13.4%	4.8%
Built 2000 to 2004	13.0%	12.7%	18.1%	24.5%	10.1%
Built 1990 to 1999	22.8%	21.4%	26.4%	33.0%	19.0%
Built 1980 to 1989	8.2%	12.0%	8.4%	14.7%	13.8%
Built 1970 to 1979	19.8%	17.7%	15.8%	9.3%	20.4%
Built 1960 to 1969	5.3%	9.6%	4.8%	0.9%	8.8%
Built 1950 to 1959	4.2%	11.2%	5.3%	0.5%	11.6%
Built 1940 to 1949	3.8%	3.1%	4.3%	1.4%	3.8%
Built 1939 or earlier	13.4%	4.6%	5.8%	2.4%	7.7%
Median year built	1984	1983	1992	1996	1979

Source: U.S. Census Bureau

5.3.4.26   Values, Owner-Occupied Units, by Utah MSAs, 2009

	Logan, UT-ID Metro Area	Ogden-Clearfield, UT Metro Area	Provo-Orem, UT Metro Area	St. George, UT Metro Area	Salt Lake City, UT Metro Area
< $50,000	4.1%	4.4%	2.9%	3.8%	3.4%
$50,000 to $99,999	3.5%	3.8%	1.4%	3.1%	1.8%
$100,000 to $149,999	20.0%	13.5%	7.2%	6.5%	6.8%
$150,000 to $199,999	24.9%	23.2%	15.9%	13.9%	17.3%
$200,000 to $299,999	32.1%	30.0%	35.7%	33.1%	33.0%
$300,000 to $499,999	10.2%	19.4%	26.4%	28.9%	25.8%
$500,000 to $999,999	3.8%	4.7%	8.4%	10.0%	9.9%
$1,000,000 or more	1.3%	1.0%	2.1%	0.7%	1.9%
Median value	$194,600	$214,100	$256,500	$262,400	$256,000

Source: U.S. Census Bureau

5.3.4.27   Renter-Occupied Units, by Year Built, Utah MSAs

	Logan, UT-ID Metro Area	Ogden-Clearfield, UT Metro Area	Provo-Orem, UT Metro Area	St. George, UT Metro Area	Salt Lake City, UT Metro Area
Total Renter occupied units	12,710	39,272	38,617	14,069	110,918
Built 2005 or later	6.4%	3.6%	6.0%	12.3%	4.6%
Built 2000 to 2004	11.6%	10.3%	8.7%	24.7%	6.5%
Built 1990 to 1999	11.8%	16.9%	24.1%	24.2%	16.0%
Built 1980 to 1989	20.1%	12.3%	10.4%	14.2%	16.6%
Built 1970 to 1979	13.3%	19.9%	22.8%	15.7%	22.9%
Built 1960 to 1969	11.5%	11.8%	11.5%	2.4%	11.5%
Built 1950 to 1959	8.6%	6.7%	5.5%	3.7%	7.4%
Built 1940 to 1949	4.8%	6.6%	3.3%	0.1%	3.8%
Built 1939 or earlier	12.0%	11.8%	7.7%	2.8%	10.8%
Median year built	1980	1977	1980	1995	1977

Source: U.S. Census Bureau

5.3.4.28   Occupants per Room, Owner-Occupied Housing, Comparison Counties

	Utah County	Davis County	Salt Lake County
.50 or fewer occupants per room	67.4%	68.7%	74.4%
0.51 to 1.00 occupants per room	30.3%	29.4%	24.0%
1.01 or more occupants per room	2.3%	1.9%	1.6%

Source: U.S. Census Bureau

5.3.4.29   Occupants per Room, Renter-Occupied Housing, Comparison Counties

	Utah County	Davis County	Salt Lake County
.50 or fewer occupants per room	43.2%	54.9%	58.7%
0.51 to 1.00 occupants per room	52.5%	40.3%	35.4%
1.01 or more occupants per room	4.3%	4.8%	5.9%

Source: U.S. Census Bureau

5.3.4.30   Rooms per Housing Unit, Owner-Occupied, Comparison Counties

	Utah County	Davis County	Salt Lake County
1 to 3 Room	0.6%	0.6%	1.6%
4 Room	5.0%	4.5%	6.7%
5 Rooms	11.1%	11.0%	13.3%
6 Rooms	12.8%	14.7%	15.5%
7 or More Rooms	70.4%	69.2%	62.9%

Source: U.S. Census Bureau

5.3.4.31   Rooms per Housing Unit, Renter-Occupied, Comparison Counties

	Utah County	Davis County	Salt Lake County
1 to 3 Room	15.7%	17.1%	32.4%
4 Room	27.9%	31.4%	28.7%
5 Rooms	23.1%	23.3%	15.7%
6 Rooms	10.8%	8.7%	7.4%
7 or More Rooms	22.6%	19.4%	15.8%

Source: U.S. Census Bureau

5.3.4.32   Owner-Occupied Housing with a Mortgage by Age of Householder, Comparison Counties

	Utah County	Davis County	Salt Lake County
15 to 34 years Old	23.0%	28.2%	24.6%
35 to 64 years Old	68.5%	63.3%	66.4%
65 Years or Older	8.4%	8.5%	9.0%

Source: U.S. Census Bureau

5.3.4.33   Owner-Occupied Housing without a Mortgage by Age of Householder, Comparison Counties

	Utah County	Davis County	Salt Lake County
15 to 34 years Old	4.3%	5.9%	5.0%
35 to 64 years Old	42.5%	39.9%	43.6%
65 Years or Older	53.2%	54.3%	51.5%

Source: U.S. Census Bureau

5.3.4.34   Ratio of Home Value to Household Income, Homes with a Mortgage, Comparison Counties

	Utah County	Davis County	Salt Lake County
< 2.0	16.4%	18.1%	14.4%
2.0 to 2.9	27.3%	32.6%	29.3%
3.0 to 3.9	22.9%	21.3%	21.9%
4.0+	32.8%	27.9%	33.8%

Source: U.S. Census Bureau

250

5.3.4.35   Ratio of Home Value to Household Income, Homes without a Mortgage, Comparison Counties

	Utah County	Davis County	Salt Lake County
< 2.0	21.3%	24.9%	18.1%
2.0 to 2.9	13.5%	18.6%	17.8%
3.0 to 3.9	14.0%	13.3%	12.1%
4.0+	50.2%	43.2%	51.3%

Source: U.S. Census Bureau

5.3.4.36   Aggregate Annual Household Income, Owner- and Renter-Occupied, by Mortgage Status, Comparison Counties

	Utah County	Davis County	Salt Lake County
Aggregate Annual Household Income	$9,841,030,300	$7,203,205,400	$24,303,185,500
Aggregate Annual Household Income, Owner-Occupied Units	$8,046,332,000	$6,322,576,800	$19,797,848,300
Aggregate Annual Household Income, Owner-Occupied Units with a Mortgage	$6,377,252,800	$5,187,359,200	$15,624,389,700
Aggregate Annual Household Income, Owner-Occupied Units without a Mortgage	$1,669,079,200	$1,135,217,600	$4,173,458,600
Aggregate Annual Household Income, Renter-Occupied Units	$1,794,698,300	$880,628,600	$4,505,337,200

Source: U.S. Census Bureau

5.3.4.37   Contract Rent, Comparison Counties

	Utah County	Davis County	Salt Lake County
< $200	1.4%	3.6%	2.5%
$200 to $299	3.1%	1.2%	1.9%
$300 to $499	9.9%	9.6%	8.2%
$500 to $749	38.7%	33.6%	38.2%
$750 to $999	19.5%	30.7%	26.4%
$1,000+	27.3%	21.3%	22.8%
Median Contract Rent	$727	$764	$745

Source: U.S. Census Bureau

5.3.5 Homelessness

5.3.5.1 2010 Utah Point-in-Time Homeless Count: Households

County	Households with Minor Children			Households without Children			Individuals			Unaccompanied Children			Total Households
	Sheltered	Unsheltered	Total	Sheltered	Unsheltered	Total	Sheltered	Unsheltered	Total	Sheltered	Unsheltered	Total	
Beaver	0	0	0	0	0	0	0	0	0	0	0	0	0
Box Elder	5	0	5	0	0	0	2	0	2	0	0	0	7
Cache	30	0	30	0	0	0	10	1	11	0	0	0	41
Carbon	1	0	1	0	0	0	17	0	17	0	0	0	18
Daggett	0	0	0	0	0	0	0	0	0	0	0	0	0
Davis	33	1	34	1	0	1	14	1	15	0	0	0	50
Duchesne	0	4	4	0	0	0	0	3	3	0	4	4	11
Emery	0	0	0	0	0	0	0	0	0	0	0	0	0
Garfield	0	0	0	0	0	0	0	0	0	0	0	0	0
Grand	7	0	7	1	0	1	2	16	18	0	0	0	26
Iron	7	0	7	0	0	0	86	0	86	0	0	0	93
Juab	0	0	0	0	0	0	0	0	0	0	0	0	0
Kane	0	0	0	0	0	0	0	0	0	0	0	0	0
Millard	0	0	0	0	0	0	0	0	0	0	0	0	0
Morgan	0	0	0	0	0	0	0	0	0	0	0	0	0
Piute	0	0	0	0	0	0	0	0	0	0	0	0	0
Rich	0	0	0	0	0	0	0	0	0	0	0	0	0
Salt Lake	222	1	223	7	2	9	1,026	206	1,232	0	0	0	1,464
San Juan	6	0	6	1	0	1	1	31	32	0	0	0	39
Sanpete	0	0	0	0	0	0	0	4	4	0	0	0	4
Sevier	8	0	8	1	0	1	10	0	10	0	0	0	19
Summit	6	0	6	0	0	0	4	0	4	0	0	0	10
Tooele	4	0	4	1	1	2	6	14	20	0	0	0	26
Uintah	3	1	4	0	0	0	5	12	17	0	0	0	21
Utah	24	2	26	3	4	7	65	184	249	0	0	0	282

	Households with Minor Children			Households without Children			Individuals			Unaccompanied Children			Total Households
	Sheltered	Unsheltered	Total	Sheltered	Unsheltered	Total	Sheltered	Unsheltered	Total	Sheltered	Unsheltered	Total	
Wasatch	0	0	0	0	0	0	0	1	1	0	0	0	1
Washington	20	0	20	2	0	2	22	0	22	0	0	0	44
Wayne	0	0	0	0	0	0	0	1	1	0	0	0	1
Weber	19	0	19	4	0	4	164	39	203	0	0	0	226
Totals	395	9	404	21	7	28	1,434	513	1,947	0	4	4	2,383

Source: Comprehensive Report on Homelessness, State of Utah, 2009 and 2010

5.3.5.2 2010 Utah Point-in-Time Homeless Count: Race

County	American Indian, Alaskan Native			Asian			Black, African American			Native Hawaiian, Pacific Islander			White			Other, Multi-racial, Unknown			Refused		
	Sheltered	Unsheltered	Total	Sheltered	Unsheltered	Total	Sheltered	Unsheltered	Total	Sheltered	Unsheltered	Total	Sheltered	Unsheltered	Total	Sheltered	Unsheltered	Total	Sheltered	Unsheltered	Total
Beaver	0	0	0	0	0	0	0	0	0	0	0	0	0	0	0	0	0	0	0	0	0
Box Elder	4	0	4	0	0	0	1	0	1	0	0	0	4	0	4	10	0	10	0	0	0
Cache	6	0	6	2	0	2	9	0	9	12	0	12	64	0	64	24	1	25	0	0	0
Carbon	0	0	0	0	0	0	0	0	0	0	0	0	19	0	19	2	0	2	0	0	0
Daggett	0	0	0	0	0	0	0	0	0	0	0	0	0	0	0	0	0	0	0	0	0
Davis	0	0	0	0	0	0	2	0	2	4	0	4	93	2	95	25	1	26	0	0	0
Duchesne	0	0	0	0	0	0	0	0	0	0	0	0	0	0	0	0	22	22	0	0	0
Emery	0	0	0	0	0	0	0	0	0	0	0	0	0	0	0	0	0	0	0	0	0
Garfield	0	0	0	0	0	0	0	0	0	0	0	0	0	0	0	0	0	0	0	0	0
Grand	0	3	3	0	0	0	0	0	0	0	0	0	24	11	35	1	2	3	0	0	0
Iron	5	0	5	0	0	0	3	0	3	1	0	1	91	0	91	3	0	3	0	0	0
Juab	0	0	0	0	0	0	0	0	0	0	0	0	0	0	0	0	0	0	0	0	0
Kane	0	0	0	0	0	0	0	0	0	0	0	0	0	0	0	0	0	0	0	0	0
Millard	0	0	0	0	0	0	0	0	0	0	0	0	0	0	0	0	0	0	0	0	0
Morgan	0	0	0	0	0	0	0	0	0	0	0	0	0	0	0	0	0	0	0	0	0
Piute	0	0	0	0	0	0	0	0	0	0	0	0	0	0	0	0	0	0	0	0	0
Rich	0	0	0	0	0	0	0	0	0	0	0	0	0	0	0	0	0	0	0	0	0
Salt Lake	73	4	77	17	0	17	185	1	186	23	0	23	1,084	66	1,150	427	141	568	0	1	1
San Juan	11	0	11	0	0	0	0	0	0	0	0	0	9	0	9	5	31	36	0	0	0
Sanpete	0	0	0	0	0	0	0	0	0	0	0	0	0	0	0	0	4	4	0	0	0
Sevier	8	0	8	0	0	0	0	0	0	0	0	0	26	0	26	4	0	4	0	0	0
Summit	0	0	0	0	0	0	1	0	1	0	0	0	11	0	11	7	0	7	0	0	0
Tooele	0	1	1	0	0	0	0	0	0	1	0	1	10	4	14	7	11	18	0	0	0
Uintah	0	0	0	0	0	0	0	0	0	0	0	0	7	0	7	9	15	24	0	0	0
Utah	6	0	6	1	0	1	2	1	3	3	0	3	109	46	155	23	152	175	0	1	1

	American Indian, Alaskan Native			Asian			Black, African American			Native Hawaiian, Pacific Islander			White			Other, Multi-racial, Unknown			Refused		
	Sheltered	Unsheltered	Total	Sheltered	Unsheltered	Total	Sheltered	Unsheltered	Total	Sheltered	Unsheltered	Total	Sheltered	Unsheltered	Total	Sheltered	Unsheltered	Total	Sheltered	Unsheltered	Total
Wasatch	0	0	0	0	0	0	0	0	0	0	0	0	0	0	0	0	0	0	0	1	1
Washington	8	0	8	0	0	0	0	0	0	1	0	1	84	0	84	4	0	4	0	0	0
Wayne	0	0	0	0	0	0	0	0	0	0	0	0	0	0	0	0	1	1	0	0	0
Weber	6	1	7	4	1	5	19	4	23	0	0	0	166	25	191	40	8	48	0	0	0
Totals	127	9	136	24	1	25	222	6	228	45	0	45	1,801	154	1,955	591	389	980	0	3	3

Source: Comprehensive Report on Homelessness, State of Utah, 2009 and 2010

5.3.5.3 2010 Utah Point-in-Time Homeless Count: Hispanic or Latino

County	Hispanic or Latino			Non-Hispanic or Non-Latino			Unknown			Refused			Totals		
	Sheltered	Unsheltered	Total	Sheltered	Unsheltered	Total	Sheltered	Unsheltered	Total	Sheltered1	Unsheltered	Total	Sheltered	Unsheltered	Total
Beaver	0	0	0	0	0	0	0	0	0	0	0	0	0	0	0
Box Elder	9	0	9	10	0	10	0	0	0	0	0	0	19	0	19
Cache	23	0	23	94	0	94	0	1	1	0	0	0	117	1	118
Carbon	3	0	3	18	0	18	0	0	0	0	0	0	21	0	21
Daggett	0	0	0	0	0	0	0	0	0	0	0	0	0	0	0
Davis	26	0	26	98	2	100	0	1	1	0	0	0	124	3	127
Duchesne	0	0	0	0	0	0	0	22	22	0	0	0	0	22	22
Emery	0	0	0	0	0	0	0	0	0	0	0	0	0	0	0
Garfield	0	0	0	0	0	0	0	0	0	0	0	0	0	0	0
Grand	1	0	1	24	12	36	0	3	3	0	1	1	25	16	41
Iron	4	0	4	99	0	99	0	0	0	0	0	0	103	0	103
Juab	0	0	0	0	0	0	0	0	0	0	0	0	0	0	0
Kane	0	0	0	0	0	0	0	0	0	0	0	0	0	0	0
Millard	0	0	0	0	0	0	0	0	0	0	0	0	0	0	0
Morgan	0	0	0	0	0	0	0	0	0	0	0	0	0	0	0
Piute	0	0	0	0	0	0	0	0	0	0	0	0	0	0	0
Rich	0	0	0	0	0	0	0	0	0	0	0	0	0	0	0
Salt Lake	446	14	460	1,345	60	1,405	18	138	156	0	1	1	1,809	213	2,022
San Juan	0	0	0	20	0	20	5	31	36	0	0	0	25	31	56
Sanpete	0	0	0	0	0	0	0	4	4	0	0	0	0	4	4
Sevier	4	0	4	33	0	33	1	0	1	0	0	0	38	0	38
Summit	7	0	7	12	0	12	0	0	0	0	0	0	19	0	19
Tooele	5	2	7	8	4	12	5	10	15	0	0	0	18	16	34
Uintah	7	0	7	9	0	9	0	15	15	0	0	0	16	15	31
Utah	22	4	26	122	46	168	0	150	150	0	0	0	144	200	344
Wasatch	0	0	0	0	0	0	0	0	0	0	1	1	0	1	1

	Hispanic or Latino			Non-Hispanic or Non-Latino			Unknown			Refused			Totals		
	Sheltered	Unsheltered	Total	Sheltered	Unsheltered	Total	Sheltered	Unsheltered	Total	Sheltered1	Unsheltered	Total	Sheltered	Unsheltered	Total
Washington	28	0	28	69	0	69	0	0	0	0	0	0	97	0	97
Wayne	0	0	0	0	0	0	0	1	1	0	0	0	0	1	1
Weber	41	4	45	193	28	221	1	7	8	0	0	0	235	39	274
Totals	626	24	650	2,154	152	2,306	30	383	413	0	3	3	2,810	562	3,372

Source: Comprehensive Report on Homelessness, State of Utah, 2009 and 2010

5.3.5.4 2010 Utah Point-it-Time Homeless Count: Subpopulations: Mental Illness, Substance Abuse, HIV/AIDS

County	Mental illness				Chronic substance abuse				HIV/AIDS			
	Sheltered	Unsheltered	Total	% of Homeless Adults	Sheltered	Unsheltered	Total	% of Homeless Adults	Sheltered	Unsheltered	Total	% of Homeless Adults
Beaver	0	0	0		0	0	0		0	0	0	
Box Elder	1	0	1		1	0	1		0	0	0	
Cache	8	0	8		3	0	3		0	0	0	
Carbon	10	0	10		9	0	9		0	0	0	
Daggett	0	0	0		0	0	0		0	0	0	
Davis	16	1	17		8	0	8		0	0	0	
Duchesne	0	0	0		0	0	0		0	0	0	
Emery	0	0	0		0	0	0		0	0	0	
Garfield	0	0	0		0	0	0		0	0	0	
Grand	0	3	3		0	6	6		0	0	0	
Iron	24	0	24		45	0	45		0	0	0	
Juab	0	0	0		0	0	0		0	0	0	
Kane	0	0	0		0	0	0		0	0	0	
Millard	0	0	0		0	0	0		0	0	0	
Morgan	0	0	0		0	0	0		0	0	0	
Piute	0	0	0		0	0	0		0	0	0	
Rich	0	0	0		0	0	0		0	0	0	
Salt Lake	350	18	368		400	13	413		8	0	8	
San Juan	0	0	0		1	0	1		0	0	0	
Sanpete	0	0	0		0	0	0		0	0	0	
Sevier	1	0	1		8	0	8		0	0	0	
Summit	2	0	2		3	0	3		0	0	0	
Tooele	2	0	2		4	0	4		0	0	0	

	Mental illness				Chronic substance abuse				HIV/AIDS			
	Sheltered	Unsheltered	Total	% of Homeless Adults	Sheltered	Unsheltered	Total	% of Homeless Adults	Sheltered	Unsheltered	Total	% of Homeless Adults
Uintah	1	0	1		3	0	3		1	0	1	
Utah	23	6	29		45	10	55		7	0	7	
Wasatch	0	0	0		0	0	0		0	0	0	
Washington	2	0	2		4	0	4		0	0	0	
Wayne	0	0	0		0	0	0		0	0	0	
Weber	47	7	54		32	12	44		0	0	0	
Totals	487	35	522	21.06	566	41	607	24.49	16	0	16	0.65

Source: Comprehensive Report on Homelessness, State of Utah, 2009 and 2010

5.3.5.5 2010 Utah Point-in-Time Homeless Count: Subpopulations: Victims of Domestic Violence, Veterans

County	Victims of domestic violence				Veterans			
	Sheltered	Unsheltered	Total	% of Homeless Adults	Sheltered	Unsheltered	Total	% of Homeless Adults
Beaver	0	0	0		0	0	0	
Box Elder	7	0	7		0	0	0	
Cache	37	0	37		0	0	0	
Carbon	1	0	1		3	0	3	
Daggett	0	0	0		0	0	0	
Davis	28	1	29		1	0	1	
Duchesne	0	0	0		0	0	0	
Emery	0	0	0		0	0	0	
Garfield	0	0	0		0	0	0	
Grand	2	4	6		0	2	2	
Iron	27	0	27		6	0	6	
Juab	0	0	0		0	0	0	
Kane	0	0	0		0	0	0	
Millard	0	0	0		0	0	0	
Morgan	0	0	0		0	0	0	
Piute	0	0	0		0	0	0	
Rich	0	0	0		0	0	0	
Salt Lake	208	17	225		229	22	251	
San Juan	9	0	9		0	0	0	
Sanpete	0	0	0		0	0	0	
Sevier	18	0	18		0	0	0	
Summit	5	0	5		1	0	1	
Tooele	5	1	6		0	0	0	
Uintah	2	0	2		1	0	1	
Utah	32	18	50		3	12	15	

	Victims of domestic violence				Veterans			
	Sheltered	Unsheltered	Total	% of Homeless Adults	Sheltered	Unsheltered	Total	% of Homeless Adults
Wasatch	0	0	0		0	0	0	
Washington	22	0	22		4	0	4	
Wayne	0	0	0		0	0	0	
Weber	42	7	49		50	5	55	
Totals	445	48	493	19.89	298	41	339	13.67

Source: Comprehensive Report on Homelessness, State of Utah, 2009 and 2010

5.3.5.6 2010 Utah Point-in-Time Homeless Count: Wasatch Front Summary, by Coordinating Committee

	WEBER & MORGAN	DAVIS	SALT LAKE	TOOELE	MOUNTAINLANDS	WASATCH FRONT TOTALS
POINT-IN-TIME						
HOMELESS - SHELTERED						
Individuals	164	14	1,026	6	69	1,279
Persons in Families	71	110	783	12	94	1,070
Unaccompanied Children	0	0	0	0	0	0
TOTAL SHELTERED	**235**	**124**	**1,809**	**18**	**163**	**2,349**
HOMELESS - UNSHELTERED						
Individuals	39	1	206	14	185	445
Persons in Families	0	2	7	2	16	27
Unaccompanied Children	0	0	0	0	0	0
TOTAL UNSHELTERED	**39**	**3**	**213**	**16**	**201**	472
TOTAL HOMELESS	**274**	**127**	**2,022**	**34**	**364**	**2,821**
Families with Children	19	34	223	4	32	312
Chronically Homeless						
Sheltered	13	1	89	2	12	117
Unsheltered	30	1	103	6	90	230
Total Chronically Homeless	**43**	**2**	**192**	**8**	**102**	347
Hospital Patients	6	0	27	0	11	44
Jail/Prison	4	18	145	0	58	225

	WEBER & MORGAN	DAVIS	SALT LAKE	TOOELE	MOUNTAINLANDS	WASATCH FRONT TOTALS
Homeless Veterans	55	1	251	0	16	323
Homeless School Children	1,214	1,073	4,086	645	2,569	9,587
ANNUALIZED HOMELESS ESTIMATES						
HOMELESS - SHELTERED						
Individuals	781	67	4,863	24	309	6,044
Persons in Families	355	550	3,915	60	470	5,350
Unaccompanied Children	0	0	0	0	0	0
TOTAL SHELTERED	**1,136**	**617**	**8,778**	**84**	**779**	**11,394**
HOMELESS - UNSHELTERED						
Individuals	105	2	721	52	655	1,535
Persons in Families	0	10	35	10	80	135
Unaccompanied Children	0	0	0	0	0	0
TOTAL UNSHELTERED	**105**	**12**	**756**	**62**	**735**	**1,670**
TOTAL HOMELESS	**1,241**	**629**	**9,534**	**146**	**1,514**	**13,064**
Families with Children	95	170	1115	20	160	**1,560**
% of 2009 Est. Population	**0.52%**	**0.20%**	**0.91%**	**0.25%**	**0.25%**	**0.58%**
Chronically Homeless	86	4	384	16	204	694

Source: Comprehensive Report on Homelessness, State of Utah, 2009 and 2010

	BEAR RIVER ASSOCIATION OF GOVERNMENTS	CARBON & EMERY	FIVE COUNTY	GRAND	SAN JUAN	SIX COUNTY	UINTAH BASIN	RURAL AREAS	STATE TOTALS
POINT-IN-TIME									
HOMELESS - SHELTERED									
Individuals	12	17	108	2	1	10	5	155	1,434
Persons in Families	124	4	92	23	24	28	11	306	1,376
Unaccompanied Children	0	0	0	0	0	0	0	0	0
TOTAL SHELTERED	**136**	**21**	**200**	**25**	**25**	**38**	**16**	**461**	**2,810**
HOMELESS - UNSHELTERED									
Individuals	1	0	0	16	31	5	15	68	513
Persons in Families	0	0	0	0	0	0	18	18	45
Unaccompanied Children	0	0	0	0	0	0	4	4	4
TOTAL UNSHELTERED	**1**	**0**	**0**	**16**	**31**	**5**	**37**	**90**	**562**
TOTAL HOMELESS	**137**	**21**	**200**	**41**	**56**	**43**	**53**	**551**	**3,372**
Families with Children	35	1	27	7	6	8	8	92	**404**
Chronically Homeless									
Sheltered	3	0	2	0	0	2	1	8	125
Unsheltered	1	0	0	11	31	5	3	51	281
Total Chronically Homeless	**4**	**0**	**2**	**11**	**31**	**7**	**4**	**59**	**406**

	BEAR RIVER ASSOCIATION OF GOVERNMENTS	CARBON & EMERY	FIVE COUNTY	GRAND	SAN JUAN	SIX COUNTY	UINTAH BASIN	RURAL AREAS	STATE TOTALS
Hospital Patients	0	0	3	0	0	0	0	3	**47**
Jail/Prison	17	0	0	3	0	20	1	41	**266**
Homeless Veterans	0	3	10	2	0	0	1	16	**339**
Homeless School Children	212	111	750	20	920	191	137	2,341	**11,928**
ANNUALIZED HOMELESS ESTIMATES									
HOMELESS - SHELTERED									
Individuals	51	85	534	10	5	44	22	751	6,795
Persons in Families	620	20	460	115	120	140	55	1,530	6,880
Unaccompanied Children	0	0	0	0	0	0	0	0	0
TOTAL SHELTERED	**671**	**105**	**994**	**125**	**125**	**184**	**77**	**2,281**	**13,675**
HOMELESS - UNSHELTERED									
Individuals	2	0	0	47	62	10	66	187	1,722
Persons in Families	0	0	0	0	0	0	90	90	225
Unaccompanied Children	0	0	0	0	0	0	20	20	20
TOTAL UNSHELTERED	**2**	**0**	**0**	**47**	**62**	**10**	**176**	**297**	**1,967**
TOTAL HOMELESS	**673**	**105**	**994**	**172**	**187**	**194**	**253**	**2,578**	**15,642**
Families with Children	175	5	135	35	30	40	40	**460**	**2,020**
% of 2009 Est. Population	**0.41%**	**0.34%**	**0.47%**	**1.81%**	**1.20%**	**0.25%**	**0.51%**	**0.46%**	**0.56%**
Chronically Homeless	**8**	**0**	**4**	**22**	**62**	**14**	**8**	**118**	**812**

Source: Comprehensive Report on Homelessness, State of Utah, 2009 and 2010

Notes:

- The sheltered and unsheltered families are annualized by multiplying by five; the chronically homeless and unsheltered individuals are annualized by multiplying by two.
- Number of homeless school children provided by Utah State Office of Education's 2010 Annual Point-in-Time Count

5.3.5.8 Utah Point-in-Time Homeless Count, 2009 and 2010, Comparison Counties

	Utah County	Davis County	Salt Lake County
2009	323	645	9,766
2010	1,414	629	9,534

Source: Comprehensive Report on Homelessness, State of Utah, 2009 and 2010

5.4 Health Data

5.4.1   Healthy Behavior

5.4.1.1 General Health Status, 2009, by Local Health District, All Districts

	General Health Status	Age Groups 18 and Older	Number of Responses	General Health Status
State Total	Excellent / Very Good / Good	Total	8,701	89.21%
State Total	Fair / Poor	Total	1,421	10.79%
Bear River LHD	Excellent / Very Good / Good	18-34 years	94*	90.1761*
Bear River LHD	Fair / Poor	18-34 years	9*	9.8239*
Bear River LHD	Total	18-34 years	103	100.00%
Bear River LHD	Excellent / Very Good / Good	35-49 years	119	87.11%
Bear River LHD	Fair / Poor	35-49 years	16	12.89%
Bear River LHD	Total	35-49 years	135	100.00%
Bear River LHD	Excellent / Very Good / Good	50-64 years	136	89.54%
Bear River LHD	Fair / Poor	50-64 years	19	10.46%
Bear River LHD	Total	50-64 years	155	100.00%
Bear River LHD	Excellent / Very Good / Good	65+ years	99	76.58%
Bear River LHD	Fair / Poor	65+ years	32	23.42%
Bear River LHD	Total	65+ years	131	100.00%
Central Utah LHD	Excellent / Very Good / Good	18-34 years	**	**
Central Utah LHD	Fair / Poor	18-34 years	**	**
Central Utah LHD	Total	18-34 years	89	100.00%
Central Utah LHD	Excellent / Very Good / Good	35-49 years	98*	90.8210*
Central Utah LHD	Fair / Poor	35-49 years	11*	9.1790*
Central Utah LHD	Total	35-49 years	109	100.00%

	General Health Status	Age Groups 18 and Older	Number of Responses	General Health Status
Central Utah LHD	Excellent / Very Good / Good	50-64 years	127	87.16%
Central Utah LHD	Fair / Poor	50-64 years	24	12.84%
Central Utah LHD	Total	50-64 years	151	100.00%
Central Utah LHD	Excellent / Very Good / Good	65+ years	103	73.82%
Central Utah LHD	Fair / Poor	65+ years	36	26.18%
Central Utah LHD	Total	65+ years	139	100.00%
Davis County LHD	Excellent / Very Good / Good	18-34 years	157*	94.0845*
Davis County LHD	Fair / Poor	18-34 years	10*	5.9155*
Davis County LHD	Total	18-34 years	167	100.00%
Davis County LHD	Excellent / Very Good / Good	35-49 years	228	93.55%
Davis County LHD	Fair / Poor	35-49 years	16	6.45%
Davis County LHD	Total	35-49 years	244	100.00%
Davis County LHD	Excellent / Very Good / Good	50-64 years	182	89.67%
Davis County LHD	Fair / Poor	50-64 years	25	10.33%
Davis County LHD	Total	50-64 years	207	100.00%
Davis County LHD	Excellent / Very Good / Good	65+ years	137	78.10%
Davis County LHD	Fair / Poor	65+ years	34	21.90%
Davis County LHD	Total	65+ years	171	100.00%
Salt Lake Valley LHD	Excellent / Very Good / Good	18-34 years	495	93.60%
Salt Lake Valley LHD	Fair / Poor	18-34 years	38	6.40%
Salt Lake Valley LHD	Total	18-34 years	533	100.00%
Salt Lake Valley LHD	Excellent / Very Good / Good	35-49 years	831	90.85%
Salt Lake Valley LHD	Fair / Poor	35-49 years	89	9.15%
Salt Lake Valley LHD	Total	35-49 years	920	100.00%

	General Health Status	Age Groups 18 and Older	Number of Responses	General Health Status
Salt Lake Valley LHD	Excellent / Very Good / Good	50-64 years	848	85.30%
Salt Lake Valley LHD	Fair / Poor	50-64 years	151	14.70%
Salt Lake Valley LHD	Total	50-64 years	999	100.00%
Salt Lake Valley LHD	Excellent / Very Good / Good	65+ years	608	79.69%
Salt Lake Valley LHD	Fair / Poor	65+ years	163	20.31%
Salt Lake Valley LHD	Total	65+ years	771	100.00%
Southeastern Utah LHD	Excellent / Very Good / Good	18-34 years	**	**
Southeastern Utah LHD	Fair / Poor	18-34 years	**	**
Southeastern Utah LHD	Total	18-34 years	85	100.00%
Southeastern Utah LHD	Excellent / Very Good / Good	35-49 years	79	84.73%
Southeastern Utah LHD	Fair / Poor	35-49 years	14	15.27%
Southeastern Utah LHD	Total	35-49 years	93	100.00%
Southeastern Utah LHD	Excellent / Very Good / Good	50-64 years	149	78.28%
Southeastern Utah LHD	Fair / Poor	50-64 years	34	21.72%
Southeastern Utah LHD	Total	50-64 years	183	100.00%
Southeastern Utah LHD	Excellent / Very Good / Good	65+ years	92	64.28%
Southeastern Utah LHD	Fair / Poor	65+ years	48	35.72%
Southeastern Utah LHD	Total	65+ years	140	100.00%
Southwest Utah LHD	Excellent / Very Good / Good	18-34 years	**	**
Southwest Utah LHD	Fair / Poor	18-34 years	**	**
Southwest Utah LHD	Total	18-34 years	70	100.00%
Southwest Utah LHD	Excellent / Very Good / Good	35-49 years	95*	91.1365*
Southwest Utah LHD	Fair / Poor	35-49 years	10*	8.8635*
Southwest Utah LHD	Total	35-49 years	105	100.00%

	General Health Status	Age Groups 18 and Older	Number of Responses	General Health Status
Southwest Utah LHD	Excellent / Very Good / Good	50-64 years	109	83.01%
Southwest Utah LHD	Fair / Poor	50-64 years	23	16.99%
Southwest Utah LHD	Total	50-64 years	132	100.00%
Southwest Utah LHD	Excellent / Very Good / Good	65+ years	149	72.67%
Southwest Utah LHD	Fair / Poor	65+ years	51	27.33%
Southwest Utah LHD	Total	65+ years	200	100.00%
Summit County LHD	Excellent / Very Good / Good	18-34 years	**	**
Summit County LHD	Fair / Poor	18-34 years	**	**
Summit County LHD	Total	18-34 years	61	100.00%
Summit County LHD	Excellent / Very Good / Good	35-49 years	**	**
Summit County LHD	Fair / Poor	35-49 years	**	**
Summit County LHD	Total	35-49 years	129	100.00%
Summit County LHD	Excellent / Very Good / Good	50-64 years	191	94.08%
Summit County LHD	Fair / Poor	50-64 years	14	5.92%
Summit County LHD	Total	50-64 years	205	100.00%
Summit County LHD	Excellent / Very Good / Good	65+ years	73*	83.4558*
Summit County LHD	Fair / Poor	65+ years	13*	16.5442*
Summit County LHD	Total	65+ years	86	100.00%
Tooele County LHD	Excellent / Very Good / Good	18-34 years	78*	91.7890*
Tooele County LHD	Fair / Poor	18-34 years	9*	8.2110*
Tooele County LHD	Total	18-34 years	87	100.00%
Tooele County LHD	Excellent / Very Good / Good	35-49 years	127*	92.9398*
Tooele County LHD	Fair / Poor	35-49 years	13*	7.0602*
Tooele County LHD	Total	35-49 years	140	100.00%

	General Health Status	Age Groups 18 and Older	Number of Responses	General Health Status
Tooele County LHD	Excellent / Very Good / Good	50-64 years	113	79.59%
Tooele County LHD	Fair / Poor	50-64 years	30	20.41%
Tooele County LHD	Total	50-64 years	143	100.00%
Tooele County LHD	Excellent / Very Good / Good	65+ years	87	74.30%
Tooele County LHD	Fair / Poor	65+ years	36	25.70%
Tooele County LHD	Total	65+ years	123	100.00%
TriCounty LHD	Excellent / Very Good / Good	18-34 years	112*	96.5564*
TriCounty LHD	Fair / Poor	18-34 years	6*	3.4436*
TriCounty LHD	Total	18-34 years	118	100.00%
TriCounty LHD	Excellent / Very Good / Good	35-49 years	107	88.34%
TriCounty LHD	Fair / Poor	35-49 years	18	11.66%
TriCounty LHD	Total	35-49 years	125	100.00%
TriCounty LHD	Excellent / Very Good / Good	50-64 years	120	82.61%
TriCounty LHD	Fair / Poor	50-64 years	25	17.39%
TriCounty LHD	Total	50-64 years	145	100.00%
TriCounty LHD	Excellent / Very Good / Good	65+ years	93	69.25%
TriCounty LHD	Fair / Poor	65+ years	41	30.75%
TriCounty LHD	Total	65+ years	134	100.00%
Utah County LHD	Excellent / Very Good / Good	18-34 years	255	92.38%
Utah County LHD	Fair / Poor	18-34 years	23	7.62%
Utah County LHD	Total	18-34 years	278	100.00%
Utah County LHD	Excellent / Very Good / Good	35-49 years	285	93.99%
Utah County LHD	Fair / Poor	35-49 years	24	6.01%
Utah County LHD	Total	35-49 years	309	100.00%

	General Health Status	Age Groups 18 and Older	Number of Responses	General Health Status
Utah County LHD	Excellent / Very Good / Good	50-64 years	213	91.70%
Utah County LHD	Fair / Poor	50-64 years	25	8.30%
Utah County LHD	Total	50-64 years	238	100.00%
Utah County LHD	Excellent / Very Good / Good	65+ years	196	80.03%
Utah County LHD	Fair / Poor	65+ years	46	19.97%
Utah County LHD	Total	65+ years	242	100.00%
Wasatch County LHD	Excellent / Very Good / Good	18-34 years	**	**
Wasatch County LHD	Fair / Poor	18-34 years	**	**
Wasatch County LHD	Total	18-34 years	85	100.00%
Wasatch County LHD	Excellent / Very Good / Good	35-49 years	139	91.59%
Wasatch County LHD	Fair / Poor	35-49 years	14	8.41%
Wasatch County LHD	Total	35-49 years	153	100.00%
Wasatch County LHD	Excellent / Very Good / Good	50-64 years	138	87.44%
Wasatch County LHD	Fair / Poor	50-64 years	20	12.56%
Wasatch County LHD	Total	50-64 years	158	100.00%
Wasatch County LHD	Excellent / Very Good / Good	65+ years	101	89.45%
Wasatch County LHD	Fair / Poor	65+ years	17	10.55%
Wasatch County LHD	Total	65+ years	118	100.00%
Weber-Morgan LHD	Excellent / Very Good / Good	18-34 years	138*	95.3866*
Weber-Morgan LHD	Fair / Poor	18-34 years	7*	4.6134*
Weber-Morgan LHD	Total	18-34 years	145	100.00%
Weber-Morgan LHD	Excellent / Very Good / Good	35-49 years	175	84.36%
Weber-Morgan LHD	Fair / Poor	35-49 years	30	15.64%
Weber-Morgan LHD	Total	35-49 years	205	100.00%

	General Health Status	Age Groups 18 and Older	Number of Responses	General Health Status
Weber-Morgan LHD	Excellent / Very Good / Good	50-64 years	192	86.52%
Weber-Morgan LHD	Fair / Poor	50-64 years	32	13.48%
Weber-Morgan LHD	Total	50-64 years	224	100.00%
Weber-Morgan LHD	Excellent / Very Good / Good	65+ years	163	75.64%
Weber-Morgan LHD	Fair / Poor	65+ years	50	24.36%
Weber-Morgan LHD	Total	65+ years	213	100.00%

Source: Utah Department of Health

5.4.1.2 Percent Receiving Influenza Vaccine, by Age Group, Comparison Counties, 2007-2009

	2007			2008			2009		
	18-49	50-64	65+	18-49	50-64	65+	18-49	50-64	65+
Utah County	30%	46%	72%	26%	50%	69%	30%	48%	68%
Davis County	35%	54%	75%	30%	49%	77%	35%	46%	69%
Salt Lake County	30%	48%	76%	34%	50%	74%	33%	50%	70%

Source: Utah Department of Health

5.4.1.3 Percent Receiving Pneumonia Vaccine, by Age Group, Comparison Counties, 2007-2009

	2007		2008		2009	
	18-64	65+	18-64	65+	18-64	65+
Utah County	15%	72%	11%	67%	15%	71%
Davis County	18%	68%	17%	73%	15%	72%
Salt Lake County	16%	70%	17%	73%	18%	72%

Source: Utah Department of Health

5.4.1.4 Percent Children Fully Immunized by Age 2, 2007-2009, Comparison Counties and State

	Utah County	Davis County	Salt Lake County	State
2007	56%	55%	67%	54%
2008	62%	53%	64%	55%
2009	47%	67%	60%	54%

Source: Utah Department of Health

5.4.1.5 Mothers Receiving First Prenatal Care During First Trimester of Pregnancy, by Hispanic Origin, 2008, Comparison Counties and State

	Utah County	Davis County	Salt Lake County	State
Hispanic	66.39%	72.41%	64.09%	65.31%
Non-Hispanic	85.00%	86.98%	80.71%	83.35%
Total	82.84%	85.62%	76.69%	80.16%

Source: U.S. Census Bureau

5.4.1.6 Mothers Receiving First Prenatal Care During First Trimester of Pregnancy, by Educational Attainment, 2008, Comparison Counties and State

	Utah County	Davis County	Salt Lake County	State
Less than High School	62.51%	67.80%	59.23%	60.58%
High School Graduate	79.44%	81.44%	73.61%	76.60%
Some College	84.88%	89.36%	82.29%	84.52%
College Graduate	87.79%	89.88%	87.59%	88.06%

Source: U.S. Census Bureau

5.4.1.7 Average Number of Prenatal Visits, by Educational Attainment, 2008, Comparison Counties and State

	Utah County	Davis County	Salt Lake County	State
Less than High School	10	10.24	9.69	9.8
High School Graduate	11.14	11.27	10.78	10.97
Some College	11.34	11.65	11.29	11.38
College Graduate	11.54	11.67	11.7	11.63
Total	11.25	11.42	10.9	11.1

Source: U.S. Census Bureau

5.4.1.8 Average Number of Prenatal Visits, by Hispanic Origin of Mother, 2008, Comparison Counties and State

	Utah County	Davis County	Salt Lake County	State
Hispanic	10.22	10.34	10	10.08
Non-Hispanic	11.38	11.54	11.23	11.34
Unknown	12.41	10.16	9.33	9.74
Total	11.25	11.42	10.9	11.1

Source: U.S. Census Bureau

5.4.1.9 Overweight and Obese, by Local Health District, 2009, Comparison Counties

	Utah County LHD	Davis County LHD	Salt Lake Valley LHD
BMI less than 25 (normal)	45.70%	42.03%	41.35%
BMI 25+ (Overweight or obese)	54.30%	57.97%	58.65%
Total	100.00%	100.00%	100.00%

Source: Utah Department of Health

5.4.1.10 Current Smokers, by Local Health District, 2009, Comparison Counties

	Utah County	Davis County	Salt Lake County
Not current smoker	94.28%	94.26%	88.68%
Current smoker	5.72%	5.74%	11.32%
Total	100.00%	100.00%	100.00%

Source: Utah Department of Health

5.4.1.11   Risk of Binge Drinking, by Local Health District, 2009, Comparison Counties

	Utah County	Davis County	Salt Lake County
Not at risk	96.54%	93.15%	88.33%
At risk (5+ drinks for men, 4+ drinks for women, 1 or more times)	3.46%	6.85%	11.67%
Total	100.00%	100.00%	100.00%

Source: Utah Department of Health

5.4.1.12   Risk of Chronic Drinking, by Local Health District, 2009, Comparison Counties

	Utah County	Davis County	Salt Lake County
Not at risk	99.11%	97.82%	96.56%
At risk (>30 for women, >60 for men)	0.89%	2.18%	3.44%
Total	100.00%	100.00%	100.00%

Source: Utah Department of Health

5.4.1.13   No or Some Physical Activity, by Local Health District, 2009, Comparison Counties

	Utah County LHD	Davis County LHD	Salt Lake Valley LHD
No leisure time activity	13.47%	14.20%	19.04%
Some activity	86.53%	85.80%	80.96%
Total	100.00%	100.00%	100.00%

Source: Utah Department of Health

5.4.1.14   Recommended or Vigorous Physical Activity, by Local Health District, 2009, Comparison Counties

	Utah County	Davis County	Salt Lake County
Recommended physical activity	60.0%	49.6%	57.5%
Vigorous physical activity	42.6%	33.4%	37.9%

Recommended: 30 minutes light or moderate physical activity a day, 5 days a week

Vigorous: At least 3 times/week for at least 20 minutes

Source: Utah Department of Health

5.4.1.15   Seat Belt Use, 2009, Comparison Counties

	Utah County	Davis County	Salt Lake County
Always, nearly always	93.59%	95.01%	95.03%
At risk (sometime, seldom, never)	6.41%	4.99%	4.97%
Total	100.00%	100.00%	100.00%

Source: Utah Department of Health

5.4.2   Health Access

5.4.2.1 Number of Healthcare Facilities, by Type, Comparison Counties

	Utah County	Davis County	Salt Lake County
Public Medical Clinics	4	3	20
Hospitals	9	5	19
Long-term Care and Assisted Living Centers	57	27	88
Local Health District Offices	3	2	6

Source: Utah Department of Health

5.4.2.2 Persons with Hospital Insurance or Medicare, Comparison Counties and State, 1998-2007

	Utah County	Davis County	Salt Lake County	State
1998	24,982	17,142	77,633	198,028
1999	25,494	17,674	78,471	201,217
2000	26,276	18,447	79,611	206,056
2001	26,858	19,216	80,679	210,400
2002	27,592	19,847	81,833	214,881
2003	28,248	20,569	83,291	220,221
2004	27,709	20,741	79,988	214,817
2005	29,843	22,307	85,353	230,009
2006	31,780	23,593	89,634	241,886
2007	33,392	24,784	93,315	252,572

Source: U.S. Census Bureau

5.4.2.3 Persons with Disabilities with Hospital Insurance or Medicare, Comparison Counties and State, 1999-2007

	Utah County	Davis County	Salt Lake County	State
1999	3,104	1,733	9,699	22,946
2000	3,251	1,785	9,789	23,539
2001	3,328	1,898	10,143	24,572
2002	3,509	2,007	10,565	25,760
2003	3,676	2,144	11,102	27,154
2004	3,840	2,300	11,093	27,789
2005	4,161	2,560	12,004	30,159
2006	4,487	2,730	13,040	32,458
2007	4,885	3,039	14,232	35,750

Source: U.S. Census Bureau

5.4.2.4 Persons without Health Insurance, By Age, Comparison Counties

	Utah County	Davis County	Salt Lake County
Persons < 18	189,309	101,495	300,679
< 18, No Insurance	16,003	5,640	33,873
Percent < 18, No Insurance	8.5%	5.6%	11.3%
Persons Age 18-64	318,156	170,257	636,231
Age 18-64, No Insurance	51,456	21,233	127,863
Percent 18 - 64, No Insurance	16.2%	12.5%	20.1%
Persons > 64	35,361	22,895	87,966
Age > 64, No Insurance	78	81	1,333
Percent >64, No Insurance	0.2%	0.4%	1.5%
Total Population	542,826	294,647	1,024,876
Total No Insurance	67,537	26,954	163,069
Total Percentage without Insurance	12.4%	9.1%	15.9%

Source: U.S. Census Bureau

5.4.2.5 Persons without Health Insurance, by Age and Gender, Comparison Counties

	Utah County		Davis County		Salt Lake County	
	Male	Female	Male	Female	Male	Female
Total Noninstitutionalized Population	269,506	273,320	147,386	147,261	518,080	506,796
< 18 Years Old	97,706	91,603	52,514	48,981	154,841	145,838
Percent	36.3%	33.5%	35.6%	33.3%	29.9%	28.8%
Number < 18 without Insurance	8,585	7,418	1,976	3,664	15,699	18,174
Percent	3.2%	2.7%	1.3%	2.5%	3.0%	3.6%
Noninstitutionalized Population Age 18-64	155,914	162,242	83,946	86,311	323,914	312,317
Percent	57.9%	59.4%	57.0%	58.6%	62.5%	61.6%
Number 18-64 without Insurance	26,527	24,929	11,131	10,102	74,535	53,328
Percent	9.8%	9.1%	7.6%	6.9%	14.4%	10.5%
Total Noninstitutionalized Population >64	15,886	19,475	10,926	11,969	39,325	48,641
Percent	5.9%	7.1%	7.4%	8.1%	7.6%	9.6%
Number > 64 without Insurance	78	0	81	0	954	379
Percent	0.0%	0.0%	0.1%	0.0%	0.2%	0.1%

Source: U.S. Census Bureau

5.4.2.6 Percent with One or More Types of Insurance, by Age Group, Utah County

	<18	18-34	35-64	65+
One	86.1%	74.8%	79.5%	21.5%
Two or More	5.5%	6.7%	7.3%	78.3%

Source: U.S. Census Bureau

5.4.2.7 Types of Health Insurance, By Age Group, Persons with One Type of Insurance Only

	<18	18-34	35-64	65+
Employer-provided	62.1%	57.1%	66.3%	1.7%
Direct purchase	8.9%	12.9%	8.5%	1.7%
Medicare	0.1%	0.1%	0.5%	19.5%
Medicaid	14.1%	4.0%	3.4%	76.8%
TRICARE/Military	0.8%	0.7%	0.3%	0.0%
VA	0.0%	0.1%	0.5%	0.0%

Source: U.S. Census Bureau

5.4.2.8 Children with One Type of Health Insurance, by Type, Comparison Counties

	Utah County	Davis County	Salt Lake County
Total Population < 18	34.9%	34.4%	29.3%
< 18, One Type of Insurance	86.1%	89.7%	83.0%
< 18, One Type of Insurance, Employer Provided	62.1%	70.3%	62.4%
< 18, One Type of Insurance, Direct Purchase	8.9%	5.1%	5.6%

Source: U.S. Census Bureau

5.4.2.9 Percent Unable to Obtain Health Care Due to Cost, 2005-2009, Comparison Counties

	Utah County	Davis County	Salt Lake County
2005	15.0%	13.6%	12.6%
2006	12.7%	8.6%	13.5%
2007	11.6%	7.0%	14.2%
2008	13.0%	9.3%	11.2%
2009	13.2%	9.1%	14.1%

Source: U.S. Census Bureau

5.4.2.10 Average Length of Hospital Stay in Days, by Local Health District, 1992-2009, All Districts

	Bear River LHD	Central Utah LHD	Davis County LHD	Salt Lake Valley LHD	Southeastern Utah LHD	Southwest Utah LHD	Summit County LHD	Tooele County LHD	TriCounty LHD	Utah County LHD	Wasatch County LHD	Weber-Morgan LHD	Other Utah, County Not Specified	Total
1992	4.6	4.7	4.6	5.5	4.7	5.5	4.11	5.7	4.1	4.7	4.2	5.4	3.8	5.1
1993	3.6	4.7	4.3	4.8	4.4	4.6	6.11*	4.6	4.1	3.7	4.1	4.5		4.5
1994	3.3	5.2	4.1	4.5	**	5.5	3.94	4.3	4	3.5	3.4	4.2	2.3	4.4
1995	3.6	3.9	4.4	5.5	4.6	3.9	3.5	5	5.1	4	3.4	4.4	1.8	4.7
1996	3.2	3.6	3.7	4	3.9	3.5	3.85	3.7	3.9	3.3	3.8	4	2.4	3.7
1997	3.2	3.6	3.6	3.9	3.5	3.6	3.57	3.9	3.9	3.2	3.8	3.9	3.1	3.7
1998	3.2	3.7	3.7	4	3.7	3.5	3.78	4	3.8	3.4	3.6	4		3.8
1999	3.4	3.7	3.7	4.2	3.6	3.6	3.73	3.8	4	3.4	3.6	4		3.9
2000	3.4	3.6	3.8	4.2	3.8	3.5	3.72	3.6	3.7	3.4	3.8	4		3.8
2001	3.3	3.6	3.8	4.1	4.3	3.5	3.58	3.4	3.6	3.3	3.5	3.9		3.8
2002	3.2	3.6	3.7	4	3.5	3.7	3.59	3.5	3.4	3.4	3.9	3.8		3.8
2003	3.2	3.6	3.6	4.1	3.6	3.4	3.81	3.7	3.6	3.4	3.5	3.9		3.8
2004	3.3	3.6	4	4.2	3.7	3.5	3.77	3.5	3.8	3.4	3.4	3.9		3.8
2005	3.3	3.7	3.7	4.1	3.5	3.4	3.77	3.7	3.5	3.5	3.8	3.8		3.8
2006	3.2	3.8	3.6	4	3.4	3.3	3.76	3.5	3.7	3.4	3.6	3.9		3.7
2007	3.2	3.6	3.6	4	3.5	3.3	3.6	3.3	3.5	3.5	3.3	3.8		3.7
2008	3.3	3.8	3.7	4	3.7	3.4	3.68	3.5	3.5	3.7	3.7	3.8		3.8
2009	3.3	3.8	3.6	3.9	3.6	3.4	3.57	3.8	3.4	3.7	3.5	3.8		3.7
Total	3.4	3.8	3.8	4.3	4.2	3.7	3.81	3.8	3.8	3.5	3.6	4	3.5	3.9

Source: Utah Department of Health

5.4.2.11   Enrollment in Women, Infants, & Children, 2009, Comparison Counties

	Utah County	Davis County	Salt Lake County
Women enrolled in WIC	3,768	1,419	7,101
Infants enrolled in WIC	3,285	1,511	7,256
Children enrolled in WIC	6,903	2,835	13,643

Source: Utah Department of Health

5.4.3   Birth

5.4.3.1 Births per 1,000 Live Persons, Comparison Counties and State, 2001-2008

	Utah County	Davis County	Salt Lake County	State
2001	26.21	20.43	19.72	20.78
2002	26.08	19.99	20.01	20.84
2003	25.38	20.78	19.38	20.65
2004	25.03	20.79	19.25	20.51
2005	24.81	20.36	19.09	20.22
2006	24.66	21.07	19.23	20.45
2007	24.5	20.81	19.18	20.4
2008	24.07	20.54	19.01	20.16

Source: Utah Department of Health

5.4.3.2 Fertility Rates: Births per 1,000 Women Age 14-54, 2000-2008, Comparison Counties and State

	Utah County	Davis County	Salt Lake County	State
2000	52.61	40.44	40.97	**42.23**
2001	52.07	41.03	39.79	**41.68**
2002	51.86	40.16	40.4	**41.81**
2003	50.5	41.78	39.14	**41.45**
2004	49.84	41.85	38.88	**41.19**
2005	49.44	41.01	38.59	**40.62**
2006	49.16	42.46	38.87	**41.09**
2007	48.9	41.97	38.79	**41.02**
2008	48.08	41.43	38.46	**40.56**

Source: Utah Department of Health

5.4.3.3 Fertility Rates, by Age Group, Utah County, 1989-2008

Mother's age group	< 15 yrs	15-17 yrs	18-19 yrs	20-24 yrs	25-29 yrs	30-34 yrs	35-39 yrs	40-44 yrs	45-49 yrs	50+ yrs	Total
1989	**	21	78.9	177	182	104	42.4	6.22	**		42.4
1990	**	16.6	76.7	181	173	107	43.7	6.58	**		41.3
1991	**	19.9	70.1	155	170	103	38.7	6.8	**		38.8
1992		17.7	87.8	154	175	109	40.2	8.15	**		40.2
1993	**	17.1	74.3	139	161	99.6	37.1	7.05	**		36.5
1994	**	19.5	69.1	136	167	103	46.8	6.27	**		37.8
1995	0.19*	18.4	72.4	138	175	107	39.4	9.31	**		38.6
1996	**	18.6	65.7	142	185	110	40.8	6.69	0.62*		39.6
1997	**	15	71.6	148	180	115	44.3	7.7	**		40.6
1998	0.16*	13.9	62.7	146	181	119	47.2	8.52	0.73*		41.1
1999		13.5	58.8	149	182	120	39.6	6.47	**		41
2000	**	14.8	55.3	142	188	123	45.2	8.06	**		40.4
2001	**	9.29	55	141	188	128	45.4	7.67			41
2002	**	9.35	56.8	141	169	122	46.7	7.02	0.49*		40.2
2003	**	10.9	51.3	137	180	131	46.8	8.28	**		41.8
2004	**	10.1	52	139	173	131	49.1	7.72	**		41.9
2005	**	8.94	48.3	135	164	130	52.7	6.72	**	**	41
2006		10.8	51.6	137	172	135	49.4	7.76	0.55*		42.5
2007	**	11	56.9	140	164	131	49	7.36	0.64*		42
2008	**	11.6	58.1	131	165	130	48.3	9.98	**		41.4
Total	0.06	14.2	62.4	144	174	119	44.8	7.57	0.37	**	40.6

*Use caution in interpreting, the estimate has a relative standard error greater than 30% and does not meet UDOH standards for reliability. Consider aggregating years to decrease the relative standard error and improve the reliability of the estimate

*The estimate has been suppressed because 1) The relative standard error is greater than 50% or when the relative standard error can't be determined. Consider aggregating years to decrease the relative standard error and improve the reliability of the estimate. For more information, please go to http://health.utah.gov/opha/IBIShelp/DataSuppression.pdf. 2) the observed number of events is very small and not appropriate for publication, or 3) it could be used to calculate the number in a cell that has been suppressed.

Source: Utah Department of Health

5.4.3.4 Fertility Rates per 1,000, Adolescent Girls Ages 10-14, by Mother's County of Residence, 1989-2008, Comparison Counties and State

	Utah County	Davis County	Salt Lake County	Total
1989	0.38*	**	0.59	**
1990	0.43*	**	0.56	**
1991	**	**	0.73	0.51
1992	0.49*		0.93	0.66
1993	0.49*	**	0.55	**
1994	0.50*	**	0.47	**
1995	**	0.53*	0.72	**
1996	**	**	0.46	0.37
1997	0.73*	**	0.55	**
1998	0.44*	0.46*	0.86	0.7
1999	0.36*		0.61	0.44
2000	**	**	0.56	0.39
2001	**	**	0.45	0.33
2002		**	0.53	**
2003	**	**	0.39	0.31
2004	**	**	0.42	0.26
2005	0.45*	**	0.69	**
2006	0.33*		0.22*	0.21
2007	0.26*	**	0.32	**
2008	0.25*	**	0.4	**
Total	0.26	0.16	0.5	0.38

*Use caution in interpreting, the estimate has a relative standard error greater than 30% and does not meet UDOH standards for reliability. Consider aggregating years to decrease the relative standard error and improve the reliability of the estimate.

**The estimate has been suppressed because 1) The relative standard error is greater than 50% or when the relative standard error can't be determined. Consider aggregating years to decrease the relative standard error and improve the reliability of the estimate. For more information, please go to http://health.utah.gov/opha/IBIShelp/DataSuppression.pdf or 2) the observed number of events is very small and not appropriate for publication

Source: Utah Department of Health

5.4.3.5 Fertility Rates per 1,000, Adolescent Girls Ages 15-17, by Mother's County of Residence, 1989-2008, Comparison Counties and State

	Utah County	Davis County	Salt Lake County	State
1989	17.23	20.97	26.52	22.99
1990	19.88	16.61	28.86	24.54
1991	22.8	19.88	30.33	26.67
1992	21.77	17.74	30.75	26.29
1993	20.9	17.1	29.56	25.27
1994	20.97	19.53	26.24	23.8
1995	21.64	18.42	27.25	24.37
1996	21.17	18.59	25.91	23.52
1997	22.81	14.95	26.99	23.88
1998	18.93	13.89	25.73	22.07
1999	19.87	13.53	25.19	21.87
2000	16.81	14.82	24.39	20.78
2001	13.38	9.29	21.64	17.31
2002	12.04	9.35	20.52	16.3
2003	10.78	10.88	18.11	14.88
2004	9.72	10.12	17.46	14.09
2005	10.19	8.94	17.31	13.9
2006	10.43	10.79	19.28	15.35
2007	14.03	11.04	22.14	17.89
2008	14.33	11.63	22.66	18.34
Total	14.71	12.8	21.97	18.49

Source: Utah Department of Health

5.4.3.6 Fertility Rates per 1,000, Adolescent Girls Ages 18-19, by Mother's County of Residence, 1989-2008, Comparison Counties and State

	Utah County	Davis County	Salt Lake County	State
1989	55.71	78.92	91.48	78.09
1990	43.52	76.74	91.62	71.1
1991	47.61	70.13	97.86	75.2
1992	41.28	87.82	94.75	73
1993	38.45	74.27	89.48	67.54
1994	37.48	69.13	85.99	64.88
1995	40.8	72.44	83.86	65.53
1996	42.59	65.7	87.01	66.86
1997	39.97	71.64	83.35	65.07
1998	38.49	62.71	82.41	62.91
1999	38.46	58.8	77.41	59.98
2000	34.64	55.26	72.06	55.61
2001	30.98	55.04	71.46	53.98
2002	32.83	56.76	68.97	53.71
2003	27.24	51.32	63.31	47.92
2004	25.82	52.01	60.56	45.96
2005	26.33	48.3	59.48	45.13
2006	28.28	51.63	69.4	51.02
2007	29.37	56.86	69.83	52.21
2008	27.28	58.07	67.2	50.17
Total	31.71	56.19	69.56	53.19

Source: Utah Department of Health

293

5.4.3.7 Fertility Rates per 1,000, Adolescent Girls Ages 15-19, by Mother's County of Residence, 1989-2008, Comparison Counties and State

	Utah County	Davis County	Salt Lake County	State
1989	33.63	41.97	51.46	44.65
1990	32.92	37.88	53.31	44.72
1991	35.92	37.09	55.43	46.74
1992	32.04	40.87	53.58	45.12
1993	30.1	35.84	50.62	42.14
1994	29.71	36	47.35	40.3
1995	32.07	36.73	47.54	41.24
1996	33.04	35.08	48.33	41.69
1997	32.45	35.42	48.15	41.5
1998	30.13	31.91	47.63	39.96
1999	30.74	30.55	46.04	39.03
2000	26.83	30.25	44.05	36.55
2001	23.24	26.64	42.48	34
2002	23.46	27.06	40.63	33.12
2003	19.69	25.69	36.52	29.5
2004	18.4	25.28	34.75	28.05
2005	18.75	23.14	34.07	27.43
2006	19.76	25.47	39.18	30.73
2007	21.98	27.78	41.16	32.74
2008	21.05	28.8	40.55	32.2
Total	23.84	28.42	40.5	33.42

Source: Utah Department of Health

5.4.4 Death

5.4.4.1 Fetal Mortality Rate per 1,000, by Cause of Death, 2008, Comparison Counties and State

	Utah County	Davis County	Salt Lake County	State
Maternal complications of pregnancy	0.21	0.29	0.45	0.35
Complications of placenta, cord, and membranes	1.62	1.57	1.45	1.52
Short gestation and low fetus weight, not elsewhere classified	0.18	0.13*	0.18	0.17
Intrauterine hypoxia and birth asphyxia	0.06*	0.07*	0.09	0.08
Congenital malformations, deformation and chromosomal abnormalities	0.79	0.61	0.63	0.68
Other than major causes	4.82	5.19	6.86	5.96
Total	7.68	7.87	9.66	8.76

Source: Utah Department of Health

5.4.4.2 Infant Mortality Rate per 1000, by Local Health District, 1989-2008, All Districts

	Bear River LHD	Central Utah LHD	Davis County LHD	Salt Lake Valley LHD	South-eastern Utah LHD	South-west Utah LHD	Summit County LHD	Tooele County LHD	Tri-County LHD	Utah County LHD	Wasatch County LHD	Weber-Morgan LHD	Total
1989	6.72	8.95*	6.9	8.4	10.48*	6.96*		**	8.75*	7	**	11.3	8
1990	7	11.88*	7.2	7.8	5.48*	4.44*	**	**	5.69*	6.8	**	9.97	7.4
1991	5.04	4.40*	4.3	7.2	11.45*	3.06*		**	**	5.8	**	7.3	6.2
1992	2.86*	9.84*	5.7	6.7	**	3.53*	14.04*	**	**	4.8	**	7.88	5.9
1993	6.78	14.78	4.3	5.3	**	6.63	12.38*	**	**	6.9	**	5.53	6
1994	6.05	5.41*	3.8	6.6	5.97*	6.44	**		10.43*	5.4	**	8.2	6.1
1995	8.25	4.92*	5.3	5	4.80*	5.13*	11.90*	**	9.19*	4.9	**	2.83*	5.2
1996	4.31	11.92	4.9	6.1	**	6.78	**	6.56*	16.67*	4.5	17.32*	7.1	5.9
1997	2.50*	4.34*	3.8	6.1	10.00*	6.19	**	**	**	7	**	6.57	5.8
1998	7.71	7.09*	6.2	6.3	**	4.73	**	5.52*	**	3.7	**	7.33	5.7
1999	4.73	8.64*	4.6	5	**	7.07	**	4.42*	8.15*	3.4	**	4.38	4.8
2000	4.71	4.45*	5.2	5.7	**	4.9	**	**	**	5.1	**	5.45	5.2
2001	2.33*	6.79*	3.6	4.9	9.77*	4.2	**	6.02*	5.07*	5.5		5.65	4.8
2002	4.8	3.59*	2.8	6.1	**	6.03	**	8.02*	6.00*	6	**	5.79	5.5
2003	5.49	4.28*	3.5	4.7	8.37*	6.85	**	5.53*	**	5.4	**	4.8	5
2004	2.70*	6.68*	4.3	5.6	7.13*	6.44	**	6.64*	6.82*	4.9		5.18	5.2
2005	3.33*	8.52*	3.9	4.4	4.86*	4.39	**	**	8.16*	4.1	**	6.81	4.5
2006	4.73	5.77*	4.6	5.2	**	5.06	**	5.46*	6.24*	4.5	15.27*	5.54	5
2007	5.62	7.40*	6.5	5.4	**	5.47		**	6.55*	3.7	9.80*	6.39	5.2
2008	3.42	6.25*	4.4	5.4	4.62*	5.54	**	7.28*	5.57*	3.7	**	4.39	4.8
Total	5.19	7.49	5.1	6.2	5.54	5.83	5.33	4.99	6.74	5.3	7.12	6.59	5.8

*Use caution in interpreting, the estimate has a relative standard error greater than 30% and does not meet UDOH standards for reliability. Consider aggregating years to decrease the relative standard error and improve the reliability of the estimate.

**The estimate has been suppressed because 1) The relative standard error is greater than 50% or when the relative standard error can't be determined. Consider aggregating years to decrease the relative standard error and improve the reliability of the estimate. For more information, please go to http://health.utah.gov/opha/IBIShelp/DataSuppression.pdf. 2) the observed number of events is very small and not appropriate for publication, or 3) it could be used to calculate the number in a cell that has been suppressed.

Source: Utah Department of Health

5.4.4.3 50 Leading Causes of Death, by Rate per 100,000 Live Persons, by Local Health District, 2008, All Districts

	Bear River LHD	Central Utah LHD	Davis County LHD	Salt Lake Valley LHD	Southeastern Utah LHD	Southwest Utah LHD	Summit County LHD	Tooele County LHD	TriCounty LHD	Utah County LHD	Wasatch County LHD	Weber-Morgan LHD	Total
Salmonella infections	**					**							**
Shigellosis and amebiasis	**												**
Tuberculosis	**	**	**	0.09*	**	**				**		**	0.07
Meningococcal infection				**						0.08*	**		0.03*
Septicemia	3.37	7.07	3.73	4.46	7.77	6.33	2.61*	7.26	7.1	3.53	3.32*	3.91	4.45
Syphilis			**										**
Viral hepatitis	0.67*	1.03*	0.7	1.38	2.2	1.66	**	2.00*	0.83*	0.74	**	1.75	1.2
Human immunodeficiency virus (HIV) disease	0.37*	0.90*	0.54	1.3	**	0.47*		**	1.04*	0.25	**	0.96	0.81
Malignant neoplasms	85.6	138.4	86.11	100.3	146.9	137	70.9	92.97	134.4	68.33	89.69	118.3	98.38
In situ neoplasms, benign neopl. & neopl. of uncertain or unknown behavior	3.92	4.89	3.26	3.33	3.72	4.62	2.35*	3.63	3.76	2.85	4.27*	3.83	3.47
Anemias	0.67*	1.93	0.87	0.85	1.35*	1.14	**	0.91*	1.67*	0.72	**	0.96	0.89
Diabetes mellitus	18.42	31.25	18.36	19.73	27.88	20.75	7.04	18.7	28.18	15.93	15.19	29.2	20.15
Nutritional deficiencies	0.92	2.83	0.67	0.83	1.69*	1.19	**	0.91*	1.46*	0.66	1.90*	0.96	**
Meningitis	0.43*	**	0.20*	0.2	**	0.21*	**	**		0.12*	**	0.17*	0.2
Parkinson's disease	7.53	7.72	6.38	6.56	5.91	7.62	2.87*	3.81	5.64	5.19	5.69	6.86	6.35
Alzheimer's disease	20.99	27	12.72	11.11	19.77	26.55	11.5	12.53	10.23	10.84	14.71	15.18	13.95
Diseases of heart	109.7	193.3	99.77	110.5	166.6	155.8	63.9	104.1	150.3	90.77	107.7	149.5	115.8

Local Health System	Bear River LHD	Central Utah LHD	Davis County LHD	Salt Lake Valley LHD	Southeastern Utah LHD	Southwest Utah LHD	Summit County LHD	Tooele County LHD	TriCounty LHD	Utah County LHD	Wasatch County LHD	Weber-Morgan LHD	Total
Essential (primary) hypertension and hypertensive renal disease	3.73	5.92	2.72	4.44	2.7	3.27	1.30*	2.72	3.55	3.84	**	4.78	**
Cerebrovascular diseases	40.02	54.91	26.86	31.71	42.42	41.02	15.9	20.52	30.68	27.28	28.47	38.06	**32.5**
Atherosclerosis	0.73	1.93	6.51	1.19	24.33	2.13	4.95	1.09*	1.88*	0.86	7.59	2.5	**2.5**
Aortic aneurysm and dissection	2.63	3.6	2.22	2.95	5.41	3.89	1.30*	3.27	3.34	1.6	**	4.08	**
Influenza and pneumonia	17.74	25.2	11.68	15.01	31.09	17.69	5.74	14.35	20.46	9.13	20.88	19.05	**14.94**
Acute bronchitis and bronchiolitis	**			0.05*		**				0.08*			**0.04***
Chronic lower respiratory diseases	18.78	38.19	17.39	25.4	41.23	27.49	8.87	25.24	38.41	12.03	21.36	33.23	**23.26**
Pneumoconioses and chemical effects	0.31*	0.51*	**	0.14	5.91	0.31*		**		0.25		**	**0.31**
Pneumonitis due to solids and liquids	2.39	4.5	2.48	4.43	5.75	3.22	1.83*	4.18	2.5	2.81	3.80*	2.54	**3.51**
Peptic ulcer	0.61*	1.54	0.27*	0.84	1.18*	0.83	**	0.73*	**	0.76	**	0.96	**0.78**
Diseases of appendix	0.24*	**	0.13*	0.10*	**	**			**	0.16*		**	**0.13**
Hernia	0.67*	0.77*	0.37*	0.42	**	0.41*	**	**	**	0.47	**	0.46*	**0.45**
Chronic liver disease and cirrhosis	4.41	4.89	4.06	5.8	8.96	6.07	2.87*	5.27	13.57	2.71	4.75*	7.4	**5.26**
Cholelithiasis and other disorders of gallbladder	0.61*	1.67	0.54	0.83	1.86*	1.19	**	**	1.04*	0.8		0.75	**0.82**
Nephritis, nephrotic syndrome and nephrosis	9.61	11.96	4.63	7.74	7.1	10.89	3.91	8.72	11.9	5.93	7.59	10.02	**7.76**
Infections of kidney	0.37*	0.90*	0.20*	0.17	**	0.47*		**	**	0.23*		0.58	**0.27**
Hyperplasia of prostate	**	**		0.15		**			**	**		0.29*	**0.12**
Inflammatory diseases of female pelvic organs			**	0.04*			**	**		**			**0.03***
Pregnancy, childbirth and the puerperium	0.31*	**	0.27*	0.22		0.31*	**		0.83*	0.21*	**	**	**0.23**

	Bear River LHD	Central Utah LHD	Davis County LHD	Salt Lake Valley LHD	Southeastern Utah LHD	Southwest Utah LHD	Summit County LHD	Tooele County LHD	TriCounty LHD	Utah County LHD	Wasatch County LHD	Weber-Morgan LHD	Total
Certain conditions originating in the perinatal period	4.22	3.47	4.63	4.76	1.52*	3.68	2.35*	3.63	4.8	4.91	5.22*	4.28	**4.46**
Congenital malformations, deformations and chromosomal abnormalities	4.59	4.5	4.36	4.68	4.73	5.19	2.09*	4.72	4.38	5.32	4.75*	5.03	**4.78**
Unintentional injuries	29.19	52.85	21.59	27.28	59.82	34.33	26.9	37.77	59.49	22	36.54	28.24	**28.69**
Intentional self-harm (suicide)	10.95	17.49	13.09	14.9	21.46	14.52	9.39	11.44	20.25	10.1	15.19	17.68	**14**
Assault (homicide)	1.1	1.8	1.14	3.15	3.04	1.4	**	2.91	2.92	0.99	**	2.91	**2.19**
Legal intervention	**		0.17*	0.3	**	**	**	**	**	**		0.21*	**0.2**
Complications of medical and surgical care	0.86	1.41*	0.74	0.98	2.2	1.24	**	0.91*	**	0.6	**	0.71	**0.9**
Other than 50 Leading Causes	84.93	111.4	92.92	126.7	125.7	118.2	48.8	95.15	118.8	74.94	75.46	140.5	**109.2**
Total	492.1	766.5	452.5	**	782.8	661.5	302	491.6	685.9	388.2	484.5	656.3	****

Source: Utah Department of Health

5.4.4.4 Leading Causes of Death, 2009, Comparison Counties and State, by Rate per 100,000

	Utah County	Davis County	Salt Lake County	State
Total	**268.14**	**330.89**	**385.75**	381.63
Diseases of heart	75.64	87.44	97.11	99.5
Malignant neoplasms	62.47	76.06	93.56	90.82
Unintentional injuries	21.45	24.38	32.15	31.11
Cerebrovascular diseases	20.89	24.38	25.52	26.21
Diabetes mellitus	11.29	13	15.83	16.32
Intentional self-harm (suicide)	11.29	18.85	17.37	15.82
Alzheimer's disease	9.22	11.38	10.08	13.14
Chronic lower respiratory diseases	8.28	14.63	23.22	20.57
Nephritis, nephrotic syndrome and nephrosis	6.21	2.93	7	7.5
Influenza and pneumonia	6.02	12.03	12.47	11.71

	Utah County	Davis County	Salt Lake County	State
Congenital malformations, deformations and chromosomal abnormalities	4.7	3.9	4.13	4.25
Certain conditions originating in the perinatal period	4.33	7.48	5.57	5.07
Parkinson's disease	3.76	7.8	6.43	6.18
Pneumonitis due to solids and liquids	3.76	1.3	5.28	3.68
In situ neoplasms, benign neopl. & neopl. of uncertain or unknown behavior	3.2	2.6	2.88	3.71

	Utah County	Davis County	Salt Lake County	State
Chronic liver disease and cirrhosis	2.82	3.58	6.05	5.39
Septicemia	2.45	5.2	3.65	4.14
Essential (primary) hypertension and hypertensive renal disease	2.26	2.28	4.7	3.75
Assault (homicide)	1.51	0.33	2.59	1.82
Aortic aneurysm and dissection	1.32	1.95	1.92	1.96
Cholelithiasis and other disorders of gallbladder	1.13		0.86	0.75
Nutritional deficiencies	0.75		0.48	0.61
Anemias	0.75	0.65	0.86	0.61
Atherosclerosis	0.56	6.18	0.67	1.93
Peptic ulcer	0.56	0.33	0.38	0.5

	Utah County	Davis County	Salt Lake County	State
Complications of medical and surgical care	0.38	0.33	0.58	0.71
Hernia	0.38	0.33	0.38	0.43
Acute bronchitis and bronchiolitis	0.38		0.1	0.18
Viral hepatitis	0.19	0.33	1.73	1.18
Pregnancy, childbirth and the puerperium	0.19		0.19	0.21
Human immunodeficiency virus (HIV) disease		0.65	0.86	0.54
Infections of kidney			0.38	0.39
Pneumoconioses and chemical effects			0.1	0.25
Legal intervention			0.38	0.25
Meningitis		0.33	0.19	0.18
Hyperplasia of prostate			0.1	0.11

	Utah County	Davis County	Salt Lake County	State
Meningococcal infection				0.04
Diseases of appendix				0.04
Tuberculosis				0.04
Inflammatory diseases of female pelvic organs		0.33		0.04

Source: Utah Department of Health

5.4.4.5 Average Age at Death, by Local Health District, 1999-2009, All Districts

	Bear River LHD	Central Utah LHD	Davis County LHD	Salt Lake Valley LHD	Southeastern Utah LHD	Southwest Utah LHD	Summit County LHD	Tooele County LHD	TriCounty LHD	Utah County LHD	Wasatch County LHD	Weber-Morgan LHD	Unknown	Total
1999	71.7	72.8	69.4	70	69.4	72.6	66.4	68	67.7	70.5	65	71.9		70.5
2000	74.3	74.7	69.1	69.8	71.6	74.5	69.2	68.5	68.9	70.8	72.9	72.1		71
2001	74.3	72.4	69.8	70.5	70.5	73.3	68.2	68.4	67.1	70.7	76.6	71.9		71
2002	72.5	74.9	71.1	70.3	72.3	73	68.5	67.3	67.9	69.8	66.8	72.8		71
2003	72.7	74.5	70.2	70.5	71.4	73	64.9	67.6	68.9	70	74.2	72		71
2004	73.7	73.3	70.7	69.7	70.7	72.9	67.4	66.6	68.9	69.7	71.1	72		70.7
2005	73.1	73.5	70.9	70.7	70.9	73.1	66.1	68.6	66	69.4	73.2	71.3		70.9
2006	72.6	71.9	70.3	70.1	71.2	72.8	66.6	66	64.3	70	67.3	72.5		70.6
2007	72.3	71.6	69.4	70	70.2	73.1	65.1	65.5	67.9	70.2	62.1	70.6		70.3
2008	73.5	72.4	70	70.3	72	73.2	70.1	66.6	66.5	70.4	68.5	71.7		70.8
2009	72.8	72.7	70	69.9	71.6	73.1	66.2	67.9	66.6	70.2	71.8	71.4	57	70.6
Total	73	73.1	70.1	70.2	71.1	73.1	67.1	67.3	67.3	70.1	70	71.8	57	70.8

Source: Utah Department of Health

305

5.4.4.6 Leading Causes of Injury Death, Rate per 100,000, 2009, Comparison Counties and State

	Utah County	Davis County	Salt Lake County	Total
Poisoning	15.43	16.25	23.22	19.88
Firearm	6.02	7.8	10.65	8.88
Fall	4.33	6.83	6.53	5.95
Motor Vehicle, Traffic - Other and Unspecified	3.39	2.28	1.92	2.39
Suffocation	3.2	7.48	6.62	5.79
Motor Vehicle, Traffic - Occupant Injured	0.94	1.63	2.21	1.75
Motor Vehicle, Traffic - Pedestrian Injured	0.56	1.63	1.25	1.12
Motor Vehicle, Traffic - Motorcyclist Injured	0.56	0.33	0.77	0.64
Fire/Flame/Smoke	0.56		0.48	0.43
Other Transport (Air, Space, Water, etc.)	0.56	0.65	0.19	0.37
Drowning/Submersion	0.19	0.98	0.96	0.74
Oth. Motor Vehicle - Non-Traffic (Not Pedal, Peds)	0.19	0.65	0.58	0.48
Pedestrian - MV Non-Traffic and Other	0.19		0.29	0.21
Pedal Cyclist - MV Non-Traffic and Other	0.19		0.29	0.21
Cut/Pierce	0.19		0.29	0.21
Struck By or Against	0.19		0.19	0.16
Machinery	0.19			0.05
Natural / Environmental		0.33	0.48	0.32
Motor Vehicle, Traffic - Pedal Cyclist Injured		0.33	0.1	0.11
Other Land Transport - Non-Traffic, Not MV			0.1	0.05
Total	39.89	49.73	61.13	53.26

Source: Utah Department of Health

5.4.4.7 Suicide Rates per 100,000, by Age and Gender, 2009, Utah County

	Male	Female
< 1	0	0
1-4	0	0
5-14	0	0
15-24	19.88	1.82
25-34	31.82	0
35-44	28.02	32.57
45-54	26.08	4.34
55-64	24.76	11.91
65-74	21.42	0
75-84	18.75	0
85+	0	0

Source: Utah Department of Health

5.4.4.8 Leading Causes of Suicide Death, Rate per 100,000, 2009, Comparison Counties and State

	Utah County	Davis County	Salt Lake County	State
Firearm	4.7	7.48	8.64	7.34
Suffocation	2.07	6.83	4.22	4.04
Poisoning	3.2	3.58	3.65	3.51
Fall	0.38		0.19	0.21
Drowning/Submersion		0.65	0.1	0.16
Cut/Pierce	0.19		0.19	0.16
Fire/Flame/Smoke			0.19	0.11
Total	11.29	18.85	17.37	15.89

Source: Utah Department of Health

5.4.5 Disease

5.4.5.1 Emergency Room Discharges ("Treat and Release"), by Diagnosis, by Health District, 2008, All Districts

	Bear River LHD	Central Utah LHD	Davis County LHD	Salt Lake Valley LHD	Southeastern Utah LHD	Southwest Utah LHD	Summit County LHD	Tooele County LHD	TriCounty LHD	Utah County LHD	Wasatch County LHD	Weber-Morgan LHD	Total
0 Ungroupable	1.51	3.21	1.96	6.03	3.26	2.63	4.61	3.6	8.55	1.37	2.3	1.31	**3.65**
1 Nervous System	143.8	197.3	136.2	160.1	232.3	131	68.65	163	271.2	165	190.6	172.1	**160.01**
2 Eye	52.79	68.53	35.45	44.12	64.48	38.33	17.46	52.04	115.1	41.06	58.25	48.3	**45.4**
3 Ear, Nose, Mouth And Throat	264.7	444.3	176.5	287.4	439.9	284	90.6	327.1	866.8	240.3	348.7	307.1	**283.62**
4 Respiratory System	139.1	195.2	104.9	159.7	210.9	150.4	48.97	159.7	383.1	120.3	127.8	160.1	**149.2**
5 Circulatory System	125.5	152.9	109.2	139.5	149.7	134.5	66.64	130.7	168.6	100.1	112.3	138.9	**127.72**
6 Digestive System	247.2	281.4	212.3	287.3	313.7	238.4	114	263.2	466.5	224.5	248.9	282.4	**262.18**
7 Hepatobiliary System And Pancreas	7.74	10.4	11.27	13.45	12.28	7.37	4.81	15.11	14.6	11.46	6.46	15.27	**12.02**
8 Musculoskeletal System And Connective Tissue	366.5	507	332.2	429.4	611.2	363.8	156.8	450	831.4	404.4	447.1	445.5	**417.46**
9 Skin, Subcutaneous Tissue And Breast	349.5	491.6	312.4	386.9	525.1	377.6	122.4	462.6	813.4	332.8	448.2	400.7	**379.32**
10 Endocrine, Nutritional And Metabolic System	30.46	30.45	20.52	30.79	35.91	29.68	10.32	34.18	49.83	22.82	20.93	25.82	**27.88**
11 Kidney And Urinary Tract	88.52	105.6	84.15	106.4	132.8	101.7	38.25	115.2	194.9	87.02	79.34	110	**100.61**

	Bear River LHD	Central Utah LHD	Davis County LHD	Salt Lake Valley LHD	Southeastern Utah LHD	Southwest Utah LHD	Summit County LHD	Tooele County LHD	TriCounty LHD	Utah County LHD	Wasatch County LHD	Weber-Morgan LHD	Total
12 Male Reproductive System	7.4	9.18	6.89	9.59	12.11	7.98	3.94	9.6	17.95	7.22	7.69	9.93	**8.76**
13 Female Reproductive System	19.76	29.95	24.71	38.46	37.16	27.48	12.24	36.78	58.36	28.61	29.85	32.91	**32.47**
14 Pregnancy, Childbirth And Puerperium	47.57	67.53	43.66	64.74	40.13	63.28	23.03	62.21	73.98	55.51	63.06	63.5	**58.65**
15 Newborn And Other Neonates (Perinatal Period)	3.17	3.98	1.82	3.3	2.91	2.72	1.89	3.25	5.64	2.76	3.58	2.7	**2.98**
16 Blood and Blood-Forming Disorders	4.4	9.13	3.78	5.46	14.29	5.18	2.33	5.78	11.48	3.96	5.82	4.94	**5.25**
17 Myeloproliferative DDs (Diff Neoplasms)	0.41	1.28	0.51	0.33	3.77	0.62	0.38	0.24	1.68	0.34	0.69	0.47	**0.51**
18 Infectious and Parasitic DDs	56.9	60.91	36.86	64.5	110.9	60.38	25.71	64.47	130.8	39.66	65.94	59.32	**57.45**
19 Mental Diseases and Disorders	37.86	45.84	45.73	58.26	32.22	39.2	20.52	53.24	63.57	35.47	46.93	63.07	**49.21**
20 Alcohol/Drug Use or Induced Mental Disorders	12.74	13.12	14.68	27.84	13.73	16.35	10.52	18.02	37.84	15.46	16.23	26.61	**21.34**
21 Injuries, Poison And Toxic Effect of Drugs	129.6	130.2	88.07	109.4	116.5	69.26	52.44	110.1	203.3	105.1	138.9	118.3	**107.35**
22 Burns	13.59	15.84	10.47	11.19	17.76	10.76	3.79	14.04	41.08	10.91	14.79	12.8	**12.1**
23 Factors Influencing Health Status	117.5	58	72.38	112.5	56.36	135.8	25.83	123.8	264.9	123.1	35.24	84.01	**107.75**
24 Multiple Significant Trauma	0.91	1.91	0.21	0.3	1.29	1.12	0.32	0.41	1.84	0.44	0.43	0.34	**0.51**
25 Human Immunodeficiency Virus Infection	0.17	0.09	0.06	0.19	0.3	0.15	0.03	0.02	0.14	0.04		0.41	**0.16**

	Bear River LHD	Central Utah LHD	Davis County LHD	Salt Lake Valley LHD	Southeastern Utah LHD	Southwest Utah LHD	Summit County LHD	Tooele County LHD	TriCounty LHD	Utah County LHD	Wasatch County LHD	Weber-Morgan LHD	Total
Total	2,269.24	2,934.78	1,886.80	2,557.16	3,190.82	2,299.61	926.51	2,678.39	5,096.44	2,179.81	2,520.14	2,586.68	2,433.56

Treat and Release: A patient that visits the ED, but is not admitted to the hospital as an inpatient. The patient does not stay overnight and is not admitted to another department of the hospital

Source: Utah Department of Health

310

5.4.5.2 Leading Incidence of Cancer, Comparison Counties and State, 2007

	Utah County	Davis County	Salt Lake County	State
Prostate	195	188	660	1,043
Breast	139	123	466	728
Melanomas of the Skin	79	68	235	382
Colon (exluding Rectum)	65	55	167	287
Rectum, Rectosigmoid Junction	50	25	83	158
Lung and Bronchus	42	39	227	308
Corpus and Uterus	34	19	93	146
Pancreas	30	19	67	116
Testis	22	18	47	87
Ovary	19	5	52	76
Oral Cavity and Pharynx	15	10	61	86
Soft Tissues, including Heart	10	11	33	54
Small Intestine	9	5	12	26
Gallbladder and Biliary Ducts	9	**	11	**
Liver and Intrahepatic Bile Duct	7	12	31	50
Bones and Joints	6	5	13	24
Cervix	6	7	21	34
Esophagus	5	5	21	31
Stomach	5	10	39	54
Other Digestive System	5	5	13	23
Other Male Genital Organs			**	**
Urinary Bladder		24	123	194
Kidney and Renal Pelvis		24	82	134
Other Urinary Organs		**	**	8
Eye and Orbit		**	9	**
Brain		13	54	93
Cranial Nerves, Other Nervous System		**	**	5
Thyroid		39	114	208
Other Endocrine including Thymus		**	**	7
Hodgkin's Lymphoma		8	20	43
Non-Hodgkins Lymphomas		47	153	264
Multiple Myeloma		7	36	54

	Utah County	Davis County	Salt Lake County	State
Lymphocytic Leukemia		18	48	84
Myeloid Leukemia		9	38	69
Monocytic Leukemia			**	**
Other Leukemia			**	**
Other sites/types (not specified above)		13	92	135
Anus, Anal Canal and Anorectum	**	**	12	15
Larynx	**	**	12	17
Other Respiratory System	**	**	15	21
Other Non-Epithelial Skin	**	6	23	**
Other Female Genital Organs	**	**	13	19
Total		858	3,211	5,165

Source: Utah Department of Health

312

5.4.5.3 Leading Rates of Cancer per 100,000, 2007, Comparison Counties and State

	Utah County	Davis County	Salt Lake County	State
Prostate	68.59	89.34	83.04	80.91
Breast	47.1	53.14	56.15	53.67
Melanomas of the Skin	24.26	29.88	28.07	27.48
Colon (exluding Rectum)	23.27	26.7	21.68	22.73
Non-Hodgkins Lymphomas	20.67	20.91	19.31	19.89
Rectum, Rectosigmoid Junction	17.9	11.53	10.58	12.3
Urinary Bladder	17.34	11.99	16.36	15.86
Lung and Bronchus	15.17	18.59	29.82	24.67
Thyroid	14.38	14.4	12.48	13.24
Pancreas	11.58	8.94	8.89	9.56
Corpus and Uterus	11.23	8.17	10.79	10.44
Other sites/types (not specified above)	10.47	6.8	12.32	11.06
Kidney and Renal Pelvis	9.25	10.9	9.76	9.85
Myeloid Leukemia	6.98	4.26	4.26	4.79
Brain	6.38	4.7	5.71	5.75
Ovary	5.96	1.85	6.27	5.47
Lymphocytic Leukemia	5.3	7.33	5.97	5.98
Oral Cavity and Pharynx	4.43	4.06	7.58	6.32
Multiple Myeloma	4.06	3.68	4.65	4.37
Testis	3.91	5.64	4.5	4.58
Gallbladder and Biliary Ducts	3.2	**	1.54	**
Hodgkin's Lymphoma	3.2	2.77	2.03	2.42
Small Intestine	2.94	2.18	1.41	1.85
Liver and Intrahepatic Bile Duct	2.58	5.45	3.51	3.61
Soft Tissues, including Heart	2.55	4.3	3.86	3.65
Eye and Orbit	2.29	**	1.08	**
Esophagus	1.58	2.67	2.79	2.48
Cervix	1.52	2.87	2.21	2.16
Stomach	1.4	4.38	4.88	4
Other Digestive System	1.39	1.93	1.78	1.74
Bones and Joints	1.28	1.66	1.45	1.46

	Utah County	Davis County	Salt Lake County	State
Other Male Genital Organs			**	**
Monocytic Leukemia			**	**
Other Leukemia			**	**
Total	358.59	384.19	396.07	385.62

Source: Utah Department of Health

5.4.5.4 Hepatitis A, Hepatitis B, Pertussis Rates per 100,000, 2009, Comparison Counties

	Utah County	Davis County	Salt Lake County	State
Hepatitis A	0	0.3	0.3	0.2
Hepatitis B	0.2	0	0.3	0.2
Pertussis	6	4.9	9.7	7.8

Source: Utah Department of Health

5.4.5.5 New HIV/AIDS Cases and Percent of State Total, 2009, Comparison Counties and State

	Utah County	Davis County	Salt Lake County	All Other Counties
Percent of State Total	5.0%	7.0%	75.0%	13.0%
# Cases	9	13	142	25

Source: Utah Department of Health

5.4.5.6 Chlamydia Cases, by Local Health District, 2005-2009, All Districts

	2005	2006	2007	2008	2009
Bear River	156	190	233	190	176
Central	61	52	54	77	60
Davis	465	535	540	567	756
Salt Lake	2,524	2,824	3,238	3,415	3,271
Southeastern	96	89	91	76	101
Southwest	193	214	263	274	245
Summit	60	36	64	62	49
Tooele	74	66	88	83	109
Tri-County	59	51	46	71	62
Utah	405	420	464	518	622
Wasatch	12	24	32	29	39
Weber-Morgan	497	589	607	657	662
State	4,602	5,090	5,720	6,019	6,152

Source: Utah Department of Health

5.4.5.7 Chlamydia Rates per 100,000, by Health District, 2009, All Districts

	2005	2006	2007	2008	2009
Bear River	103.4	123.6	146.8	116.7	106.0
Central	85.8	72.0	73.0	102.3	78.4
Davis	167.1	186.7	182.4	187.8	245.7
Salt Lake	258.0	283.4	317.8	331.4	313.9
Southeastern	180.4	166.0	168.1	138.2	181.2
Southwest	103.9	109.3	129.2	130.9	116.2
Summit	165.4	97.6	166.6	155.2	121.1
Tooele	141.9	121.4	155.7	142.6	184.4
Tri-County	136.9	115.2	100.1	147.4	124.9
Utah	88.8	88.3	92.5	99.7	117.0
Wasatch	60.0	114.0	145.8	126.9	166.5
Weber-Morgan	223.7	262.1	263.9	280.6	279.1
State	180.7	194.6	211.9	218.3	219.7

Source: Utah Department of Health

5.4.5.8 Gonorrhea Cases, by Local Health District, 2005-2009, All Districts

	2005	2006	2007	2008	2009
Bear River	13	26	12	3	6
Central	15	8	5	0	0
Davis	62	58	54	24	36
Salt Lake	451	612	552	334	241
Southeastern	6	11	5	2	5
Southwest	27	17	15	14	12
Summit	3	6	6	4	2
Tooele	7	10	14	10	1
Tri-County	4	10	1	2	0
Utah	53	45	34	13	16
Wasatch	3	2	1	0	0
Weber-Morgan	83	83	122	71	22
State	727	888	821	477	341

Source: Utah Department of Health

5.4.5.9 Gonorrhea Rates per 100,000, by Local Health District, 2005-2009, All Districts

	2005	2006	2007	2008	2009
Bear River	8.6	16.9	7.6	1.8	3.6
Central	21.1	11.1	6.8	0.0	0.0
Davis	22.3	20.2	18.2	7.9	11.7
Salt Lake	46.1	61.4	54.2	32.4	23.1
Southeastern	11.3	20.5	9.2	3.6	9.0
Southwest	14.5	8.7	7.4	6.7	5.7
Summit	8.3	16.3	15.6	10.0	4.9
Tooele	13.4	18.4	24.8	17.2	1.7
Tri-County	9.3	22.6	2.2	4.2	0.0
Utah	11.6	9.5	6.8	2.5	3.0
Wasatch	15.0	9.5	4.6	0.0	0.0
Weber-Morgan	37.4	36.9	53.0	30.3	9.3
State	28.5	34.0	30.4	17.3	12.2

Source: Utah Department of Health

5.4.5.10   Primary and Secondary Syphilis Cases, by Local Health District, 2005-2009, All Districts

	2005	2006	2007	2008	2009
Bear River	0	0	0	0	0
Central	0	0	0	0	0
Davis	0	2	1	1	0
Salt Lake	9	15	19	22	28
Southeastern	0	0	0	0	0
Southwest	0	0	0	0	0
Summit	0	0	0	0	0
Tooele	0	0	0	1	0
Tri-County	0	0	0	0	0
Utah	1	4	0	1	0
Wasatch	0	0	0	0	0
Weber-Morgan	0	0	0	0	3
State	10	21	20	25	31

Source: Utah Department of Health

5.4.5.11   Primary and Secondary Syphilis Rates per 100,000, by Local Health District, 2005-2009, All Districts

	2005	2006	2007	2008	2009
Bear River	0.0	0.0	0.0	0.0	0.0
Central	0.0	0.0	0.0	0.0	0.0
Davis	0.0	0.7	0.3	0.3	0.0
Salt Lake	0.9	1.5	1.9	2.1	2.7
Southeastern	0.0	0.0	0.0	0.0	0.0
Southwest	0.0	0.0	0.0	0.0	0.0
Summit	0.0	0.0	0.0	0.0	0.0
Tooele	0.0	0.0	0.0	1.7	0.0
Tri-County	0.0	0.0	0.0	0.0	0.0
Utah	0.2	0.8	0.0	0.2	0.0
Wasatch	0.0	0.0	0.0	0.0	0.0
Weber-Morgan	0.0	0.0	0.0	0.0	1.3
State	0.4	0.8	0.7	0.9	1.1

Source: Utah Department of Health

5.4.6   Violence

5.4.6.1 Domestic Violence Indicators, 2009, Comparison Counties

	Utah County	Davis County	Salt Lake County
Protective Orders Granted	197	148	747
Civil Stalking Injunctions Granted	19	27	49
Domestic Violence Charges Filed	655	274	2,079
Domestic Violence Hotline Calls	209	233	1,501

Source: Utah Domestic Violence Council

5.4.6.2 Domestic Violence Indicators, Rate per 100,000, 2009, Comparison Counties

	Utah County	Davis County	Salt Lake County
Protective Orders Granted	36.1	47.0	70.4
Civil Stalking Injunctions Granted	3.5	8.6	4.6
Domestic Violence Charges Filed	120.2	87.0	196.0

Source: Utah Domestic Violence Council

5.4.6.3 Deaths due to Domestic Violence, 2006-2010, Comparison Counties

	Utah County	Davis County	Salt Lake County
2006	2	3	7
2007	1	0	10
2008	2	3	8
2009	6	0	12
2010	2	0	12

Source: Utah Domestic Violence Council

5.4.7.2 Primary Substance at Admission, County Divisions of Substance Abuse, 2009, Comparison Counties

	Utah County				Davis County				Salt Lake County			
	Male	Female	Total	% of Total	Male	Female	Total	% of Total	Male	Female	Total	% of Total
Alcohol	256	136	392	24.6%	158	89	247	23.4%	2884	737	3621	38.2%
Cocain / Crack	27	32	59	3.7%	54	16	70	6.6%	644	275	919	9.7%
Marijuana/ Hashish	162	60	222	13.9%	132	41	173	16.4%	968	265	1233	13.0%
Heroin	198	151	349	21.9%	89	20	109	10.3%	1016	526	1542	16.3%
Other Opiates/ Synthetics	5	16	21	1.3%	14	18	32	3.0%	136	140	276	2.9%
Hallucinogens	5	0	5	0.3%	0	0	0	0.0%	3	4	7	0.1%
Meth- amphetamine	136	172	308	19.3%	163	157	320	30.4%	820	765	1585	16.7%
Other Stimulants	4	0	4	0.3%	3	0	3	0.3%	12	29	41	0.4%
Benzodiazepines	9	15	24	1.5%	0	1	1	0.1%	13	13	26	0.3%
Tranquilizers/ Sedatives	0	3	3	0.2%	0	1	1	0.1%	3	14	17	0.2%
Inhalants	0	0	0	0.0%	2	2	4	0.4%	3	1	4	0.0%
Oxycodone	94	103	197	12.4%	48	44	92	8.7%	106	74	180	1.9%
Club Drugs	3	0	3	0.2%	0	0	0	0.0%	6	4	10	0.1%
Over-the- Counter	0	3	3	0.2%	2	0	2	0.2%	0	2	2	0.0%
Other	1	2	3	0.2%	0	0	0	0.0%	3	1	4	0.0%
Unknown	0	0	0	0.0%	0	0	0	0.0%	0	0	0	0.0%
Total	900	693	1593		665	389	1054		6617	2850	9467	

Source: Utah Division of Substance Abuse and Mental Health, Annual Report 2009

5.4.7.3 Mental Health Diagnosis, County Mental Health Units, by Youth and Adults, 2009, Comparison Counties

	Utah County				Davis County				Salt Lake County			
	Youth	Youth %	Adult	Adult %	Youth	Youth %	Adults	Adult %	Youth	Youth %	Adults	Adult %
Mood Disorders	730	26.3%	2145	66.6%	512	45.1%	1560	76.3%	1601	33.7%	5865	55.7%
Anxiety Disorders	887	32.0%	2073	64.3%	371	32.7%	1253	61.3%	1537	32.3%	3663	34.8%
Personality Disorders	15	0.5%	828	25.7%	8	0.7%	319	15.6%	22	0.5%	2713	25.8%
Substance Abuse	133	4.8%	1032	32.0%	61	5.4%	497	24.3%	615	12.9%	5970	56.7%
Adjustment Disorders	423	15.2%	94	2.9%	172	15.1%	102	5.0%	682	14.3%	251	2.4%
Cognitive Disorders	69	2.5%	374	11.6%	15	1.3%	71	3.5%	117	2.5%	431	4.1%
Schizophrenia and Other Psychotic	41	1.5%	833	25.9%	26	2.3%	454	22.2%	80	1.7%	2260	21.5%
Attention Deficit	681	24.5%	281	8.7%	441	38.8%	129	6.3%	1577	33.2%	494	4.7%
Autism	316	11.4%	94	2.9%	117	10.3%	40	2.0%	548	11.5%	136	1.3%
Impulse Disorders	55	2.0%	134	4.2%	24	2.1%	32	1.6%	21	0.4%	132	1.3%
Neglect or Abuse	612	22.1%	154	4.8%	435	38.3%	28	1.4%	766	16.1%	36	0.3%
Conduct Disorders	87	3.1%	8	0.2%	61	5.4%	15	0.7%	231	4.9%	21	0.2%
Other	1585	57.1%	1524	47.3%	884	77.8%	990	48.4%	2453	51.6%	1617	15.4%
V Codes	1174	42.3%	600	18.6%	220	19.4%	89	4.4%	838	17.6%	1830	17.4%
Total	6808		10174		3347		5579		11088		25419	

Source: Utah Division of Substance Abuse and Mental Health, Annual Report 2009

5.4.7.4 Emergency Department Admissions for Mental Diseases and Disorders, Rate per 10,000, 2004-2008, Comparison Counties and State

	Utah County	Davis County	Salt Lake County	State
2004	16.11	16.59	8.84	12.01
2005	17.06	16.78	8.54	12.15
2006	15.78	18.43	8.85	12.28
2007	15.89	17.5	8.67	12.1
2008	13.99	15.77	9.42	11.74

Source: Utah Division of Substance Abuse and Mental Health, Annual Report 2009

5.4.7.5 Emergency Department Admissions for Alcohol/Drug Use or Induced Mental Disorders, Rate per 10,000, 2004-2008, Comparison Counties and State

	Utah County	Davis County	Salt Lake County	State
2004	5.92	4.98	3.89	4.6
2005	5.68	4.82	4.3	4.75
2006	5.45	6.32	4.41	5
2007	4.31	5.17	4.69	4.66
2008	3.71	4.84	4.93	4.57

Source: Utah Division of Substance Abuse and Mental Health, Annual Report 2009

5.4.7.6 Mental Health Outcomes Questionnaire, 2009, Comparison Counties and State

	Utah County	Davis County	Salt Lake County	State
Participating in Survey	55.0%	16.0%	29.0%	35.0%
Recovered	24.1%	14.5%	22.2%	22.6%
Stablized or Improved	60.1%	69.5%	61.8%	62.1%

Source: Utah Division of Substance Abuse and Mental Health, Annual Report 2009

5.4.7.7 Youth Mental Health Outcomes Questionnaire, 2009, Comparison Counties and State

	Utah County	Davis County	Salt Lake County	State
Participating in Survey	47.0%	14.0%	34.0%	38.0%
Recovered	38.1%	14.6%	25.1%	26.9%
Stablized or Improved	38.1%	65.8%	58.5%	58.4%

Source: Utah Division of Substance Abuse and Mental Health, Annual Report 2009

5.4.8   Disability

5.4.8.1 Persons with Disabilities by Gender

SEX	Total	With a disability	Percent with a disability
Male	269,506	22,779	8.5%
Female	273,320	19,962	7.3%

Source: U.S. Census Bureau

5.4.8.2 Persons with Disabilities by Age

Subject	Total	With a disability	Percent with a disability
Total civilian noninstitutionalized population	542,826	42,741	7.9%
Population under 5 years	60,873	648	1.1%
With a hearing difficulty	(X)	414	0.7%
With a vision difficulty	(X)	441	0.7%
Population 5 to 17 years	128,436	6,208	4.8%
With a hearing difficulty	(X)	1,120	0.9%
With a vision difficulty	(X)	850	0.7%
With a cognitive difficulty	(X)	4,664	3.6%
With an ambulatory difficulty	(X)	1,246	1.0%
With a self-care difficulty	(X)	1,452	1.1%
Population 18 to 64 years	318,156	22,898	7.2%
With a hearing difficulty	(X)	7,437	2.3%
With a vision difficulty	(X)	3,408	1.1%
With a cognitive difficulty	(X)	10,864	3.4%
With an ambulatory difficulty	(X)	7,856	2.5%
With a self-care difficulty	(X)	3,502	1.1%
With an independent living difficulty	(X)	7,331	2.3%
Population 65 years and over	35,361	12,987	36.7%
With a hearing difficulty	(X)	5,070	14.3%
With a vision difficulty	(X)	2,648	7.5%
With a cognitive difficulty	(X)	3,971	11.2%
With an ambulatory difficulty	(X)	8,516	24.1%
With a self-care difficulty	(X)	2,991	8.5%
With an independent living difficulty	(X)	6,297	17.8%

Source: U.S. Census Bureau

5.4.8.3 Persons with Disabilities by Age and Gender

	Utah County		Davis County		Salt Lake County	
	Male	Female	Male	Female	Male	Female
Population	269,506	273,320	147,386	147,261	518,080	506,796
<18 years old	97,706	91,603	52,514	48,981	154,841	145,838
<18 years old with a disability	4,393	2,463	2,113	961	5,113	3,802
Percent <18 years old with a disability	4.5%	2.7%	4.0%	2.0%	3.3%	2.6%
18-64 years old	155,914.0	162,242.0	83,946.0	86,311.0	323,914.0	312,317.0
18-64 years old with a disability	13,060.0	9,838.0	4,933.0	6,989.0	25,617.0	24,639.0
Percent 18-64 years old with a disability	8.4%	6.1%	5.9%	8.1%	7.9%	7.9%
>64 years old	15,886	19,475	10,926	11,969	39,325	48,641
>64 years old with a disability	5,326	7,661	4,018	4,540	12,324	17,550
Percent >64 years old with a disability	33.5%	39.3%	36.8%	37.9%	31.3%	36.1%

Source: U.S. Census Bureau

5.4.8.4 Persons with Disabilities by Race and Ethnicity

RACE AND HISPANIC OR LATINO ORIGIN	Total	With a disability	Percent with a disability
One Race	N	N	N
White alone	494,034	39,447	8.0%
Black or African American alone	N	N	N
American Indian and Alaska Native alone	N	N	N
Asian alone	N	N	N
Native Hawaiian and Other Pacific Islander alone	N	N	N
Some other race alone	N	N	N
Two or more races	12,453	598	4.8%
White alone, not Hispanic or Latino	461,803	37,100	8.0%
Hispanic or Latino (of any race)	53,354	3,631	6.8%

Source: U.S. Census Bureau

5.4.8.5 Persons with Disabilities by Employment Status

EMPLOYMENT STATUS	Percent	With a Disability	No Disability
Employed	63.4%	31.5%	67.0%
Not in Labor Force	30.9%	61.3%	27.6%

	Number	With a Disability	No Disability
Employed Population Age 16 and Over	235,219	11,638	223,581

5.4.8.6 Persons with Disabilities by Class of Worker

CLASS OF WORKER	Percent	With a Disability	No Disability
Private for-profit wage and salary workers	71.4%	60.6%	72.0%
Employee of private company workers	66.8%	55.7%	67.4%
Self-employed in own incorporated business workers	4.6%	4.9%	4.6%
Private not-for-profit wage and salary workers	11.7%	15.8%	11.5%
Local government workers	6.7%	12.6%	6.4%
State government workers	4.3%	6.5%	4.2%
Federal government workers	1.1%	1.2%	1.1%
Self-employed in own not incorporated business workers	4.7%	2.2%	4.9%
Unpaid family workers	0.2%	1.1%	0.1%

Source: U.S. Census Bureau

5.4.8.7 Persons with Disabilities by Occupation

OCCUPATION	Percent	With a Disability	No Disability
Management, professional, and related occupations	36.0%	29.7%	36.3%
Service occupations	16.1%	20.5%	15.9%
Sales and office occupations	29.9%	21.6%	30.3%
Farming, fishing, and forestry occupations	0.2%	0.6%	0.2%
Construction, extraction, maintenance, and repair occupations	7.6%	13.6%	7.3%
Production, transportation, and material moving occupations	10.2%	14.1%	10.0%

Source: U.S. Census Bureau

5.4.8.8 Persons with Disabilities by Industry

INDUSTRY	Percent	With a Disability	No Disability
Agriculture, forestry, fishing and hunting, and mining	1.0%	1.7%	1.0%
Construction	6.8%	7.5%	6.8%
Manufacturing	10.8%	5.7%	11.0%
Wholesale trade	2.9%	5.2%	2.8%
Retail trade	14.3%	14.5%	14.2%
Transportation and warehousing, and utilities	2.4%	3.0%	2.4%
Information	2.2%	0.0%	2.3%
Finance and insurance, and real estate and rental and leasing	6.2%	7.8%	6.1%
Professional, scientific, and management, and administrative and waste management services	11.7%	10.7%	11.7%
Educational services, and health care and social assistance	25.1%	31.0%	24.8%
Arts, entertainment, and recreation, and accommodation and food services	8.8%	7.0%	8.9%
Other services (except public administration)	4.6%	3.1%	4.7%
Public administration	3.2%	2.7%	3.2%

Source: U.S. Census Bureau

5.4.8.9 Persons with Disabilities by Commuting to Work

COMMUTING TO WORK	Total	With a Disability	No Disability
Workers Age 16 and Over	**230,081**	**10,987**	**219,094**
Car, truck, or van - drove alone	73.6%	61.3%	74.3%
Car, truck, or van - carpooled	11.2%	17.9%	10.9%
Public transportation (excluding taxicab)	2.6%	8.7%	2.3%
Walked	5.2%	7.1%	5.1%
Taxicab, motorcycle, bicycle, or other means	2.0%	2.3%	2.0%
Worked at home	5.3%	2.8%	5.5%

Source: U.S. Census Bureau

5.4.8.10   Persons with Disabilities by Educational Attainment

EDUCATIONAL ATTAINMENT	Total	With a Disability	No Disability
Population Age 25 and Over	**245,433**	**31,107**	**214,326**
Less than high school graduate	6.7%	14.7%	5.5%
High school graduate, GED, or alternative	17.5%	28.0%	15.9%
Some college or associate's degree	42.0%	40.2%	42.2%
Bachelor's degree or higher	33.9%	17.2%	36.3%

Source: U.S. Census Bureau

5.4.8.11   Persons with Disabilities by Earnings

EARNINGS IN PAST 12 MONTHS (IN 2009 INFLATION ADJUSTED DOLLARS)	Total	With a Disability	No Disability
Population Age 16 and over with earnings	**278,645**	**14,197**	**264,448**
$1 to $4,999 or loss	35.3%	37.7%	35.2%
$5,000 to $14,999	10.2%	8.8%	10.2%
$15,000 to $24,999	12.8%	14.0%	12.7%
$25,000 to $34,999	10.6%	9.6%	10.6%
$35,000 to $49,999	11.5%	9.0%	11.6%
$50,000 to $74,999	9.8%	12.2%	9.7%
$75,000 or more	9.9%	8.7%	9.9%
Median Earnings	18,863	17,412	18,932

Source: U.S. Census Bureau

5.4.8.12   Persons with Disabilities by Poverty Status

POVERTY STATUS IN THE PAST 12 MONTHS	Total	With a Disability	No Disability
Population Age 16 and over for whom poverty status is determined	**365,071**	**36,819**	**328,252**
Below 100 percent of the poverty level	16.0%	15.1%	16.1%
100 to 149 percent of the poverty level	8.5%	12.5%	8.0%
At or above 150 percent of the poverty level	75.5%	72.4%	75.8%

Source: U.S. Census Bureau

5.5 Looking Forward

5.5.1 Utah County Population Projections, 2000-2060, by Gender, by Age Group

G	Age	2000	2001	2002	2003	2004	2005	2006	2007	2008	2009	2010
F	0-4	20,054	21,628	23,053	24,501	25,507	26,338	27,318	28,271	29,009	29,517	29,787
F	5-9	16,573	17,120	17,713	18,595	19,708	21,250	22,896	24,719	26,405	27,739	28,452
F	10-14	15,326	15,874	16,407	16,904	17,244	17,839	18,473	19,502	20,622	22,055	23,459
F	15-19	21,727	21,663	21,383	21,474	21,785	22,279	22,839	23,768	24,544	25,247	25,639
F	20-24	29,198	30,758	31,777	32,216	32,144	31,820	31,422	31,247	31,587	32,167	32,488
F	25-29	15,772	17,302	18,739	20,380	21,958	23,439	24,549	25,710	26,281	26,244	25,868
F	30-34	11,452	12,088	12,621	13,323	14,097	15,403	16,848	18,699	20,550	22,415	23,763
F	35-39	10,110	10,437	10,798	11,126	11,306	11,598	12,255	13,258	14,142	15,235	16,400
F	40-44	9,491	10,005	10,244	10,717	11,000	11,455	11,845	12,648	13,134	13,598	13,744
F	45-49	8,231	8,802	9,361	9,871	10,162	10,614	11,200	11,825	12,379	12,888	13,196
F	50-54	6,923	7,461	7,793	8,223	8,577	9,154	9,764	10,640	11,195	11,643	11,961
F	55-59	5,262	5,731	6,219	6,625	7,009	7,648	8,199	8,795	9,204	9,644	10,090
F	60-64	3,986	4,180	4,482	4,975	5,385	5,751	6,236	6,906	7,244	7,646	8,160
F	65-69	3,560	3,691	3,761	3,930	4,043	4,260	4,483	4,898	5,306	5,682	5,924
F	70-74	3,145	3,237	3,338	3,405	3,477	3,604	3,732	3,865	3,979	4,085	4,231
F	75-79	2,680	2,689	2,707	2,728	2,753	2,831	2,887	3,012	3,091	3,198	3,300
F	80-84	2,074	2,029	2,018	1,986	2,004	1,976	1,996	1,948	2,044	2,114	2,220
F	85 +	1,920	1,924	1,915	1,899	1,865	1,831	1,760	1,614	1,633	1,695	1,750
M	0-4	21,140	22,892	24,357	25,854	26,866	27,708	28,265	29,582	30,338	30,980	31,328
M	5-9	17,446	18,022	18,667	19,660	20,788	22,333	24,153	26,016	27,748	29,089	29,824
M	10-14	16,286	16,903	17,332	17,775	18,055	18,709	19,371	20,450	21,681	23,123	24,529
M	15-19	19,495	19,227	18,881	18,941	19,082	19,561	20,266	21,200	21,915	22,564	23,008
M	20-24	26,712	28,211	29,166	29,563	29,476	29,437	29,040	28,999	29,361	29,894	30,169
M	25-29	17,874	19,515	21,048	22,755	24,437	25,670	26,757	27,868	28,435	28,467	28,353
M	30-34	11,985	12,505	12,998	13,679	14,509	15,842	17,328	19,203	21,085	22,991	24,116
M	35-39	10,476	10,993	11,353	11,714	11,881	12,183	12,714	13,666	14,536	15,673	16,855
M	40-44	9,411	9,919	10,414	10,984	11,265	11,775	12,373	13,167	13,676	14,136	14,294
M	45-49	8,109	8,732	9,141	9,646	9,981	10,503	11,071	11,948	12,609	13,116	13,482
M	50-54	6,509	7,043	7,494	7,992	8,415	8,994	9,662	10,387	10,910	11,384	11,767
M	55-59	4,930	5,327	5,750	6,234	6,600	7,193	7,757	8,452	8,917	9,422	9,865
M	60-64	3,672	3,937	4,209	4,558	4,953	5,367	5,791	6,394	6,813	7,209	7,664
M	65-69	3,139	3,304	3,461	3,636	3,729	3,916	4,152	4,561	4,818	5,179	5,457
M	70-74	2,749	2,795	2,831	2,865	2,941	3,104	3,297	3,500	3,630	3,716	3,817
M	75-79	2,084	2,124	2,166	2,233	2,318	2,392	2,433	2,527	2,563	2,669	2,798
M	80-84	1,386	1,363	1,378	1,356	1,388	1,404	1,438	1,424	1,599	1,714	1,815
M	85 +	1,007	1,016	1,002	963	919	892	855	778	809	863	938

334

G	Age	2011	2012	2013	2014	2015	2016	2017	2018	2019	2020
F	0-4	29,799	29,937	30,091	30,298	30,529	30,737	30,955	31,202	31,499	31,827
F	5-9	29,312	29,923	30,417	30,733	31,056	31,095	31,251	31,408	31,608	31,822
F	10-14	24,976	26,445	27,882	29,025	29,794	30,676	31,303	31,796	32,104	32,411
F	15-19	26,081	26,676	27,508	28,725	30,189	31,734	33,216	34,651	35,781	36,527
F	20-24	32,925	33,457	33,881	34,323	34,794	35,268	35,884	36,719	37,920	39,361
F	25-29	25,519	25,143	25,117	25,406	25,804	26,278	26,837	27,270	27,700	28,147
F	30-34	24,769	25,503	25,738	25,439	25,138	24,824	24,474	24,457	24,738	25,118
F	35-39	17,698	19,087	20,641	22,275	23,678	24,705	25,457	25,700	25,394	25,082
F	40-44	14,232	14,780	15,419	16,308	17,517	18,833	20,231	21,783	23,397	24,777
F	45-49	13,432	13,816	14,105	14,410	14,600	15,102	15,659	16,298	17,181	18,373
F	50-54	12,388	12,641	13,038	13,420	13,753	14,003	14,398	14,687	14,989	15,173
F	55-59	10,550	11,093	11,537	11,893	12,231	12,665	12,923	13,320	13,694	14,020
F	60-64	8,578	8,895	9,239	9,622	10,065	10,521	11,059	11,496	11,849	12,180
F	65-69	6,268	6,684	6,997	7,372	7,874	8,279	8,588	8,927	9,302	9,737
F	70-74	4,344	4,578	4,970	5,329	5,560	5,886	6,282	6,585	6,944	7,423
F	75-79	3,391	3,446	3,550	3,649	3,790	3,898	4,118	4,477	4,806	5,023
F	80-84	2,318	2,444	2,516	2,604	2,697	2,779	2,835	2,929	3,015	3,142
F	85 +	1,829	1,885	1,962	2,050	2,158	2,276	2,393	2,484	2,597	2,727
M	0-4	31,682	31,571	31,742	31,962	32,203	32,421	32,652	32,912	33,225	33,574
M	5-9	30,272	31,243	31,754	32,204	32,607	32,981	32,887	33,058	33,273	33,498
M	10-14	26,220	27,731	29,220	30,374	31,165	31,638	32,622	33,132	33,576	33,961
M	15-19	23,478	24,122	25,066	26,297	27,764	29,480	31,007	32,496	33,637	34,406
M	20-24	30,670	31,097	31,461	31,846	32,367	32,871	33,534	34,476	35,692	37,133
M	25-29	27,953	27,634	27,627	27,873	28,228	28,767	29,221	29,589	29,959	30,458
M	30-34	25,127	25,855	26,086	25,854	25,814	25,447	25,153	25,156	25,393	25,728
M	35-39	18,187	19,599	21,178	22,845	24,023	25,056	25,799	26,037	25,804	25,751
M	40-44	14,666	15,162	15,783	16,717	17,941	19,287	20,705	22,279	23,927	25,082
M	45-49	13,905	14,288	14,595	14,892	15,093	15,482	15,984	16,605	17,527	18,726
M	50-54	12,175	12,682	13,187	13,567	13,956	14,387	14,781	15,089	15,378	15,568
M	55-59	10,370	10,758	11,172	11,550	11,951	12,369	12,873	13,371	13,745	14,129
M	60-64	8,079	8,473	8,867	9,307	9,748	10,241	10,627	11,035	11,407	11,798
M	65-69	5,740	6,097	6,483	6,847	7,285	7,685	8,064	8,443	8,868	9,296
M	70-74	3,953	4,172	4,415	4,752	5,016	5,278	5,613	5,977	6,324	6,734
M	75-79	2,945	3,043	3,160	3,240	3,332	3,459	3,658	3,881	4,185	4,423
M	80-84	1,877	1,970	2,005	2,094	2,206	2,327	2,416	2,512	2,582	2,668
M	85 +	1,025	1,108	1,233	1,320	1,416	1,493	1,595	1,686	1,791	1,915

G	Age	2021	2022	2023	2024	2025	2026	2027	2028	2029	2030
F	0-4	32,252	32,794	33,400	34,089	34,874	35,711	36,581	37,501	38,464	39,423
F	5-9	32,015	32,216	32,443	32,723	33,035	33,443	33,967	34,563	35,240	36,006
F	10-14	32,436	32,571	32,707	32,888	33,086	33,266	33,448	33,660	33,931	34,221
F	15-19	37,390	37,997	38,469	38,753	39,039	39,043	39,158	39,279	39,451	39,626
F	20-24	40,872	42,324	43,727	44,830	45,556	46,399	46,985	47,440	47,710	47,969
F	25-29	28,600	29,189	29,991	31,158	32,566	34,053	35,483	36,870	37,964	38,660
F	30-34	25,566	26,103	26,508	26,912	27,335	27,764	28,330	29,112	30,265	31,646
F	35-39	24,752	24,380	24,342	24,604	24,963	25,396	25,912	26,303	26,696	27,098
F	40-44	25,786	26,518	26,741	26,423	26,093	25,755	25,372	25,329	25,584	25,926
F	45-49	19,666	21,043	22,563	24,154	25,511	26,501	27,222	27,441	27,121	26,785
F	50-54	15,665	16,210	16,834	17,695	18,865	20,140	21,501	23,002	24,577	25,917
F	55-59	14,264	14,647	14,932	15,226	15,401	15,886	16,420	17,039	17,891	19,045
F	60-64	12,608	12,868	13,259	13,627	13,947	14,188	14,562	14,848	15,143	15,315
F	65-69	10,179	10,705	11,134	11,482	11,811	12,230	12,488	12,872	13,233	13,549
F	70-74	7,807	8,105	8,436	8,801	9,224	9,650	10,157	10,573	10,913	11,238
F	75-79	5,321	5,686	5,972	6,312	6,756	7,119	7,404	7,717	8,063	8,465
F	80-84	3,240	3,433	3,747	4,039	4,232	4,493	4,816	5,081	5,388	5,784
F	85 +	2,859	2,970	3,102	3,248	3,444	3,617	3,847	4,177	4,493	4,760
M	0-4	34,023	34,598	35,237	35,966	36,796	37,683	38,607	39,583	40,603	41,618
M	5-9	33,707	33,922	34,161	34,455	34,786	35,217	35,771	36,398	37,116	37,925
M	10-14	34,318	34,205	34,357	34,555	34,765	34,957	35,151	35,379	35,665	35,973
M	15-19	34,856	35,820	36,304	36,725	37,087	37,427	37,299	37,432	37,619	37,808
M	20-24	38,821	40,315	41,768	42,875	43,620	44,053	44,991	45,462	45,874	46,211
M	25-29	30,938	31,575	32,488	33,671	35,078	36,739	38,208	39,646	40,745	41,467
M	30-34	26,242	26,673	27,017	27,364	27,839	28,298	28,911	29,804	30,974	32,356
M	35-39	25,366	25,054	25,038	25,255	25,570	26,068	26,481	26,813	27,149	27,601
M	40-44	26,095	26,821	27,037	26,789	26,723	26,332	26,009	25,988	26,199	26,501
M	45-49	20,048	21,439	22,985	24,605	25,740	26,736	27,451	27,660	27,415	27,340
M	50-54	15,942	16,434	17,041	17,940	19,121	20,423	21,791	23,308	24,904	26,018
M	55-59	14,547	14,924	15,224	15,510	15,700	16,067	16,548	17,145	18,027	19,180
M	60-64	12,204	12,698	13,187	13,555	13,927	14,339	14,710	15,001	15,286	15,474
M	65-69	9,769	10,141	10,541	10,903	11,289	11,687	12,169	12,644	13,004	13,367
M	70-74	7,112	7,471	7,833	8,238	8,643	9,095	9,458	9,842	10,190	10,562
M	75-79	4,660	4,967	5,302	5,622	6,003	6,353	6,690	7,026	7,406	7,784
M	80-84	2,781	2,951	3,144	3,401	3,608	3,813	4,083	4,373	4,658	4,991
M	85 +	2,034	2,146	2,269	2,388	2,533	2,694	2,894	3,109	3,367	3,601

G	Age	2031	2032	2033	2034	2035	2036	2037	2038	2039	2040
F	0-4	40,377	41,289	42,160	42,988	43,770	44,489	45,156	45,765	46,317	46,763
F	5-9	36,805	37,629	38,492	39,392	40,300	41,208	42,081	42,923	43,726	44,433
F	10-14	34,591	35,069	35,609	36,225	36,936	37,686	38,472	39,304	40,182	41,008
F	15-19	39,756	39,879	40,026	40,222	40,450	40,765	41,194	41,695	42,279	42,895
F	20-24	47,914	47,958	48,003	48,089	48,187	48,254	48,323	48,430	48,589	48,710
F	25-29	39,448	39,967	40,342	40,523	40,701	40,583	40,576	40,576	40,627	40,616
F	30-34	33,082	34,451	35,767	36,780	37,407	38,136	38,608	38,939	39,088	39,170
F	35-39	27,485	28,000	28,721	29,801	31,120	32,505	33,829	35,110	36,093	36,639
F	40-44	26,328	26,806	27,150	27,486	27,836	28,183	28,664	29,357	30,416	31,663
F	45-49	26,430	26,023	25,947	26,160	26,466	26,832	27,282	27,602	27,918	28,215
F	50-54	26,880	27,574	27,765	27,418	27,060	26,688	26,268	26,178	26,376	26,644
F	55-59	20,294	21,621	23,089	24,621	25,925	26,863	27,542	27,724	27,376	27,000
F	60-64	15,788	16,305	16,907	17,733	18,861	20,086	21,393	22,837	24,346	25,620
F	65-69	13,790	14,161	14,444	14,736	14,905	15,370	15,882	16,473	17,284	18,390
F	70-74	11,646	11,903	12,281	12,633	12,944	13,181	13,545	13,825	14,112	14,279
F	75-79	8,874	9,355	9,751	10,076	10,390	10,781	11,031	11,396	11,734	12,035
F	80-84	6,104	6,366	6,650	6,969	7,341	7,712	8,148	8,507	8,802	9,093
F	85 +	5,063	5,460	5,888	6,334	6,810	7,245	7,708	8,216	8,768	9,384
M	0-4	42,627	43,592	44,515	45,392	46,221	46,982	47,691	48,338	48,923	49,397
M	5-9	38,777	39,655	40,576	41,534	42,500	43,465	44,389	45,283	46,134	46,888
M	10-14	36,366	36,872	37,443	38,098	38,854	39,656	40,498	41,390	42,327	43,209
M	15-19	37,953	38,089	38,250	38,461	38,706	39,042	39,501	40,033	40,657	41,319
M	20-24	46,492	46,297	46,356	46,459	46,574	46,660	46,743	46,866	47,042	47,178
M	25-29	41,847	42,716	43,110	43,431	43,688	43,904	43,663	43,680	43,750	43,763
M	30-34	33,970	35,384	36,749	37,763	38,412	38,733	39,552	39,905	40,197	40,362
M	35-39	28,025	28,593	29,432	30,532	31,849	33,403	34,769	36,095	37,079	37,645
M	40-44	26,966	27,340	27,625	27,906	28,313	28,695	29,226	30,033	31,106	32,351
M	45-49	26,931	26,586	26,530	26,697	26,957	27,387	27,734	27,996	28,259	28,614
M	50-54	26,982	27,666	27,851	27,582	27,483	27,063	26,706	26,635	26,790	27,011
M	55-59	20,447	21,783	23,263	24,816	25,894	26,831	27,497	27,673	27,403	27,286
M	60-64	15,832	16,301	16,884	17,740	18,865	20,100	21,402	22,846	24,363	25,408
M	65-69	13,771	14,136	14,426	14,704	14,889	15,243	15,705	16,276	17,110	18,203
M	70-74	10,950	11,417	11,877	12,227	12,579	12,973	13,328	13,613	13,888	14,072
M	75-79	8,204	8,545	8,909	9,238	9,592	9,959	10,399	10,832	11,167	11,502
M	80-84	5,292	5,590	5,891	6,233	6,571	6,943	7,246	7,570	7,869	8,189
M	85 +	3,846	4,171	4,516	4,887	5,274	5,640	6,066	6,508	6,999	7,496

G	Age	2041	2042	2043	2044	2045	2046	2047	2048	2049	2050
F	0-4	47,174	47,539	47,866	48,159	48,438	48,744	49,085	49,471	49,922	50,412
F	5-9	45,083	45,679	46,213	46,679	47,077	47,460	47,819	48,157	48,475	48,805
F	10-14	41,839	42,640	43,407	44,123	44,775	45,394	45,987	46,531	47,026	47,477
F	15-19	43,555	44,251	44,991	45,767	46,527	47,328	48,123	48,901	49,656	50,369
F	20-24	48,924	49,248	49,638	50,100	50,639	51,262	51,949	52,706	53,526	54,364
F	25-29	40,581	40,550	40,547	40,579	40,624	40,801	41,113	41,515	42,013	42,632
F	30-34	38,964	38,863	38,766	38,703	38,630	38,557	38,515	38,521	38,595	38,715
F	35-39	37,292	37,682	37,923	37,973	38,002	37,766	37,658	37,570	37,536	37,522
F	40-44	32,980	34,234	35,443	36,339	36,836	37,452	37,827	38,068	38,141	38,225
F	45-49	28,511	28,940	29,577	30,562	31,767	33,059	34,297	35,498	36,403	36,931
F	50-54	26,975	27,386	27,663	27,929	28,200	28,480	28,903	29,536	30,525	31,748
F	55-59	26,614	26,175	26,062	26,227	26,483	26,803	27,210	27,487	27,762	28,050
F	60-64	26,536	27,197	27,366	27,011	26,631	26,244	25,815	25,713	25,885	26,153
F	65-69	19,592	20,868	22,279	23,750	24,999	25,901	26,547	26,708	26,365	26,007
F	70-74	14,735	15,235	15,812	16,602	17,672	18,836	20,075	21,443	22,869	24,076
F	75-79	12,266	12,616	12,888	13,165	13,330	13,770	14,251	14,804	15,555	16,570
F	80-84	9,453	9,691	10,028	10,337	10,617	10,834	11,153	11,410	11,673	11,831
F	85 +	9,959	10,611	11,228	11,829	12,480	13,153	13,786	14,478	15,134	15,813
M	0-4	49,833	50,217	50,564	50,875	51,171	51,492	51,853	52,261	52,736	53,252
M	5-9	47,581	48,219	48,789	49,288	49,714	50,120	50,499	50,856	51,193	51,542
M	10-14	44,095	44,949	45,766	46,530	47,228	47,891	48,524	49,104	49,634	50,114
M	15-19	42,032	42,781	43,581	44,415	45,232	46,088	46,936	47,766	48,564	49,325
M	20-24	47,411	47,764	48,184	48,683	49,264	49,937	50,671	51,482	52,359	53,252
M	25-29	43,750	43,733	43,745	43,795	43,856	44,049	44,385	44,812	45,347	46,004
M	30-34	40,492	40,163	40,085	40,042	39,992	39,936	39,902	39,918	40,004	40,133
M	35-39	37,894	38,633	38,903	39,097	39,210	39,305	38,962	38,886	38,867	38,875
M	40-44	33,835	35,131	36,383	37,279	37,803	38,023	38,747	39,017	39,227	39,385
M	45-49	28,946	29,424	30,173	31,172	32,376	33,831	35,113	36,358	37,270	37,823
M	50-54	27,403	27,711	27,932	28,146	28,476	28,796	29,269	30,017	31,025	32,250
M	55-59	26,856	26,485	26,389	26,506	26,709	27,086	27,392	27,617	27,843	28,198
M	60-64	26,317	26,963	27,128	26,857	26,738	26,317	25,956	25,866	25,992	26,206
M	65-69	19,408	20,673	22,074	23,542	24,559	25,443	26,071	26,235	25,978	25,878
M	70-74	14,418	14,871	15,426	16,229	17,274	18,430	19,644	20,983	22,386	23,360
M	75-79	11,876	12,216	12,492	12,751	12,932	13,264	13,698	14,226	14,982	15,954
M	80-84	8,522	8,918	9,311	9,613	9,912	10,249	10,561	10,817	11,053	11,222
M	85 +	8,003	8,499	9,026	9,571	10,141	10,722	11,346	11,988	12,571	13,180

338

G	Age	2051	2052	2053	2054	2055	2056	2057	2058	2059	2060
F	0-4	50,890	51,360	51,808	52,202	52,544	52,876	53,202	53,517	53,823	54,122
F	5-9	49,146	49,510	49,914	50,373	50,875	51,362	51,845	52,304	52,713	53,067
F	10-14	47,897	48,282	48,633	48,958	49,295	49,647	50,024	50,443	50,922	51,440
F	15-19	51,030	51,655	52,217	52,727	53,188	53,618	54,015	54,381	54,726	55,081
F	20-24	55,214	56,045	56,848	57,615	58,337	59,013	59,651	60,233	60,763	61,248
F	25-29	43,309	44,037	44,818	45,648	46,496	47,361	48,205	49,022	49,808	50,558
F	30-34	38,939	39,287	39,713	40,223	40,852	41,539	42,279	43,077	43,926	44,791
F	35-39	37,495	37,484	37,511	37,599	37,730	37,966	38,321	38,760	39,286	39,934
F	40-44	38,027	37,947	37,880	37,855	37,851	37,835	37,834	37,874	37,978	38,123
F	45-49	37,574	37,975	38,229	38,313	38,407	38,220	38,151	38,092	38,081	38,089
F	50-54	33,049	34,297	35,504	36,410	36,945	37,594	37,991	38,254	38,351	38,452
F	55-59	28,341	28,767	29,401	30,390	31,610	32,907	34,147	35,345	36,247	36,785
F	60-64	26,481	26,889	27,169	27,441	27,730	28,018	28,443	29,074	30,058	31,269
F	65-69	25,641	25,232	25,138	25,310	25,575	25,903	26,305	26,580	26,848	27,133
F	70-74	24,948	25,576	25,735	25,415	25,075	24,728	24,341	24,259	24,437	24,703
F	75-79	17,676	18,851	20,146	21,492	22,633	23,459	24,057	24,214	23,917	23,612
F	80-84	12,236	12,682	13,192	13,884	14,800	15,810	16,879	18,058	19,284	20,318
F	85 +	16,458	17,143	17,837	18,522	19,127	19,922	20,803	21,729	22,786	23,974
M	0-4	53,757	54,252	54,726	55,142	55,506	55,860	56,204	56,535	56,858	57,175
M	5-9	51,899	52,284	52,706	53,189	53,714	54,227	54,737	55,222	55,655	56,033
M	10-14	50,556	50,962	51,337	51,682	52,039	52,406	52,798	53,231	53,727	54,266
M	15-19	50,031	50,694	51,295	51,839	52,328	52,782	53,199	53,586	53,951	54,326
M	20-24	54,159	55,045	55,898	56,709	57,478	58,199	58,875	59,496	60,060	60,572
M	25-29	46,724	47,501	48,337	49,228	50,134	51,057	51,957	52,826	53,654	54,445
M	30-34	40,376	40,750	41,201	41,749	42,418	43,150	43,936	44,792	45,704	46,627
M	35-39	38,868	38,867	38,906	39,001	39,141	39,397	39,783	40,247	40,809	41,495
M	40-44	39,514	39,203	39,150	39,146	39,163	39,164	39,175	39,225	39,341	39,497
M	45-49	38,069	38,804	39,088	39,305	39,475	39,616	39,317	39,274	39,281	39,310
M	50-54	33,709	34,991	36,234	37,139	37,699	37,948	38,682	38,974	39,202	39,384
M	55-59	28,536	29,018	29,762	30,763	31,977	33,418	34,689	35,925	36,826	37,382
M	60-64	26,595	26,904	27,131	27,357	27,709	28,048	28,526	29,264	30,254	31,453
M	65-69	25,480	25,139	25,061	25,194	25,406	25,790	26,099	26,322	26,548	26,900
M	70-74	24,211	24,822	24,987	24,749	24,660	24,288	23,973	23,912	24,051	24,270
M	75-79	17,037	18,172	19,423	20,741	21,646	22,446	23,022	23,188	22,981	22,905
M	80-84	11,533	11,931	12,411	13,090	13,949	14,915	15,933	17,048	18,223	19,034
M	85 +	13,829	14,475	15,105	15,688	16,231	16,928	17,712	18,538	19,472	20,527

G	Age	2000	2001	2002	2003	2004	2005	2006	2007	2008	2009	2010
Total	0-4	41,194	44,520	47,410	50,355	52,373	54,046	55,583	57,853	59,347	60,497	61,115
Total	5-9	34,019	35,142	36,380	38,255	40,496	43,583	47,049	50,735	54,153	56,828	58,276
Total	10-14	31,612	32,777	33,739	34,679	35,299	36,548	37,844	39,952	42,303	45,178	47,988
Total	15-19	41,222	40,890	40,264	40,415	40,867	41,840	43,105	44,968	46,459	47,811	48,647
Total	20-24	55,910	58,969	60,943	61,779	61,620	61,257	60,462	60,246	60,948	62,061	62,657
Total	25-29	33,646	36,817	39,787	43,135	46,395	49,109	51,306	53,578	54,716	54,711	54,221
Total	30-34	23,437	24,593	25,619	27,002	28,606	31,245	34,176	37,902	41,635	45,406	47,879
Total	35-39	20,586	21,430	22,151	22,840	23,187	23,781	24,969	26,924	28,678	30,908	33,255
Total	40-44	18,902	19,924	20,658	21,701	22,265	23,230	24,218	25,815	26,810	27,734	28,038
Total	45-49	16,340	17,534	18,502	19,517	20,143	21,117	22,271	23,773	24,988	26,004	26,678
Total	50-54	13,432	14,504	15,287	16,215	16,992	18,148	19,426	21,027	22,105	23,027	23,728
Total	55-59	10,192	11,058	11,969	12,859	13,609	14,841	15,956	17,247	18,121	19,066	19,955
Total	60-64	7,658	8,117	8,691	9,533	10,338	11,118	12,027	13,300	14,057	14,855	15,824
Total	65-69	6,699	6,995	7,222	7,566	7,772	8,176	8,635	9,459	10,124	10,861	11,381
Total	70-74	5,894	6,032	6,169	6,270	6,418	6,708	7,029	7,365	7,609	7,801	8,048
Total	75-79	4,764	4,813	4,873	4,961	5,071	5,223	5,320	5,539	5,654	5,867	6,098
Total	80-84	3,460	3,392	3,396	3,342	3,392	3,380	3,434	3,372	3,643	3,828	4,035
Total	85 +	2,927	2,940	2,917	2,862	2,784	2,723	2,615	2,392	2,442	2,558	2,688

G	Age	2011	2012	2013	2014	2015	2016	2017	2018	2019	2020
Total	0-4	61,481	61,508	61,833	62,260	62,732	63,158	63,607	64,114	64,724	65,401
Total	5-9	59,584	61,166	62,171	62,937	63,663	64,076	64,138	64,466	64,881	65,320
Total	10-14	51,196	54,176	57,102	59,399	60,959	62,314	63,925	64,928	65,680	66,372
Total	15-19	49,559	50,798	52,574	55,022	57,953	61,214	64,223	67,147	69,418	70,933
Total	20-24	63,595	64,554	65,342	66,169	67,161	68,139	69,418	71,195	73,612	76,494
Total	25-29	53,472	52,777	52,744	53,279	54,032	55,045	56,058	56,859	57,659	58,605
Total	30-34	49,896	51,358	51,824	51,293	50,952	50,271	49,627	49,613	50,131	50,846
Total	35-39	35,885	38,686	41,819	45,120	47,701	49,761	51,256	51,737	51,198	50,833
Total	40-44	28,898	29,942	31,202	33,025	35,458	38,120	40,936	44,062	47,324	49,859
Total	45-49	27,337	28,104	28,700	29,302	29,693	30,584	31,643	32,903	34,708	37,099
Total	50-54	24,563	25,323	26,225	26,987	27,709	28,390	29,179	29,776	30,367	30,741
Total	55-59	20,920	21,851	22,709	23,443	24,182	25,034	25,796	26,691	27,439	28,149
Total	60-64	16,657	17,368	18,106	18,929	19,813	20,762	21,686	22,531	23,256	23,978
Total	65-69	12,008	12,781	13,480	14,219	15,159	15,964	16,652	17,370	18,170	19,033
Total	70-74	8,297	8,750	9,385	10,081	10,576	11,164	11,895	12,562	13,268	14,157
Total	75-79	6,336	6,489	6,710	6,889	7,122	7,357	7,776	8,358	8,991	9,446
Total	80-84	4,195	4,414	4,521	4,698	4,903	5,106	5,251	5,441	5,597	5,810
Total	85 +	2,854	2,993	3,195	3,370	3,574	3,769	3,988	4,170	4,388	4,642

G	Age	2021	2022	2023	2024	2025	2026	2027	2028	2029	2030
Total	0-4	66,275	67,392	68,637	70,055	71,670	73,394	75,188	77,084	79,067	81,041
Total	5-9	65,722	66,138	66,604	67,178	67,821	68,660	69,738	70,961	72,356	73,931
Total	10-14	66,754	66,776	67,064	67,443	67,851	68,223	68,599	69,039	69,596	70,194
Total	15-19	72,246	73,817	74,773	75,478	76,126	76,470	76,457	76,711	77,070	77,434
Total	20-24	79,693	82,639	85,495	87,705	89,176	90,452	91,976	92,902	93,584	94,180
Total	25-29	59,538	60,764	62,479	64,829	67,644	70,792	73,691	76,516	78,709	80,127
Total	30-34	51,808	52,776	53,525	54,276	55,174	56,062	57,241	58,916	61,239	64,002
Total	35-39	50,118	49,434	49,380	49,859	50,533	51,464	52,393	53,116	53,845	54,699
Total	40-44	51,881	53,339	53,778	53,212	52,816	52,087	51,381	51,317	51,783	52,427
Total	45-49	39,714	42,482	45,548	48,759	51,251	53,237	54,673	55,101	54,536	54,125
Total	50-54	31,607	32,644	33,875	35,635	37,986	40,563	43,292	46,310	49,481	51,935
Total	55-59	28,811	29,571	30,156	30,736	31,101	31,953	32,968	34,184	35,918	38,225
Total	60-64	24,812	25,566	26,446	27,182	27,874	28,527	29,272	29,849	30,429	30,789
Total	65-69	19,948	20,846	21,675	22,385	23,100	23,917	24,657	25,516	26,237	26,916
Total	70-74	14,919	15,576	16,269	17,039	17,867	18,745	19,615	20,415	21,103	21,800
Total	75-79	9,981	10,653	11,274	11,934	12,759	13,472	14,094	14,743	15,469	16,249
Total	80-84	6,021	6,384	6,891	7,440	7,840	8,306	8,899	9,454	10,046	10,775
Total	85 +	4,893	5,116	5,371	5,636	5,977	6,311	6,741	7,286	7,860	8,361

G	Age	2031	2032	2033	2034	2035	2036	2037	2038	2039	2040
Total	0-4	83,004	84,881	86,675	88,380	89,991	91,471	92,847	94,103	95,240	96,160
Total	5-9	75,582	77,284	79,068	80,926	82,800	84,673	86,470	88,206	89,860	91,321
Total	10-14	70,957	71,941	73,052	74,323	75,790	77,342	78,970	80,694	82,509	84,217
Total	15-19	77,709	77,968	78,276	78,683	79,156	79,807	80,695	81,728	82,936	84,214
Total	20-24	94,406	94,255	94,359	94,548	94,761	94,914	95,066	95,296	95,631	95,888
Total	25-29	81,295	82,683	83,452	83,954	84,389	84,487	84,239	84,256	84,377	84,379
Total	30-34	67,052	69,835	72,516	74,543	75,819	76,869	78,160	78,844	79,285	79,532
Total	35-39	55,510	56,593	58,153	60,333	62,969	65,908	68,598	71,205	73,172	74,284
Total	40-44	53,294	54,146	54,775	55,392	56,149	56,878	57,890	59,390	61,522	64,014
Total	45-49	53,361	52,609	52,477	52,857	53,423	54,219	55,016	55,598	56,177	56,829
Total	50-54	53,862	55,240	55,616	55,000	54,543	53,751	52,974	52,813	53,166	53,655
Total	55-59	40,741	43,404	46,352	49,437	51,819	53,694	55,039	55,397	54,779	54,286
Total	60-64	31,620	32,606	33,791	35,473	37,726	40,186	42,795	45,683	48,709	51,028
Total	65-69	27,561	28,297	28,870	29,440	29,794	30,613	31,587	32,749	34,394	36,593
Total	70-74	22,596	23,320	24,158	24,860	25,523	26,154	26,873	27,438	28,000	28,351
Total	75-79	17,078	17,900	18,660	19,314	19,982	20,740	21,430	22,228	22,901	23,537
Total	80-84	11,396	11,956	12,541	13,202	13,912	14,655	15,394	16,077	16,671	17,282
Total	85 +	8,909	9,631	10,404	11,221	12,084	12,885	13,774	14,724	15,767	16,880

G	Age	2041	2042	2043	2044	2045	2046	2047	2048	2049	2050
Total	0-4	97,007	97,756	98,430	99,034	99,609	100,236	100,938	101,732	102,658	103,664
Total	5-9	92,664	93,898	95,002	95,967	96,791	97,580	98,318	99,013	99,668	100,347
Total	10-14	85,934	87,589	89,173	90,653	92,003	93,285	94,511	95,635	96,660	97,591
Total	15-19	85,587	87,032	88,572	90,182	91,759	93,416	95,059	96,667	98,220	99,694
Total	20-24	96,335	97,012	97,822	98,783	99,903	101,199	102,620	104,188	105,885	107,616
Total	25-29	84,331	84,283	84,292	84,374	84,480	84,850	85,498	86,327	87,360	88,636
Total	30-34	79,456	79,026	78,851	78,745	78,622	78,493	78,417	78,439	78,599	78,848
Total	35-39	75,186	76,315	76,826	77,070	77,212	77,071	76,620	76,456	76,403	76,397
Total	40-44	66,815	69,365	71,826	73,618	74,639	75,475	76,574	77,085	77,368	77,610
Total	45-49	57,457	58,364	59,750	61,734	64,143	66,890	69,410	71,856	73,673	74,754
Total	50-54	54,378	55,097	55,595	56,075	56,676	57,276	58,172	59,553	61,550	63,998
Total	55-59	53,470	52,660	52,451	52,733	53,192	53,889	54,602	55,104	55,605	56,248
Total	60-64	52,853	54,160	54,494	53,868	53,369	52,561	51,771	51,579	51,877	52,359
Total	65-69	39,000	41,541	44,353	47,292	49,558	51,344	52,618	52,943	52,343	51,885
Total	70-74	29,153	30,106	31,238	32,831	34,946	37,266	39,719	42,426	45,255	47,436
Total	75-79	24,142	24,832	25,380	25,916	26,262	27,034	27,949	29,030	30,537	32,524
Total	80-84	17,975	18,609	19,339	19,950	20,529	21,083	21,714	22,227	22,726	23,053
Total	85 +	17,962	19,110	20,254	21,400	22,621	23,875	25,132	26,466	27,705	28,993

G	Age	2051	2052	2053	2054	2055	2056	2057	2058	2059	2060
Total	0-4	104,647	105,612	106,534	107,344	108,050	108,736	109,406	110,052	110,681	111,297
Total	5-9	101,045	101,794	102,620	103,562	104,589	105,589	106,582	107,526	108,368	109,100
Total	10-14	98,453	99,244	99,970	100,640	101,334	102,053	102,822	103,674	104,649	105,706
Total	15-19	101,061	102,349	103,512	104,566	105,516	106,400	107,214	107,967	108,677	109,407
Total	20-24	109,373	111,090	112,746	114,324	115,815	117,212	118,526	119,729	120,823	121,820
Total	25-29	90,033	91,538	93,155	94,876	96,630	98,418	100,162	101,848	103,462	105,003
Total	30-34	79,315	80,037	80,914	81,972	83,270	84,689	86,215	87,869	89,630	91,418
Total	35-39	76,363	76,351	76,417	76,600	76,871	77,363	78,104	79,007	80,095	81,429
Total	40-44	77,541	77,150	77,030	77,001	77,014	76,999	77,009	77,099	77,319	77,620
Total	45-49	75,643	76,779	77,317	77,618	77,882	77,836	77,468	77,366	77,362	77,399
Total	50-54	66,758	69,288	71,738	73,549	74,644	75,542	76,673	77,228	77,553	77,836
Total	55-59	56,877	57,785	59,163	61,153	63,587	66,325	68,836	71,270	73,073	74,167
Total	60-64	53,076	53,793	54,300	54,798	55,439	56,066	56,969	58,338	60,312	62,722
Total	65-69	51,121	50,371	50,199	50,504	50,981	51,693	52,404	52,902	53,396	54,033
Total	70-74	49,159	50,398	50,722	50,164	49,735	49,016	48,314	48,171	48,488	48,973
Total	75-79	34,713	37,023	39,569	42,233	44,279	45,905	47,079	47,402	46,898	46,517
Total	80-84	23,769	24,613	25,603	26,974	28,749	30,725	32,812	35,106	37,507	39,352
Total	85 +	30,287	31,618	32,942	34,210	35,358	36,850	38,515	40,267	42,258	44,501

Source: Utah Governor's Office of Planning and Budget

5.5.2 State of Utah Population Projections, 2000-2060, by Gender, by Age Group

G	Age	2,000	2,001	2,002	2,003	2,004	2,005	2,006	2,007	2,008	2,009	2,010
F	0-4	103,034	107,395	111,229	115,226	118,759	121,664	124,067	127,250	129,858	131,435	133,710
F	5-9	93,608	94,760	96,334	98,603	101,895	106,520	111,144	116,011	121,022	125,329	128,003
F	10-14	93,835	94,569	95,253	95,797	95,993	97,392	98,826	101,514	104,841	108,856	113,223
F	15-19	108,103	107,764	105,998	104,847	104,849	106,259	107,209	109,021	110,841	111,853	112,898
F	20-24	113,380	117,456	120,183	121,895	122,604	123,051	122,515	121,810	121,931	122,603	123,633
F	25-29	86,275	89,857	94,226	99,235	103,981	109,180	112,825	116,837	119,830	121,122	121,344
F	30-34	72,657	76,040	78,935	81,723	84,421	88,636	92,349	98,019	104,266	109,864	114,675
F	35-39	73,904	73,115	72,413	72,124	72,765	75,632	79,288	83,455	87,297	90,816	94,601
F	40-44	74,182	75,828	76,708	77,362	77,575	77,771	77,287	77,696	78,304	79,632	82,007
F	45-49	66,254	68,968	71,355	73,436	74,922	77,293	79,203	81,070	82,378	83,147	82,903
F	50-54	54,145	57,817	59,988	62,408	65,306	68,695	71,596	74,770	77,316	79,156	81,071
F	55-59	41,030	42,978	46,304	49,216	51,858	56,047	59,829	62,624	65,234	68,317	71,163
F	60-64	32,631	33,956	35,592	37,790	40,145	42,215	44,299	48,042	51,007	53,642	57,249
F	65-69	28,335	28,921	29,609	30,657	31,694	33,043	34,445	36,352	38,478	40,789	42,369
F	70-74	25,771	26,159	26,490	26,820	27,082	27,807	28,418	29,280	30,308	31,371	32,387
F	75-79	22,475	22,631	22,783	22,873	23,131	23,544	24,002	24,322	24,775	25,144	25,725
F	80-84	16,315	16,678	17,122	17,391	17,705	17,981	18,170	18,288	18,665	19,076	19,578
F	85 +	14,755	14,944	15,058	15,274	15,501	15,770	16,110	16,307	16,730	17,289	17,913
M	0-4	109,068	113,475	117,391	121,372	124,589	127,503	130,200	134,079	136,939	139,189	141,596
M	5-9	99,735	100,753	102,412	104,690	107,864	112,509	117,194	122,152	127,162	131,158	133,856
M	10-14	98,730	99,772	100,563	101,400	101,799	103,485	104,788	107,551	110,882	114,777	119,164
M	15-19	107,552	106,659	104,743	103,073	102,484	103,797	105,182	107,292	109,375	110,594	111,925
M	20-24	112,854	116,381	118,755	120,593	121,399	122,278	121,559	120,890	120,659	120,966	121,798
M	25-29	93,466	97,534	102,012	106,996	111,957	116,820	120,035	123,624	126,761	128,163	128,816
M	30-34	77,813	81,271	84,127	86,817	89,514	93,383	97,495	103,226	109,380	115,101	119,540
M	35-39	76,352	75,999	75,826	76,224	77,256	80,585	84,285	88,401	92,161	95,664	99,074
M	40-44	75,445	77,119	78,247	78,996	79,313	79,837	79,857	80,862	82,158	83,916	86,782
M	45-49	66,778	69,704	72,100	74,084	75,726	78,136	80,038	82,176	83,605	84,512	84,649
M	50-54	53,865	57,447	59,766	62,316	65,135	68,745	71,846	75,043	77,501	79,470	81,376
M	55-59	39,807	42,003	45,252	48,173	51,047	55,266	58,940	61,818	64,589	67,604	70,676
M	60-64	30,459	31,821	33,656	36,003	38,168	40,452	42,783	46,431	49,382	52,283	55,922
M	65-69	25,689	26,272	26,986	28,041	29,213	30,426	31,796	33,890	36,131	38,253	40,023
M	70-74	22,278	22,659	23,075	23,413	23,703	24,567	25,221	26,137	27,193	28,375	29,295
M	75-79	17,514	17,925	18,170	18,571	19,012	19,558	20,058	20,504	21,039	21,487	22,232
M	80-84	11,142	11,517	11,955	12,220	12,596	12,986	13,386	13,641	14,407	15,058	15,667
M	85 +	7,317	7,505	7,714	7,959	8,269	8,556	8,884	9,169	9,549	10,147	10,800

G	Age	2,011	2,012	2,013	2,014	2,015	2,016	2,017	2,018	2,019	2,020
F	0-4	135,408	136,863	138,443	140,155	141,609	142,849	143,966	145,031	146,163	147,255
F	5-9	130,570	133,309	135,441	136,835	139,098	140,748	142,192	143,761	145,436	146,844
F	10-14	117,979	122,394	126,906	131,040	133,709	136,237	138,947	141,051	142,411	144,622
F	15-19	114,453	116,552	119,279	123,106	127,443	132,175	136,565	141,039	145,100	147,691
F	20-24	124,867	126,190	127,286	128,069	129,118	130,645	132,736	135,432	139,212	143,474
F	25-29	121,349	120,373	119,754	120,172	121,195	122,404	123,708	124,816	125,571	126,540
F	30-34	118,599	122,008	124,301	125,386	125,593	125,563	124,584	123,946	124,335	125,314
F	35-39	98,444	103,434	109,063	114,460	119,261	123,157	126,552	128,814	129,843	130,012
F	40-44	85,676	89,152	92,492	95,838	99,595	103,396	108,360	113,966	119,316	124,057
F	45-49	82,411	82,187	82,391	83,591	85,965	89,602	93,053	96,379	99,691	103,392
F	50-54	82,872	84,130	85,137	85,831	85,621	85,152	84,964	85,187	86,388	88,744
F	55-59	73,861	76,456	78,758	80,528	82,432	84,233	85,518	86,550	87,256	87,068
F	60-64	60,751	63,017	65,447	68,462	71,282	73,972	76,553	78,849	80,621	82,507
F	65-69	44,178	47,348	50,195	52,771	56,281	59,683	61,926	64,313	67,256	70,040
F	70-74	33,554	35,088	37,135	39,363	40,895	42,641	45,685	48,405	50,874	54,227
F	75-79	26,316	27,048	28,016	29,005	29,989	31,106	32,560	34,478	36,547	37,985
F	80-84	20,070	20,475	20,921	21,271	21,848	22,413	23,089	23,966	24,848	25,764
F	85 +	18,476	19,103	19,678	20,417	21,270	22,089	22,882	23,669	24,544	25,664
M	0-4	143,355	144,359	146,055	147,864	149,408	150,734	151,907	153,021	154,239	155,392
M	5-9	136,720	140,158	142,529	144,606	146,997	148,707	149,701	151,373	153,153	154,660
M	10-14	124,001	128,508	133,030	136,855	139,543	142,368	145,802	148,145	150,175	152,517
M	15-19	113,320	115,489	118,229	121,932	126,298	131,109	135,582	140,065	143,840	146,450
M	20-24	123,363	124,808	126,170	127,162	128,478	129,855	132,016	134,726	138,372	142,653
M	25-29	128,592	127,539	126,563	126,620	127,460	129,004	130,430	131,781	132,741	133,978
M	30-34	123,068	126,161	128,602	129,783	130,408	130,142	129,085	128,105	128,155	128,941
M	35-39	103,275	108,321	113,831	119,328	123,736	127,204	130,272	132,680	133,839	134,438
M	40-44	90,505	93,900	97,158	100,491	103,872	108,034	113,048	118,521	123,968	128,311
M	45-49	84,633	85,020	85,888	87,502	90,358	94,049	97,427	100,666	103,964	107,284
M	50-54	83,183	84,706	85,827	86,647	86,822	86,824	87,244	88,125	89,717	92,534
M	55-59	73,575	76,193	78,405	80,289	82,191	84,006	85,545	86,683	87,520	87,701
M	60-64	59,314	61,635	64,204	67,137	70,180	73,027	75,604	77,794	79,674	81,569
M	65-69	42,014	45,104	47,923	50,720	54,196	57,457	59,702	62,190	65,033	67,980
M	70-74	30,477	32,175	34,281	36,300	37,974	39,844	42,749	45,404	48,047	51,330
M	75-79	22,845	23,629	24,591	25,685	26,547	27,645	29,211	31,152	32,979	34,503
M	80-84	16,240	16,736	17,208	17,624	18,281	18,854	19,560	20,403	21,363	22,137
M	85 +	11,502	12,180	12,907	13,718	14,553	15,416	16,191	17,017	17,890	18,969

G	Age	2,021	2,022	2,023	2,024	2,025	2,026	2,027	2,028	2,029	2,030
F	0-4	148,553	150,108	151,813	153,740	156,024	158,498	161,105	163,959	167,038	170,179
F	5-9	148,053	149,104	150,119	151,168	152,174	153,400	154,864	156,476	158,306	160,490
F	10-14	146,234	147,619	149,118	150,720	152,046	153,172	154,123	155,027	155,999	156,911
F	15-19	150,152	152,799	154,825	156,095	158,223	159,732	161,002	162,382	163,870	165,099
F	20-24	148,098	152,390	156,759	160,728	163,204	165,546	168,061	169,959	171,114	173,081
F	25-29	127,974	129,972	132,566	136,237	140,391	144,887	149,054	153,279	157,115	159,459
F	30-34	126,438	127,669	128,684	129,351	130,222	131,551	133,436	135,907	139,480	143,525
F	35-39	129,951	128,901	128,195	128,519	129,415	130,459	131,588	132,498	133,080	133,848
F	40-44	127,909	131,255	133,449	134,444	134,542	134,424	133,293	132,537	132,780	133,590
F	45-49	107,135	112,044	117,572	122,861	127,530	131,301	134,578	136,708	137,625	137,672
F	50-54	92,322	95,724	98,981	102,228	105,879	109,585	114,428	119,881	125,088	129,667
F	55-59	86,615	86,451	86,692	87,881	90,197	93,714	97,029	100,232	103,440	107,037
F	60-64	84,306	85,600	86,651	87,371	87,199	86,774	86,613	86,867	88,040	90,314
F	65-69	72,667	75,201	77,449	79,208	81,060	82,835	84,115	85,160	85,876	85,756
F	70-74	57,483	59,650	61,966	64,806	67,493	70,036	72,478	74,634	76,353	78,163
F	75-79	39,596	42,433	44,999	47,321	50,458	53,485	55,542	57,769	60,424	62,977
F	80-84	26,777	28,088	29,802	31,629	32,917	34,341	36,888	39,197	41,306	44,085
F	85 +	26,745	27,892	29,200	30,593	32,202	33,862	35,781	38,137	40,601	42,774
M	0-4	156,767	158,428	160,231	162,261	164,669	167,314	170,077	173,101	176,358	179,677
M	5-9	155,963	157,071	158,141	159,262	160,320	161,609	163,172	164,900	166,841	169,161
M	10-14	154,185	155,113	156,719	158,426	159,846	161,054	162,065	163,040	164,092	165,053
M	15-19	149,189	152,556	154,821	156,760	159,016	160,579	161,396	162,873	164,483	165,799
M	20-24	147,355	151,715	156,090	159,753	162,253	164,885	168,119	170,247	172,082	174,191
M	25-29	135,271	137,340	139,939	143,482	147,644	152,221	156,438	160,678	164,200	166,572
M	30-34	130,388	131,753	133,049	133,929	135,080	136,271	138,206	140,677	144,118	148,169
M	35-39	134,147	133,043	132,015	131,996	132,731	134,099	135,372	136,575	137,366	138,397
M	40-44	131,739	134,750	137,089	138,203	138,730	138,385	137,221	136,144	136,076	136,752
M	45-49	111,379	116,327	121,705	127,077	131,342	134,703	137,650	139,926	140,978	141,442
M	50-54	96,153	99,480	102,660	105,872	109,147	113,167	118,003	123,297	128,577	132,763
M	55-59	87,712	88,137	89,004	90,588	93,355	96,890	100,133	103,247	106,390	109,599
M	60-64	83,355	84,876	86,014	86,840	87,036	87,088	87,509	88,371	89,947	92,663
M	65-69	70,749	73,242	75,381	77,243	79,114	80,869	82,374	83,502	84,332	84,577
M	70-74	54,422	56,591	58,984	61,700	64,507	67,148	69,536	71,594	73,393	75,215
M	75-79	36,227	38,910	41,394	43,832	46,819	49,632	51,676	53,919	56,444	59,073
M	80-84	23,097	24,453	26,143	27,723	29,047	30,519	32,873	35,067	37,216	39,823
M	85 +	19,988	21,051	22,254	23,579	24,938	26,391	28,161	30,273	32,361	34,278

346

G	Age	2,031	2,032	2,033	2,034	2,035	2,036	2,037	2,038	2,039	2,040
F	0-4	173,492	176,843	180,236	183,644	186,991	190,243	193,426	196,467	199,375	202,059
F	5-9	162,863	165,395	168,198	171,232	174,341	177,653	181,006	184,427	187,848	191,192
F	10-14	158,029	159,433	160,994	162,782	164,927	167,286	169,829	172,642	175,717	178,817
F	15-19	166,104	166,966	167,812	168,743	169,622	170,723	172,134	173,698	175,519	177,662
F	20-24	174,439	175,586	176,893	178,340	179,524	180,511	181,372	182,246	183,200	184,056
F	25-29	161,652	164,040	165,839	166,925	168,870	170,196	171,339	172,668	174,140	175,310
F	30-34	147,891	151,953	156,103	159,873	162,159	164,323	166,714	168,514	169,619	171,554
F	35-39	135,087	136,882	139,283	142,815	146,822	151,178	155,234	159,378	163,145	165,420
F	40-44	134,533	135,603	136,460	137,006	137,746	138,976	140,780	143,212	146,773	150,757
F	45-49	137,490	136,313	135,544	135,759	136,564	137,502	138,570	139,429	139,974	140,715
F	50-54	133,344	136,567	138,627	139,533	139,561	139,379	138,248	137,506	137,749	138,568
F	55-59	110,672	115,419	120,810	125,934	130,446	134,096	137,275	139,333	140,232	140,263
F	60-64	93,757	97,017	100,162	103,320	106,876	110,463	115,167	120,500	125,563	130,025
F	65-69	85,357	85,228	85,483	86,672	88,913	92,295	95,494	98,588	101,692	105,191
F	70-74	79,911	81,197	82,245	82,998	82,921	82,590	82,494	82,781	83,987	86,197
F	75-79	65,389	67,722	69,803	71,457	73,244	74,941	76,227	77,296	78,054	78,052
F	80-84	46,756	48,657	50,730	53,163	55,528	57,730	59,894	61,838	63,419	65,125
F	85 +	45,123	48,617	52,195	55,684	59,442	63,213	67,153	71,321	75,718	80,276
M	0-4	183,169	186,732	190,335	193,938	197,475	200,922	204,298	207,511	210,583	213,416
M	5-9	171,703	174,387	177,359	180,563	183,863	187,354	190,919	194,542	198,173	201,703
M	10-14	166,237	167,733	169,395	171,302	173,590	176,117	178,813	181,804	185,046	188,330
M	15-19	166,902	167,822	168,739	169,732	170,679	171,845	173,346	175,016	176,963	179,243
M	20-24	175,596	176,310	177,706	179,273	180,560	181,673	182,626	183,567	184,607	185,528
M	25-29	169,075	172,170	174,225	176,004	178,087	179,491	180,233	181,668	183,273	184,553
M	30-34	152,609	156,721	160,890	164,360	166,707	169,179	172,277	174,351	176,176	178,258
M	35-39	139,492	141,344	143,756	147,142	151,150	155,580	159,703	163,876	167,361	169,690
M	40-44	138,003	139,208	140,350	141,098	142,113	143,198	145,074	147,508	150,918	154,907
M	45-49	141,061	139,862	138,774	138,686	139,341	140,600	141,799	142,947	143,721	144,740
M	50-54	136,041	138,924	141,177	142,206	142,679	142,319	141,179	140,120	140,056	140,738
M	55-59	113,551	118,324	123,539	128,726	132,840	136,094	138,987	141,243	142,304	142,780
M	60-64	96,124	99,307	102,362	105,463	108,639	112,530	117,212	122,344	127,448	131,509
M	65-69	84,660	85,125	85,992	87,558	90,219	93,608	96,738	99,720	102,756	105,873
M	70-74	76,927	78,407	79,519	80,388	80,688	80,832	81,334	82,220	83,788	86,396
M	75-79	61,553	63,799	65,767	67,473	69,249	70,919	72,374	73,504	74,381	74,745
M	80-84	42,259	44,123	46,191	48,473	50,845	53,076	55,107	56,924	58,508	60,186
M	85 +	36,398	39,462	42,607	45,694	48,983	52,265	55,846	59,658	63,499	67,557

G	Age	2,041	2,042	2,043	2,044	2,045	2,046	2,047	2,048	2,049	2,050
F	0-4	204,652	207,090	209,397	211,587	213,763	215,893	218,071	220,270	222,612	224,949
F	5-9	194,439	197,640	200,696	203,560	206,234	208,833	211,288	213,628	215,836	218,053
F	10-14	182,133	185,482	188,904	192,301	195,622	198,872	202,100	205,174	208,076	210,790
F	15-19	180,014	182,571	185,359	188,373	191,456	194,798	198,185	201,638	205,089	208,478
F	20-24	185,177	186,576	188,117	189,901	192,003	194,377	196,995	199,830	202,912	206,086
F	25-29	176,303	177,162	178,011	178,909	179,758	180,875	182,306	183,910	185,757	187,961
F	30-34	172,895	174,037	175,341	176,778	177,931	178,930	179,810	180,681	181,630	182,576
F	35-39	167,581	169,983	171,757	172,825	174,761	176,113	177,267	178,603	180,072	181,288
F	40-44	155,098	159,132	163,257	166,978	169,213	171,374	173,787	175,566	176,660	178,632
F	45-49	141,946	143,745	146,161	149,674	153,637	157,971	161,993	166,116	169,831	172,082
F	50-54	139,508	140,580	141,412	141,940	142,686	143,928	145,747	148,152	151,664	155,644
F	55-59	140,118	139,027	138,322	138,568	139,377	140,311	141,372	142,225	142,760	143,514
F	60-64	133,644	136,798	138,834	139,723	139,759	139,629	138,569	137,898	138,151	138,959
F	65-69	108,755	113,353	118,581	123,545	127,930	131,483	134,583	136,575	137,452	137,519
F	70-74	89,496	92,616	95,598	98,636	102,030	105,489	109,948	114,990	119,804	124,038
F	75-79	77,813	77,798	78,148	79,327	81,496	84,642	87,614	90,449	93,316	96,542
F	80-84	66,729	67,987	69,028	69,772	69,844	69,705	69,767	70,189	71,342	73,379
F	85 +	84,696	89,281	93,884	98,375	103,090	107,622	112,021	116,288	120,245	123,864
M	0-4	216,145	218,735	221,188	223,510	225,811	228,065	230,355	232,670	235,141	237,602
M	5-9	205,166	208,554	211,779	214,795	217,621	220,351	222,952	225,427	227,769	230,102
M	10-14	191,815	195,383	199,000	202,597	206,123	209,594	213,001	216,235	219,291	222,158
M	15-19	181,774	184,471	187,464	190,652	193,917	197,411	201,005	204,647	208,285	211,888
M	20-24	186,693	188,185	189,830	191,749	194,002	196,551	199,295	202,343	205,589	208,930
M	25-29	185,675	186,625	187,545	188,531	189,458	190,642	192,162	193,836	195,803	198,141
M	30-34	179,663	180,420	181,830	183,391	184,666	185,795	186,779	187,722	188,767	189,767
M	35-39	172,168	175,269	177,336	179,112	181,165	182,575	183,317	184,762	186,344	187,695
M	40-44	159,309	163,431	167,571	170,972	173,289	175,778	178,881	180,952	182,742	184,821
M	45-49	145,831	147,709	150,131	153,511	157,461	161,848	165,952	170,096	173,515	175,861
M	50-54	142,006	143,200	144,331	145,089	146,130	147,248	149,128	151,548	154,923	158,867
M	55-59	142,456	141,356	140,330	140,265	140,939	142,209	143,421	144,549	145,323	146,375
M	60-64	134,748	137,621	139,859	140,932	141,441	141,138	140,085	139,100	139,041	139,720
M	65-69	109,674	114,231	119,245	124,231	128,193	131,374	134,174	136,358	137,421	137,933
M	70-74	89,688	92,712	95,551	98,470	101,474	105,154	109,566	114,372	119,139	122,934
M	75-79	74,944	75,494	76,418	77,928	80,434	83,536	86,386	89,078	91,815	94,661
M	80-84	61,756	63,135	64,214	65,061	65,456	65,704	66,280	67,193	68,633	70,936
M	85 +	71,485	75,505	79,541	83,512	87,727	91,754	95,701	99,448	102,985	106,344

348

G	Age	2,051	2,052	2,053	2,054	2,055	2,056	2,057	2,058	2,059	2,060
F	0-4	227,250	229,558	231,860	234,082	236,217	238,362	240,512	242,647	244,769	246,869
F	5-9	220,238	222,451	224,684	227,029	229,399	231,726	234,082	236,454	238,741	240,950
F	10-14	213,438	215,927	218,282	220,522	222,790	225,004	227,246	229,534	231,957	234,388
F	15-19	211,773	215,038	218,128	221,075	223,839	226,546	229,095	231,513	233,806	236,156
F	20-24	209,450	212,866	216,365	219,867	223,323	226,689	230,020	233,199	236,213	239,038
F	25-29	190,422	193,061	195,924	199,040	202,261	205,697	209,196	212,778	216,353	219,892
F	30-34	183,740	185,216	186,877	188,766	191,032	193,542	196,231	199,142	202,318	205,614
F	35-39	182,319	183,223	184,129	185,101	186,090	187,325	188,860	190,579	192,513	194,832
F	40-44	180,014	181,195	182,550	184,045	185,295	186,352	187,280	188,233	189,281	190,344
F	45-49	174,259	176,696	178,483	179,584	181,569	182,975	184,187	185,573	187,071	188,337
F	50-54	159,958	163,965	168,053	171,760	174,022	176,190	178,622	180,415	181,537	183,536
F	55-59	144,759	146,571	148,980	152,482	156,443	160,734	164,703	168,750	172,416	174,682
F	60-64	139,893	140,913	141,759	142,291	143,038	144,277	146,072	148,476	151,950	155,867
F	65-69	137,390	136,352	135,677	135,908	136,690	137,591	138,588	139,409	139,918	140,658
F	70-74	127,466	130,494	132,423	133,295	133,367	133,234	132,225	131,567	131,809	132,579
F	75-79	99,854	104,082	108,859	113,396	117,427	120,700	123,594	125,453	126,289	126,385
F	80-84	76,241	78,938	81,533	84,145	87,093	90,145	94,045	98,420	102,561	106,236
F	85 +	127,206	130,601	134,233	138,249	142,727	147,671	152,503	157,370	162,613	168,512
M	0-4	240,025	242,476	244,913	247,253	249,531	251,797	254,064	256,324	258,566	260,799
M	5-9	232,405	234,721	237,059	239,549	242,046	244,506	247,011	249,536	251,936	254,276
M	10-14	224,937	227,572	230,067	232,434	234,823	237,158	239,509	241,912	244,462	247,038
M	15-19	215,395	218,839	222,102	225,228	228,144	230,988	233,674	236,236	238,664	241,133
M	20-24	212,433	216,056	219,733	223,417	227,079	230,685	234,202	237,548	240,739	243,717
M	25-29	200,753	203,531	206,615	209,899	213,287	216,877	220,573	224,339	228,096	231,832
M	30-34	190,996	192,562	194,280	196,256	198,655	201,333	204,156	207,303	210,649	214,113
M	35-39	188,861	189,858	190,830	191,908	192,954	194,235	195,871	197,639	199,677	202,112
M	40-44	186,253	187,038	188,509	190,121	191,507	192,687	193,702	194,718	195,859	196,979
M	45-49	178,346	181,444	183,506	185,302	187,384	188,847	189,661	191,165	192,785	194,201
M	50-54	163,210	167,267	171,378	174,767	177,135	179,636	182,740	184,787	186,590	188,691
M	55-59	147,497	149,365	151,764	155,098	159,006	163,290	167,317	171,423	174,794	177,147
M	60-64	140,984	142,171	143,282	144,035	145,065	146,187	148,026	150,371	153,667	157,529
M	65-69	137,639	136,596	135,637	135,597	136,268	137,502	138,658	139,731	140,468	141,475
M	70-74	125,986	128,694	130,795	131,816	132,311	132,035	131,068	130,168	130,161	130,839
M	75-79	98,143	102,296	106,815	111,251	114,816	117,694	120,255	122,277	123,307	123,793
M	80-84	73,756	76,313	78,729	81,162	83,723	86,904	90,689	94,756	98,728	101,936
M	85 +	109,464	112,800	116,244	119,958	124,280	128,787	133,261	137,663	142,374	147,702

G	Age	2,000	2,001	2,002	2,003	2,004	2,005	2,006	2,007	2,008	2,009	2,010
Total	0-4	212,102	220,870	228,620	236,598	243,348	249,167	254,267	261,329	266,797	270,624	275,306
Total	5-9	193,343	195,513	198,746	203,293	209,759	219,029	228,338	238,163	248,184	256,487	261,859
Total	10-14	192,565	194,341	195,816	197,197	197,792	200,877	203,614	209,065	215,723	223,633	232,387
Total	15-19	215,655	214,423	210,741	207,920	207,333	210,056	212,391	216,313	220,216	222,447	224,823
Total	20-24	226,234	233,837	238,938	242,488	244,003	245,329	244,074	242,700	242,590	243,569	245,431
Total	25-29	179,741	187,391	196,238	206,231	215,938	226,000	232,860	240,461	246,591	249,285	250,160
Total	30-34	150,470	157,311	163,062	168,540	173,935	182,019	189,844	201,245	213,646	224,965	234,215
Total	35-39	150,256	149,114	148,239	148,348	150,021	156,217	163,573	171,856	179,458	186,480	193,675
Total	40-44	149,627	152,947	154,955	156,358	156,888	157,608	157,144	158,558	160,462	163,548	168,789
Total	45-49	133,032	138,672	143,455	147,520	150,648	155,429	159,241	163,246	165,983	167,659	167,552
Total	50-54	108,010	115,264	119,754	124,724	130,441	137,440	143,442	149,813	154,817	158,626	162,447
Total	55-59	80,837	84,981	91,556	97,389	102,905	111,313	118,769	124,442	129,823	135,921	141,839
Total	60-64	63,090	65,777	69,248	73,793	78,313	82,667	87,082	94,473	100,389	105,925	113,171
Total	65-69	54,024	55,193	56,595	58,698	60,907	63,469	66,241	70,242	74,609	79,042	82,392
Total	70-74	48,049	48,818	49,565	50,233	50,785	52,374	53,639	55,417	57,501	59,746	61,682
Total	75-79	39,989	40,556	40,953	41,444	42,143	43,102	44,060	44,826	45,814	46,631	47,957
Total	80-84	27,457	28,195	29,077	29,611	30,301	30,967	31,556	31,929	33,072	34,134	35,245
Total	85 +	22,072	22,449	22,772	23,233	23,770	24,326	24,994	25,476	26,279	27,436	28,713

G	Age	2,011	2,012	2,013	2,014	2,015	2,016	2,017	2,018	2,019	2,020
Total	0-4	278,763	281,222	284,498	288,019	291,017	293,583	295,873	298,052	300,402	302,647
Total	5-9	267,290	273,467	277,970	281,441	286,095	289,455	291,893	295,134	298,589	301,504
Total	10-14	241,980	250,902	259,936	267,895	273,252	278,605	284,749	289,196	292,586	297,139
Total	15-19	227,773	232,041	237,508	245,038	253,741	263,284	272,147	281,104	288,940	294,141
Total	20-24	248,230	250,998	253,456	255,231	257,596	260,500	264,752	270,158	277,584	286,127
Total	25-29	249,941	247,912	246,317	246,792	248,655	251,408	254,138	256,597	258,312	260,518
Total	30-34	241,667	248,169	252,903	255,169	256,001	255,705	253,669	252,051	252,490	254,255
Total	35-39	201,719	211,755	222,894	233,788	242,997	250,361	256,824	261,494	263,682	264,450
Total	40-44	176,181	183,052	189,650	196,329	203,467	211,430	221,408	232,487	243,284	252,368
Total	45-49	167,044	167,207	168,279	171,093	176,323	183,651	190,480	197,045	203,655	210,676
Total	50-54	166,055	168,836	170,964	172,478	172,443	171,976	172,208	173,312	176,105	181,278
Total	55-59	147,436	152,649	157,163	160,817	164,623	168,239	171,063	173,233	174,776	174,769
Total	60-64	120,065	124,652	129,651	135,599	141,462	146,999	152,157	156,643	160,295	164,076
Total	65-69	86,192	92,452	98,118	103,491	110,477	117,140	121,628	126,503	132,289	138,020
Total	70-74	64,031	67,263	71,416	75,663	78,869	82,485	88,434	93,809	98,921	105,557
Total	75-79	49,161	50,677	52,607	54,690	56,536	58,751	61,771	65,630	69,526	72,488
Total	80-84	36,310	37,211	38,129	38,895	40,129	41,267	42,649	44,369	46,211	47,901
Total	85 +	29,978	31,283	32,585	34,135	35,823	37,505	39,073	40,686	42,434	44,633

G	Age	2,021	2,022	2,023	2,024	2,025	2,026	2,027	2,028	2,029	2,030
Total	0-4	305,320	308,536	312,044	316,001	320,693	325,812	331,182	337,060	343,396	349,856
Total	5-9	304,016	306,175	308,260	310,430	312,494	315,009	318,036	321,376	325,147	329,651
Total	10-14	300,419	302,732	305,837	309,146	311,892	314,226	316,188	318,067	320,091	321,964
Total	15-19	299,341	305,355	309,646	312,855	317,239	320,311	322,398	325,255	328,353	330,898
Total	20-24	295,453	304,105	312,849	320,481	325,457	330,431	336,180	340,206	343,196	347,272
Total	25-29	263,245	267,312	272,505	279,719	288,035	297,108	305,492	313,957	321,315	326,031
Total	30-34	256,826	259,422	261,733	263,280	265,302	267,822	271,642	276,584	283,598	291,694
Total	35-39	264,098	261,944	260,210	260,515	262,146	264,558	266,960	269,073	270,446	272,245
Total	40-44	259,648	266,005	270,538	272,647	273,272	272,809	270,514	268,681	268,856	270,342
Total	45-49	218,514	228,371	239,277	249,938	258,872	266,004	272,228	276,634	278,603	279,114
Total	50-54	188,475	195,204	201,641	208,100	215,026	222,752	232,431	243,178	253,665	262,430
Total	55-59	174,327	174,588	175,696	178,469	183,552	190,604	197,162	203,479	209,830	216,636
Total	60-64	167,661	170,476	172,665	174,211	174,235	173,862	174,122	175,238	177,987	182,977
Total	65-69	143,416	148,443	152,830	156,451	160,174	163,704	166,489	168,662	170,208	170,333
Total	70-74	111,905	116,241	120,950	126,506	132,000	137,184	142,014	146,228	149,746	153,378
Total	75-79	75,823	81,343	86,393	91,153	97,277	103,117	107,218	111,688	116,868	122,050
Total	80-84	49,874	52,541	55,945	59,352	61,964	64,860	69,761	74,264	78,522	83,908
Total	85 +	46,733	48,943	51,454	54,172	57,140	60,253	63,942	68,410	72,962	77,052

G	Age	2,031	2,032	2,033	2,034	2,035	2,036	2,037	2,038	2,039	2,040
Total	0-4	356,661	363,575	370,571	377,582	384,466	391,165	397,724	403,978	409,958	415,475
Total	5-9	334,566	339,782	345,557	351,795	358,204	365,007	371,925	378,969	386,021	392,895
Total	10-14	324,266	327,166	330,389	334,084	338,517	343,403	348,642	354,446	360,763	367,147
Total	15-19	333,006	334,788	336,551	338,475	340,301	342,568	345,480	348,714	352,482	356,905
Total	20-24	350,035	351,896	354,599	357,613	360,084	362,184	363,998	365,813	367,807	369,584
Total	25-29	330,727	336,210	340,064	342,929	346,957	349,687	351,572	354,336	357,413	359,863
Total	30-34	300,500	308,674	316,993	324,233	328,866	333,502	338,991	342,865	345,795	349,812
Total	35-39	274,579	278,226	283,039	289,957	297,972	306,758	314,937	323,254	330,506	335,110
Total	40-44	272,536	274,811	276,810	278,104	279,859	282,174	285,854	290,720	297,691	305,664
Total	45-49	278,551	276,175	274,318	274,445	275,905	278,102	280,369	282,376	283,695	285,455
Total	50-54	269,385	275,491	279,804	281,739	282,240	281,698	279,427	277,626	277,805	279,306
Total	55-59	224,223	233,743	244,349	254,660	263,286	270,190	276,262	280,576	282,536	283,043
Total	60-64	189,881	196,324	202,524	208,783	215,515	222,993	232,379	242,844	253,011	261,534
Total	65-69	170,017	170,353	171,475	174,230	179,132	185,903	192,232	198,308	204,448	211,064
Total	70-74	156,838	159,604	161,764	163,386	163,609	163,422	163,828	165,001	167,775	172,593
Total	75-79	126,942	131,521	135,570	138,930	142,493	145,860	148,601	150,800	152,435	152,797
Total	80-84	89,015	92,780	96,921	101,636	106,373	110,806	115,001	118,762	121,927	125,311
Total	85 +	81,521	88,079	94,802	101,378	108,425	115,478	122,999	130,979	139,217	147,833

G	Age	2,041	2,042	2,043	2,044	2,045	2,046	2,047	2,048	2,049	2,050
Total	0-4	420,797	425,825	430,585	435,097	439,574	443,958	448,426	452,940	457,753	462,551
Total	5-9	399,605	406,194	412,475	418,355	423,855	429,184	434,240	439,055	443,605	448,155
Total	10-14	373,948	380,865	387,904	394,898	401,745	408,466	415,101	421,409	427,367	432,948
Total	15-19	361,788	367,042	372,823	379,025	385,373	392,209	399,190	406,285	413,374	420,366
Total	20-24	371,870	374,761	377,947	381,650	386,005	390,928	396,290	402,173	408,501	415,016
Total	25-29	361,978	363,787	365,556	367,440	369,216	371,517	374,468	377,746	381,560	386,102
Total	30-34	352,558	354,457	357,171	360,169	362,597	364,725	366,589	368,403	370,397	372,343
Total	35-39	339,749	345,252	349,093	351,937	355,926	358,688	360,584	363,365	366,416	368,983
Total	40-44	314,407	322,563	330,828	337,950	342,502	347,152	352,668	356,518	359,402	363,453
Total	45-49	287,777	291,454	296,292	303,185	311,098	319,819	327,945	336,212	343,346	347,943
Total	50-54	281,514	283,780	285,743	287,029	288,816	291,176	294,875	299,700	306,587	314,511
Total	55-59	282,574	280,383	278,652	278,833	280,316	282,520	284,793	286,774	288,083	289,889
Total	60-64	268,392	274,419	278,693	280,655	281,200	280,767	278,654	276,998	277,192	278,679
Total	65-69	218,429	227,584	237,826	247,776	256,123	262,857	268,757	272,933	274,873	275,452
Total	70-74	179,184	185,328	191,149	197,106	203,504	210,643	219,514	229,362	238,943	246,972
Total	75-79	152,757	153,292	154,566	157,255	161,930	168,178	174,000	179,527	185,131	191,203
Total	80-84	128,485	131,122	133,242	134,833	135,300	135,409	136,047	137,382	139,975	144,315
Total	85 +	156,181	164,786	173,425	181,887	190,817	199,376	207,722	215,736	223,230	230,208

G	Age	2,051	2,052	2,053	2,054	2,055	2,056	2,057	2,058	2,059	2,060
Total	0-4	467,275	472,034	476,773	481,335	485,748	490,159	494,576	498,971	503,335	507,668
Total	5-9	452,643	457,172	461,743	466,578	471,445	476,232	481,093	485,990	490,677	495,226
Total	10-14	438,375	443,499	448,349	452,956	457,613	462,162	466,755	471,446	476,419	481,426
Total	15-19	427,168	433,877	440,230	446,303	451,983	457,534	462,769	467,749	472,470	477,289
Total	20-24	421,883	428,922	436,098	443,284	450,402	457,374	464,222	470,747	476,952	482,755
Total	25-29	391,175	396,592	402,539	408,939	415,548	422,574	429,769	437,117	444,449	451,724
Total	30-34	374,736	377,778	381,157	385,022	389,687	394,875	400,387	406,445	412,967	419,727
Total	35-39	371,180	373,081	374,959	377,009	379,044	381,560	384,731	388,218	392,190	396,944
Total	40-44	366,267	368,233	371,059	374,166	376,802	379,039	380,982	382,951	385,140	387,323
Total	45-49	352,605	358,140	361,989	364,886	368,953	371,822	373,848	376,738	379,856	382,538
Total	50-54	323,168	331,232	339,431	346,527	351,157	355,826	361,362	365,202	368,127	372,227
Total	55-59	292,256	295,936	300,744	307,580	315,449	324,024	332,020	340,173	347,210	351,829
Total	60-64	280,877	283,084	285,041	286,326	288,103	290,464	294,098	298,847	305,617	313,396
Total	65-69	275,029	272,948	271,314	271,505	272,958	275,093	277,246	279,140	280,386	282,133
Total	70-74	253,452	259,188	263,218	265,111	265,678	265,269	263,293	261,735	261,970	263,418
Total	75-79	197,997	206,378	215,674	224,647	232,243	238,394	243,849	247,730	249,596	250,178
Total	80-84	149,997	155,251	160,262	165,307	170,816	177,049	184,734	193,176	201,289	208,172
Total	85 +	236,670	243,401	250,477	258,207	267,007	276,458	285,764	295,033	304,987	316,214

Source: Utah Governor's Office of Planning and Budget

5.5.3 United States Population Projections, 2000-2060, by Gender, by Age Group

G	Age	2000	2001	2002	2003	2004	2005	2006	2007	2008	2009	2010
F	0-4	9371769	9454573	9546739	9664157	9802212	9941365	10012706	10124567	10236681	10349467	10452831
F	5-9	9990491	9873135	9749927	9649345	9580605	9533812	9595395	9668400	9774257	9902821	10042515
F	10-14	10054658	10189213	10296617	10339627	10307570	10181757	10057882	9924164	9810603	9728992	9681779
F	15-19	9842784	9851679	9888488	9964570	10092051	10268234	10412105	10527166	10577816	10554755	10431421
F	20-24	9348418	9668301	9903785	10085111	10169701	10171284	10163898	10193116	10275770	10418361	10597538
F	25-29	9539230	9331062	9295687	9376922	9562793	9803723	10106996	10322509	10481583	10552335	10559213
F	30-34	10200498	10289687	10318389	10266012	10127610	9927774	9705986	9655772	9728006	9913286	10156874
F	35-39	11359504	11148481	10916838	10682265	10480333	10440766	10520047	10539491	10481455	10344757	10148742
F	40-44	11353549	11508695	11551050	11570056	11591724	11487472	11273335	11037587	10800946	10600192	10563072
F	45-49	10267145	10509970	10794299	11032003	11203891	11379555	11530743	11569603	11586628	11609850	11507859
F	50-54	9074037	9529401	9550285	9729389	9960786	10210077	10448539	10727846	10961111	11130732	11304455
F	55-59	7005483	7193040	7772890	8096677	8487134	8931175	9379602	9401080	9579493	9808206	10053175
F	60-64	5693701	5821418	6027634	6342534	6590985	6804659	6991350	7562461	7882057	8265299	8695161
F	65-69	5123049	5122537	5141057	5219286	5324869	5411240	5538118	5740606	6048026	6290297	6495391
F	70-74	4946533	4897348	4836117	4774219	4717422	4706157	4714926	4738894	4817123	4919316	5003782
F	75-79	4380699	4375713	4366190	4363230	4318227	4303022	4275257	4235051	4192432	4152504	4150843
F	80-84	3132274	3217000	3305376	3361102	3443505	3491132	3509001	3520610	3533987	3512940	3511740
F	85 +	3039931	3110785	3180983	3275682	3360021	3534499	3701234	3864077	4010434	4161355	4308738
M	0-4	9815615	9894823	9990483	10114009	10258460	10380600	10439772	10539726	10635284	10739861	10846318
M	5-9	10485842	10360028	10226078	10111653	10033431	9980490	10037075	10113178	10223623	10351034	10473648
M	10-14	10565429	10701790	10810954	10859623	10823881	10689553	10556829	10410557	10281596	10188967	10135987
M	15-19	10418948	10454269	10477514	10522905	10632254	10807203	10954322	11077118	11140571	11120236	10990878
M	20-24	9777904	10132699	10433978	10683153	10803688	10794445	10770917	10747289	10772178	10882664	11058593
M	25-29	9766840	9606167	9618273	9755603	9991956	10240760	10544490	10782366	10964596	11034130	11027235
M	30-34	10339935	10440432	10496771	10460370	10339610	10141530	9951360	9930084	10038686	10251588	10504562
M	35-39	11300648	11130311	10923237	10730676	10569858	10549157	10622971	10652845	10595090	10464865	10274803
M	40-44	11170751	11334207	11396320	11421285	11463136	11371047	11190826	10970878	10764865	10592217	10576590
M	45-49	9954897	10198653	10480373	10733329	10917081	11104408	11259820	11314833	11332882	11369362	11281855
M	50-54	8700802	9132679	9145811	9311992	9535042	9786667	10021738	10294779	10540406	10719439	10905047
M	55-59	6553737	6740443	7310094	7626221	8000457	8423620	8841412	8852930	9015176	9231210	9476851
M	60-64	5163111	5282917	5473394	5768129	5997568	6204480	6386252	6938592	7244264	7602513	8004063
M	65-69	4394593	4408751	4440039	4525674	4634812	4722663	4839333	5021032	5301613	5518273	5710896
M	70-74	3905258	3893421	3864938	3831919	3801151	3813683	3838460	3876159	3960188	4062074	4144874
M	75-79	3054939	3067108	3084061	3104859	3104404	3121941	3125971	3115514	3100998	3086227	3105309
M	80-84	1854248	1930312	2004152	2056087	2121197	2160368	2181527	2204811	2229280	2238003	2259901
M	85 +	1246227	1306875	1365978	1440331	1507417	1604563	1698817	1790167	1872077	1952644	2032042

G	Age	2,011	2,012	2,013	2,014	2,015	2,016	2,017	2,018	2,019	2,020
F	0-4	10,562,792	10,674,307	10,782,494	10,883,486	10,974,933	11,056,198	11,128,487	11,193,452	11,253,381	11,310,419
F	5-9	10,114,987	10,228,297	10,341,892	10,456,101	10,560,226	10,670,911	10,782,993	10,891,786	10,993,341	11,085,520
F	10-14	9,742,985	9,816,168	9,922,822	10,052,557	10,193,776	10,267,793	10,382,387	10,497,049	10,612,201	10,717,193
F	15-19	10,309,730	10,178,260	10,066,841	9,987,570	9,942,831	10,006,223	10,081,487	10,190,049	10,321,415	10,464,286
F	20-24	10,744,812	10,863,337	10,917,595	10,898,392	10,778,618	10,660,512	10,532,547	10,424,646	10,348,962	10,307,606
F	25-29	10,556,724	10,590,067	10,676,186	10,821,699	11,004,028	11,154,575	11,276,566	11,334,431	11,319,104	11,203,162
F	30-34	10,462,594	10,680,960	10,843,188	10,916,917	10,926,804	10,927,495	10,964,002	11,052,994	11,201,292	11,386,614
F	35-39	9,930,681	9,883,062	9,957,009	10,143,347	10,387,734	10,694,056	10,913,517	11,077,277	11,153,081	11,165,590
F	40-44	10,643,642	10,664,592	10,608,555	10,474,559	10,281,934	10,067,432	10,022,044	10,097,468	10,284,372	10,529,140
F	45-49	11,296,885	11,064,867	10,832,397	10,635,665	10,601,083	10,682,821	10,705,291	10,651,139	10,519,803	10,330,933
F	50-54	11,453,938	11,492,922	11,510,427	11,534,611	11,435,677	11,229,027	11,001,863	10,774,779	10,583,242	10,551,822
F	55-59	10,287,148	10,561,192	10,790,429	10,957,465	11,129,448	11,277,538	11,317,595	11,336,575	11,362,512	11,268,183
F	60-64	9,128,650	9,153,009	9,328,414	9,552,664	9,793,251	10,022,589	10,290,719	10,515,583	10,680,210	10,850,456
F	65-69	6,673,680	7,221,052	7,529,444	7,896,107	8,306,424	8,719,238	8,748,111	8,919,834	9,138,017	9,372,179
F	70-74	5,125,164	5,316,492	5,606,522	5,834,530	6,028,168	6,195,577	6,710,443	7,003,288	7,347,763	7,731,944
F	75-79	4,165,233	4,192,655	4,268,457	4,364,439	4,446,975	4,561,565	4,738,558	5,005,742	5,215,253	5,393,812
F	80-84	3,498,084	3,474,144	3,448,001	3,422,887	3,432,753	3,453,831	3,485,212	3,557,243	3,644,643	3,723,407
F	85 +	4,429,043	4,543,490	4,648,987	4,733,944	4,834,386	4,906,311	4,968,273	5,024,208	5,067,420	5,152,955
M	0-4	10,959,688	11,074,929	11,187,065	11,291,856	11,386,569	11,470,798	11,545,812	11,613,148	11,675,114	11,734,111
M	5-9	10,533,909	10,635,382	10,732,076	10,837,895	10,945,275	11,059,645	11,175,254	11,287,976	11,393,432	11,489,181
M	10-14	10,192,601	10,268,923	10,380,271	10,508,892	10,633,288	10,695,107	10,798,037	10,895,976	11,002,958	11,111,199
M	15-19	10,862,474	10,720,181	10,594,692	10,505,249	10,455,279	10,514,499	10,593,115	10,706,532	10,836,931	10,963,152
M	20-24	11,207,796	11,333,688	11,401,216	11,385,702	11,261,036	11,137,480	11,000,191	10,879,382	10,794,312	10,748,390
M	25-29	11,006,036	10,984,876	11,012,264	11,125,124	11,304,099	11,456,585	11,585,944	11,657,339	11,646,236	11,526,342
M	30-34	10,811,442	11,052,416	11,237,698	11,310,719	11,307,841	11,290,689	11,273,901	11,305,420	11,421,590	11,603,801
M	35-39	10,092,264	10,076,248	10,187,806	10,401,714	10,654,734	10,961,444	11,202,775	11,388,986	11,464,415	11,465,191
M	40-44	10,653,955	10,687,217	10,633,611	10,508,060	10,323,451	10,145,793	10,132,306	10,244,520	10,457,925	10,709,888
M	45-49	11,107,321	10,893,962	10,694,699	10,528,606	10,517,059	10,596,281	10,631,615	10,581,286	10,460,021	10,281,089
M	50-54	11,059,081	11,115,269	11,135,258	11,173,833	11,091,647	10,923,767	10,718,205	10,526,882	10,368,583	10,361,768
M	55-59	9,705,601	9,971,102	10,210,538	10,385,576	10,568,213	10,719,766	10,777,103	10,799,397	10,840,207	10,764,948
M	60-64	8,399,176	8,415,215	8,572,963	8,781,682	9,019,519	9,240,054	9,495,827	9,727,180	9,897,172	10,075,874
M	65-69	5,878,924	6,393,480	6,680,620	7,012,861	7,384,047	7,747,380	7,769,711	7,920,953	8,119,036	8,345,263
M	70-74	4,252,099	4,416,807	4,670,491	4,865,456	5,039,040	5,189,247	5,652,547	5,914,477	6,212,805	6,544,247
M	75-79	3,132,731	3,170,329	3,246,440	3,335,813	3,411,917	3,507,110	3,650,278	3,869,775	4,037,369	4,186,776
M	80-84	2,270,188	2,270,267	2,267,232	2,263,349	2,287,501	2,316,166	2,351,943	2,416,854	2,490,181	2,556,092
M	85 +	2,098,521	2,165,658	2,228,650	2,281,661	2,344,416	2,391,680	2,433,898	2,472,599	2,505,408	2,565,438

G	Age	2,021	2,022	2,023	2,024	2,025	2,026	2,027	2,028	2,029	2,030
F	0-4	11,366,062	11,420,968	11,475,052	11,528,970	11,583,367	11,636,736	11,690,292	11,745,525	11,803,452	11,864,256
F	5-9	11,167,475	11,240,532	11,306,118	11,366,609	11,423,899	11,479,681	11,534,558	11,588,706	11,642,662	11,697,242
F	10-14	10,828,432	10,940,798	11,049,739	11,151,381	11,243,713	11,325,751	11,398,946	11,464,622	11,525,251	11,582,605
F	15-19	10,539,243	10,653,865	10,767,765	10,881,763	10,985,364	11,095,339	11,206,399	11,314,345	11,415,099	11,506,656
F	20-24	10,373,504	10,450,983	10,561,193	10,693,342	10,836,121	10,911,449	11,026,378	11,140,520	11,254,845	11,358,908
F	25-29	11,088,733	10,964,104	10,859,148	10,785,880	10,746,604	10,814,139	10,893,220	11,004,804	11,138,313	11,282,410
F	30-34	11,540,365	11,665,408	11,726,586	11,714,733	11,602,282	11,491,217	11,370,088	11,268,512	11,198,514	11,162,259
F	35-39	11,168,929	11,208,101	11,299,524	11,450,027	11,637,536	11,793,669	11,921,135	11,984,944	11,975,936	11,866,839
F	40-44	10,835,420	11,055,552	11,220,270	11,297,720	11,312,470	11,318,214	11,359,579	11,452,860	11,604,774	11,793,674
F	45-49	10,120,672	10,077,943	10,154,974	10,342,549	10,587,778	10,893,793	11,114,395	11,280,007	11,359,215	11,376,366
F	50-54	10,634,933	10,659,372	10,608,118	10,480,957	10,297,807	10,093,610	10,054,592	10,133,609	10,321,604	10,566,849
F	55-59	11,068,109	10,848,363	10,629,441	10,446,196	10,420,503	10,506,302	10,533,751	10,486,578	10,364,916	10,189,153
F	60-64	10,997,335	11,039,841	11,062,268	11,091,962	11,005,378	10,815,416	10,606,514	10,398,836	10,226,412	10,207,700
F	65-69	9,594,886	9,854,960	10,073,994	10,235,802	10,404,304	10,549,740	10,595,689	10,622,498	10,656,526	10,579,883
F	70-74	8,117,091	8,151,406	8,317,573	8,526,855	8,751,733	8,964,987	9,213,476	9,423,732	9,580,510	9,744,845
F	75-79	5,547,364	6,019,136	6,291,650	6,606,682	6,956,391	7,304,022	7,344,997	7,502,977	7,699,634	7,911,243
F	80-84	3,827,575	3,984,375	4,219,757	4,402,866	4,559,150	4,693,089	5,106,316	5,349,822	5,624,828	5,927,714
F	85 +	5,225,259	5,298,313	5,399,117	5,501,676	5,630,743	5,769,766	5,951,232	6,216,342	6,438,472	6,658,151
M	0-4	11,791,920	11,849,034	11,905,302	11,961,538	12,018,446	12,074,171	12,129,942	12,187,477	12,247,903	12,311,275
M	5-9	11,573,921	11,649,712	11,717,829	11,780,651	11,839,888	11,898,068	11,955,547	12,012,378	12,068,800	12,126,107
M	10-14	11,226,064	11,341,889	11,454,783	11,560,185	11,656,082	11,740,916	11,816,938	11,885,114	11,948,164	12,007,529
M	15-19	11,025,723	11,128,005	11,224,224	11,328,932	11,434,298	11,546,654	11,660,048	11,770,853	11,874,354	11,968,634
M	20-24	10,810,820	10,892,125	11,007,658	11,139,384	11,266,098	11,329,509	11,432,224	11,528,946	11,634,177	11,739,903
M	25-29	11,407,384	11,274,428	11,157,242	11,075,045	11,031,469	11,095,278	11,177,650	11,293,883	11,426,089	11,553,274
M	30-34	11,759,908	11,892,914	11,968,151	11,961,285	11,846,292	11,732,193	11,604,156	11,491,687	11,414,018	11,374,532
M	35-39	11,451,730	11,438,800	11,474,253	11,593,825	11,778,876	11,937,813	12,073,864	12,152,712	12,149,939	12,039,898
M	40-44	11,015,194	11,256,104	11,442,817	11,520,101	11,523,851	11,513,535	11,504,008	11,542,159	11,663,491	11,849,742
M	45-49	10,109,017	10,098,510	10,211,762	10,424,595	10,675,972	10,979,825	11,220,151	11,406,937	11,485,908	11,492,708
M	50-54	10,443,197	10,481,176	10,435,061	10,319,731	10,148,984	9,984,762	9,978,490	10,093,069	10,305,112	10,555,222
M	55-59	10,606,308	10,411,737	10,231,718	10,084,896	10,085,952	10,171,035	10,212,694	10,172,090	10,064,352	9,904,296
M	60-64	10,224,593	10,284,592	10,311,775	10,357,425	10,293,789	10,149,320	9,970,547	9,806,087	9,674,545	9,685,280
M	65-69	8,554,301	8,796,926	9,017,720	9,181,912	9,357,082	9,502,679	9,566,702	9,600,402	9,651,675	9,602,622
M	70-74	6,866,346	6,896,134	7,038,575	7,223,100	7,434,536	7,628,875	7,853,841	8,059,755	8,214,878	8,382,475
M	75-79	4,315,408	4,714,413	4,945,260	5,201,674	5,484,920	5,756,619	5,795,500	5,926,607	6,092,963	6,284,014
M	80-84	2,635,223	2,751,204	2,927,894	3,061,950	3,182,203	3,285,646	3,605,875	3,796,270	4,001,510	4,226,464
M	85 +	2,618,613	2,673,982	2,747,695	2,823,371	2,913,137	3,006,892	3,127,452	3,302,335	3,446,952	3,590,891

G	Age	2,031	2,032	2,033	2,034	2,035	2,036	2,037	2,038	2,039	2,040
F	0-4	11,930,474	12,001,977	12,078,610	12,159,413	12,244,059	12,331,264	12,420,483	12,510,593	12,601,103	12,691,043
F	5-9	11,750,457	11,803,737	11,858,492	11,915,872	11,976,001	12,041,917	12,113,275	12,189,916	12,270,736	12,355,466
F	10-14	11,638,255	11,692,723	11,746,248	11,799,360	11,852,882	11,905,185	11,957,731	12,011,887	12,068,793	12,128,584
F	15-19	11,587,821	11,660,256	11,725,233	11,785,110	11,841,515	11,896,324	11,950,073	12,002,967	12,055,395	12,108,387
F	20-24	11,468,831	11,579,278	11,686,229	11,785,882	11,876,290	11,956,369	12,027,802	12,092,003	12,151,240	12,207,010
F	25-29	11,358,556	11,473,461	11,587,108	11,700,357	11,803,000	11,911,548	12,020,856	12,126,744	12,225,607	12,315,288
F	30-34	11,231,573	11,311,547	11,423,172	11,555,745	11,698,236	11,773,240	11,886,947	11,999,392	12,111,593	12,213,328
F	35-39	11,758,519	11,639,535	11,539,228	11,469,715	11,432,968	11,501,269	11,580,206	11,690,800	11,822,224	11,963,620
F	40-44	11,950,843	12,079,044	12,143,446	12,135,086	12,026,655	11,918,989	11,800,632	11,700,883	11,631,685	11,595,081
F	45-49	11,384,163	11,426,892	11,520,764	11,672,290	11,860,269	12,016,753	12,144,456	12,208,688	12,200,720	12,093,504
F	50-54	10,871,488	11,091,282	11,256,246	11,335,602	11,353,592	11,362,326	11,405,511	11,499,300	11,650,038	11,837,024
F	55-59	9,992,363	9,957,204	10,037,259	10,223,714	10,466,437	10,767,261	10,984,526	11,147,719	11,226,880	11,246,239
F	60-64	10,296,025	10,326,253	10,282,897	10,166,769	9,998,918	9,810,573	9,779,333	9,859,905	10,043,990	10,283,484
F	65-69	10,402,834	10,207,327	10,013,332	9,854,011	9,842,592	9,932,123	9,964,263	9,925,033	9,816,137	9,659,745
F	70-74	9,886,447	9,935,156	9,965,805	10,002,992	9,936,740	9,775,202	9,596,433	9,419,821	9,277,071	9,274,309
F	75-79	8,111,176	8,343,231	8,540,633	8,689,226	8,846,394	8,981,567	9,033,016	9,068,188	9,109,300	9,057,113
F	80-84	6,224,688	6,272,667	6,418,133	6,596,406	6,788,638	6,969,252	7,178,229	7,357,433	7,494,597	7,641,712
F	85 +	6,865,477	7,329,745	7,718,513	8,092,756	8,483,465	8,854,424	9,227,989	9,616,222	10,016,323	10,438,918
M	0-4	12,380,223	12,454,733	12,534,717	12,618,984	12,707,135	12,797,952	12,891,026	12,984,967	13,079,184	13,172,860
M	5-9	12,182,094	12,238,088	12,295,277	12,355,443	12,418,549	12,487,631	12,562,017	12,642,100	12,726,547	12,815,029
M	10-14	12,065,744	12,122,858	12,179,301	12,235,072	12,291,597	12,346,755	12,402,273	12,459,034	12,518,969	12,581,771
M	15-19	12,052,058	12,127,005	12,194,253	12,256,546	12,315,121	12,372,704	12,429,188	12,485,124	12,540,429	12,596,660
M	20-24	11,851,870	11,964,383	12,073,936	12,175,883	12,268,683	12,350,960	12,424,974	12,491,394	12,552,978	12,610,994
M	25-29	11,616,933	11,719,048	11,814,843	11,918,736	12,022,571	12,132,731	12,243,693	12,351,929	12,452,779	12,544,715
M	30-34	11,440,658	11,524,353	11,641,053	11,772,873	11,899,122	11,962,389	12,063,986	12,159,322	12,262,652	12,365,876
M	35-39	11,930,350	11,806,391	11,696,951	11,621,165	11,582,548	11,648,715	11,732,096	11,848,170	11,979,359	12,105,315
M	40-44	12,009,810	12,146,604	12,226,378	12,225,016	12,117,271	12,009,809	11,888,059	11,780,681	11,706,712	11,669,308
M	45-49	11,485,341	11,478,387	11,518,282	11,639,831	11,825,293	11,984,633	12,120,926	12,200,828	12,200,647	12,095,517
M	50-54	10,856,115	11,094,309	11,279,486	11,358,654	11,367,193	11,361,808	11,356,846	11,398,031	11,519,293	11,703,585
M	55-59	9,749,997	9,748,443	9,863,534	10,072,695	10,319,009	10,614,142	10,848,275	11,030,499	11,109,561	11,120,556
M	60-64	9,774,142	9,819,609	9,785,198	9,686,393	9,539,211	9,397,080	9,400,939	9,515,862	9,720,741	9,962,020
M	65-69	9,475,969	9,316,962	9,172,034	9,059,262	9,080,757	9,172,123	9,220,490	9,193,009	9,105,818	8,976,695
M	70-74	8,521,378	8,587,949	8,627,207	8,682,353	8,648,327	8,542,526	8,407,425	8,286,016	8,195,526	8,228,342
M	75-79	6,458,292	6,659,352	6,844,539	6,985,999	7,141,411	7,269,701	7,337,519	7,382,373	7,440,993	7,425,174
M	80-84	4,438,374	4,484,351	4,598,871	4,740,620	4,903,648	5,051,255	5,221,210	5,379,046	5,502,331	5,640,622
M	85 +	3,724,658	4,030,831	4,279,698	4,515,213	4,763,123	4,992,197	5,224,844	5,465,050	5,714,963	5,989,700

357

G	Age	2,041	2,042	2,043	2,044	2,045	2,046	2,047	2,048	2,049	2,050
F	0-4	12,780,002	12,867,128	12,952,202	13,034,840	13,114,797	13,191,869	13,266,825	13,339,370	13,409,645	13,478,517
F	5-9	12,442,662	12,531,928	12,622,004	12,712,566	12,802,434	12,891,427	12,978,500	13,063,639	13,146,260	13,226,134
F	10-14	12,194,335	12,265,574	12,342,145	12,422,912	12,507,659	12,594,800	12,684,014	12,773,971	12,864,466	12,953,962
F	15-19	12,160,359	12,212,606	12,266,432	12,323,164	12,382,903	12,448,659	12,519,795	12,596,411	12,677,243	12,761,801
F	20-24	12,261,191	12,314,500	12,367,000	12,419,031	12,471,662	12,523,448	12,575,697	12,629,464	12,686,158	12,745,806
F	25-29	12,394,847	12,465,852	12,529,780	12,588,681	12,644,224	12,698,213	12,751,423	12,803,781	12,855,863	12,908,531
F	30-34	12,321,087	12,429,538	12,534,752	12,633,026	12,722,322	12,801,463	12,872,151	12,935,845	12,994,608	13,049,901
F	35-39	12,037,897	12,150,826	12,262,444	12,373,889	12,474,884	12,582,010	12,689,828	12,794,502	12,892,219	12,981,253
F	40-44	11,662,904	11,741,328	11,851,245	11,981,821	12,122,363	12,196,306	12,308,627	12,419,666	12,530,551	12,631,186
F	45-49	11,987,062	11,869,851	11,771,078	11,702,690	11,666,680	11,734,235	11,812,269	11,921,659	12,051,594	12,191,406
F	50-54	11,992,732	12,119,909	12,184,191	12,177,018	12,071,823	11,967,366	11,852,141	11,755,105	11,688,095	11,653,170
F	55-59	11,256,532	11,300,607	11,394,435	11,544,346	11,730,274	11,885,169	12,011,791	12,076,390	12,070,644	11,968,554
F	60-64	10,579,028	10,792,921	10,953,917	11,033,021	11,054,413	11,067,046	11,112,609	11,206,765	11,355,606	11,540,088
F	65-69	9,483,675	9,458,172	9,539,461	9,719,970	9,954,673	10,242,372	10,451,013	10,608,273	10,686,903	10,711,317
F	70-74	9,364,668	9,399,274	9,365,823	9,267,018	9,125,770	8,965,868	8,947,435	9,028,959	9,203,805	9,430,851
F	75-79	8,916,585	8,760,139	8,606,730	8,485,884	8,494,640	8,585,865	8,623,721	8,597,839	8,512,385	8,391,192
F	80-84	7,767,638	7,822,168	7,862,949	7,908,813	7,874,753	7,761,765	7,634,724	7,511,681	7,419,305	7,442,459
F	85 +	10,833,348	11,251,626	11,656,223	12,035,374	12,442,470	12,809,050	13,137,659	13,446,008	13,741,030	13,996,552
M	0-4	13,265,639	13,356,468	13,445,040	13,531,121	13,614,518	13,694,838	13,772,872	13,848,446	13,921,773	13,993,504
M	5-9	12,905,748	12,998,857	13,092,888	13,187,376	13,280,906	13,373,713	13,464,632	13,553,495	13,639,436	13,722,751
M	10-14	12,650,797	12,725,086	12,805,222	12,889,522	12,978,033	13,068,654	13,161,793	13,255,637	13,350,089	13,443,207
M	15-19	12,651,554	12,706,933	12,763,563	12,823,502	12,886,316	12,955,440	13,029,768	13,110,011	13,194,380	13,282,666
M	20-24	12,668,205	12,724,281	12,779,871	12,834,943	12,891,148	12,946,022	13,001,438	13,058,254	13,118,519	13,181,253
M	25-29	12,626,312	12,699,899	12,765,974	12,827,245	12,885,087	12,942,282	12,998,361	13,054,003	13,109,296	13,165,738
M	30-34	12,475,652	12,586,269	12,694,255	12,794,947	12,886,978	12,968,803	13,042,662	13,109,067	13,170,878	13,229,779
M	35-39	12,168,683	12,270,013	12,365,229	12,468,523	12,571,536	12,681,003	12,791,512	12,899,598	13,000,303	13,092,800
M	40-44	11,735,607	11,818,873	11,934,737	12,065,386	12,190,905	12,254,519	12,355,891	12,450,996	12,554,178	12,657,326
M	45-49	11,990,776	11,871,831	11,766,994	11,695,029	11,659,226	11,725,870	11,809,185	11,924,693	12,054,854	12,180,142
M	50-54	11,861,998	11,997,601	12,077,749	12,079,227	11,977,807	11,876,727	11,761,490	11,660,093	11,590,975	11,557,674
M	55-59	11,118,050	11,115,988	11,159,081	11,280,193	11,463,340	11,620,846	11,755,784	11,836,467	11,840,430	11,744,433
M	60-64	10,249,406	10,478,043	10,656,441	10,735,541	10,750,141	10,751,813	10,754,037	10,800,044	10,921,239	11,103,044
M	65-69	8,851,781	8,863,026	8,977,276	9,175,439	9,409,011	9,684,303	9,903,978	10,075,627	10,153,718	10,172,719
M	70-74	8,320,987	8,372,343	8,353,561	8,281,350	8,174,611	8,071,085	8,090,365	8,202,033	8,389,602	8,610,871
M	75-79	7,345,136	7,239,433	7,146,915	7,083,419	7,129,067	7,222,001	7,275,913	7,267,347	7,213,398	7,134,240
M	80-84	5,754,154	5,821,396	5,870,961	5,931,723	5,935,113	5,884,299	5,812,439	5,752,820	5,719,036	5,776,189
M	85 +	6,238,704	6,507,108	6,772,651	7,020,298	7,299,586	7,541,549	7,765,264	7,975,854	8,184,140	8,375,899

G	Age	2,051	2,052	2,053	2,054	2,055	2,056	2,057	2,058	2,059	2,060
F	0-4	13,525,601	13,566,074	13,601,784	13,638,758	13,681,599	13,737,431	13,794,787	13,853,964	13,915,228	13,978,769
F	5-9	13,316,577	13,405,653	13,491,987	13,569,372	13,635,097	13,681,737	13,721,721	13,756,933	13,793,407	13,835,744
F	10-14	13,043,056	13,132,515	13,222,031	13,312,672	13,403,985	13,493,728	13,582,110	13,667,750	13,744,455	13,809,511
F	15-19	12,840,620	12,924,961	13,012,663	13,101,054	13,187,554	13,275,503	13,363,818	13,452,189	13,541,678	13,631,837
F	20-24	12,811,755	12,878,289	12,945,096	13,011,077	13,083,785	13,161,306	13,244,324	13,330,685	13,417,730	13,502,895
F	25-29	12,937,430	12,969,754	13,008,860	13,060,916	13,118,928	13,183,525	13,248,704	13,314,154	13,378,781	13,450,101
F	30-34	13,088,353	13,126,123	13,162,734	13,195,923	13,228,322	13,256,052	13,287,200	13,325,098	13,375,866	13,432,529
F	35-39	13,046,141	13,101,832	13,149,782	13,192,301	13,229,001	13,266,349	13,303,019	13,338,540	13,370,672	13,402,024
F	40-44	12,724,982	12,819,352	12,910,316	12,993,074	13,067,404	13,131,140	13,185,772	13,232,740	13,274,331	13,310,158
F	45-49	12,249,956	12,347,562	12,444,716	12,542,311	12,628,745	12,721,082	12,813,974	12,903,496	12,984,903	13,057,979
F	50-54	11,702,759	11,763,693	11,856,026	11,969,085	12,092,948	12,152,788	12,251,007	12,348,816	12,447,101	12,534,449
F	55-59	11,839,425	11,702,537	11,586,445	11,502,650	11,452,277	11,504,539	11,567,524	11,661,095	11,774,830	11,899,194
F	60-64	11,650,806	11,788,441	11,856,303	11,845,885	11,731,325	11,607,530	11,476,159	11,364,975	11,285,206	11,237,775
F	65-69	10,666,497	10,716,902	10,818,984	10,978,439	11,178,118	11,352,326	11,490,724	11,560,886	11,554,969	11,449,140
F	70-74	9,626,291	9,803,721	9,937,651	10,003,612	10,026,405	10,047,074	10,102,097	10,205,807	10,363,455	10,560,386
F	75-79	8,143,474	8,079,833	8,115,196	8,241,921	8,425,563	8,656,252	8,823,299	8,950,213	9,016,211	9,046,834
F	80-84	7,400,741	7,354,313	7,258,602	7,122,030	6,969,341	6,811,831	6,769,979	6,809,879	6,926,225	7,093,060
F	85 +	14,130,707	14,289,439	14,427,699	14,572,188	14,769,640	14,936,080	15,026,792	15,064,906	15,079,575	15,128,370
M	0-4	14,046,549	14,093,981	14,138,005	14,182,084	14,231,705	14,289,945	14,349,767	14,411,488	14,475,388	14,541,654
M	5-9	13,815,904	13,905,992	13,991,846	14,070,710	14,138,032	14,190,770	14,237,847	14,281,509	14,325,223	14,374,473
M	10-14	13,537,274	13,632,571	13,728,825	13,824,821	13,921,098	14,013,696	14,103,238	14,188,551	14,266,884	14,333,691
M	15-19	13,359,351	13,444,043	13,531,431	13,620,445	13,708,926	13,802,040	13,896,376	13,991,663	14,086,696	14,182,006
M	20-24	13,262,246	13,339,076	13,416,842	13,490,948	13,568,520	13,644,308	13,728,060	13,814,498	13,902,556	13,990,084
M	25-29	13,214,991	13,267,953	13,325,757	13,395,086	13,467,925	13,548,000	13,623,933	13,700,796	13,774,015	13,850,685
M	30-34	13,273,387	13,317,362	13,360,885	13,405,016	13,456,436	13,507,529	13,562,331	13,621,970	13,693,093	13,767,729
M	35-39	13,171,585	13,241,953	13,304,121	13,360,081	13,406,019	13,452,775	13,499,927	13,546,657	13,594,023	13,648,637
M	40-44	12,764,447	12,871,123	12,975,505	13,071,822	13,160,020	13,237,732	13,307,110	13,368,371	13,423,487	13,468,679
M	45-49	12,240,112	12,338,082	12,430,730	12,531,468	12,632,250	12,737,917	12,843,132	12,946,073	13,041,039	13,127,981
M	50-54	11,621,638	11,701,625	11,810,908	11,933,702	12,050,826	12,109,741	12,205,930	12,296,908	12,395,837	12,494,818
M	55-59	11,645,103	11,531,213	11,430,860	11,361,539	11,326,637	11,389,469	11,467,577	11,574,192	11,693,834	11,807,935
M	60-64	11,302,017	11,468,057	11,570,028	11,585,636	11,490,570	11,395,906	11,287,088	11,191,278	11,125,674	11,093,336
M	65-69	10,232,759	10,293,576	10,396,585	10,571,702	10,806,655	11,005,414	11,171,226	11,274,493	11,293,826	11,206,996
M	70-74	8,914,273	9,169,603	9,381,979	9,510,178	9,586,137	9,651,632	9,718,007	9,824,619	9,999,313	10,231,786
M	75-79	7,089,540	7,152,022	7,297,414	7,512,941	7,766,007	8,053,179	8,296,896	8,501,467	8,629,992	8,713,994
M	80-84	5,899,363	5,986,175	6,020,423	6,017,805	5,997,242	5,976,604	6,046,532	6,185,848	6,385,058	6,619,061
M	85 +	8,556,302	8,715,766	8,882,968	9,075,210	9,332,403	9,565,043	9,750,588	9,900,879	10,044,535	10,230,194

G	Age	2,000	2,001	2,002	2,003	2,004	2,005	2,006	2,007	2,008	2,009	2,010
Total	0-4	19,187,384	19,349,396	19,537,222	19,778,166	20,060,672	20,321,965	20,452,478	20,664,293	20,871,965	21,089,328	21,299,149
	5-9	20,476,333	20,233,163	19,976,005	19,760,998	19,614,036	19,514,302	19,632,470	19,781,578	19,997,880	20,253,855	20,516,163
	10-14	20,620,087	20,891,003	21,107,571	21,199,250	21,131,451	20,871,310	20,614,711	20,334,721	20,092,199	19,917,959	19,817,766
	15-19	20,261,732	20,305,948	20,366,002	20,487,475	20,724,305	21,075,437	21,366,427	21,604,284	21,718,387	21,674,991	21,422,299
Total	20-24	19,126,322	19,801,000	20,337,763	20,768,264	20,973,389	20,965,729	20,934,815	20,940,405	21,047,948	21,301,025	21,656,131
	25-29	19,306,070	18,937,229	18,913,960	19,132,525	19,554,749	20,044,483	20,651,486	21,104,875	21,446,179	21,586,465	21,586,448
	30-34	20,540,433	20,730,119	20,815,160	20,726,382	20,467,220	20,069,304	19,657,346	19,585,856	19,766,692	20,164,874	20,661,436
	35-39	22,660,152	22,278,792	21,840,075	21,412,941	21,050,191	20,989,923	21,143,018	21,192,336	21,076,545	20,809,622	20,423,545
Total	40-44	22,524,300	22,842,902	22,947,370	22,991,341	23,054,860	22,858,519	22,464,161	22,008,465	21,565,811	21,192,409	21,139,662
	45-49	20,222,042	20,708,623	21,274,672	21,765,332	22,120,972	22,483,963	22,790,563	22,884,436	22,919,510	22,979,212	22,789,714
	50-54	17,774,839	18,662,080	18,696,096	19,041,381	19,495,828	19,996,744	20,470,277	21,022,625	21,501,517	21,850,171	22,209,502
	55-59	13,559,220	13,933,483	15,082,984	15,722,898	16,487,591	17,354,795	18,221,014	18,254,010	18,594,669	19,039,416	19,530,026
Total	60-64	10,856,812	11,104,335	11,501,028	12,110,663	12,588,553	13,009,139	13,377,602	14,501,053	15,126,321	15,867,812	16,699,224
	65-69	9,517,642	9,531,288	9,581,096	9,744,960	9,959,681	10,133,903	10,377,451	10,761,638	11,349,639	11,808,570	12,206,287
	70-74	8,851,791	8,790,769	8,701,055	8,606,138	8,518,573	8,519,840	8,553,386	8,615,053	8,777,311	8,981,390	9,148,656
	75-79	7,435,638	7,442,821	7,450,251	7,468,089	7,422,631	7,424,963	7,401,228	7,350,565	7,293,430	7,238,731	7,256,152
	80-84	4,986,522	5,147,312	5,309,528	5,417,189	5,564,702	5,651,500	5,690,528	5,725,421	5,763,267	5,750,943	5,771,641
	85 +	4,286,158	4,417,660	4,546,961	4,716,013	4,867,438	5,139,062	5,400,051	5,654,244	5,882,511	6,113,999	6,340,780

G	Age	2,011	2,012	2,013	2,014	2,015	2,016	2,017	2,018	2,019	2,020
Total	0-4	21,522,480	21,749,236	21,969,559	22,175,342	22,361,502	22,526,996	22,674,299	22,806,600	22,928,495	23,044,530
	5-9	20,648,896	20,863,679	21,073,968	21,293,996	21,505,501	21,730,556	21,958,247	22,179,762	22,386,773	22,574,701
	10-14	19,935,586	20,085,091	20,303,093	20,561,449	20,827,064	20,962,900	21,180,424	21,393,025	21,615,159	21,828,392
	15-19	21,172,204	20,898,441	20,661,533	20,492,819	20,398,110	20,520,722	20,674,602	20,896,581	21,158,346	21,427,438
Total	20-24	21,952,608	22,197,025	22,318,811	22,284,094	22,039,654	21,797,992	21,532,738	21,304,028	21,143,274	21,055,996
	25-29	21,562,760	21,574,943	21,688,450	21,946,823	22,308,127	22,611,160	22,862,510	22,991,770	22,965,340	22,729,504
	30-34	21,274,036	21,733,376	22,080,886	22,227,636	22,234,645	22,218,184	22,237,903	22,358,414	22,622,882	22,990,415
	35-39	20,022,945	19,959,310	20,144,815	20,545,061	21,042,468	21,655,500	22,116,292	22,466,263	22,617,496	22,630,781
Total	40-44	21,297,597	21,351,809	21,242,166	20,982,619	20,605,385	20,213,225	20,154,350	20,341,988	20,742,297	21,239,028
	45-49	22,404,206	21,958,829	21,527,096	21,164,271	21,118,142	21,279,102	21,336,906	21,232,425	20,979,824	20,612,022
	50-54	22,513,019	22,608,191	22,645,685	22,708,444	22,527,324	22,152,794	21,720,068	21,301,661	20,951,825	20,913,590
	55-59	19,992,749	20,532,294	21,000,967	21,343,041	21,697,661	21,997,304	22,094,698	22,135,972	22,202,719	22,033,131
Total	60-64	17,527,826	17,568,224	17,901,377	18,334,346	18,812,770	19,262,643	19,786,546	20,242,763	20,577,382	20,926,330
	65-69	12,552,604	13,614,532	14,210,064	14,908,968	15,690,471	16,466,618	16,517,822	16,840,787	17,257,053	17,717,442
	70-74	9,377,263	9,733,299	10,277,013	10,699,986	11,067,208	11,384,824	12,362,990	12,917,765	13,560,568	14,276,191
	75-79	7,297,964	7,362,984	7,514,897	7,700,252	7,858,892	8,068,675	8,388,836	8,875,517	9,252,622	9,580,588
	80-84	5,768,272	5,744,411	5,715,233	5,686,236	5,720,254	5,769,997	5,837,155	5,974,097	6,134,824	6,279,499
	85 +	6,527,564	6,709,148	6,877,637	7,015,605	7,178,802	7,297,991	7,402,171	7,496,807	7,572,828	7,718,393

G	Age	2,021	2,022	2,023	2,024	2,025	2,026	2,027	2,028	2,029	2,030
Total	0-4	23,157,982	23,270,002	23,380,354	23,490,508	23,601,813	23,710,907	23,820,234	23,933,002	24,051,355	24,175,531
	5-9	22,741,396	22,890,244	23,023,947	23,147,260	23,263,787	23,377,749	23,490,105	23,601,084	23,711,462	23,823,349
	10-14	22,054,496	22,282,687	22,504,522	22,711,566	22,899,795	23,066,667	23,215,884	23,349,736	23,473,415	23,590,134
	15-19	21,564,966	21,781,870	21,991,989	22,210,695	22,419,662	22,641,993	22,866,447	23,085,198	23,289,453	23,475,290
Total	20-24	21,184,324	21,343,108	21,568,851	21,832,726	22,102,219	22,240,958	22,458,602	22,669,466	22,889,022	23,098,811
	25-29	22,496,117	22,238,532	22,016,390	21,860,925	21,778,073	21,909,417	22,070,870	22,298,687	22,564,402	22,835,684
	30-34	23,300,273	23,558,322	23,694,737	23,676,018	23,448,574	23,223,410	22,974,244	22,760,199	22,612,532	22,536,791
	35-39	22,620,659	22,646,901	22,773,777	23,043,852	23,416,412	23,731,482	23,994,999	24,137,656	24,125,875	23,906,737
Total	40-44	21,850,614	22,311,656	22,663,087	22,817,821	22,836,321	22,831,749	22,863,587	22,995,019	23,268,265	23,643,416
	45-49	20,229,689	20,176,453	20,366,736	20,767,144	21,263,750	21,873,618	22,334,546	22,686,944	22,845,123	22,869,074
	50-54	21,078,130	21,140,548	21,043,179	20,800,688	20,446,791	20,078,372	20,033,082	20,226,678	20,626,716	21,122,071
	55-59	21,674,417	21,260,100	20,861,159	20,531,092	20,506,455	20,677,337	20,746,445	20,658,668	20,429,268	20,093,449
Total	60-64	21,221,928	21,324,433	21,374,043	21,449,387	21,299,167	20,964,736	20,577,061	20,204,923	19,900,957	19,892,980
	65-69	18,149,187	18,651,886	19,091,714	19,417,714	19,761,386	20,052,419	20,162,391	20,222,900	20,308,201	20,182,505
	70-74	14,983,437	15,047,540	15,356,148	15,749,955	16,186,269	16,593,862	17,067,317	17,483,487	17,795,388	18,127,320
	75-79	9,862,772	10,733,549	11,236,910	11,808,356	12,441,311	13,060,641	13,140,497	13,429,584	13,792,597	14,195,257
	80-84	6,462,798	6,735,579	7,147,651	7,464,816	7,741,353	7,978,735	8,712,191	9,146,092	9,626,338	10,154,178
	85 +	7,843,872	7,972,295	8,146,812	8,325,047	8,543,880	8,776,658	9,078,684	9,518,677	9,885,424	10,249,042

G	Age	2,031	2,032	2,033	2,034	2,035	2,036	2,037	2,038	2,039	2,040
Total	0-4	24,310,697	24,456,710	24,613,327	24,778,397	24,951,194	25,129,216	25,311,509	25,495,560	25,680,287	25,863,903
	5-9	23,932,551	24,041,825	24,153,769	24,271,315	24,394,550	24,529,548	24,675,292	24,832,016	24,997,283	25,170,495
	10-14	23,703,999	23,815,581	23,925,549	24,034,432	24,144,479	24,251,940	24,360,004	24,470,921	24,587,762	24,710,355
	15-19	23,639,879	23,787,261	23,919,486	24,041,656	24,156,636	24,269,028	24,379,261	24,488,091	24,595,824	24,705,047
Total	20-24	23,320,701	23,543,661	23,760,165	23,961,765	24,144,973	24,307,329	24,452,776	24,583,397	24,704,218	24,818,004
	25-29	22,975,489	23,192,509	23,401,951	23,619,093	23,825,571	24,044,279	24,264,549	24,478,673	24,678,386	24,860,003
	30-34	22,672,231	22,835,900	23,064,225	23,328,618	23,597,358	23,735,629	23,950,933	24,158,714	24,374,245	24,579,204
	35-39	23,688,869	23,445,926	23,236,179	23,090,880	23,015,516	23,149,984	23,312,302	23,538,970	23,801,583	24,068,935
Total	40-44	23,960,653	24,225,648	24,369,824	24,360,102	24,143,926	23,928,798	23,688,691	23,481,564	23,338,397	23,264,389
	45-49	22,869,504	22,905,279	23,039,046	23,312,121	23,685,562	24,001,386	24,265,382	24,409,516	24,401,367	24,189,021
	50-54	21,727,603	22,185,591	22,535,732	22,694,256	22,720,785	22,724,134	22,762,357	22,897,331	23,169,331	23,540,609
	55-59	19,742,360	19,705,647	19,900,793	20,296,409	20,785,446	21,381,403	21,832,801	22,178,218	22,336,441	22,366,795
Total	60-64	20,070,167	20,145,862	20,068,095	19,853,162	19,538,129	19,207,653	19,180,272	19,375,767	19,764,731	20,245,504
	65-69	19,878,803	19,524,289	19,185,366	18,913,273	18,923,349	19,104,246	19,184,753	19,118,042	18,921,955	18,636,440
	70-74	18,407,825	18,523,105	18,593,012	18,685,345	18,585,067	18,317,728	18,003,858	17,705,837	17,472,597	17,502,651
	75-79	14,569,468	15,002,583	15,385,172	15,675,225	15,987,805	16,251,268	16,370,535	16,450,561	16,550,293	16,482,287
	80-84	10,663,062	10,757,018	11,017,004	11,337,026	11,692,286	12,020,507	12,399,439	12,736,479	12,996,928	13,282,334
	85 +	10,590,135	11,360,576	11,998,211	12,607,969	13,246,588	13,846,621	14,452,833	15,081,272	15,731,286	16,428,618

G	Age	2,041	2,042	2,043	2,044	2,045	2,046	2,047	2,048	2,049	2,050
Total	0-4	26,045,641	26,223,596	26,397,242	26,565,961	26,729,315	26,886,707	27,039,697	27,187,816	27,331,418	27,472,021
	5-9	25,348,410	25,530,785	25,714,892	25,899,942	26,083,340	26,265,140	26,443,132	26,617,134	26,785,696	26,948,885
	10-14	24,845,132	24,990,660	25,147,367	25,312,434	25,485,692	25,663,454	25,845,807	26,029,608	26,214,555	26,397,169
	15-19	24,811,913	24,919,539	25,029,995	25,146,666	25,269,219	25,404,099	25,549,563	25,706,422	25,871,623	26,044,467
Total	20-24	24,929,396	25,038,781	25,146,871	25,253,974	25,362,810	25,469,470	25,577,135	25,687,718	25,804,677	25,927,059
	25-29	25,021,159	25,165,751	25,295,754	25,415,926	25,529,311	25,640,495	25,749,784	25,857,784	25,965,159	26,074,269
	30-34	24,796,739	25,015,807	25,229,007	25,427,973	25,609,300	25,770,266	25,914,813	26,044,912	26,165,486	26,279,680
	35-39	24,206,580	24,420,839	24,627,673	24,842,412	25,046,420	25,263,013	25,481,340	25,694,100	25,892,522	26,074,053
Total	40-44	23,398,511	23,560,201	23,785,982	24,047,207	24,313,268	24,450,825	24,664,518	24,870,662	25,084,729	25,288,512
	45-49	23,977,838	23,741,682	23,538,072	23,397,719	23,325,906	23,460,105	23,621,454	23,846,352	24,106,448	24,371,548
	50-54	23,854,730	24,117,510	24,261,940	24,256,245	24,049,630	23,844,093	23,613,631	23,415,198	23,279,070	23,210,844
	55-59	22,374,582	22,416,595	22,553,516	22,824,539	23,193,614	23,506,015	23,767,575	23,912,857	23,911,074	23,712,987
Total	60-64	20,828,434	21,270,964	21,610,358	21,768,562	21,804,554	21,818,859	21,866,646	22,006,809	22,276,845	22,643,132
	65-69	18,335,456	18,321,198	18,516,737	18,895,409	19,363,684	19,926,675	20,354,991	20,683,900	20,840,621	20,884,036
	70-74	17,685,655	17,771,617	17,719,384	17,548,368	17,300,381	17,036,953	17,037,800	17,230,992	17,593,407	18,041,722
	75-79	16,261,721	15,999,572	15,753,645	15,569,303	15,623,707	15,807,866	15,899,634	15,865,186	15,725,783	15,525,432
	80-84	13,521,792	13,643,564	13,733,910	13,840,536	13,809,866	13,646,064	13,447,163	13,264,501	13,138,341	13,218,648
	85 +	17,072,052	17,758,734	18,428,874	19,055,672	19,742,056	20,350,599	20,902,923	21,421,862	21,925,170	22,372,451

G	Age	2,051	2,052	2,053	2,054	2,055	2,056	2,057	2,058	2,059	2,060
Total	0-4	27,572,150	27,660,055	27,739,789	27,820,842	27,913,304	28,027,376	28,144,554	28,265,452	28,390,616	28,520,423
	5-9	27,132,481	27,311,645	27,483,833	27,640,082	27,773,129	27,872,507	27,959,568	28,038,442	28,118,630	28,210,217
	10-14	26,580,330	26,765,086	26,950,856	27,137,493	27,325,083	27,507,424	27,685,348	27,856,301	28,011,339	28,143,202
	15-19	26,199,971	26,369,004	26,544,094	26,721,499	26,896,480	27,077,543	27,260,194	27,443,852	27,628,374	27,813,843
Total	20-24	26,074,001	26,217,365	26,361,938	26,502,025	26,652,305	26,805,614	26,972,384	27,145,183	27,320,286	27,492,979
	25-29	26,152,421	26,237,707	26,334,617	26,456,002	26,586,853	26,731,525	26,872,637	27,014,950	27,152,796	27,300,786
	30-34	26,361,740	26,443,485	26,523,619	26,600,939	26,684,758	26,763,581	26,849,531	26,947,068	27,068,959	27,200,258
	35-39	26,217,726	26,343,785	26,453,903	26,552,382	26,635,020	26,719,124	26,802,946	26,885,197	26,964,695	27,050,661
Total	40-44	25,489,429	25,690,475	25,885,821	26,064,896	26,227,424	26,368,872	26,492,882	26,601,111	26,697,818	26,778,837
	45-49	24,490,068	24,685,644	24,875,446	25,073,779	25,260,995	25,458,999	25,657,106	25,849,569	26,025,942	26,185,960
	50-54	23,324,397	23,465,318	23,666,934	23,902,787	24,143,774	24,262,529	24,456,937	24,645,724	24,842,938	25,029,267
	55-59	23,484,528	23,233,750	23,017,305	22,864,189	22,778,914	22,894,008	23,035,101	23,235,287	23,468,664	23,707,129
Total	60-64	22,952,823	23,256,498	23,426,331	23,431,521	23,221,895	23,003,436	22,763,247	22,556,253	22,410,880	22,331,111
	65-69	20,899,256	21,010,478	21,215,569	21,550,141	21,984,773	22,357,740	22,661,950	22,835,379	22,848,795	22,656,136
	70-74	18,540,564	18,973,324	19,319,630	19,513,790	19,612,542	19,698,706	19,820,104	20,030,426	20,362,768	20,792,172
	75-79	15,233,014	15,231,855	15,412,610	15,754,862	16,191,570	16,709,431	17,120,195	17,451,680	17,646,203	17,760,828
	80-84	13,300,104	13,340,488	13,279,025	13,139,835	12,966,583	12,788,435	12,816,511	12,995,727	13,311,283	13,712,121
	85 +	22,687,009	23,005,205	23,310,667	23,647,398	24,102,043	24,501,123	24,777,380	24,965,785	25,124,110	25,358,564

Source: Utah Governor's Office of Planning and Budget

5.5.4 County and Subcounty Decennial Population Projections, 2000-2060, All Counties

Geography	Census 2000	2006	2010	2020	2030	2040	2050	2060	AARC 2000-2060
Beaver County	6,005	6,428	6,674	9,178	13,293	17,418	21,971	27,298	2.6%
Beaver city	2,454	2,631	2,904	3,992	5,782	7,577	9,557	11,875	2.7%
Milford city	1,451	1,441	1,524	2,093	3,031	3,971	5,009	6,224	2.5%
Minersville town	817	848	881	1,210	1,753	2,296	2,897	3,599	2.5%
Balance of Beaver County	1,283	1,508	1,365	1,883	2,727	3,574	4,508	5,601	2.5%
Box Elder County	42,745	45,987	49,953	59,215	70,393	84,034	102,910	126,925	1.8%
Bear River City city	750	802	872	1,034	1,228	1,467	1,798	2,218	1.8%
Brigham City city	17,411	18,463	20,055	23,774	28,263	33,741	41,321	50,963	1.8%
Corinne city	621	640	695	824	979	1,169	1,432	1,767	1.8%
Deweyville town	278	332	361	428	508	606	742	916	2.0%
Elwood town	678	799	869	1,031	1,224	1,463	1,792	2,210	2.0%
Fielding town	448	431	468	555	658	785	961	1,186	1.6%
Garland city	1,943	1,994	2,166	2,569	3,053	3,645	4,465	5,507	1.8%
Honeyville city	1,214	1,316	1,429	1,693	2,012	2,402	2,942	3,627	1.8%
Howell town	221	229	249	295	351	419	513	633	1.8%
Mantua town	791	769	835	989	1,176	1,405	1,720	2,121	1.7%
Perry city	2,383	3,407	3,700	4,387	5,215	6,225	7,624	9,404	2.3%
Plymouth town	328	372	404	477	567	677	830	1,023	1.9%
Portage town	257	271	295	350	417	497	608	750	1.8%
Snowville town	177	167	181	215	255	305	374	461	1.6%
Tremonton city	5,592	6,289	6,832	8,099	9,627	11,492	14,074	17,359	1.9%
Willard city	1,630	1,674	1,819	2,157	2,565	3,062	3,751	4,627	1.8%
Balance of Box Elder County	8,023	8,032	8,723	10,338	12,295	14,674	17,963	22,153	1.7%

Geography	Census 2000	2006	2010	2020	2030	2040	2050	2060	AARC 2000-2060
Cache County	91,391	105,671	117,758	149,322	181,921	223,442	274,527	331,594	2.2%
Amalga town	427	468	509	538	582	620	664	702	0.8%
Clarkston town	688	737	772	809	841	890	947	992	0.6%
Cornish town	259	276	289	308	320	331	349	365	0.6%
Hyde Park city	2,955	3,579	3,992	5,421	6,201	8,665	10,495	13,577	2.6%
Hyrum city	6,316	7,471	8,342	10,917	13,471	16,895	20,984	24,793	2.3%
Lewiston city	1,877	1,999	2,228	2,824	3,441	4,226	5,193	6,272	2.0%
Logan city	42,670	47,359	52,776	67,122	81,530	101,238	122,253	149,097	2.1%
Mendon city	898	1,175	1,030	1,305	1,589	1,954	2,401	2,900	2.0%
Millville city	1,507	1,786	2,027	2,915	3,808	4,877	6,341	7,905	2.8%
Newton town	699	793	817	859	911	1,017	1,121	1,268	1.0%
Nibley city	2,045	3,773	4,224	5,923	7,199	9,075	10,498	14,035	3.3%
North Logan city	6,163	7,545	8,432	11,001	13,728	17,054	21,302	25,977	2.4%
Paradise town	759	881	982	1,247	1,519	1,864	2,290	2,766	2.2%
Providence city	4,377	6,076	6,795	8,885	11,098	11,947	17,536	21,367	2.7%
Richmond city	2,051	2,312	2,576	3,268	3,983	4,893	7,713	7,263	2.1%
River Heights city	1,496	1,670	1,705	1,742	1,783	1,837	1,899	1,962	0.5%
Smithfield city	7,261	8,774	9,808	12,511	15,874	19,652	24,493	29,831	2.4%
Trenton town	449	495	522	565	625	711	794	878	1.1%
Wellsville city	2,728	3,187	3,575	4,558	6,197	7,840	9,281	10,804	2.3%
Balance of Cache County	5,766	5,315	6,357	6,604	7,221	7,856	7,973	8,840	0.7%
Carbon County	20,422	19,504	20,317	24,843	27,106	27,447	28,275	29,338	0.6%
East Carbon city	1,393	1,280	1,334	1,632	1,780	1,803	1,858	1,928	0.5%
Helper city	2,025	1,886	1,965	2,403	2,621	2,653	2,733	2,836	0.6%
Price city	8,402	8,010	8,344	10,203	11,134	11,273	11,612	12,049	0.6%
Scofield town	28	26	27	37	39	39	39	39	0.6%
Sunnyside city	404	378	393	482	526	532	548	568	0.6%
Wellington city	1,666	1,570	1,635	1,999	2,182	2,208	2,275	2,360	0.6%
Balance of Carbon County	6,504	6,354	6,619	8,087	8,824	8,939	9,210	9,558	0.6%
Daggett County	921	949	992	1,076	1,155	1,231	1,351	1,520	0.8%
Manila town	308	303	316	343	370	397	437	493	0.8%
Balance of Daggett County	613	646	676	733	785	834	914	1,027	0.9%

Geography	Census								AARC
	2000	2006	2010	2020	2030	2040	2050	2060	2000-2060
Davis County	238,994	286,547	323,087	369,467	390,159	407,238	424,318	441,398	1.0%
Bountiful city	41,301	43,576	43,956	43,284	42,786	41,729	41,912	42,682	0.1%
Centerville city	14,585	15,075	16,213	17,051	17,378	17,301	17,815	18,471	0.4%
Clearfield city	25,974	27,241	29,840	31,698	34,034	34,847	35,534	36,325	0.6%
Clinton city	12,585	18,811	25,613	29,878	31,449	31,940	33,017	34,233	1.7%
Farmington city	12,081	15,540	16,312	19,877	22,012	24,973	25,300	26,232	1.3%
Fruit Heights city	4,701	4,910	5,065	5,943	6,807	7,418	7,745	8,173	0.9%
Kaysville city	20,351	23,563	26,024	31,074	32,731	35,044	37,821	39,214	1.1%
Layton city	58,474	62,716	70,502	80,106	86,543	90,461	91,113	94,341	0.8%
North Salt Lake city	8,749	11,598	14,837	15,354	15,558	15,301	15,489	15,892	1.0%
South Weber city	4,260	5,807	8,455	12,108	12,349	12,388	13,211	13,622	2.0%
Sunset city	5,204	4,910	5,099	5,124	4,904	4,649	4,587	4,756	-0.1%
Syracuse city	9,398	19,534	26,656	33,184	34,034	34,704	40,090	44,540	2.6%
West Bountiful city	4,484	5,185	5,654	6,341	6,731	6,994	7,458	7,732	0.9%
West Point city	6,033	8,186	12,600	20,081	24,499	31,016	34,139	35,396	3.0%
Woods Cross city	6,419	8,168	10,200	11,300	11,103	11,124	11,414	11,834	1.0%
Balance of Davis County	4,395	11,727	6,062	7,063	7,241	7,349	7,671	7,954	1.0%
Duchesne County	14,371	15,585	17,336	20,130	21,533	22,561	24,586	27,499	1.1%
Altamont town	178	185	206	239	255	267	291	325	1.0%
Duchesne city	1,408	1,506	1,676	1,946	2,082	2,183	2,378	2,663	1.1%
Myton city	539	567	631	732	782	818	891	996	1.0%
Roosevelt city	4,299	4,681	5,208	6,048	6,468	6,777	7,383	8,258	1.1%
Tabiona town	149	155	173	201	215	225	245	274	1.0%
Balance of Duchesne County	7,798	8,491	9,442	10,964	11,731	12,291	13,398	14,983	1.1%
Emery County	10,860	10,438	10,698	12,673	13,119	12,854	13,313	13,791	0.4%
Castle Dale city	1,657	1,617	1,658	1,963	2,033	1,992	2,061	2,136	0.4%
Clawson town	153	173	177	210	219	213	222	232	0.7%
Cleveland town	508	507	519	615	637	624	647	670	0.5%
Elmo town	368	366	376	447	462	452	468	485	0.5%
Emery town	308	303	311	366	378	371	385	398	0.4%
Ferron city	1,623	1,569	1,608	1,906	1,973	1,934	2,003	2,075	0.4%
Green River city	868	949	972	1,152	1,194	1,171	1,212	1,255	0.6%
Huntington city	2,131	2,061	2,113	2,504	2,592	2,540	2,630	2,724	0.4%
Orangeville city	1,398	1,344	1,377	1,632	1,687	1,653	1,711	1,772	0.4%
Balance of Emery County	1,846	1,549	1,587	1,878	1,944	1,904	1,974	2,044	0.2%

Geography	Census 2000	2006	2010	2020	2030	2040	2050	2060	AARC 2000-2060
Garfield County	4,735	4,772	5,092	5,843	6,823	7,656	8,738	10,356	1.3%
Antimony town	122	112	119	137	157	177	202	239	1.1%
Boulder town	180	178	191	220	259	289	329	390	1.3%
Bryce Canyon City	X	138	147	170	200	223	255	301	1.3%
Cannonville town	148	136	145	168	198	220	251	297	1.2%
Escalante city	818	750	801	920	1,075	1,205	1,375	1,631	1.2%
Hatch town	127	116	123	141	161	181	207	244	1.1%
Henrieville town	159	145	154	178	208	236	270	320	1.2%
Panguitch city	1,623	1,485	1,585	1,817	2,122	2,383	2,719	3,222	1.1%
Tropic town	508	467	499	573	670	752	859	1,018	1.2%
Balance of Garfield County	1,050	1,245	1,328	1,519	1,773	1,990	2,271	2,694	1.6%
Grand County	8,485	9,024	9,693	11,007	11,827	12,559	13,781	15,542	1.0%
Castle Valley town	349	364	391	444	477	509	558	629	1.0%
Moab city	4,779	4,875	5,237	5,946	6,388	6,783	7,443	8,394	0.9%
Balance of Grand County	3,357	3,785	4,065	4,617	4,962	5,267	5,780	6,519	1.1%
Iron County	33,779	43,424	50,601	68,315	87,644	110,257	137,240	168,383	2.7%
Brian Head town	118	117	137	186	237	299	373	458	2.3%
Cedar City city	20,527	25,665	29,907	40,376	51,799	65,165	81,113	99,516	2.7%
Enoch city	3,467	4,550	5,302	7,157	9,181	11,551	14,379	17,642	2.7%
Kanarraville town	311	305	356	482	618	778	969	1,189	2.3%
Paragonah town	470	465	541	730	937	1,179	1,468	1,802	2.3%
Parowan city	2,565	2,549	2,971	4,012	5,150	6,478	8,063	9,893	2.3%
Balance of Iron County	6,321	9,773	11,387	15,372	19,722	24,807	30,875	37,883	3.0%
Juab County	8,238	9,315	10,519	14,158	18,004	22,950	29,728	38,446	2.6%
Eureka city	766	798	901	1,212	1,541	1,965	2,544	3,290	2.5%
Levan town	688	834	941	1,266	1,611	2,056	2,664	3,445	2.7%
Mona city	850	1,198	1,353	1,821	2,313	2,949	3,819	4,939	3.0%
Nephi city	4,733	5,207	5,879	7,913	10,064	12,827	16,615	21,489	2.6%
Rocky Ridge town	403	485	548	738	938	1,196	1,551	2,006	2.7%
Santaquin city (pt.)	0	8	8	8	8	8	8	8	0.0%
Balance of Juab County	798	785	889	1,200	1,529	1,949	2,527	3,269	2.4%

Geography	Census 2000	2006	2010	2020	2030	2040	2050	2060	AARC 2000-2060
Kane County	6,046	6,294	6,893	8,746	10,394	12,034	14,267	17,276	1.8%
Alton town	134	140	153	193	232	268	318	384	1.8%
Big Water town	417	413	452	573	680	788	933	1,128	1.7%
Glendale town	355	350	384	488	578	669	794	962	1.7%
Kanab city	3,564	3,754	4,111	5,216	6,198	7,177	8,509	10,304	1.8%
Orderville town	596	606	664	841	998	1,156	1,371	1,660	1.7%
Balance of Kane County	980	1,031	1,129	1,435	1,708	1,976	2,342	2,838	1.8%
Millard County	12,405	13,230	13,863	16,868	19,682	22,754	28,538	37,549	1.9%
Delta city	3,209	3,125	3,274	3,984	4,649	5,376	6,743	8,873	1.7%
Fillmore city	2,253	2,204	2,309	2,809	3,277	3,789	4,753	6,253	1.7%
Hinckley town	698	734	769	935	1,090	1,261	1,581	2,080	1.8%
Holden town	400	388	407	495	579	668	841	1,106	1.7%
Kanosh town	485	481	504	612	715	827	1,037	1,365	1.7%
Leamington town	217	212	222	272	318	367	461	606	1.7%
Lynndyl town	134	125	131	161	190	220	275	362	1.7%
Meadow town	254	247	259	316	370	428	538	708	1.7%
Oak City town	650	624	654	795	929	1,076	1,350	1,776	1.7%
Scipio town	290	301	315	384	450	521	655	862	1.8%
Balance of Millard County	3,815	4,789	5,019	6,105	7,115	8,221	10,304	13,558	2.1%

Geography	Census 2000	2006	2010	2020	2030	2040	2050	2060	AARC 2000-2060
Morgan County	7,129	8,888	10,589	16,756	24,478	34,407	48,662	68,246	3.8%
Morgan city	2,635	3,101	3,695	4,329	4,812	5,432	6,052	6,903	1.6%
Balance of Morgan County	4,494	5,787	6,894	12,427	19,666	28,975	42,610	61,343	4.5%
Piute County	1,435	1,373	1,396	1,526	1,690	1,817	2,035	2,404	0.9%
Circleville town	505	466	474	518	573	616	690	815	0.8%
Junction town	177	164	166	182	203	218	243	287	0.8%
Kingston town	142	131	133	146	162	173	194	229	0.8%
Marysvale town	381	342	348	379	417	447	500	591	0.7%
Balance of Piute County	230	270	275	301	335	363	408	482	1.2%
Rich County	1,961	2,121	2,235	2,606	2,842	3,040	3,473	4,147	1.3%
Garden City town	357	396	418	487	531	569	648	773	1.3%
Laketown town	188	181	191	223	244	259	296	353	1.1%
Randolph city	483	464	489	570	623	666	760	907	1.1%
Woodruff town	194	187	198	232	253	269	308	368	1.1%
Balance of Rich County	739	893	939	1,094	1,191	1,277	1,461	1,746	1.4%

Geography	Census 2000	2006	2010	2020	2030	2040	2050	2060	AARC 2000-2060
Salt Lake County	898,387	996,374	1,079,679	1,273,929	1,468,615	1,671,627	1,853,891	2,004,773	1.3%
Alta town	370	365	359	375	378	390	400	400	0.1%
Bluffdale city	4,700	7,088	28,154	43,988	55,219	60,065	62,844	62,988	4.4%
Cottonwood Heights city	35,168	34,954	35,475	40,645	45,920	48,052	50,681	50,990	0.6%
Draper city (pt.)	25,220	36,099	40,076	51,286	54,006	56,060	57,776	57,989	1.4%
Herriman city	1,523	14,643	23,462	39,100	47,689	63,473	77,473	82,637	6.9%
Holladay city	14,561	25,308	28,474	32,264	34,333	38,514	41,727	44,508	1.9%
Midvale city	27,029	27,249	35,111	44,024	46,566	54,953	61,404	65,497	1.5%
Murray city	34,024	44,844	50,076	64,516	73,792	76,082	78,048	77,985	1.4%
Riverton city	25,011	35,543	38,253	46,018	54,063	66,470	77,497	82,663	2.0%
Salt Lake City city	181,743	178,858	180,086	199,329	208,822	218,235	225,023	225,956	0.4%
Sandy city	88,418	94,203	94,544	94,683	98,298	106,657	112,828	120,348	0.5%
South Jordan city	29,437	44,009	56,144	83,088	102,406	106,114	121,634	139,973	2.6%
South Salt Lake city	22,038	21,354	22,274	27,799	32,391	38,818	44,560	47,530	1.3%
Taylorsville city	57,439	58,048	58,482	66,334	70,062	78,487	84,824	90,477	0.8%
West Jordan city	68,336	100,280	108,204	121,211	138,549	163,725	172,315	174,966	1.6%
West Valley City city	108,896	120,235	122,003	141,739	160,637	170,183	179,410	179,965	0.8%
Balance of Salt Lake County	174,474	153,294	158,502	177,530	245,484	325,350	405,446	499,902	1.8%
San Juan County	14,413	14,647	15,053	15,319	16,653	18,051	20,083	23,174	0.8%
Blanding city	3,162	3,169	3,257	3,314	3,604	3,908	4,349	5,019	0.8%
Monticello city	1,958	1,922	1,975	2,011	2,186	2,370	2,637	3,043	0.7%
Balance of San Juan County	9,293	9,556	9,821	9,994	10,863	11,773	13,097	15,112	0.8%

Geography	Census 2000	2006	2010	2020	2030	2040	2050	2060	AARC 2000-2060
Sanpete County	22,763	25,799	27,557	31,519	36,120	40,196	45,624	53,066	1.4%
Centerfield town	1,048	1,049	1,120	1,282	1,469	1,634	1,854	2,155	1.2%
Ephraim city	4,505	5,085	5,432	6,214	7,122	7,924	8,996	10,466	1.4%
Fairview city	1,160	1,161	1,240	1,419	1,626	1,811	2,055	2,390	1.2%
Fayette town	204	203	217	249	287	317	361	419	1.2%
Fountain Green city	945	939	1,003	1,147	1,314	1,463	1,660	1,930	1.2%
Gunnison city	2,394	2,717	2,902	3,321	3,806	4,235	4,808	5,592	1.4%
Manti city	3,040	3,180	3,397	3,885	4,453	4,955	5,624	6,541	1.3%
Mayfield town	420	424	453	519	595	663	752	874	1.2%
Moroni city	1,280	1,273	1,359	1,554	1,782	1,982	2,249	2,614	1.2%
Mount Pleasant city	2,707	2,698	2,882	3,298	3,780	4,205	4,772	5,550	1.2%
Spring City city	956	1,001	1,069	1,222	1,399	1,558	1,767	2,055	1.3%
Sterling town	235	251	268	307	353	393	447	520	1.3%
Wales town	219	224	239	274	314	349	395	460	1.2%
Balance of Sanpete County	3,650	5,594	5,976	6,828	7,820	8,707	9,884	11,500	1.9%
Sevier County	18,842	19,984	21,249	23,583	25,177	26,775	29,828	33,740	1.0%
Annabella town	603	648	689	764	816	869	969	1,097	1.0%
Aurora city	947	947	1,007	1,119	1,195	1,270	1,415	1,600	0.9%
Central Valley town	406	413	439	489	521	554	618	699	0.9%
Elsinore town	733	740	787	873	933	992	1,103	1,248	0.9%
Glenwood town	437	436	463	513	549	583	648	734	0.9%
Joseph town	269	271	287	317	339	360	401	454	0.9%
Koosharem town	276	390	415	461	492	522	582	659	1.5%
Monroe city	1,845	1,842	1,959	2,175	2,322	2,469	2,750	3,111	0.9%
Redmond town	788	798	849	942	1,006	1,069	1,190	1,346	0.9%
Richfield city	6,847	7,104	7,553	8,383	8,951	9,519	10,604	11,994	0.9%
Salina city	2,393	2,399	2,551	2,830	3,022	3,212	3,577	4,045	0.9%
Sigurd town	430	429	456	506	540	574	639	722	0.9%
Balance of Sevier County	2,868	3,567	3,794	4,211	4,491	4,782	5,332	6,031	1.2%

371

Geography	Census 2000	2006	2010	2020	2030	2040	2050	2060	AARC 2000-2060
Summit County	29,736	36,871	42,320	61,738	83,252	104,620	131,594	165,029	2.9%
Coalville city	1,382	1,419	1,587	2,031	2,383	2,400	2,500	2,600	1.1%
Francis town	698	889	1,077	1,919	2,748	4,300	6,000	8,300	4.2%
Henefer town	684	722	875	1,558	2,729	3,500	3,800	4,100	3.0%
Kamas city	1,274	1,493	1,810	2,779	3,982	4,100	4,500	4,900	2.3%
Oakley city	948	1,299	1,601	2,851	4,993	6,300	7,000	7,600	3.5%
Park City city (pt.)	7,371	8,041	9,185	13,382	15,838	16,600	18,000	19,400	1.6%
Balance of Summit County	17,379	23,008	26,185	37,217	50,580	67,420	89,794	118,129	3.2%
Tooele County	40,735	54,375	63,777	91,849	119,871	152,734	192,007	235,839	3.0%
Grantsville city	6,015	8,016	9,435	15,217	19,315	24,842	33,900	46,857	3.5%
Ophir town	23	27	27	30	30	30	32	36	0.8%
Rush Valley town	453	569	670	1,079	1,368	1,760	2,401	3,318	3.4%
Stockton town	443	579	681	1,100	1,397	1,797	2,453	3,389	3.4%
Tooele city	22,502	29,062	34,205	44,949	45,904	49,644	59,881	70,079	1.9%
Vernon town	236	296	348	558	708	911	1,243	1,718	3.4%
Wendover city	1,537	1,632	1,706	1,966	1,967	2,041	2,275	2,628	0.9%
Balance of Tooele County	9,526	14,194	16,703	26,949	49,183	71,709	89,821	107,813	4.1%
Uintah County	25,224	27,747	31,379	37,950	40,638	42,536	46,445	51,300	1.2%
Ballard town	566	633	717	866	927	970	1,060	1,171	1.2%
Naples city	1,300	1,502	1,698	2,055	2,201	2,302	2,514	2,777	1.3%
Vernal city	7,714	8,163	9,232	11,163	11,954	12,513	13,663	15,091	1.1%
Balance of Uintah County	15,644	17,449	19,732	23,866	25,556	26,751	29,208	32,261	1.2%

Geography	Census 2000	2006	2010	2020	2030	2040	2050	2060	AARC 2000-2060
Utah County	368,536	475,425	560,511	727,718	907,210	1,092,450	1,261,653	1,438,300	2.3%
Alpine city	7,146	9,204	9,884	11,340	12,105	12,800	12,900	13,000	1.0%
American Fork city	21,941	25,596	29,434	36,139	42,100	46,600	48,200	48,300	1.3%
Cedar Fort town	341	396	416	2,485	9,175	15,900	23,600	35,000	8.0%
Cedar Hills city	3,094	8,410	11,737	12,295	12,552	12,600	12,700	12,800	2.4%
Draper city (pt.)	0	774	2,400	4,856	6,307	8,100	9,600	10,100	4.4%
Eagle Mountain city	2,157	17,391	26,239	45,653	76,376	113,200	149,900	180,000	7.7%
Elk Ridge city	1,838	2,296	3,133	5,578	6,963	7,100	7,200	7,300	2.3%
Fairfield town	139	146	146	470	1,585	4,800	12,000	19,000	8.5%
Genola town	965	997	1,494	2,886	5,078	7,500	10,000	15,400	4.7%
Goshen town	874	911	937	1,294	1,702	1,800	2,900	6,000	3.3%
Highland city	8,172	13,889	18,107	21,735	22,775	23,900	24,400	24,500	1.8%
Lehi city	19,028	36,021	47,555	66,967	82,487	100,700	114,300	127,700	3.2%
Lindon city	8,363	9,758	11,318	13,722	14,500	14,700	14,800	14,900	1.0%
Mapleton city	5,809	7,157	8,764	11,644	16,358	17,500	17,600	17,700	1.9%
Orem city	84,324	90,857	94,725	98,732	105,000	109,500	114,000	115,000	0.5%
Payson city	12,716	16,748	19,221	30,234	43,790	55,300	63,100	71,900	2.9%
Pleasant Grove city	23,468	30,729	34,446	38,578	42,877	48,200	52,600	55,500	1.4%
Provo city	105,166	116,217	121,330	131,258	138,450	141,800	141,900	142,000	0.5%
Salem city	4,372	5,632	9,004	17,022	28,651	38,000	45,000	51,100	4.2%
Santaquin city (pt.)	4,834	7,027	10,882	20,219	29,113	39,300	47,500	55,700	4.2%
Saratoga Springs city	1,003	10,750	17,936	38,325	70,386	94,200	115,200	122,000	8.3%
Spanish Fork city	20,246	27,717	34,173	46,042	56,651	66,300	69,400	72,700	2.2%
Springville city	20,424	25,998	30,536	44,438	50,741	58,000	58,700	59,200	1.8%
Vineyard town	150	148	1,955	10,526	15,832	22,000	23,100	24,000	8.8%
Woodland Hills city	941	1,269	1,461	1,558	2,245	2,900	3,000	3,000	2.0%
Balance of Utah County	11,025	9,387	13,276	13,723	13,412	29,750	68,053	134,500	4.3%

Geography	Census 2000	2006	2010	2020	2030	2040	2050	2060	AARC 2000-2060
Wasatch County	15,215	21,053	24,950	36,181	48,693	64,631	86,393	113,910	3.4%
Charleston town	378	436	518	751	1,011	1,340	1,792	2,363	3.1%
Daniel town	X	726	861	1,250	1,684	2,237	2,988	3,938	2.9%
Heber city	7,291	9,775	11,584	16,797	22,607	30,008	40,113	52,890	3.4%
Midway city	2,121	3,117	3,695	5,359	7,211	9,572	12,795	16,871	3.5%
Park City city (pt.)	0	3	3	3	3	3	3	3	0.0%
Wallsburg town	274	298	354	513	691	917	1,226	1,616	3.0%
Balance of Wasatch County	5,151	6,698	7,935	11,508	15,486	20,554	27,476	36,229	3.3%
Washington County	90,354	134,899	168,078	279,864	415,510	559,670	709,674	860,378	3.8%
Apple Valley town	X	582	826	1,371	2,036	2,742	3,477	4,216	3.4%
Enterprise city	1,285	1,489	1,854	3,079	4,583	6,173	7,828	9,490	3.4%
Hildale city	1,895	1,950	2,430	4,058	6,008	8,092	10,261	12,440	3.2%
Hurricane city	8,250	12,084	16,381	27,287	40,512	54,568	69,193	83,887	3.9%
Ivins city	4,450	7,205	10,477	17,436	25,886	34,867	44,213	53,602	4.2%
La Verkin city	3,392	4,142	5,162	8,592	12,756	17,182	21,787	26,413	3.5%
Leeds town	547	720	980	1,623	2,410	3,246	4,116	4,990	3.8%
New Harmony town	190	193	241	392	595	801	1,016	1,232	3.2%
Rockville town	247	257	319	532	789	1,063	1,348	1,634	3.2%
Santa Clara city	4,630	6,280	9,325	15,532	23,061	31,062	39,387	47,751	4.0%
Springdale town	457	551	687	924	1,163	1,399	1,632	1,721	2.2%
St. George city	49,663	67,614	84,245	140,268	208,254	280,507	355,703	431,239	3.7%
Toquerville town	910	1,215	1,514	2,519	3,742	5,040	6,391	7,748	3.6%
Virgin town	394	508	634	1,063	1,566	2,109	2,675	3,243	3.6%
Washington city	8,186	15,217	22,858	38,285	57,050	77,011	97,793	118,818	4.6%
Balance of Washington County	5,858	14,892	10,145	16,904	25,099	33,807	42,854	51,954	3.7%

Geography	Census 2000	2006	2010	2020	2030	2040	2050	2060	AARC 2000-2060
Wayne County	2,509	2,535	2,698	2,912	3,395	3,879	4,556	5,608	1.3%
Bicknell town	353	346	368	398	464	529	622	766	1.3%
Hanksville town	204	203	216	233	272	312	366	451	1.3%
Loa town	525	515	548	593	690	788	926	1,139	1.3%
Lyman town	234	230	244	262	305	348	409	503	1.3%
Torrey town	171	190	202	217	254	290	341	420	1.5%
Balance of Wayne County	1,022	1,051	1,120	1,209	1,410	1,612	1,892	2,329	1.4%
Weber County	196,533	215,870	232,696	278,256	320,634	370,523	429,628	493,358	1.5%
Farr West city	3,094	4,828	5,170	5,703	7,374	11,767	12,419	13,348	2.5%
Harrisville city	3,645	5,247	6,225	8,232	9,520	10,814	14,018	16,721	2.6%
Hooper city	4,058	4,649	7,091	10,398	13,812	14,098	23,313	27,809	3.3%
Huntsville town	649	650	545	589	630	657	716	788	0.3%
Marriott-Slaterville city	1,425	1,474	1,600	2,147	2,854	5,065	5,278	5,590	2.3%
North Ogden city	15,026	16,798	18,986	23,744	27,256	38,416	40,361	46,019	1.9%
Ogden city	77,226	78,086	82,522	94,329	106,062	109,539	116,943	124,163	0.8%
Plain City city	3,489	4,352	4,872	6,704	8,115	10,070	12,430	14,827	2.4%
Pleasant View city	5,632	6,486	8,909	9,627	10,743	11,448	15,523	21,500	2.3%
Riverdale city	7,656	7,979	8,385	9,526	9,720	9,742	10,142	10,750	0.6%
Roy city	32,885	35,100	35,457	37,382	39,567	40,787	46,156	55,057	0.9%
South Ogden city	14,377	15,328	18,479	20,268	21,486	22,434	30,174	35,993	1.5%
Uintah town	1,127	1,215	1,266	1,703	2,019	2,071	3,030	3,615	2.0%
Washington Terrace city	8,551	8,292	9,106	11,082	12,466	14,098	17,143	20,449	1.5%
West Haven city	3,976	6,122	7,082	12,399	18,209	31,054	33,117	38,441	3.9%
Balance of Weber County	13,717	19,264	17,000	24,424	30,802	38,460	48,865	58,288	2.4%

Source: Utah Governor's Office of Planning and Budget

5.5.5 Projected Number of Households, 2000-2060, Utah Counties, State, and USA

County	2000	2001	2002	2003	2004	2005
Beaver	1,982	2,041	2,080	2,097	2,104	2,114
Box Elder	13,198	13,474	13,772	13,968	14,290	14,592
Cache	27,853	28,369	29,065	29,907	30,483	31,507
Carbon	7,425	7,320	7,373	7,303	7,270	7,279
Daggett	346	354	355	356	374	378
Davis	71,698	74,351	77,437	80,076	82,614	85,939
Duchesne	4,565	4,690	4,805	4,801	4,920	5,040
Emery	3,454	3,421	3,483	3,510	3,556	3,590
Garfield	1,590	1,569	1,578	1,580	1,612	1,651
Grand	3,462	3,458	3,492	3,515	3,596	3,704
Iron	10,777	11,273	11,498	11,990	12,439	13,222
Juab	2,483	2,577	2,625	2,661	2,709	2,769
Kane	2,231	2,251	2,256	2,272	2,327	2,381
Millard	3,864	3,930	4,060	4,185	4,252	4,310
Morgan	2,069	2,192	2,264	2,380	2,504	2,604
Piute	507	505	508	496	500	503
Rich	641	662	692	706	708	716
Salt Lake	297,064	303,660	308,344	313,860	319,826	328,508
San Juan	4,090	4,063	4,169	4,254	4,364	4,511
Sanpete	6,597	6,846	7,176	7,321	7,447	7,619
Sevier	6,110	6,253	6,330	6,415	6,469	6,569
Summit	10,441	10,945	11,380	12,065	12,523	13,024
Tooele	12,931	13,879	14,718	15,389	15,788	16,497
Uintah	8,222	8,561	8,623	8,712	8,838	9,100
Utah	101,368	106,762	111,336	116,314	120,435	125,840
Wasatch	4,811	5,101	5,473	5,816	6,039	6,324
Washington	30,225	32,571	35,299	37,710	40,619	44,431
Wayne	892	896	898	900	917	915
Weber	66,082	67,331	68,464	69,518	70,842	72,356
State	706,978	729,305	749,553	770,077	790,365	817,993
USA	105,838,447	107,227,429	108,649,085	110,065,057	111,462,218	112,898,864

376

County	2006	2007	2008	2009	2010	2011	2012	2013	2014
Beaver	2,152	2,173	2,210	2,232	2,281	2,340	2,405	2,477	2,552
Box Elder	14,900	15,473	15,847	16,187	16,502	16,851	17,204	17,541	17,909
Cache	32,149	33,185	34,530	35,819	37,088	38,246	39,451	40,626	41,732
Carbon	7,360	7,447	7,534	7,596	7,809	8,001	8,176	8,329	8,456
Daggett	378	386	403	406	414	419	424	430	438
Davis	88,900	92,239	95,915	99,343	102,444	105,240	107,662	109,805	111,891
Duchesne	5,185	5,382	5,528	5,662	5,806	5,940	6,067	6,180	6,292
Emery	3,609	3,644	3,664	3,664	3,764	3,855	3,935	3,997	4,061
Garfield	1,682	1,723	1,756	1,790	1,819	1,849	1,881	1,906	1,936
Grand	3,797	3,853	3,938	4,015	4,112	4,195	4,274	4,349	4,421
Iron	13,864	14,302	14,904	15,535	16,135	16,699	17,366	17,983	18,537
Juab	2,882	3,011	3,112	3,208	3,343	3,478	3,624	3,762	3,906
Kane	2,425	2,479	2,527	2,571	2,639	2,713	2,779	2,841	2,905
Millard	4,386	4,470	4,531	4,586	4,718	4,852	4,980	5,095	5,218
Morgan	2,734	2,869	3,010	3,146	3,348	3,533	3,729	3,925	4,131
Piute	506	514	525	524	528	534	537	546	554
Rich	740	767	791	805	826	846	869	887	909
Salt Lake	335,664	343,982	353,182	361,448	369,665	378,080	386,499	394,754	403,145
San Juan	4,618	4,764	4,871	4,974	5,043	5,114	5,197	5,270	5,347
Sanpete	7,756	8,004	8,278	8,529	8,750	8,964	9,206	9,444	9,653
Sevier	6,694	6,856	6,989	7,096	7,216	7,336	7,448	7,542	7,643
Summit	13,361	13,976	14,465	14,929	15,545	16,181	16,820	17,480	18,175
Tooele	17,250	18,004	18,863	19,687	20,772	21,848	22,947	24,035	25,137
Uintah	9,413	9,759	10,042	10,292	10,634	10,957	11,232	11,469	11,688
Utah	131,486	139,049	145,413	151,906	158,203	164,040	170,399	176,538	182,090
Wasatch	6,684	6,996	7,350	7,694	8,070	8,466	8,850	9,236	9,635
Washington	47,289	49,504	52,855	56,161	59,396	62,701	66,132	69,643	73,267
Wayne	931	965	990	1,004	1,016	1,025	1,044	1,058	1,073
Weber	73,321	75,116	76,880	78,424	80,279	82,197	84,101	85,944	87,839
State	842,116	870,892	900,903	929,233	958,165	986,500	1,015,238	1,043,092	1,070,540
USA	114,306,322	115,717,049	117,132,026	118,547,145	120,015,349	121,470,427	122,924,662	124,359,548	125,783,735

County	2015	2016	2017	2018	2019	2020	2021	2022	2023
Beaver	2,636	2,725	2,818	2,920	3,028	3,145	3,267	3,390	3,521
Box Elder	18,290	18,666	19,049	19,438	19,839	20,259	20,679	21,111	21,554
Cache	42,873	44,027	45,243	46,530	47,822	49,168	50,546	51,995	53,480
Carbon	8,579	8,708	8,853	8,988	9,123	9,247	9,353	9,470	9,568
Daggett	441	448	455	458	466	469	474	478	480
Davis	113,879	115,644	117,331	118,911	120,468	122,029	123,515	124,962	126,367
Duchesne	6,399	6,488	6,578	6,665	6,748	6,824	6,904	6,980	7,059
Emery	4,125	4,190	4,254	4,314	4,373	4,443	4,498	4,544	4,591
Garfield	1,965	1,996	2,024	2,052	2,084	2,117	2,145	2,177	2,208
Grand	4,490	4,559	4,633	4,697	4,765	4,834	4,896	4,967	5,029
Iron	19,172	19,801	20,403	21,034	21,691	22,367	23,064	23,800	24,545
Juab	4,060	4,212	4,371	4,521	4,672	4,828	4,988	5,147	5,301
Kane	2,960	3,024	3,081	3,134	3,191	3,246	3,297	3,352	3,410
Millard	5,350	5,464	5,573	5,678	5,783	5,899	6,000	6,110	6,221
Morgan	4,347	4,564	4,791	5,026	5,269	5,517	5,760	6,008	6,268
Piute	563	571	576	587	596	603	610	618	626
Rich	932	953	973	995	1,017	1,039	1,061	1,076	1,092
Salt Lake	411,589	419,940	428,320	436,750	445,328	453,993	462,770	471,667	480,625
San Juan	5,429	5,524	5,624	5,713	5,812	5,912	6,019	6,126	6,228
Sanpete	9,838	10,021	10,226	10,435	10,650	10,855	11,062	11,284	11,514
Sevier	7,747	7,841	7,936	8,023	8,121	8,216	8,315	8,417	8,506
Summit	18,907	19,657	20,429	21,230	22,077	22,961	23,849	24,727	25,605
Tooele	26,248	27,352	28,513	29,685	30,860	32,056	33,236	34,437	35,644
Uintah	11,897	12,094	12,286	12,466	12,644	12,828	13,002	13,178	13,345
Utah	188,203	194,310	200,487	206,839	213,218	220,036	226,983	234,004	241,188
Wasatch	10,045	10,456	10,872	11,284	11,716	12,156	12,601	13,050	13,515
Washington	76,960	80,749	84,645	88,620	92,667	96,788	101,003	105,357	109,766
Wayne	1,089	1,113	1,133	1,155	1,174	1,196	1,219	1,246	1,268
Weber	89,740	91,642	93,572	95,502	97,458	99,428	101,419	103,444	105,451
State	1,098,753	1,126,739	1,155,049	1,183,650	1,212,660	1,242,459	1,272,535	1,303,122	1,333,975
USA	127,217,923	128,612,782	129,994,252	131,350,127	132,692,349	134,037,864	135,372,763	136,707,395	138,031,892

County	2025	2026	2027	2028	2029	2030	2031	2032	2033	2034
Beaver	3,797	3,938	4,083	4,219	4,351	4,482	4,611	4,741	4,870	4,999
Box Elder	22,470	22,936	23,420	23,913	24,411	24,921	25,448	25,975	26,521	27,068
Cache	56,526	58,074	59,633	61,185	62,739	64,292	65,837	67,389	68,937	70,484
Carbon	9,761	9,850	9,953	10,027	10,114	10,188	10,257	10,328	10,387	10,441
Daggett	489	490	500	505	508	512	516	516	519	522
Davis	129,204	130,555	131,839	133,144	134,464	135,759	137,039	138,293	139,480	140,628
Duchesne	7,224	7,299	7,388	7,468	7,546	7,634	7,711	7,794	7,880	7,963
Emery	4,644	4,671	4,694	4,719	4,745	4,775	4,804	4,830	4,851	4,872
Garfield	2,275	2,310	2,347	2,380	2,411	2,441	2,473	2,506	2,533	2,562
Grand	5,161	5,223	5,285	5,345	5,404	5,458	5,512	5,565	5,614	5,662
Iron	26,095	26,884	27,683	28,485	29,296	30,131	30,963	31,799	32,642	33,504
Juab	5,629	5,791	5,960	6,128	6,299	6,468	6,656	6,835	7,017	7,204
Kane	3,525	3,586	3,647	3,709	3,762	3,825	3,884	3,948	4,010	4,075
Millard	6,447	6,553	6,667	6,778	6,893	7,011	7,126	7,246	7,368	7,495
Morgan	6,777	7,044	7,321	7,603	7,899	8,198	8,506	8,820	9,141	9,472
Piute	640	646	661	667	676	686	692	704	708	718
Rich	1,125	1,139	1,154	1,170	1,187	1,200	1,214	1,226	1,235	1,244
Salt Lake	498,875	508,138	517,259	526,344	535,409	544,378	553,311	562,175	570,999	579,807
San Juan	6,437	6,539	6,636	6,729	6,825	6,920	7,017	7,103	7,186	7,273
Sanpete	11,963	12,175	12,393	12,610	12,817	13,020	13,220	13,425	13,624	13,823
Sevier	8,699	8,789	8,877	8,957	9,036	9,114	9,194	9,269	9,348	9,429
Summit	27,356	28,214	29,072	29,919	30,776	31,635	32,481	33,333	34,188	35,060
Tooele	38,074	39,312	40,554	41,820	43,099	44,391	45,707	47,049	48,405	49,789
Uintah	13,677	13,846	14,013	14,178	14,343	14,509	14,673	14,828	14,975	15,125
Utah	255,963	263,582	271,178	278,814	286,488	294,223	301,942	309,596	317,186	324,660
Wasatch	14,459	14,937	15,421	15,916	16,428	16,939	17,454	17,982	18,529	19,088
Washington	118,904	123,591	128,325	133,157	138,022	142,916	147,875	152,897	157,986	163,140
Wayne	1,320	1,343	1,369	1,388	1,412	1,434	1,452	1,471	1,490	1,509
Weber	109,492	111,494	113,509	115,493	117,497	119,489	121,483	123,511	125,537	127,590
State	1,397,008	1,428,949	1,460,841	1,492,770	1,524,857	1,556,949	1,589,058	1,621,154	1,653,166	1,685,206
USA	140,663,008	141,981,196	143,277,563	144,549,923	145,822,001	147,106,908	148,379,758	149,590,695	150,795,917	151,986,425

County	2035	2036	2037	2038	2039	2040	2041	2042	2043	2044
Beaver	5,125	5,249	5,380	5,510	5,641	5,777	5,906	6,040	6,178	6,319
Box Elder	27,626	28,200	28,782	29,373	29,977	30,595	31,223	31,861	32,513	33,177
Cache	72,038	73,584	75,151	76,713	78,301	79,925	81,578	83,266	84,998	86,791
Carbon	10,486	10,526	10,566	10,596	10,630	10,663	10,692	10,714	10,734	10,752
Daggett	521	520	522	526	527	535	543	544	546	552
Davis	141,791	142,897	143,935	144,887	145,775	146,646	147,456	148,208	148,925	149,613
Duchesne	8,043	8,119	8,202	8,280	8,360	8,435	8,509	8,582	8,656	8,728
Emery	4,890	4,915	4,938	4,960	4,980	5,000	5,020	5,036	5,050	5,067
Garfield	2,593	2,623	2,654	2,687	2,718	2,754	2,788	2,821	2,860	2,895
Grand	5,710	5,759	5,806	5,856	5,909	5,960	6,011	6,066	6,120	6,176
Iron	34,368	35,249	36,159	37,074	37,994	38,944	39,906	40,841	41,791	42,782
Juab	7,399	7,596	7,795	7,999	8,214	8,431	8,653	8,880	9,115	9,357
Kane	4,150	4,221	4,292	4,359	4,434	4,509	4,589	4,669	4,756	4,843
Millard	7,625	7,756	7,897	8,038	8,187	8,344	8,505	8,671	8,849	9,041
Morgan	9,818	10,175	10,549	10,938	11,336	11,748	12,176	12,619	13,078	13,558
Piute	720	722	727	731	736	737	736	739	741	740
Rich	1,254	1,264	1,277	1,291	1,305	1,317	1,331	1,342	1,355	1,371
Salt Lake	588,446	596,955	605,374	613,660	621,852	629,950	637,944	645,839	653,652	661,393
San Juan	7,356	7,447	7,539	7,633	7,728	7,821	7,915	8,010	8,105	8,206
Sanpete	14,017	14,212	14,422	14,633	14,836	15,040	15,243	15,455	15,666	15,880
Sevier	9,518	9,616	9,707	9,804	9,909	10,008	10,113	10,219	10,328	10,432
Summit	35,946	36,831	37,735	38,657	39,590	40,548	41,518	42,503	43,505	44,530
Tooele	51,192	52,603	54,039	55,502	56,987	58,494	60,008	61,540	63,103	64,675
Uintah	15,271	15,409	15,549	15,687	15,822	15,954	16,089	16,235	16,370	16,509
Utah	332,133	339,581	346,974	354,288	361,513	368,681	375,783	382,848	389,883	396,762
Wasatch	19,658	20,242	20,844	21,454	22,088	22,738	23,403	24,089	24,798	25,530
Washington	168,334	173,614	178,939	184,327	189,749	195,188	200,658	206,144	211,654	217,194
Wayne	1,530	1,554	1,577	1,597	1,618	1,642	1,668	1,687	1,711	1,734
Weber	129,666	131,765	133,908	136,071	138,260	140,478	142,706	144,952	147,199	149,466
State	1,717,224	1,749,204	1,781,239	1,813,131	1,844,976	1,876,862	1,908,670	1,940,420	1,972,239	2,004,073
USA	153,170,664	154,335,839	155,478,030	156,598,505	157,701,012	158,793,480	159,870,162	160,923,251	161,962,365	162,996,552

380

County	2045	2046	2047	2048	2049	2050	2051	2052	2053	2054
Beaver	6,467	6,612	6,766	6,921	7,080	7,241	7,398	7,565	7,726	7,885
Box Elder	33,863	34,569	35,287	36,024	36,782	37,560	38,363	39,186	40,037	40,896
Cache	88,632	90,530	92,470	94,456	96,474	98,530	100,637	102,789	104,984	107,198
Carbon	10,771	10,791	10,820	10,843	10,858	10,879	10,908	10,955	10,993	11,023
Daggett	557	559	567	575	578	586	596	600	609	620
Davis	150,292	150,955	151,603	152,254	152,953	153,706	154,459	155,248	156,087	156,955
Duchesne	8,798	8,872	8,949	9,039	9,132	9,227	9,328	9,442	9,552	9,672
Emery	5,084	5,102	5,123	5,146	5,171	5,192	5,214	5,242	5,268	5,295
Garfield	2,927	2,967	3,008	3,051	3,090	3,134	3,177	3,222	3,275	3,325
Grand	6,231	6,288	6,347	6,410	6,474	6,545	6,618	6,696	6,775	6,860
Iron	43,796	44,850	45,951	47,051	48,122	49,250	50,405	51,532	52,695	53,906
Juab	9,603	9,856	10,113	10,375	10,650	10,930	11,212	11,500	11,800	12,105
Kane	4,930	5,017	5,107	5,199	5,293	5,395	5,494	5,603	5,705	5,815
Millard	9,240	9,449	9,666	9,898	10,136	10,378	10,631	10,893	11,165	11,446
Morgan	14,057	14,575	15,107	15,664	16,236	16,838	17,452	18,086	18,734	19,402
Piute	745	752	757	763	770	779	789	806	820	833
Rich	1,385	1,406	1,418	1,435	1,455	1,477	1,494	1,518	1,546	1,576
Salt Lake	669,034	676,645	684,217	691,752	699,270	706,750	714,239	721,682	729,033	736,297
San Juan	8,306	8,409	8,509	8,612	8,720	8,835	8,956	9,078	9,201	9,332
Sanpete	16,099	16,319	16,546	16,785	17,041	17,316	17,589	17,882	18,183	18,471
Sevier	10,536	10,647	10,760	10,874	10,993	11,114	11,240	11,370	11,503	11,642
Summit	45,582	46,648	47,743	48,856	49,992	51,160	52,351	53,567	54,806	56,079
Tooele	66,263	67,876	69,515	71,166	72,838	74,527	76,224	77,947	79,689	81,468
Uintah	16,653	16,804	16,957	17,123	17,284	17,442	17,616	17,805	17,996	18,198
Utah	403,686	410,634	417,530	424,517	431,610	438,857	446,230	453,617	461,055	468,592
Wasatch	26,276	27,033	27,823	28,621	29,439	30,281	31,136	32,019	32,928	33,849
Washington	222,738	228,318	233,932	239,562	245,225	250,904	256,618	262,353	268,114	273,907
Wayne	1,757	1,782	1,805	1,833	1,858	1,891	1,926	1,956	1,988	2,020
Weber	151,742	154,035	156,365	158,732	161,131	163,561	166,041	168,563	171,115	173,698
State	2,036,050	2,068,300	2,100,761	2,133,537	2,166,655	2,200,285	2,234,341	2,268,722	2,303,382	2,338,365
USA	164,028,236	165,057,566	166,084,284	167,108,336	168,133,774	169,176,822	170,026,391	171,098,812	172,183,740	173,278,410

County	2055	2056	2057	2058	2059	2060
Beaver	8,048	8,213	8,375	8,538	8,701	8,875
Box Elder	41,773	42,671	43,592	44,530	45,495	46,482
Cache	109,455	111,768	114,127	116,536	118,963	121,428
Carbon	11,062	11,106	11,170	11,239	11,302	11,361
Daggett	629	636	641	653	664	674
Davis	157,853	158,790	159,768	160,750	161,773	162,844
Duchesne	9,795	9,915	10,042	10,172	10,303	10,439
Emery	5,318	5,351	5,384	5,415	5,448	5,488
Garfield	3,370	3,423	3,476	3,531	3,584	3,638
Grand	6,943	7,030	7,116	7,207	7,299	7,397
Iron	55,126	56,359	57,635	58,916	60,211	61,530
Juab	12,416	12,737	13,059	13,390	13,721	14,058
Kane	5,926	6,040	6,161	6,278	6,400	6,527
Millard	11,740	12,047	12,363	12,681	13,034	13,398
Morgan	20,081	20,782	21,504	22,241	22,990	23,760
Piute	849	862	879	897	917	936
Rich	1,604	1,632	1,657	1,687	1,714	1,740
Salt Lake	743,453	750,530	757,534	764,437	771,261	778,002
San Juan	9,467	9,593	9,731	9,867	10,000	10,137
Sanpete	18,752	19,045	19,358	19,671	19,983	20,303
Sevier	11,788	11,941	12,094	12,253	12,418	12,590
Summit	57,383	58,701	60,040	61,404	62,803	64,229
Tooele	83,272	85,106	86,969	88,857	90,769	92,706
Uintah	18,403	18,625	18,856	19,085	19,327	19,581
Utah	476,208	483,869	491,616	499,351	507,004	514,811
Wasatch	34,799	35,783	36,774	37,790	38,827	39,884
Washington	279,723	285,574	291,452	297,360	303,302	309,273
Wayne	2,054	2,089	2,128	2,166	2,202	2,243
Weber	176,305	178,937	181,598	184,279	186,989	189,727
State	2,373,595	2,409,155	2,445,099	2,481,181	2,517,404	2,554,061
USA	174,380,484	175,497,686	176,636,351	177,795,212	178,971,276	180,159,197

Source: Utah Governor's Office of Planning and Budget

5.5.6 Projected Average Household Size, 2000-2060, Utah Counties, State, USA

County	2000	2001	2002	2003	2004	2005	2006	2007	2008	2009
Beaver	2.94	2.93	2.91	2.89	2.89	2.89	2.88	2.87	2.84	2.83
Box Elder	3.22	3.18	3.15	3.12	3.10	3.08	3.06	3.04	3.03	3.01
Cache	3.22	3.22	3.21	3.21	3.22	3.22	3.22	3.22	3.19	3.15
Carbon	2.68	2.64	2.62	2.61	2.60	2.59	2.58	2.58	2.56	2.54
Daggett	2.46	2.44	2.38	2.39	2.35	2.35	2.33	2.32	2.29	2.26
Davis	3.30	3.27	3.25	3.22	3.21	3.19	3.18	3.16	3.14	3.12
Duchesne	3.11	3.08	3.04	3.02	2.99	2.98	2.96	2.96	2.95	2.94
Emery	3.09	3.03	3.00	2.96	2.92	2.89	2.86	2.84	2.82	2.81
Garfield	2.91	2.87	2.83	2.79	2.79	2.77	2.75	2.74	2.74	2.73
Grand	2.44	2.41	2.39	2.38	2.36	2.35	2.35	2.34	2.34	2.33
Iron	3.10	3.09	3.08	3.07	3.07	3.07	3.07	3.07	3.09	3.10
Juab	3.31	3.28	3.25	3.23	3.22	3.20	3.19	3.17	3.15	3.13
Kane	2.68	2.65	2.61	2.58	2.57	2.58	2.56	2.57	2.57	2.58
Millard	3.19	3.14	3.10	3.08	3.04	3.01	2.97	2.96	2.94	2.91
Morgan	3.47	3.44	3.37	3.34	3.29	3.27	3.25	3.23	3.20	3.18
Piute	2.80	2.75	2.75	2.71	2.71	2.69	2.69	2.67	2.64	2.63
Rich	3.02	2.97	2.93	2.92	2.90	2.85	2.84	2.80	2.75	2.72
Salt Lake	2.99	2.98	2.96	2.95	2.94	2.93	2.92	2.92	2.90	2.89
San Juan	3.45	3.40	3.35	3.28	3.23	3.17	3.11	3.04	3.01	2.96
Sanpete	3.25	3.23	3.20	3.17	3.15	3.13	3.11	3.09	3.05	3.00
Sevier	3.03	3.00	2.97	2.95	2.94	2.93	2.92	2.92	2.91	2.90
Summit	2.87	2.85	2.83	2.82	2.80	2.78	2.75	2.74	2.73	2.72
Tooele	3.11	3.10	3.09	3.08	3.07	3.06	3.05	3.04	3.02	3.00
Uintah	3.05	3.01	2.98	2.96	2.94	2.92	2.92	2.92	2.92	2.92
Utah	3.58	3.57	3.56	3.55	3.55	3.54	3.53	3.53	3.52	3.51
Wasatch	3.18	3.17	3.17	3.16	3.15	3.14	3.12	3.11	3.10	3.08
Washington	2.97	2.93	2.89	2.86	2.84	2.81	2.80	2.80	2.79	2.78
Wayne	2.81	2.79	2.78	2.76	2.74	2.73	2.72	2.72	2.69	2.68
Weber	2.94	2.93	2.93	2.92	2.91	2.91	2.90	2.90	2.88	2.87
State	3.12	3.10	3.09	3.08	3.07	3.06	3.05	3.05	3.03	3.02
USA	2.59	2.59	2.58	2.57	2.56	2.55	2.54	2.54	2.53	2.52

County	2010	2011	2012	2013	2014	2015	2016	2017	2018	2019	2020	2021	2022	2023	2024
Beaver	2.82	2.81	2.81	2.80	2.80	2.80	2.80	2.80	2.80	2.80	2.80	2.80	2.80	2.80	2.81
Box Elder	3.00	2.98	2.97	2.96	2.95	2.93	2.92	2.92	2.91	2.90	2.89	2.89	2.88	2.87	2.86
Cache	3.12	3.11	3.09	3.08	3.07	3.06	3.05	3.04	3.02	3.01	2.99	2.96	2.94	2.91	2.89
Carbon	2.54	2.55	2.56	2.57	2.58	2.59	2.60	2.61	2.62	2.63	2.63	2.64	2.64	2.65	2.65
Daggett	2.23	2.22	2.22	2.21	2.18	2.19	2.17	2.16	2.16	2.14	2.13	2.12	2.12	2.12	2.12
Davis	3.11	3.09	3.08	3.07	3.05	3.04	3.03	3.02	3.01	3.00	2.98	2.97	2.95	2.94	2.92
Duchesne	2.94	2.93	2.93	2.92	2.92	2.91	2.91	2.91	2.91	2.91	2.91	2.90	2.90	2.89	2.88
Emery	2.81	2.82	2.82	2.83	2.83	2.83	2.83	2.83	2.83	2.83	2.82	2.81	2.81	2.80	2.79
Garfield	2.71	2.69	2.68	2.68	2.67	2.67	2.66	2.66	2.67	2.67	2.67	2.68	2.68	2.69	2.69
Grand	2.33	2.32	2.32	2.31	2.30	2.30	2.29	2.28	2.27	2.26	2.25	2.24	2.22	2.21	2.20
Iron	3.08	3.07	3.05	3.04	3.04	3.03	3.03	3.02	3.02	3.01	3.00	2.99	2.97	2.96	2.94
Juab	3.11	3.09	3.07	3.05	3.03	3.01	2.98	2.96	2.94	2.92	2.90	2.88	2.86	2.84	2.82
Kane	2.58	2.58	2.59	2.60	2.60	2.62	2.62	2.64	2.65	2.66	2.66	2.67	2.68	2.68	2.69
Millard	2.89	2.88	2.86	2.86	2.85	2.83	2.83	2.83	2.82	2.82	2.82	2.82	2.81	2.81	2.81
Morgan	3.16	3.14	3.12	3.11	3.10	3.08	3.08	3.07	3.06	3.05	3.04	3.03	3.03	3.02	3.02
Piute	2.62	2.60	2.60	2.57	2.55	2.54	2.53	2.54	2.52	2.51	2.51	2.52	2.52	2.51	2.53
Rich	2.68	2.66	2.62	2.61	2.59	2.56	2.55	2.54	2.52	2.51	2.49	2.47	2.46	2.45	2.44
Salt Lake	2.88	2.86	2.85	2.84	2.83	2.82	2.81	2.80	2.79	2.77	2.76	2.75	2.74	2.72	2.71
San Juan	2.92	2.87	2.82	2.78	2.74	2.70	2.66	2.62	2.59	2.56	2.53	2.50	2.48	2.46	2.43
Sanpete	2.95	2.91	2.87	2.84	2.81	2.80	2.79	2.77	2.75	2.74	2.73	2.72	2.71	2.69	2.68
Sevier	2.88	2.87	2.86	2.85	2.84	2.83	2.83	2.82	2.82	2.81	2.81	2.80	2.79	2.78	2.77
Summit	2.72	2.71	2.70	2.70	2.69	2.69	2.69	2.69	2.69	2.69	2.68	2.68	2.68	2.67	2.67
Tooele	2.98	2.96	2.94	2.92	2.90	2.88	2.86	2.84	2.82	2.80	2.78	2.77	2.75	2.73	2.71
Uintah	2.92	2.92	2.92	2.92	2.92	2.93	2.93	2.93	2.93	2.93	2.93	2.92	2.91	2.90	2.88
Utah	3.47	3.45	3.41	3.39	3.37	3.35	3.33	3.31	3.29	3.26	3.24	3.21	3.19	3.16	3.14
Wasatch	3.07	3.05	3.03	3.02	3.01	3.00	2.99	2.98	2.97	2.96	2.95	2.94	2.93	2.91	2.90
Washington	2.78	2.78	2.78	2.79	2.80	2.80	2.81	2.82	2.83	2.84	2.85	2.85	2.86	2.86	2.87
Wayne	2.65	2.63	2.58	2.56	2.53	2.52	2.48	2.47	2.45	2.44	2.42	2.41	2.39	2.39	2.38
Weber	2.86	2.84	2.83	2.83	2.82	2.81	2.80	2.79	2.78	2.77	2.75	2.74	2.73	2.72	2.70
State	3.00	2.99	2.98	2.96	2.95	2.94	2.93	2.92	2.91	2.90	2.89	2.88	2.86	2.85	2.84
USA	2.51	2.51	2.50	2.49	2.49	2.48	2.48	2.47	2.47	2.47	2.46	2.46	2.45	2.45	2.45

County	2025	2026	2027	2028	2029	2030	2031	2032	2033	2034	2035	2036	2037	2038	2039
Beaver	2.80	2.81	2.81	2.82	2.83	2.84	2.85	2.85	2.86	2.86	2.87	2.88	2.88	2.89	2.89
Box Elder	2.85	2.84	2.83	2.82	2.80	2.79	2.78	2.77	2.76	2.75	2.74	2.73	2.73	2.72	2.72
Cache	2.87	2.85	2.83	2.81	2.79	2.78	2.77	2.76	2.75	2.75	2.75	2.74	2.74	2.74	2.74
Carbon	2.65	2.64	2.63	2.62	2.61	2.60	2.59	2.57	2.56	2.55	2.54	2.53	2.52	2.51	2.51
Daggett	2.11	2.12	2.09	2.08	2.09	2.08	2.08	2.08	2.08	2.08	2.09	2.10	2.10	2.09	2.10
Davis	2.91	2.89	2.87	2.86	2.84	2.82	2.81	2.79	2.78	2.77	2.76	2.75	2.74	2.73	2.72
Duchesne	2.86	2.85	2.83	2.82	2.80	2.78	2.76	2.74	2.72	2.71	2.69	2.68	2.66	2.65	2.64
Emery	2.79	2.78	2.77	2.75	2.73	2.70	2.68	2.66	2.63	2.61	2.59	2.57	2.55	2.53	2.52
Garfield	2.69	2.69	2.69	2.69	2.70	2.70	2.70	2.70	2.70	2.70	2.70	2.70	2.69	2.69	2.69
Grand	2.19	2.18	2.17	2.16	2.14	2.14	2.13	2.12	2.11	2.10	2.09	2.09	2.08	2.08	2.08
Iron	2.92	2.91	2.89	2.88	2.87	2.86	2.84	2.84	2.83	2.82	2.81	2.81	2.80	2.79	2.79
Juab	2.81	2.79	2.78	2.77	2.76	2.75	2.73	2.72	2.72	2.71	2.70	2.70	2.69	2.69	2.68
Kane	2.69	2.69	2.69	2.69	2.69	2.68	2.68	2.68	2.67	2.67	2.66	2.65	2.65	2.64	2.64
Millard	2.80	2.80	2.79	2.79	2.78	2.76	2.75	2.74	2.73	2.72	2.71	2.70	2.69	2.69	2.68
Morgan	3.02	3.01	3.01	3.00	2.99	2.99	2.98	2.97	2.97	2.96	2.96	2.95	2.95	2.94	2.93
Piute	2.52	2.52	2.48	2.48	2.46	2.45	2.45	2.42	2.43	2.41	2.42	2.42	2.42	2.43	2.43
Rich	2.43	2.42	2.40	2.38	2.36	2.35	2.33	2.32	2.32	2.31	2.31	2.30	2.30	2.29	2.29
Salt Lake	2.70	2.69	2.68	2.67	2.66	2.65	2.64	2.64	2.63	2.63	2.62	2.62	2.61	2.61	2.61
San Juan	2.42	2.40	2.39	2.37	2.36	2.35	2.33	2.32	2.31	2.30	2.29	2.28	2.27	2.26	2.25
Sanpete	2.67	2.66	2.65	2.64	2.63	2.62	2.61	2.60	2.59	2.58	2.57	2.56	2.55	2.55	2.54
Sevier	2.76	2.75	2.73	2.72	2.71	2.70	2.68	2.67	2.66	2.65	2.64	2.63	2.62	2.62	2.61
Summit	2.66	2.66	2.65	2.64	2.63	2.63	2.62	2.61	2.61	2.60	2.60	2.59	2.59	2.58	2.58
Tooele	2.70	2.68	2.67	2.65	2.64	2.62	2.61	2.60	2.59	2.58	2.57	2.57	2.56	2.55	2.55
Uintah	2.87	2.85	2.83	2.81	2.79	2.76	2.74	2.72	2.70	2.68	2.67	2.65	2.64	2.63	2.63
Utah	3.12	3.09	3.07	3.05	3.04	3.02	3.00	2.99	2.98	2.96	2.95	2.94	2.93	2.92	2.92
Wasatch	2.89	2.88	2.87	2.86	2.85	2.85	2.84	2.84	2.83	2.82	2.82	2.82	2.82	2.81	2.81
Washington	2.87	2.87	2.87	2.87	2.87	2.86	2.86	2.86	2.85	2.85	2.84	2.84	2.84	2.83	2.83
Wayne	2.37	2.37	2.36	2.36	2.36	2.36	2.36	2.36	2.36	2.36	2.36	2.35	2.35	2.35	2.35
Weber	2.69	2.68	2.67	2.66	2.65	2.64	2.63	2.62	2.62	2.61	2.61	2.60	2.60	2.59	2.59
State	2.82	2.81	2.80	2.79	2.78	2.77	2.76	2.75	2.74	2.73	2.73	2.72	2.72	2.71	2.71
USA	2.44	2.44	2.44	2.43	2.43	2.43	2.42	2.42	2.42	2.41	2.41	2.41	2.41	2.41	2.40

County	2040	2041	2042	2043	2044	2045	2046	2047	2048	2049	2050	2051	2052	2053	2054
Beaver	2.89	2.90	2.90	2.90	2.91	2.91	2.91	2.91	2.91	2.91	2.91	2.91	2.91	2.92	2.92
Box Elder	2.71	2.71	2.71	2.70	2.70	2.70	2.70	2.70	2.70	2.70	2.70	2.70	2.70	2.70	2.70
Cache	2.75	2.75	2.75	2.75	2.75	2.75	2.75	2.74	2.74	2.74	2.73	2.73	2.72	2.72	2.71
Carbon	2.51	2.51	2.51	2.51	2.51	2.51	2.52	2.52	2.52	2.53	2.53	2.53	2.53	2.53	2.53
Daggett	2.08	2.06	2.07	2.07	2.06	2.06	2.07	2.07	2.05	2.06	2.05	2.04	2.05	2.04	2.03
Davis	2.72	2.71	2.71	2.71	2.71	2.71	2.70	2.70	2.70	2.70	2.70	2.69	2.69	2.68	2.68
Duchesne	2.64	2.63	2.63	2.63	2.63	2.63	2.63	2.63	2.63	2.63	2.63	2.63	2.62	2.62	2.61
Emery	2.52	2.51	2.51	2.51	2.51	2.51	2.51	2.51	2.51	2.51	2.50	2.50	2.49	2.49	2.48
Garfield	2.68	2.68	2.68	2.68	2.68	2.68	2.68	2.68	2.69	2.69	2.70	2.70	2.71	2.71	2.71
Grand	2.07	2.07	2.07	2.07	2.07	2.07	2.07	2.07	2.07	2.07	2.07	2.07	2.07	2.07	2.07
Iron	2.78	2.77	2.77	2.77	2.76	2.76	2.76	2.75	2.74	2.74	2.73	2.73	2.72	2.72	2.71
Juab	2.68	2.68	2.68	2.68	2.67	2.67	2.67	2.67	2.68	2.67	2.67	2.68	2.68	2.68	2.68
Kane	2.63	2.63	2.63	2.62	2.62	2.61	2.61	2.61	2.61	2.61	2.61	2.61	2.61	2.61	2.61
Millard	2.68	2.68	2.68	2.68	2.68	2.68	2.68	2.69	2.69	2.70	2.70	2.71	2.71	2.72	2.73
Morgan	2.93	2.92	2.92	2.92	2.91	2.91	2.90	2.90	2.90	2.89	2.89	2.89	2.88	2.88	2.88
Piute	2.45	2.47	2.48	2.50	2.53	2.54	2.55	2.57	2.58	2.59	2.60	2.60	2.58	2.58	2.58
Rich	2.29	2.29	2.29	2.30	2.30	2.31	2.30	2.31	2.32	2.32	2.33	2.34	2.34	2.34	2.33
Salt Lake	2.60	2.60	2.60	2.59	2.59	2.59	2.58	2.58	2.58	2.57	2.57	2.56	2.56	2.55	2.55
San Juan	2.24	2.24	2.23	2.22	2.22	2.22	2.21	2.21	2.21	2.21	2.21	2.20	2.20	2.20	2.20
Sanpete	2.53	2.53	2.52	2.52	2.51	2.51	2.51	2.51	2.51	2.51	2.50	2.50	2.49	2.49	2.49
Sevier	2.61	2.61	2.60	2.60	2.60	2.61	2.61	2.61	2.61	2.62	2.62	2.62	2.62	2.62	2.62
Summit	2.58	2.57	2.57	2.57	2.57	2.57	2.57	2.57	2.57	2.57	2.57	2.57	2.57	2.57	2.57
Tooele	2.54	2.54	2.53	2.53	2.53	2.52	2.52	2.52	2.52	2.51	2.51	2.51	2.50	2.50	2.50
Uintah	2.62	2.62	2.62	2.62	2.62	2.62	2.62	2.62	2.62	2.62	2.62	2.62	2.61	2.61	2.60
Utah	2.91	2.90	2.89	2.88	2.87	2.86	2.85	2.84	2.83	2.82	2.82	2.81	2.80	2.79	2.78
Wasatch	2.81	2.81	2.81	2.81	2.81	2.82	2.82	2.82	2.82	2.82	2.82	2.82	2.82	2.82	2.82
Washington	2.82	2.82	2.82	2.81	2.81	2.80	2.80	2.80	2.79	2.79	2.78	2.78	2.77	2.77	2.77
Wayne	2.35	2.35	2.35	2.35	2.36	2.36	2.37	2.38	2.38	2.39	2.40	2.40	2.41	2.42	2.43
Weber	2.59	2.59	2.59	2.58	2.58	2.58	2.58	2.58	2.58	2.58	2.58	2.57	2.57	2.57	2.56
State	2.70	2.70	2.70	2.69	2.69	2.69	2.68	2.68	2.68	2.67	2.67	2.66	2.66	2.66	2.65
USA	2.40	2.40	2.40	2.40	2.40	2.40	2.40	2.40	2.40	2.40	2.40	2.40	2.40	2.40	2.39

County	2055	2056	2057	2058	2059	2060
Beaver	2.92	2.93	2.93	2.94	2.94	2.95
Box Elder	2.70	2.70	2.70	2.70	2.69	2.69
Cache	2.71	2.70	2.69	2.69	2.68	2.67
Carbon	2.53	2.53	2.53	2.52	2.52	2.51
Daggett	2.02	2.03	2.04	2.03	2.02	2.02
Davis	2.67	2.67	2.66	2.65	2.64	2.64
Duchesne	2.61	2.61	2.60	2.60	2.60	2.60
Emery	2.48	2.48	2.47	2.46	2.46	2.45
Garfield	2.72	2.72	2.73	2.73	2.74	2.75
Grand	2.07	2.07	2.07	2.07	2.07	2.06
Iron	2.71	2.70	2.70	2.69	2.69	2.68
Juab	2.68	2.68	2.68	2.68	2.68	2.68
Kane	2.61	2.61	2.61	2.61	2.61	2.61
Millard	2.73	2.74	2.74	2.75	2.75	2.76
Morgan	2.88	2.88	2.87	2.87	2.87	2.87
Piute	2.58	2.58	2.58	2.57	2.56	2.55
Rich	2.33	2.33	2.34	2.34	2.35	2.36
Salt Lake	2.55	2.54	2.53	2.53	2.52	2.52
San Juan	2.20	2.21	2.21	2.21	2.21	2.21
Sanpete	2.49	2.49	2.48	2.48	2.48	2.48
Sevier	2.62	2.62	2.62	2.61	2.61	2.61
Summit	2.57	2.57	2.57	2.57	2.57	2.56
Tooele	2.49	2.49	2.49	2.48	2.48	2.48
Uintah	2.60	2.60	2.59	2.58	2.58	2.57
Utah	2.77	2.76	2.76	2.75	2.74	2.73
Wasatch	2.82	2.82	2.82	2.82	2.82	2.82
Washington	2.76	2.76	2.75	2.75	2.74	2.74
Wayne	2.44	2.45	2.46	2.47	2.48	2.49
Weber	2.56	2.56	2.56	2.55	2.55	2.55
State	2.65	2.64	2.64	2.63	2.63	2.62
USA	2.39	2.39	2.39	2.39	2.39	2.39

Source: Utah Governor's Office of Planning and Budget

5.5.7　Projected Employment, by Industry, 2000-2060, Utah County

	2001	2002	2003	2004
Total Employment	202957	203507	206243	215820
Natural Resources	629	591	546	555
Mining	211	192	230	260
Utilities	256	262	252	261
Construction	15145	14874	14977	16165
Manufacturing	20748	18273	17606	18295
Wholesale Trade	4917	4580	4458	4848
Retail Trade	24334	24872	25340	26209
Transportation & Warehousing	2357	2456	2419	2437
Information	8268	7475	7733	8229
Finance & Insurance	8529	9172	9635	10037
Real Estate, Rental & Leasing	7478	7473	7692	8138
Professional & Technical Services	14406	14428	14874	15433
Management of Companies	1710	1793	1545	1611
Administrative & Waste Services	10595	10574	10826	12398
Educational Services	16061	16979	17114	17239
Health & Social Services	15663	16314	17156	18110
Arts, Entertainment & Recreation	4319	3811	3843	4081
Accomodation & Food Services	10431	10952	11033	11487
Other Services	10700	11512	11661	11962
State & Local Government	20475	21289	21556	22445
Federal Civilian	1081	1077	1047	1012
Federal Military	1998	2025	2086	2030
Farm	2646	2533	2614	2578
State Government	5973	6092	6026	6365
Local Government	14502	15197	15530	16080

388

	2005	2006	2007	2008	2009
Total Employment	226945	239911	252480	261978	268648
Natural Resources	600	608	604	595	593
Mining	78	34	37	38	39
Utilities	274	289	303	310	314
Construction	18245	19463	20103	20727	21344
Manufacturing	17943	18399	18755	18910	19198
Wholesale Trade	4917	5122	5323	5472	5570
Retail Trade	28028	29809	31572	32973	33556
Transportation & Warehousing	2513	2646	2763	2837	2882
Information	8416	8821	9250	9583	9823
Finance & Insurance	10319	10682	11089	11332	11415
Real Estate, Rental & Leasing	8608	9113	9615	10002	10247
Professional & Technical Services	16381	17496	18573	19448	20155
Management of Companies	1652	1732	1805	1854	1891
Administrative & Waste Services	13304	14365	15439	16321	17025
Educational Services	18294	19605	21021	22077	22751
Health & Social Services	19186	20377	21751	22761	23514
Arts, Entertainment & Recreation	4405	4720	5053	5306	5469
Accomodation & Food Services	12658	13709	14717	15492	15872
Other Services	12572	13285	14049	14576	14857
State & Local Government	22889	23996	24959	25661	26421
Federal Civilian	1033	1081	1110	1130	1139
Federal Military	2035	2003	2051	2054	2073
Farm	2595	2556	2538	2519	2500
State Government	6491	6804	7078	7276	7492
Local Government	16399	17192	17881	18385	18929

	2010	2011	2012	2013	2014
Total Employment	283915	297243	308008	316745	325389
Natural Resources	586	580	573	565	555
Mining	32	31	30	29	28
Utilities	328	337	343	347	349
Construction	22615	23700	24544	25177	25779
Manufacturing	20141	20969	21620	22151	22692
Wholesale Trade	5853	6099	6293	6447	6600
Retail Trade	35180	36527	37495	38188	38856
Transportation & Warehousing	3017	3127	3207	3261	3310
Information	10396	10915	11350	11735	12118
Finance & Insurance	11860	12224	12472	12635	12798
Real Estate, Rental & Leasing	10818	11314	11711	12025	12332
Professional & Technical Services	21521	22754	23786	24662	25530
Management of Companies	1989	2073	2140	2192	2244
Administrative & Waste Services	18302	19490	20539	21473	22425
Educational Services	24155	25397	26438	27306	28172
Health & Social Services	25031	26426	27616	28619	29597
Arts, Entertainment & Recreation	5803	6096	6331	6525	6718
Accomodation & Food Services	16747	17503	18097	18568	19045
Other Services	15600	16222	16690	17035	17374
State & Local Government	28066	29545	30792	31842	32884
Federal Civilian	1184	1222	1250	1270	1289
Federal Military	2192	2213	2233	2255	2276
Farm	2499	2479	2458	2438	2418
State Government	7959	8378	8732	9029	9325
Local Government	20107	21168	22061	22813	23559

	2015	2016	2017	2018	2019
Total Employment	334110	342132	350111	358056	365965
Natural Resources	567	577	587	598	607
Mining	28	28	28	28	28
Utilities	360	369	378	386	395
Construction	26375	26845	27276	27678	28064
Manufacturing	23319	23891	24451	25005	25555
Wholesale Trade	6684	6749	6813	6875	6934
Retail Trade	39466	39955	40429	40880	41307
Transportation & Warehousing	3381	3444	3506	3565	3624
Information	12253	12397	12516	12634	12741
Finance & Insurance	12956	13091	13236	13392	13566
Real Estate, Rental & Leasing	12654	12942	13228	13511	13791
Professional & Technical Services	26320	27036	27732	28409	29075
Management of Companies	2275	2300	2325	2349	2372
Administrative & Waste Services	23163	23848	24537	25227	25913
Educational Services	29337	30478	31665	32894	34162
Health & Social Services	30774	31945	33160	34398	35641
Arts, Entertainment & Recreation	6897	7059	7223	7387	7552
Accomodation & Food Services	19567	20047	20540	21038	21546
Other Services	17827	18239	18660	19083	19508
State & Local Government	33971	35006	35983	36927	37835
Federal Civilian	1299	1309	1318	1329	1341
Federal Military	2251	2224	2197	2171	2147
Farm	2386	2353	2323	2292	2261
State Government	9633	9926	10203	10472	10729
Local Government	24338	25080	25780	26456	27106

	2020	2021	2022	2023	2024
Total Employment	373848	381715	389574	397821	406098
Natural Resources	615	625	633	641	650
Mining	28	27	27	27	26
Utilities	404	411	420	429	437
Construction	28439	28807	29174	29568	29967
Manufacturing	26097	26633	27160	27720	28278
Wholesale Trade	6991	7044	7096	7155	7213
Retail Trade	41706	42079	42425	42782	43125
Transportation & Warehousing	3680	3736	3788	3845	3901
Information	12866	12966	13069	13178	13282
Finance & Insurance	13736	13911	14100	14304	14506
Real Estate, Rental & Leasing	14069	14345	14617	14902	15188
Professional & Technical Services	29727	30362	30991	31641	32291
Management of Companies	2394	2415	2434	2457	2479
Administrative & Waste Services	26597	27280	27960	28671	29384
Educational Services	35469	36810	38184	39644	41146
Health & Social Services	36902	38224	39569	40974	42385
Arts, Entertainment & Recreation	7717	7881	8047	8218	8392
Accomodation & Food Services	22059	22579	23105	23656	24223
Other Services	19935	20363	20790	21240	21693
State & Local Government	38710	39549	40353	41165	41955
Federal Civilian	1352	1363	1376	1389	1402
Federal Military	2125	2104	2085	2072	2060
Farm	2230	2201	2171	2143	2115
State Government	10977	11215	11442	11673	11897
Local Government	27734	28334	28910	29493	30060

	2025	2026	2027	2028	2029
Total Employment	414402	423135	431906	440930	450425
Natural Resources	659	667	677	685	695
Mining	26	26	25	25	24
Utilities	446	453	462	471	479
Construction	30364	30804	31265	31766	32318
Manufacturing	28848	29423	30001	30574	31198
Wholesale Trade	7270	7332	7391	7453	7519
Retail Trade	43429	43765	44078	44391	44722
Transportation & Warehousing	3956	4011	4067	4121	4177
Information	13409	13525	13626	13747	13852
Finance & Insurance	14717	14941	15163	15401	15661
Real Estate, Rental & Leasing	15469	15769	16064	16369	16690
Professional & Technical Services	32947	33624	34294	34969	35677
Management of Companies	2501	2523	2544	2564	2587
Administrative & Waste Services	30096	30840	31580	32335	33122
Educational Services	42686	44306	45965	47675	49477
Health & Social Services	43807	45335	46895	48508	50176
Arts, Entertainment & Recreation	8563	8747	8932	9120	9318
Accomodation & Food Services	24787	25395	26010	26653	27325
Other Services	22143	22620	23098	23588	24099
State & Local Government	42725	43493	44250	45010	45809
Federal Civilian	1418	1432	1447	1462	1480
Federal Military	2050	2045	2041	2039	2043
Farm	2086	2059	2031	2004	1977
State Government	12115	12334	12548	12763	12990
Local Government	30609	31160	31702	32247	32820

	2030	2031	2032	2033	2034
Total Employment	459981	469559	479125	488626	498489
Natural Resources	704	712	720	728	737
Mining	24	24	23	23	22
Utilities	488	496	505	513	521
Construction	32889	33491	34139	34830	35581
Manufacturing	31786	32351	32920	33435	33994
Wholesale Trade	7583	7643	7699	7749	7805
Retail Trade	45027	45324	45607	45866	46145
Transportation & Warehousing	4234	4286	4335	4381	4428
Information	13989	14087	14174	14290	14345
Finance & Insurance	15910	16167	16410	16653	16895
Real Estate, Rental & Leasing	17012	17328	17640	17946	18270
Professional & Technical Services	36380	37072	37735	38381	39051
Management of Companies	2609	2628	2646	2661	2677
Administrative & Waste Services	33908	34686	35453	36206	36985
Educational Services	51317	53189	55083	57003	59033
Health & Social Services	51876	53628	55376	57079	58755
Arts, Entertainment & Recreation	9515	9715	9917	10118	10330
Accomodation & Food Services	28010	28712	29432	30160	30923
Other Services	24612	25127	25641	26152	26686
State & Local Government	46611	47401	48179	48964	49815
Federal Civilian	1497	1514	1530	1545	1561
Federal Military	2049	2054	2062	2070	2081
Farm	1951	1924	1899	1873	1849
State Government	13217	13441	13661	13884	14126
Local Government	33394	33960	34518	35080	35689

	2035	2036	2037	2038	2039
Total Employment	508237	518154	528482	538743	549437
Natural Resources	744	752	759	766	775
Mining	22	21	21	20	20
Utilities	529	537	546	553	563
Construction	36323	37096	37933	38833	39847
Manufacturing	34531	35031	35555	36031	36494
Wholesale Trade	7856	7907	7961	8008	8059
Retail Trade	46379	46619	46890	47178	47514
Transportation & Warehousing	4474	4518	4563	4604	4643
Information	14430	14540	14615	14686	14783
Finance & Insurance	17133	17388	17641	17895	18173
Real Estate, Rental & Leasing	18586	18903	19231	19552	19883
Professional & Technical Services	39717	40368	41045	41686	42334
Management of Companies	2692	2706	2719	2729	2739
Administrative & Waste Services	37747	38511	39296	40061	40840
Educational Services	61110	63245	65486	67742	70099
Health & Social Services	60360	61983	63645	65240	66795
Arts, Entertainment & Recreation	10533	10745	10969	11200	11449
Accomodation & Food Services	31675	32460	33290	34163	35095
Other Services	27209	27743	28303	28869	29468
State & Local Government	50693	51580	52505	53410	54336
Federal Civilian	1578	1595	1611	1627	1641
Federal Military	2092	2106	2122	2138	2158
Farm	1824	1800	1776	1752	1729
State Government	14375	14626	14888	15146	15408
Local Government	36318	36953	37617	38266	38928

	2040	2041	2042	2043	2044
Total Employment	560058	570646	581195	591690	602118
Natural Resources	783	791	800	808	815
Mining	19	19	18	18	17
Utilities	572	582	593	601	611
Construction	40952	42171	43501	44925	46352
Manufacturing	36899	37242	37539	37793	38029
Wholesale Trade	8105	8145	8178	8206	8234
Retail Trade	47876	48269	48676	49098	49478
Transportation & Warehousing	4676	4702	4722	4735	4750
Information	14831	14854	14875	14870	14876
Finance & Insurance	18436	18719	18989	19270	19525
Real Estate, Rental & Leasing	20205	20514	20814	21101	21383
Professional & Technical Services	42965	43538	44082	44596	45102
Management of Companies	2748	2752	2752	2751	2749
Administrative & Waste Services	41599	42329	43032	43712	44380
Educational Services	72487	74873	77267	79651	82075
Health & Social Services	68266	69722	71133	72491	73799
Arts, Entertainment & Recreation	11709	11982	12264	12558	12844
Accomodation & Food Services	36082	37126	38214	39346	40470
Other Services	30079	30703	31332	31974	32609
State & Local Government	55233	56069	56864	57633	58463
Federal Civilian	1653	1664	1672	1678	1685
Federal Military	2177	2197	2217	2236	2256
Farm	1706	1683	1661	1639	1616
State Government	15662	15898	16124	16342	16577
Local Government	39571	40171	40739	41291	41885

	2045	2046	2047	2048	2049
Total Employment	612464	623082	633664	644498	655304
Natural Resources	822	828	835	840	844
Mining	17	16	16	15	15
Utilities	617	626	634	639	645
Construction	47677	48965	50117	51076	51788
Manufacturing	38277	38524	38807	39144	39536
Wholesale Trade	8259	8287	8315	8346	8380
Retail Trade	49781	50130	50375	50543	50615
Transportation & Warehousing	4767	4783	4804	4832	4868
Information	14918	14926	14911	14946	15029
Finance & Insurance	19775	20053	20308	20565	20807
Real Estate, Rental & Leasing	21657	21924	22186	22459	22725
Professional & Technical Services	45622	46138	46677	47249	47840
Management of Companies	2746	2744	2744	2748	2753
Administrative & Waste Services	45046	45718	46404	47120	47854
Educational Services	84573	87161	89894	92827	95940
Health & Social Services	75083	76436	77835	79306	80785
Arts, Entertainment & Recreation	13117	13413	13687	13946	14186
Accomodation & Food Services	41560	42732	43837	44899	45900
Other Services	33230	33891	34526	35156	35767
State & Local Government	59353	60211	61161	62230	63393
Federal Civilian	1696	1705	1720	1738	1759
Federal Military	2276	2297	2318	2342	2364
Farm	1595	1574	1553	1532	1511
State Government	16831	17074	17342	17645	17975
Local Government	42523	43137	43818	44583	45417

	2050	2051	2052	2053	2054
Total Employment	666085	676943	687871	698872	709937
Natural Resources	849	855	862	869	875
Mining	14	14	13	13	12
Utilities	650	660	671	682	693
Construction	52305	53163	54027	54896	55771
Manufacturing	39967	40623	41283	41948	42616
Wholesale Trade	8416	8554	8693	8833	8973
Retail Trade	50661	51492	52329	53171	54018
Transportation & Warehousing	4907	4988	5069	5151	5233
Information	15037	15284	15533	15783	16034
Finance & Insurance	21036	21381	21728	22078	22430
Real Estate, Rental & Leasing	22993	23370	23750	24132	24517
Professional & Technical Services	48438	49233	50033	50838	51648
Management of Companies	2760	2806	2851	2897	2943
Administrative & Waste Services	48597	49394	50197	51004	51817
Educational Services	99201	100828	102467	104116	105775
Health & Social Services	82281	83632	84990	86358	87735
Arts, Entertainment & Recreation	14424	14661	14899	15139	15380
Accomodation & Food Services	46908	47678	48452	49232	50017
Other Services	36392	36989	37590	38195	38804
State & Local Government	64585	65645	66712	67785	68866
Federal Civilian	1785	1814	1844	1874	1903
Federal Military	2388	2409	2430	2451	2472
Farm	1491	1470	1448	1427	1405
State Government	18315	18615	18918	19222	19529
Local Government	46272	47031	47796	48565	49339

	2055	2056	2057	2058	2059	2060
Total Employment	721082	732292	743577	754930	766355	777851
Natural Resources	882	889	895	902	909	915
Mining	12	12	11	11	10	10
Utilities	704	715	726	737	748	759
Construction	56652	57538	58430	59328	60231	61140
Manufacturing	43289	43966	44648	45334	46024	46718
Wholesale Trade	9115	9258	9401	9546	9691	9837
Retail Trade	54871	55730	56594	57463	58338	59218
Transportation & Warehousing	5315	5398	5482	5566	5651	5736
Information	16287	16542	16799	17057	17316	17578
Finance & Insurance	22784	23140	23499	23860	24223	24589
Real Estate, Rental & Leasing	24904	25294	25686	26080	26477	26877
Professional & Technical Services	52464	53285	54111	54942	55778	56620
Management of Companies	2990	3037	3084	3131	3179	3227
Administrative & Waste Services	52636	53459	54288	55122	55961	56805
Educational Services	107446	109126	110818	112520	114233	115957
Health & Social Services	89120	90514	91918	93329	94750	96180
Arts, Entertainment & Recreation	15623	15867	16113	16361	16610	16860
Accomodation & Food Services	50807	51601	52401	53206	54016	54831
Other Services	39417	40033	40654	41278	41907	42539
State & Local Government	69953	71048	72149	73257	74372	75494
Federal Civilian	1934	1964	1994	2025	2056	2087
Federal Military	2493	2514	2535	2556	2577	2598
Farm	1384	1362	1341	1319	1298	1276
State Government	19837	20147	20460	20774	21090	21408
Local Government	50118	50902	51691	52485	53284	54088

Source: Utah Governor's Office of Planning and Budget